Praise for *Two Souls: Four Lives*

"A remarkable tapestry of spiritual destiny."

—**Brad and Sherry Steiger**, authors of *Real Miracles, Divine Intervention* and *Feats of Incredible Survival*

"*Two Souls: Four Lives* tantalizes your intellect, stirs your soul, and challenges you to re-look at your current, even multiple-life mission. . . . Makes reincarnation come alive."

—**Barbara Lane, Ph.D**, author of *16 Clues to Your Past Lives, Echoes from the Battlefield*, and *Echoes from Medieval Halls*

"[A] fascinating narrative."

—**Dr. Bob Hieronimus**, author of *United Symbolism of America*, host of *21st Century Radio*

"A very thoughtful and enjoyable book. I loved it!"

—**Walter Cruttenden**, author of *Lost Star of Myth and Time*

"Helps open the door to understanding and enlightenment."

—**Michael R. Hathaway, D.C.H.**, director, White Mountain Hypnosis Center, author of *It's Time to Simplify Your Soul's Code* and *A Complete Idiot's Guide to Past-Life Regression*

"Well-researched, authoritative and totally convincing. . . . I'm convinced this book will become a classic."

—**Richard Webster**, author of *Soul Mates* and *Practical Guide to Past-Life Memories*

"There are powerful lessons in this book that plead for us to heed. What is more, they are woven superbly into a fascinating and irresistible story."

—**Surendra James Conti**, manager, East West Bookstore, Mountain View, California

"The astounding similarities revealed make it hard to doubt that these are, indeed, two souls moving triumphantly together through four lives."

—**Savitri Simpson**, author of *Chakras for Starters* and *The Chakras Workbook*, and *The Meaning of Dreaming: Paramhansa Yogananda's Teachings on Why We Dream and What Our Dreams Mean*

"The similarities between Henry I and Swami Kriyananda are astonishing, and the parallels between their relationships with William the Conqueror/Paramhansa Yogananda are incontrovertible."

—**Devi Novak**, spiritual teacher and author of *Faith Is My Armor: The Life of Swami Kriyananda*

"*Two Souls: Four Lives* takes the subject of reincarnation into never-explored areas of subtlety, meaning, and historical verification. The facts are at hand and the evidence is irrefutable, not only of reincarnation, but also of the workings of a subtle "Divine Plan" guiding this world in ways almost never imagined. Truth is stranger than fiction and far more interesting."

—**Asha Praver**, spiritual teacher and author of *Swami Kriyananda: As We Have Known Him*

"*Two Souls: Four Lives* will expand your consciousness and your mental horizons. You will understand inner greatness and how it can manifest in this world. Open this book and get swept away on a spiritual and historical adventure par excellence."

—**Richard Salva**, author of *The Reincarnation of Abraham Lincoln* and *Walking with William of Normandy*

"Inspirational both as historical text and a metaphysical work that clearly demonstrates karma and reincarnation."

—**Robert S. Morrison, DCH**, founder of the Institute of Hypnosis and Past Life Regressions

"A fascinating exploration of the currents of karma and spiritual destiny."

—**Susan Wisehart, MS, LMFT**, psychotherapist and author of *Soul Visioning: Clear the Past, Create Your Future*

"For those [who] appreciate learning about history and are interested in the development of souls, *Two Souls: Four Lives* will be a rewarding read."

—**Jed Shlackman, LMHC, C.Ht.**, counselor, regression therapist, and author of *Consciousness, Creation, and Existence: A Guide to the Grand Adventure*

"Raises many interesting questions for students of reincarnation and karma . . . I strongly recommend [*Two Souls: Four Lives*] to historians and spiritual seekers alike."

—**Ann Merivale**, author of *Karmic Release: Journeying Back to the Self* and *Souls United: The Power of Divine Connection*

"Fascinating, compelling and challenging."

—**Katherine Diehl**, journalist

"Profound [and] well-researched."

—**Dr. Linda R. Backman**, licensed psychologist, regression therapist, and author of *Bringing Your Soul to Light: Healing through Past Lives and the Time Between*

"An insight to history and the confirmation of spiritual truths."

—**A.L. Ward, CHt**, author of *The Inner Mind Revisited: Researching the Soul*

"Well-researched and . . . a cracking good read."

—**Ian Lawton**, Rational Spirituality Press, author of *The Wisdom of the Soul*

"A must-read for anyone who wants to know what really happened during the Norman 'Conquest.'"

—**Ray Noble**, descendant of one of William the Conqueror's companions

"The most inspiring history book I've ever read."

—**Nabha Cosley**, monk, yogi, and webmaster

"Brings a new light to the field of past-life regressions through the testimonials of great souls and their karmic path."

—**Kaiser Shroff**, reiki master, spiritual teacher, and regression therapist

"*Two Souls: Four Lives* is at once an accurate history with fresh insightful conclusions about a much-misinterpreted period, and a very useful spiritual explanation of how reincarnation plays a role in life. Most of all, Catherine Kairavi has given us a book that is very readable—a real treat to be enjoyed."

—**Tom Cerussi, BASc**, amateur historian

Two Souls: Four Lives

TWO SOULS: FOUR LIVES

The Lives and Former Lives of Paramhansa Yogananda and His Disciple, Swami Kriyananda

Catherine Kairavi

Crystal Clarity Publishers
Nevada City, California

Crystal Clarity Publishers, Nevada City, CA 95959
Copyright © 2010 Catherine Kairavi
All rights reserved. Published 2010
Printed in China
ISBN: 978-1-56589-244-6

Cover design and layout by Renée Glenn Designs
Interior design and layout by Crystal Clarity Publishers
Special thanks to the many photographers who have given their contributions to this
work. Photographs are used with permission from the individual photographers.
Individual credits are listed under each photograph.

Library of Congress Cataloging-in-Publication Data

Kairavi, Catherine.
  Two Souls : Four Lives / by Catherine Kairavi.
     p. cm.
  ISBN 978-1-56589-244-6 (tradepaper)
  1. Yogananda, Paramhansa, 1893-1952. 2. Yogis—India—Biography. 3. William
I, King of England, 1027 or 8-1087—Miscellanea. 4. Kriyananda, Swami.
5. Gurus—United States—Biography. 6. Henry I, King of England, 1068-1135—
Miscellanea. I. Title.

  BP605.S43Y675 2009
  133.901'350922—dc22
  [B]   2009034137

www.crystalclarity.com
800-424-1055
clarity@crystalclarity.com

CONTENTS

TWO SOULS: FOUR LIVES

FOREWORD

By Swami Kriyananda

Historians see the advance of civilization in terms of progressive sophistication from primitive "hunter-gatherers" to farmers, to city dwellers, to our own age of unprecedented scientific achievement. Their teaching is that basic human nature has remained more or less the same throughout history. They quite naturally dismiss the possibility that man, though he lives in a cosmic environment, is affected by cosmic influences.

Paramhansa Yogananda's guru, Swami Sri Yukteswar, gave us a very different view of history, based on the reality of those influences. He said the earth passes repeatedly through great cycles of increasing and diminishing awareness—from deep ignorance to steadily greater enlightenment, then back again to its former depths. Relying on ancient tradition as well as on his own intuition, Sri Yukteswar attributed these cycles to the sun's movement around a dual, a revolution which brings our solar system alternately closer to and farther away from a cosmic center of highly conscious energy, or Vishnunabhi.

Interestingly, numerous ancient peoples throughout the world believed in these cycles of time. They even divided each of them into four ages, which Greek tradition symbolized with the words gold, silver, copper, and iron. Orthodox historians today, of course, don't admit the possibility that such cycles exist. Yet it is from history itself that we get the first glimpses of those cycles' reality.

These great cycles of time, as Sri Yukteswar explained them, reached their nadir, or lowest point, in the year 500 AD. Indeed, one discerns in the centuries prior to that year a gradual decrease of knowledge, awareness, and sensitivity, amounting to a steady decline in human awareness. Since 500 AD, moreover, there has clearly been a steady increase in that awareness, resulting in ever-greater clarity.

The possibility of the earth's going through a cycle of ascending and descending ages gives credence to the evidence, rapidly accumulating in our own day, that high civilizations existed in the past. Many books today make a case for some of those civilizations, at least, having reached far higher heights than our own. As for there being cycles of time due to the movement within the galaxy of our sun, at least two books so far address this subject in depth: *Lost Star of Myth and Time*, by Walter Cruttenden, and *The Yugas**, by Joseph Selbie and Byasa Steinmetz.

Consider one simple, known reality which points to the general debasement of consciousness approaching 500 AD: the Roman "games," in which gladiators ferociously slaughtered one another in the Colosseum, to the applause and delight of many thousands. Today it seems hardly credible, but even Saint Augustine, in his youth, was addicted to those games.

Consider also the widespread poverty and squalor of those times; the general illiteracy; the violence and insensitivity; the brevity of life combined with the prevalence of disease. These and many other symptoms of emotional and intellectual darkness prevailed everywhere.

Since 500 AD, there has been a general rise in human consciousness. Sri Yukteswar corrected old *Kali Yuga* reckonings as to the correct length of each age, which assigned to *Kali Yuga* a duration of 432,000 years. Sri Yukteswar said that, in fact, a whole cycle lasts only 24,000 years, and the darkest age lasts only 1,200 descending, and 1,200 ascending years.

The present age, *Dwapara Yuga*, will, he said, endure a total of 2,400 years. A *sandhya*, or bridge, occurs between each *yuga* and

*– Available in October 2010 from Crystal Clarity Publishers.

the next: 100 years at the end of ascending *Kali Yuga*, followed by
a 200-year bridge into ascending *Dwapara*.

Thus, the bridge leading out of *Kali Yuga*, which brought the first
hints of approaching *Dwapara*, occurred from 1600–1700 AD. This
century was followed by two more, from 1700–1900 AD, that led
into *Dwapara* proper. There were "rumblings" of the end of deepest
Kali Yuga as early as the Italian Renaissance, but the sixteen hundreds saw the true dawn of a new understanding with those pio-
neers of modern physics: Galileo Galilei, Isaac Newton, and many
others. These men introduced the scientific method, which was
a completely new way of thinking based not on a priori assumptions, but on demonstrated facts.

During the next two-hundred-year bridge, or *sandhya*, into
Dwapara proper, we see the Industrial Revolution; the acceptance
and increasing use of electricity; social upheaval to affirm the natural dignity of man; the Michelson-Morley experiment (in 1887),
which revealed that light is both a particle and a wave; and the
dawning realization that the universe is not a giant mechanism, as
scientists had believed, but is a manifestation of far subtler realities.
Matter itself was seen to be a manifestation of energy. These were
but a few of the radical changes human understanding underwent
during the *sandhya* into *Dwapara Yuga* proper.

Today (2009) man is well into the second century of ascending
Dwapara Yuga. Conflict is increasing between old, *Kali Yuga* ways of
thinking and those of *Dwapara*: between self-aggrandizement and
a more generous wish for universal upliftment; between the wish
to control situations, things, and people and an impulse to flow
with wholesome change in one's own life, and in the lives of others; between the tendency to close one's mind to anything new,
and an opposite tendency to be open to improvement. The conflict
is bringing increasing tension to the human spirit, one that may
well soon explode into widespread and major social upheavals:
a deep economic depression; global warfare; perhaps even earth
cataclysms. After the "dust" has settled, however, I believe that
things will simmer down peaceably, and this new Age of Energy

will begin in earnest with its more fluid view of life, of human existence, and of objective reality.

The age of William the Conqueror was much darker than our own. Historians, unaware of these great cycles of time, have no choice but to believe that human consciousness itself hasn't changed much over the centuries. From the knowledge they possess, they cannot but believe that what people did in the past they would do as readily today, if society had not advanced to levels that have made such behavior unacceptable. Naturally, too, people without special knowledge of the *yugas* believe that what people understood centuries ago has changed only to the extent that gradual, linear developments in society itself have influenced human understanding. How, indeed, could anyone imagine another explanation for the great changes that have affected society over the past one thousand—indeed, fifteen hundred—years, since 500 AD?

In this book, Catherine Kairavi describes a society much more primitive than our own in both knowledge and consciousness. Historians will inevitably object that mankind was the same in William's day as it is today. They will give facts and figures to defend that belief. For they are intellectual scholars, and there is no aspect of human consciousness more disposed to argument than the intellect. It is kept vital and alive, after all, by argument. Indeed, historians—experts in their field—may well need at least a generation to change this view. In that case, it will probably be other historians who grow up with this new and broader perspective on their subject.

Catherine depicts the days of William and Henry as having been far more brutal than our own, despite the much greater capacity for destruction of modern weaponry. The developing consciousness of our age, however, is certainly toward deeper concern and respect for others, with an increasing desire for worldwide peace and harmony. Ms. Kairavi's statement that the difference lies in a change toward increasing expansion of human consciousness itself, and not in mere social developments, cannot but be opposed by historians who (by their own lights, necessarily so) reject any thought that human consciousness itself can be essentially improved.

Historians will certainly protest also against some of Catherine's "value judgments"—for example, her description of Harold Godwinson as a "scoundrel." Yet she takes the trouble in these pages to explain at length her reason for this adjective. Historians claim to *know* the whole story of the Conquest, yet many different conclusions can be drawn from the same set of facts. Scholars who are prejudiced on the Anglo-Saxon side naturally view Harold as an Anglo-Saxon hero, and ignore—whether deliberately so or not—such inconvenient facts as his own mixed Anglo-Saxon and Danish blood, and his truly scurrilous family heritage. Those on the other hand who, like Hillaire Belloc, favor the French side underscore William's very real greatness. A case can be made for either side. The novels of Sir Walter Scott and others, however, who staunchly defended the Anglo-Saxon "cause," must be classed simply as romances.

I myself was raised, until the age of thirteen, in the English system, and was conditioned to consider William the Conqueror one of history's great villains. Imagine my shock, therefore, to find (at the age of twenty-two) that the man to whom, after prolonged and anguished searching, I had pledged my life as a disciple, had himself been, in a past life, that great warrior king, William the Conqueror! Yogananda made this statement to his disciples quite openly. Needless to say, I had to revise my opinion of William, for my own experience of my Guru, Paramhansa Yogananda, was—yes, certainly—that he was gifted with the strong personality of a born leader, but also that he emanated powerfully the supreme virtues: kindness—indeed, compassion—humility, gentleness, truthfulness, universal respect, and all the marks of true spiritual greatness.

What had been his purpose, I asked myself, in even making such a statement?

Years later, when Warren Hollister's book, *Henry I,* came out, I felt the time had come to explore this issue in greater detail. For by then I had also come to believe deeply that I myself had been

William's youngest son, Henry I, whose role it was to complete his father's mission.

The thought of my identity with Henry had been growing in me steadily for years. Indeed, in all my reading about Henry, I found that I saw the world *through* his eyes, rather than looking at him in the third person. When I read about "Conan's Leap"—you'll read that story in these pages—I found my heart racing with the stress and excitement of that day. When Henry appeared at Winchester after his brother's death in the New Forest, and claimed the royal treasury, and was confronted there by William of Breteuil as he sought to prevent Henry's entry, I felt I was myself on the scene at that crucial moment.

Historians will surely oppose much that Catherine has written in this book, as, on many issues, they oppose even one another. Nevertheless, Catherine devoted ten years of her life to carefully researching her subject. For the rest, I think Paramhansa Yogananda's statement that he himself *was* William will outweigh, for many readers, any intellectual beliefs, doubts, and challenges that may be presented to disprove certain statements in this book.

On the other hand, if you don't believe this account, then I suggest you take it as a fascinating slant on a well-known period of history. Read it—if you prefer—as a novel! At any rate, read it. To me it is intensely real, but if to you it seems too large a chunk to swallow whole, read it at least as a first-class adventure story! I think it will give you, among other things, a completely new take on present and future trends in modern society.

ACKNOWLEDGEMENTS

I would like to express my gratitude to the many conscientious scholars whose careful research made this work possible. Especially I would like to thank C. Warren Hollister and his student, Amanda Clark Frost, for their monumental work, *Henry I.* It was more than nine years ago that Swami Kriyananda (J. Donald Walters), after reading their book, suggested that I consider undertaking doing the research for, and writing, another book, based on theirs, but intended for a more general readership.

Their work was obviously intended especially for the benefit of fellow scholars. Its nearly five hundred pages contained some 2500 footnotes, some of which included untranslated passages in the original French, Latin, or Greek. Obviously their work, though groundbreaking, was intended for a restricted readership. Swami Kriyananda proposed that I research and write a work for a broader audience.

I want also to thank the following individuals: Devi Novak and Asha Praver, for their insights into similarities between Henry and Kriyananda; Richard Salva, who brought his own scholarship and love for the subject to the job of indexing; and Anandi Cornell, for her editorial help.

Above all, I want to express my profound gratitude to Swami Kriyananda, my dear teacher and friend, who gave unstintingly of his time to help edit and shorten material that might otherwise, because of my enthusiasm for the subject, have overwhelmed the poor reader with too many facts! I want to thank him also for giving me the courage to produce what may be viewed in time as a new kind of history.

Two Souls: Four Lives

Part One

WILLIAM: CONQUEROR OR REFORMER?

CHAPTER 1

The Past Revealed

This book will explore an astonishing statement made by Paramhansa Yogananda, a universally revered spiritual teacher of modern times. It was, to the best of my knowledge, the first time that a Self-realized master (one who has been liberated from all the egoic desires which compel man to reincarnate) revealed that he had been, in a previous incarnation, a historical figure about whom a great deal is known: William the Conqueror.

Yogananda's *Autobiography of a Yogi*, one of the world's most widely read and translated of spiritual classics, has convinced millions of rational, modern minds of the existence of spiritual truths, and of the universal value of the teachings of India, including the twin teachings of karma and reincarnation. Even those of us who at first had to "back burner" a few of the miracles we encountered in *Autobiography of a Yogi* found ourselves accepting innumerable, completely new possibilities regarding the nature of God, Creation, and man's place in the greater scheme of things—all entirely because of the purity and personal spiritual authority that come through so palpably in the character of Paramhansa Yogananda.

What Yogananda shares with his readers in *Autobiography of a Yogi* has struck a deep chord in virtually all who have read it. As the master himself very often said, "One cannot *learn* spiritual truths: one can only *recognize* them."

Even those who entertain deep reverence for Yogananda, however, have had difficulty with the question, "How can someone of his spiritual stature have willingly played out such a life as that of William the Conqueror, a life that called for spectacular bloodshed?" It is safe to say, certainly, that there isn't one reader of Yogananda's autobiography who, on hearing for the first time that Paramhansa Yogananda was William the Conqueror, has reacted with the thought, "Well, that does make sense!"

Even if you yourself know nothing about Paramhansa Yogananda, you have probably formed some notion of William the Conqueror's role in history, and of the manner of man he was. If you were schooled under the English system, you may have been taught that William, duke of Normandy, was one of the great villains of history. And although most Americans have only vague notions about the Conqueror, they, too, would readily agree that words like "fierce" and "merciless" fit what they do know about the Norman warrior who defeated Harold Godwinson at the Battle of Hastings, subdued all of England, and, as a result, changed the course of Western civilization.

In these pages, I shall investigate the manner of man he was. Was he a warrior driven by ambition for territorial conquest? Or was he a deeply pious leader, dedicated to the greater good of humanity, whose decisions can only be understood by appreciating the loftiness of his vision?

I shall also investigate the history of his youngest son, Henry, who—alone among those who walked in the footsteps of the Conqueror—understood the Conqueror's vision and brought it to completion. The life span of William was not enough to instill in his kingdom and duchy all the dreams he held of a stability that would endure beyond the Middle Ages, and usher in a new age of expanding knowledge. In investigating Henry's life, I shall attempt in addition to discern whether he might not, in this lifetime also, have joined Yogananda to bring that master's vast mission to fulfillment.

Using essentially the same facts as those available to every historian, let us see whether we cannot find William's deeds and motivations to have been consonant with the life and teachings of Paramhansa Yogananda, and Henry's, with the role of one of his disciples.

CHAPTER 2

A Righteous Warrior, and a Noble Cause

The **Norman Conquest of** England was a watershed event for the whole of Europe. When England came under the rule of a Norman king, the balance of power in Western Christendom shifted. The Conquest also strengthened the papacy in its efforts to unify and reform the church. William wrenched England out from the orbit of Scandinavia, and aligned it with the Latin West and with the Roman church.

William the Conqueror has been excoriated for his exceptional brutality in subduing England. Interestingly, students of those times always express—though sometimes grudgingly—their awe at his feats, and at the indomitable will he brought to bear in their accomplishment. Usually, at the same time, they decry what looks to them like his unusual savagery in accomplishing them. I must ask the reader, therefore, to bear in mind at the outset these salient facts:

The historian today, writing of those times (one imagines him puffing on his pipe in a cozy study, with no one to "command" but a secretary to whom he always expresses himself politely), cannot easily imagine the times of William, and the exigencies he faced as a warrior and as the ruler of a nation.

Hand-to-hand combat, for one thing, may be almost inconceivable to the historian, though he may be able to visualize it clearly enough for the purposes of his work. Imagine, however, the realities of that era. Try to see with your mind's eye, and to experience mentally through your senses, a time when disease was common; when people had little concept of sanitation; when muddy streets were difficult to navigate and filthy with garbage; when there was no street lighting; when most people lived in squalor; when few lived to old age; and when most nobles treated the common people like cattle.

It was a time when voluntary cooperation was almost unimaginable; when most people lived only for themselves; when violence was the recognized way of settling a disagreement; when harshness was understood but kindness was equated with weakness; when a thought seemed "reasonable" only if it agreed with one's own desires.

It is true that great and noble individuals appear also in every age, whose lofty natures lift them above the negative influences of their times. Such a man, as I shall show, was William, duke of Normandy.

One of the traits that still causes him to be generally misunderstood was his utter lack of any personal motive. Even today, those few who want nothing for themselves are suspected of being furtive and unnatural. *Of course* (so goes the reasoning) everybody wants *something*. If a person shows himself to be wholly without personal motives, it must mean his motives (which everyone of course has) are *dark* ones. People who say they want nothing for themselves are often persecuted as though they wanted to accomplish their inevitably selfish ends underhandedly. Yogananda said, of those who renounce everything for God, that they receive (as Jesus put it) "an hundredfold, *and persecution*—and, in the world to come, eternal life."

I will answer the charges historians have laid against the Conqueror for the supposed villainy of the role he had to play—for example, in his widely deprecated "Harrying of the North." First, however, it is important for me to make a few more general observations on the nature of eleventh century Western Europe, thus to place William's actions more clearly in context.

Life on the whole continent of Europe was only then emerging from centuries of darkness, following the final collapse of the

Roman empire. Life then was squalid, brief, and brutal. Viking marauders, slavers, murderous highwaymen, unchecked cheating (motivated by avarice), and petty wars of vengeance between local despots—which always involved acute suffering for their dependents—made life a precarious affair, lived always on a knife's edge. In fact, the most common cause of death then was not disease, childbirth, or malnourishment, but, instead, violence in some form—whether in battle or by murder. Those who died of old age were rare. The failure of a single crop could result in starvation for a whole community.

To our modern sensibilities, not only was eleventh century warfare brutal, but so also were a host of other customs: medical practice, building construction, personal hygiene, child raising, the treatment of vassals and peasants (what to speak of domestic animals!)—in fact, virtually every aspect of life. Could you and I be transported back magically to Normandy and England in those times, we would be horrified by virtually everything we saw. Even the way a prelate scolded an altar boy would earn from us the epithet "brutal," including as it usually did a few kicks and blows from the prelate's staff.

In order to learn what we may from Yogananda's statement that he was William the Conqueror, we have to resolve to our satisfaction history's assessment that William was harsh and merciless in the way he brought England under his control. What do historians mean by such epithets? Do they mean that William was more drastic than other successful medieval rulers? Do they imagine that kindness would have won over the boors who warred with one another constantly, or that sweet smiles would have secured his "conquest" from a completely selfish populace? Did he employ tactics that were uniquely brutal for his age? Are the textbooks suggesting that he derived some dark pleasure from the power he wielded? William was a man with a mission, and it will become clear as we proceed that he brought about vital changes in the Western world.

Interestingly, no historian to my knowledge would readily agree to the extreme judgments I have suggested. One must conclude, therefore, that these non-specific charges against him are the result, again, of overlaying modern sensibilities onto the life of a warrior king of the eleventh century. Though many historians would protest that they are not "in the business" of generating military policies and tactics, it would be very refreshing to encounter one historian who, after exclaiming, for example, on William's "Harrying of the North," followed his description with a counter-suggestion of what the Conqueror might have done instead—more "humanely"—to secure the kingdom against Scandinavian invasion and constant treachery from his subjects in the North, especially given the fact that the men and the resources the Conqueror could command were stretched very thin.

Whatever various writers have had in mind in making their sweeping statements, the same "evidence" of William's character has also led them to conclude that he was, certainly, highly effective, and—unlike such a warrior general as Genghis Khan—was widely admired. Surely, in light of Paramhansa Yogananda's statement that he himself was William, that lifetime needs careful reexamination.

The Conqueror's actions were, as I shall show, completely appropriate to the times and to the mission he had been sent by God to accomplish.

CHAPTER 3

"A Lie Agreed Upon"

The first question that must be settled is whether any conquest can be justified, ever. Is it right to defend one's country? Is it even right, spiritually, to defend one's home? What, exactly, are the merits of passive surrender—let us say, to a ruthless invader? When Genghis Khan swept over Asia, slaying the populations of whole cities, he even left soldiers in concealment after his departure, who later emerged and killed the remaining citizens who emerged from hiding. Proudly, Genghis Khan left mounds of skulls outside every town he conquered.

Which would have been more spiritually right: to defend oneself, to the death if necessary, or to surrender and await one's fate passively? People who believe in passive resistance might respond, "Love conquers all." It would take a mighty love, however, to overcome such cruelty as Genghis Khan's.

Life itself is a battle. Those who never struggle against wrongs, or against evil in themselves, become weak-willed and lose their spiritual strength.

Mahatma Gandhi is a modern example of one who conquered a whole nation through the quality of *ahimsa* (harmlessness). He was once asked, "What would you do if a killer came to your village and threatened to slay everybody?" His reply was, "I'd let him kill me, first."

Fine. Then what if, after he had killed you, he went on to slaughter everyone else? Would you have accomplished anything worthwhile by stepping to the head of that line?

Spiritually speaking, it is better for one man to die than for many. Had Gandhi practiced his non-violence on a nation that was less well-intentioned than England, the results of his movement might have been very different. To begin with, he would have been killed himself, first; the opposition wouldn't have bothered to send him to prison. Second, if the whole nation continued in this folly, millions would have been killed.

Yogananda commented on India's peaceful victory: "It was because the British are gentlemen. Had he practiced non-violence on Russia, he would have failed." Yogananda continued, "Love is powerful only to the extent that you actually feel it. But if what you really feel is fear, not love? If you confront a tiger with a quaking heart, you'll only finish practicing your 'non-violence' inside its stomach."

William the Conqueror was only as violent as he needed to be, to achieve his goals.

The next obvious question, then, must be, "Were those goals right? Is aggression ever right?" Obviously, had it been truly aggression, it would not have been right. Self-defense is spiritually acceptable, but was William practicing self-defense? If his invasion of England had been merely a conquest, it would certainly have been spiritually wrong.

In this book I shall show that William came to England not as a conqueror (though for the sake of convenience in referring to him, I will often use that traditional epithet). He came as its rightful ruler and king, to correct a situation that threatened lasting misery for the whole island.

There is another, much more important principle involved here than the simple defense of one's human rights. To defend truth, justice, and high spiritual principles is a higher right. In the great Indian scripture, the Bhagavad Gita (chapter 4 verse 8), this truth is stated: "O Bharata (Arjuna), whenever virtue (*dharma*, or right action) declines, and vice (*adharma*) is in the ascendant, I [the Divine Lord] incarnate Myself on earth (as an *avatar*, or descended master). Appearing from age to age in visible form, I come to destroy evil and to re-establish virtue."

William was born with a much higher mission than merely to reclaim a kingship. His life-purpose went far beyond even establishing new and beneficial trends in an important European country. He came as a divine instrument, long since liberated from all karma of his own, to destroy evil and re-establish virtue at a time when mankind, generally, had fallen far from virtue.

There is another aspect to consider. When a whole people embroil themselves in vice and error, we never find God trying to help them. Sodom and Gomorrah are excellent examples. God said that if even fifty good men could be found therein, He would spare those cities; but there weren't even ten. In other words, there must also be in men's hearts a certain openness to virtue, before God will descend and offer them help. Normandy and England at the time of which I speak (I cannot speak for the whole of Europe) were experiencing a rise of consciousness. There was a dawning desire for God and righteousness. William was born to shift England's focus away from the quasi-pagan influence of Scandinavia, and to bring it under the influence of Christian Rome. He came to instill law and order. The English people of our times often think of Harold Godwinson as a good man. In fact he was a scoundrel, born into a family of unscrupulous opportunists. England itself had been divided into several large, warring earldoms and warring noble families, because of which the common man suffered greatly. William's duty was to bring unity to that country, and a more godly way of life— also, and very importantly, to prepare them for a great destiny. England, separated as it was from the rest of Europe, could more easily be brought into a new way of living.

Paramhansa Yogananda tried his best, similarly, to encourage people to live in little, self-sustaining intentional communities. As Henry completed William's mission, bringing peace and lawful governance to England and ensuring its glorious future, so Swami Kriyananda, a close disciple of Yogananda's, brought his guru's mission and teachings to the world and created those communities, for which the time was not yet ripe during the master's life.

Was Kriyananda, in a former life, King Henry I of England? We shall explore this possibility. Curiously, again, it wasn't until William's youngest son Henry was crowned the king of England that he, alone of William's children, was able to complete William's mission. And it wasn't until Kriyananda was put out on his own by those who were senior to him as disciples, but who didn't share his vision of Yogananda's worldwide mission, that Kriyananda was able to begin the work which Yogananda had given him.

William, however, in order to fulfill his mission, could only work with the materials, the social realities, and the general, low level of refinement of his times. The relatively coarse mentality of that age was the unavoidable backdrop for William's mission.

Thus, as William struggled to bring England under his control as its new king, he was constrained to exercise authority in the way medieval man could understand: siege, battle, pillage, and other methods that are far from acceptable nowadays. The methods to which he resorted were unquestionably necessary for those times, however. In order to unite England, it was necessary to establish the kingship itself as the central power in a country which, until then, had been groupings of several self-centered, self-ambitious earldoms. The remarkable thing about William is that he very rarely imposed the death penalty himself; in those few cases, it was for treachery.

Unchecked violence, everywhere in Europe, had been a fact of life since the collapse of the Roman Empire. Fighting was necessary if one didn't want simply to be slaughtered. The barbarians who overran Rome, after its moral collapse, represented a strain of mindlessness which, in its violence, was utterly unstoppable. They tormented Western Europe until Charlemagne's empire imposed on people a brief period of restraint. That those northern hordes didn't destroy everything was partly because they didn't understand Rome's civilization. The men from the North hadn't the knowledge to destroy Rome's great monuments, roads, aqueducts, coliseum, or its temples. All these were therefore, for the most part, left standing, though they served people for centuries as rock quarries. The monuments stood because the invaders didn't have the technical skill to destroy them.

Kenneth Clark points out in his work *Civilisation* that relatively soon after Rome's collapse the ragtag bands who lived in the shelter of those great stone ruins assumed that the old structures had been constructed by a vanished race of giants. The knowledge of how to build monumentally in stone remained lost for centuries.

Fighting was an absolute necessity during those centuries; it was the only way of defending the tiny, first shoots of communal stability which, toward the end of the first millennium AD, were beginning to appear.

If we can accept the fact that Paramhansa Yogananda, a Self-realized master, accepted a divinely ordained mission as William the Conqueror, can we then view William's life, as it has been reported to us not only by modern historians but by his own contemporaries, as the great master who later became Paramhansa Yogananda? Were Yogananda's achievements, when he was William the Conqueror, in any way "setting the stage" for his mission in the twentieth century?

What follows is a quick overview of William's life, and what he achieved in England and Normandy. Thus I shall try to lay the foundation for a clear answer to those questions. Even though some of William's less savory deeds are difficult for us, a thousand years later, to "square" with what we know of Paramhansa Yogananda, did the Conqueror really commit, or perhaps only order to be committed, the atrocities that history has ascribed to him?

Paramhansa Yogananda himself would undoubtedly have agreed with Napoleon Bonaparte's observation, "History is a lie agreed upon."

When dealing with truths that transcend the material world, the rational mind will never be able to piece together all the hard evidence needed. Reason is a tricky tool: it can justify many sides of an equation. Intuition, then, born of receptivity to divine truth, will always be necessary.

Let me close this chapter with an interesting claim, made within the Roman Catholic Church—one that has come down through an abbey in Belgium. The tradition states that the prayer for which Saint Francis of Assisi is best known—"Make me an instrument of Thy peace"—was in fact written by "William of Normandy," and was found in William the Conqueror's breviary:

Lord, make me an instrument of Thy peace;
Where there is hatred, let me sow love;
Where there is injury: pardon;
Where there is error: truth;
Where there is doubt: faith;
Where there is despair: hope;
Where there is darkness: light;
And where there is sadness: joy.

O Divine Master,
Grant that I may not so much
Seek to be consoled, as to console;
To be understood, as to understand;
To be loved, as to love.

For it is in giving that we receive;
In pardoning, that we are pardoned,
And in dying that we are born to eternal life.
Amen.

Interesting also, Yogananda often spoke of Saint Francis as his "patron saint."

CHAPTER 4

"A Flowering Youth"–Intimations of Greatness

If **we examine the** life of William, duke of Normandy and king of England, through the "lens" of what his youngest son, Henry, aspired to—and, indeed, achieved—the Conqueror emerges as a very different person from the ruthlessly ambitious warrior of historians' insistence. For William was the fountainhead of every aspiration that his son Henry, too, struggled to fulfill within the Anglo-Norman kingdom.

The highly effective reign of King Henry I became feasible because he was faithful to his father's vision. Henry's chief desire was for peace, which he actually accomplished with spectacular success. For thirty-three years England enjoyed, under his reign, a period of peace that had not been known in that country since Roman times. Even great rulers like Alfred the Great had been unable to curtail private warfare so completely as Henry did.

We must try, then, to understand King Henry I also, and in a new way, so as fully to understand his father. The evidence I shall offer on Henry is supported by the interpretive skills and scholarship of his recent biographer, C. Warren Hollister.

First, however, let us investigate the life of the father, William.

William was a young child when his father, Duke Robert I, set him among his barons and declared the child to be his chosen heir. He demanded that his great men then and there perform homage to William as their future overlord. Having received from them the promise he'd demanded, Duke Robert announced his intention of undertaking a penitential pilgrimage to the Holy Land.

The barons' worst fears were soon realized, when word came to Normandy, in 1035, that Duke Robert "the Magnificent" had died. He owed his death, as had many before him, to the rigors of the journey. Robert I's son and heir, William, was only seven years old at the time. An uncle of his (also bearing the name, Robert), who for decades had been archbishop of Rouen, wisely sought and received approval from King Henry I of France, the duke of Normandy's feudal overlord, for the boy William to succeed his father.

Even so, the boy's very survival depended for the next eight years on loyal relatives, and on the very few noblemen who remained faithful to their promise to Duke Robert. William had more than once to be snatched from his bed in the dead of night, hardly moments before an assassin's knife could strike him, and hurried off to concealment in some poor peasant's hovel. The duchy itself was sinking rapidly into chaos. It would be William's task, when he reached his majority, to bring back order to the dukedom. Even before his majority, however, he was already leading men into battle. The chaos was so pervasive that the interests of bishops, too, were so closely identified with their baronial overlords (often their kinsmen) that those churchmen did nothing to intervene for the prevention of inter-baronial warfare.

Around the year 1042, when the young duke was about fourteen years old, the monk chronicler William of Jumieges wrote: "Duke William, while in the prime of his flowering youth, began to devote himself wholeheartedly to the worship of God; so by avoiding the company of ignorant men and listening to wise advice he was powerful in wars as well as wise and able in secular affairs." The victory that established his power came at the battle of Val-ès-Dunes in 1047.

There is every indication, in the testimony of contemporary chroniclers, that William was precociously astute in his understanding of affairs of state, and was already able, at a remarkably young age, to discern who among his counselors were serving his best interests and those of the duchy, and who were not. The young duke's discrimination was tested mightily, long before he officially came into his majority.

Immediately thereafter, in October of 1047, the duchy's most influential prelates met Duke William near the battlefield outside of Caen. The purpose for the meeting was to endorse, with due solemnity, the Truce of God, which just five years earlier had failed to gain substantial support within the duchy. This Truce forbade battle, or any kind of fighting, from Wednesday evening of each week until the following Monday morning. It defined certain longer periods of peace which had to be observed, in addition, during Lent, Advent, and other holy seasons. Violators of this Truce of God were to be excommunicated and banned from participating in any of the sacraments or services of the church.

At this October 1047 ceremony outside Caen, however, the nineteen-year-old Duke William added something new to the enforcement of the Truce: penalties and punishments that would be exacted by the secular as well as the ecclesiastical arms of the duchy. The church recognized for its part that the duke (as also the king of France) should be exempt from penalties connected with violating the Truce of God, since these men were needed as a peacekeeping force. Up to this time, as David Douglas writes, the church had been the sole instrument for enforcing the Truce of God, largely through its use of ecclesiastical sanctions.

Duke William's decision to include, as a natural aspect of his own ducal responsibilities, the policing and punishment of those who engaged in private warfare in violation of the Truce of God introduced an innovation that created, over time, what came to be honored throughout Normandy as the *pax ducis*: the "peace of the duke."

CHAPTER 5

The Testing Ground of Normandy

William's foremost biographer in the English language, David C. Douglas, took some pains to impress on students of the Conqueror's life that the period from 1047 to 1060 was, for William, a time of great insecurity, with almost constant warfare. Even securing the surrender of the leader of the rebel barons who were defeated at Val-ès-Dunes required three whole years, during which time William was compelled to remain in Lower Normandy, in a state of the greatest vigilance.

What might have been, for a lesser man, a time of frustration and increasing impatience was for William a golden opportunity. He was forced to stay in precisely that part of the duchy which had most recently come under ducal control. There had been a long-standing division between Upper and Lower Normandy, and the ducal influence was least felt in just that area where William was now stationed, as he continued his siege of the fortress of Brionne. Since he was constrained to remain in that part of Normandy, William energetically explored the strengths of the area, and looked for ways to develop it so that a greater unity might develop between Upper and Lower Normandy.

Among other things, Duke William encouraged the growth of the small town of Caen, which was—both militarily and from a mercantile point of view—strategically well placed at the confluence of two major rivers. William himself planned and paid for the construction of a defensive stone wall around the town, and erected a castle which he eventually turned also into an important ducal residence. Some years later, he and his wife, Matilda of Flanders, each built a magnificent abbey at Caen—one for monks, the other for nuns.

Within William's lifetime, Caen rose to become the second most important city in Normandy. It is significant that William, contrary to ducal tradition, asked that he be buried there rather than in Rouen, the ducal seat. With Duke William's active promotion of Caen, he established a strong presence in the growing town, and made it a lively center of trade in Lower Normandy, thereby changing it from an area that had been traditionally a center of rebellion. Thus, the youthful duke demonstrated extraordinary maturity and creativity in political problem-solving, and achieved what no duke had previously succeeded in doing: uniting Upper and Lower Normandy under ducal authority.

The chroniclers tell us that, throughout William's several, and necessary, campaigns, he was "surrounded by treachery." Any misstep on his part would have led inevitably to widespread revolt. William was proving himself no mean strategist: cool-headed and subtle in his understanding of the diplomatic ramifications of all that was unfolding in the neighboring counties.

He was also beginning to win the loyalty of many true men. Thus, although in the autumn of 1053 King Henry of France and the count of Ponthieu moved against him (in order to relieve William of Arques, whose castle William was besieging), William's problem was decided for him by his now-loyal followers. A contingent of Duke William's men ambushed a portion of the invading French army and, catching the French totally unprepared, inflicted heavy casualties.

Late in 1053, William of Arques, Duke William's uncle, surrendered, asking only that his garrison be treated mercifully. The duke granted his kinsman what historians have called a very lenient punishment: banishment for the rest of his days. A very relieved (and humiliated) William of Arques fled immediately for refuge to the count of Boulogne.

However, Duke William's success in taking Arques and banishing his uncle, who had been a pretender to the dukedom of Normandy, did not win the war. There were further invasions, further betrayals. One invasion, which included men from all over France, was formidable. The French monarchy had mobilized an enormous array of its feudal strength against Normandy.

The timing of this invasion, however, proved fortunate for Duke William. He had recently captured the fortress of Arques, and expelled his most dangerous internal enemy. This victory was vitally important, for it meant that the duke could now draw on the feudal army of Normandy—the military service owed to him—with no serious, unresolved challenges to his overlordship dividing the loyalties of the duchy's landholders. Nor did William need to split his forces between a treacherous Norman baron, rebelling against him, in order to deal with external invaders. Additionally, the fact that the impact of the invasion was obviously intended to be far-reaching must have helped to whip those Norman barons into action who up to now had not had any real connection with Duke William.

The feudal army raised by the duke in early 1054 was large enough to be split into two significant contingents. One ducal force was sent to confront that part of the French army which was under the leadership of the count of Ponthieu and of the French king's brother; they entered Normandy from the east. Duke William himself led the second contingent to confront the larger French and Angevin army, which was now making terrible progress through the Evrecin.

The first contact with either of the two invading armies was made by the Norman army under the command of Robert, count of Eu. The French contingent, entering the duchy from the east, gave themselves over to unrestrained rape and pillage. The French, in consequence, were taken utterly by surprise by the disciplined Norman army. The French casualties were enormous, and the French army was unable to pull itself together sufficiently to make a concerted stand, though the battle raged for hours. The king's brother escaped by the skin of his teeth, while Guy, the new count of Ponthieu, was not so fortunate.

News of this encounter, which was disastrous for the French, reached both Duke William and King Henry of France as they were moving toward their own decisive encounter. Once again, the French king decided he did not want to risk a full scale pitched battle with Duke William, and hastily marched his army back toward the French border.

Duke William's control of Normandy had been saved once again—this time entirely by his own astuteness and strength of will. Many of Normandy's chief men fought in common cause on the side of their duke, and experienced his strength and sagacity at first hand. The more perceptive of them showed themselves willing, now, to submit to their duke's authority, for they realized that he was, indeed—as the phrase of the High Middle Ages expressed it—their "natural lord."

Peace negotiations with King Henry of France were concluded near the end of 1055. Significantly, the French king confirmed that the duke of Normandy was now fully in charge of those lands which he had won in Maine from Geoffrey of Anjou—notably Domfront and the area surrounding this town.

CHAPTER 6

The Strength to Mold His Times

It **was during those** tumultuous years that Duke William married Matilda, daughter of Baldwin V, count of Flanders. Diplomatically the marriage made perfect sense. David Douglas writes that William's barons encouraged the match, since it would gain a powerful ally for the duke in the person of the count of Flanders, a rising force in Western Europe.

Sometime, then, in 1050 or 1051, Matilda, then in her late teens, was met near the Normandy border, and was escorted by close family members to Eu, where the couple were married. From everything said by the chroniclers, theirs was apparently a very harmonious marriage, with no indication that William was ever unfaithful to Matilda—a fact nearly unheard of in that era. Four sons and five or six daughters were born to the couple.

The Conqueror's preeminent biographer, David Douglas, insists that even the casual student pause a moment here, to contemplate what it took for William to have come this far. Douglas points out that the usual qualities for which William is praised—his skill as a warrior and general, his occasional and highly effective, if draconian, methods, and his good luck—are not in any way adequate to explain the young duke's outstanding accomplishments. William faced enormous adversity throughout his life: attempts on his life beginning in infancy, treachery throughout his adolescence, and continual warfare for many years. In the final analysis, Douglas credits his success to be a triumph of character.

Invariably, in all the histories of the time, two other factors are named as particular to this extraordinary period of Norman achievement, even though Duke William's character overshadows all other considerations. The first of these is the aristocracy he gathered about him during these years: wonderfully vital, intelligent, and energetic.

Traditionally the *vicomte*, or baron, was the duke's main administrator in each county of Normandy. The next task before Duke William was, therefore, crucial: it was to link his own interests with those of the aristocrats around him in such a way as ultimately to dominate the developing social order.

While the characteristics of this remarkable aristocracy have been discussed by many historians, Douglas drives home the point that this group of men was unique: while highly capable and intelligent, they were also fiercely independent and proud of their own powerful masculine strength.

The fact that William was able dominate them by his personality and train them to be true statesman on his behalf is extremely impressive. Douglas considers one of the great achievements of William the Conqueror to be winning to his cause the divergent interests and ambitions of one of the most exceptional groups of aristocrats in eleventh-century Europe.

CHAPTER 7

Rebuilding the Moral Authority of the Church

The second factor that is particular to this extraordinary time in Norman history is the gathering strength of the church in Normandy under the leadership of men of outstanding ability and true sanctity. Just one hundred years before the accession of Duke William there had not been a single monastery left standing in the ecclesiastical province of Rouen, the borders of which were basically contiguous with those of Normandy itself. The collapse of the church was one consequence of the chaos that had ensued after the collapse of Charlemagne's empire. However, by the time of the Conquest in 1066, Normandy had an abundance of abbeys including Bec, the second greatest ecclesiastical learning center in Gaul after Cluny. The duke himself, moreover, in concert with Maurilius, the saintly archbishop of Rouen, regularly convened important church councils.

Formerly, and especially during William's minority, the aristocracy had spoliated the church. Now, under William, those same great families became highly identified with the church in the lands under their control. Non-inheriting sons of the great dynasties that arose under Duke William found positions of influence in church administration, including in the great bishoprics. Thus, as many scholars have pointed out, the tight interweaving of those same family members, who controlled both the secular and the ecclesiastical centers of power, had the effect over time of again enriching the church—through the generosity of those very families which,

25

quite recently, had been her despoilers. No fewer than twenty new monasteries were founded, and to some degree endowed, between 1035 and 1066. And only two of these were founded by William and Matilda themselves.

Here again the character of Duke William himself—in this case, his own very deep piety—tipped the trend even further. Not only did the great families who tied their future to his shooting star found and endow many new monasteries in Normandy, but they sought abbots for them who were of real spirituality, as well as competent in lay affairs. William added a tremendous impetus, making it clear that he wanted sincere piety to be the basis for the whole church in Normandy.

Duke William himself appointed his own half-brother Odo to the bishopric of Bayeux. Odo was probably nineteen years old at the time, but William desperately needed as many positions of authority as possible to be filled by men he could trust. Bayeux, moreover, was a central town in Lower Normandy, where William was trying to increase the ducal influence. Bishop Odo, an extremely capable administrator, also did not neglect his duties as a bishop, and served as one of the duke's key commanders at the Battle of Hastings. Eventually, he built a cathedral of great splendor at Bayeux.

Orderic Vitalis wrote of Odo, "He was a man in whom vice and virtue were strangely co-mingled." Orderic would certainly have said that Odo, like William, possessed endless energy, and was capable of great and even visionary deeds. However, quite unlike William, Odo's consciousness of his own importance was, all too often, the real driving force behind his expansive thinking.

Of the many church councils convened—numbering many more than ever before—no notes survive, but we know that the duke insisted on attending all of them personally. His faithfulness in this respect prompted the chronicler, William of Jumieges, to state that the duke was "unwilling to learn at secondhand about matters which he held to be of such importance to the welfare of his duchy."

In this same time period Duke William gradually drew into his circle of advisors the great scholar and monk, Lanfranc of Pavia, whose presence at the monastery of Bec had made it an illustrious center of learning. William's relationship with Lanfranc was the single most important collaboration for the future Anglo-Norman kingdom. Lanfranc had come to Bec above all in search of a simple life, in strict seclusion. He was appointed prior, however, by the abbot Herluin.

In 1060, Anselm, another monk of genius and deep devotion, was admitted to Bec, and became a student of Lanfranc. Lanfranc and Anselm were the two men whom William the Conqueror and, later on, his youngest son King Henry I, most trusted. Lanfranc and Anselm came together for three years as teacher and student, and also as brothers in the monastic life at Bec, where they laid the spiritual groundwork by which these great men shaped the church in England as successive archbishops of Canterbury under William, and under Henry.

Through its hold on the bishoprics by the great baronial families, and through William's close working relationship with the primate of the church in Normandy, the Norman church in the years leading up to the Conquest began to work in full cooperation with Duke William and with his policies. William's ability to keep the peace, the disruption of which had destroyed the church a century earlier, was never taken for granted by the ecclesiastical community of this period. The church in Normandy was desperate for law and order, and gave grateful support to any prince who could bring about a cessation of violence.

However, in addition to the appreciation of the churchmen for their duke, William had proved himself, by 1060, to be a champion of church reform. He himself lived a life of probity, morality, and sincere, regular participation in church sacraments—all of which contributed to the integrity and power of the many ecclesiastical councils on the reform of prelates which he convened as duke. In other words, Duke William was the very model of the ideal Christian prince, as the church community itself would have defined such a man.

The duke also understood that his era needed above all a greater order and restraint of its lawless elements, through the centralization of power—both secular and ecclesiastic. To a great degree, therefore, William supported the pope's efforts to create a center of authority for the whole of western Christendom.

On another point, however, William disagreed very strongly with those reforming popes who sought to usurp the rights and prerogatives of lay princes. As we shall see, William felt that the church was overstepping its bounds in this matter, and endangering its true spiritual function.

To me, there seems also a much deeper reason for William's incarnating to "destroy evil and re-establish virtue," as the Bhagavad Gita puts it. I shall take up this subject in a later chapter, but I want to state now that, in my opinion, the incarnation of a great soul would not have been needed merely to accomplish England's re-orientation to the influence of Rome. He came for the upliftment of an entire civilization. England was simply the place where, owing to its relative isolation from the mainland, it would be possible to establish new ideals, new ways of looking at things, new harmony, and a more cooperative spirit.

CHAPTER 8

A Tangled Web—The English Kings Preceding William

W hile **Duke William was** first struggling to survive his minority, and then to establish and consolidate his ducal authority—in the face, also, of French and Anjou aggression— another drama was unfolding across the channel, in England.

It will help if we understand the various circumstances that had placed King Edward the Confessor on the throne of England, and the question of the succession as it stood in the opening days of 1066, when Edward died. Duke William was not alone in his invasion of England in that year. He himself came, not as its conqueror, and not only as its rightful heir—a claim he shared with others— but as the God-ordained successor to King Edward the Confessor, for the well-being of England.

The great Viking leaders of the ninth century frequently transferred their base of operations back and forth across the channel between England and Normandy. The Danelaw of England, and also large settlements of Danes and Norwegians outside the Danelaw, were shaped by that same Scandinavian culture which had formed Normandy. Normandy and England of the tenth and eleventh centuries shared much together, and had seen significant intermarriages between the royal, ducal, and noble families on both sides of the Channel.

When England's King Ethelred II, of the West Saxon royal dynasty, found himself sorely pressed by Viking raiders at the end of the tenth century, he turned for aid to Normandy's ducal family.

29

Since the Viking raids and violence concerned all of Europe, an extraordinary council met in Rouen in March 991, with a papal legate at its head. There, a pact was signed in which England and Normandy agreed not to aid or harbor each other's enemies.

This agreement was promising. Unfortunately, it was not entirely successful. and more tokens of good faith had to be given. At this point a marriage took place that was to have great importance: In 1002, Emma, the sister of Normandy's Duke Richard II (William the Conqueror's grandfather), was given in marriage to King Ethelred II of England. Emma bore this king two sons, Edward and Alfred. The Viking raids continued, however, and in 1013, Sweyn Forkbeard, England's frequent nemesis, launched a great attack, overwhelming Anglo-Saxon England's powers of defense and driving the West Saxon royal house into exile.

Queen Emma of England, and the athelings (princes) Edward and Alfred, naturally sought refuge at the court of the duke of Normandy. They arrived in the autumn of 1013, and King Ethelred soon joined them there. The very next month King Ethelred, with Norman backing, returned to England and led a counter-attack against Sweyn's son, Cnut the Great.

Over the next two years, the fortunes of England's West Saxon royal house hung by a thread. Treachery within Ethelred's own court seems to have engineered his death in 1016. Cnut, who was also king of Denmark, sought legitimacy in England by marrying King Ethelred's widow, Emma. Her sons, princes Edward and Alfred, who (not surprisingly) played no role at King Cnut's English court, returned to Normandy, where they resumed their life of exile at the court of their uncle, Duke Richard.

There is evidence that the two princes remained mostly in the background during Duke Richard's life. When William's father, however, Duke Robert I, assumed the ducal title, we learn that the English princes were "much in attendance on the duke." Duke Robert was certainly prepared to support their claim to the English throne, and would have done so had he lived. As it happened, however, both he and Cnut the Great died in 1035.

Perhaps owing to King Cnut's death, Prince Alfred decided to visit his mother, Emma, in England. King Cnut had named Harthacnut, his son by Emma, as his heir. Harthacnut, however, was abroad in Denmark when his father died, and his brother, Harold "Harefoot," seized the throne despite the opposition of Queen Emma and of Godwin, the powerful earl of Wessex, though of Danish descent.

Godwin had risen to become an earl because of his energetic service to England's Danish King Cnut. Prince Alfred's visit was, as historians have remarked, an embarrassment to the many English noblemen, who had quickly abandoned the Saxon royal dynasty of Wessex, as well as to King Harold "Harefoot," whose right to the throne was already in question because his older brother, Harthacnut, was still living, and had been appointed heir by their mutual father.

Before Prince Alfred ever reached his mother, Earl Godwin intercepted him. Most of Alfred's companions were slain outright, but Alfred himself was turned over to some of Harefoot's men, who put his eyes out. Alfred died only days later, in consequence of this mutilation.

The blinding and death of Alfred the atheling shocked his contemporaries. Though the eleventh century may appear to us as having no moral code at all, in fact this act was "beyond the pale." Thugs and brutes like Earl Godwin transgressed that code, but to their contemporaries this murder by mutilation was a dark deed of almost Biblical proportions, and an expression of evil that cried out for retribution.

Though his brother Edward was too weak, even after he'd become the king of England, to inflict that retribution, the outrage remained. As a final, bitterly ironic flourish, many years later King Edward appears to have been forced, as he lay dying, to name Earl Godwin's son Harold as his heir to the throne of England.

If Duke William's father, Robert, had been still alive, he would almost certainly have mounted an attack on both "Harefoot" and Earl Godwin. However, Prince Alfred's murder occurred when

Normandy was passing through the dark days of William's minority; no succor could come from the Norman side of Prince Alfred's family. Earl Godwin's clear complicity in the death of Edward's brother Alfred was one reason King Edward loathed Godwin.

In 1040, King Harold "Harefoot" died under less than clear circumstances, and his brother Harthacnut succeeded to the throne of England. Perhaps the English nobility, including many Danes who for generations had been living in England, were weary of sharing their king with Denmark. Some of them began, anyway, to seek other candidates as Harthacnut's successor. It was under these circumstances that Edward, Alfred's brother, was invited to come over from Normandy to join the court of King Harthacnut.

Douglas aptly observes that it must have taken considerable courage for Edward to take this step, considering what had happened to his brother. Was this merely a ploy to eliminate King Ethelred's second and last son by Emma? Duke William was not close enough to his majority to take full control of Normandy, otherwise he would surely have promoted Edward's cause. In this case, Edward might have waited for William's backing before he took such a perilous step. But Duke William was then only twelve years old.

King Harthacnut, Edward's half-brother, died just two years later, in 1042, under circumstances that seem very much like poisoning, though (strange to say) no chronicler makes that suggestion. The entry in the *Anglo-Saxon Chronicle* reads:

"Here [in this year] Harthacnut died as he stood at his drink, and he suddenly fell to the earth with an awful convulsion; and those who were close by took hold of him, and he spoke no word afterwards, and he passed away on 8 June. And all the people then received Edward as king, as was his natural right."

Edward, now about forty years old, was recognized almost universally in England as the king. His rule, however, was not uncontested outside the country. The now-dead Harthacnut had made an agreement with Sweyn Estrithson of Denmark, his cousin, and with Magnus, king of Norway, that if either of them died without an heir, the other would succeed him as heir to the throne of England. This pact continued to cause problems until the very end of the Conqueror's reign in England.

There were strong pockets of support within the Danelaw of England for both Sweyn and Magnus, kings of Denmark and Norway respectively. Edward was constrained to spend the first two years of his reign in preparation for an imminent attack from Scandinavia. Those who were sympathetic to the Scandinavian cause included even Edward's own mother, Emma, whom he was forced to put under house arrest, and whose lands and treasure he confiscated because of her scheming to aid Magnus in his bid to become the next English king.

Not surprisingly, Edward was immediately, and throughout his reign, embroiled in power struggles with Earl Godwin and his ambitious, bellicose sons. Earl Godwin had chosen for himself the role of not-so-discreet power behind the throne, but had done so only because he could not legitimately sit on the throne himself. Godwin, utterly ruthless and opportunistic, considered the new king effeminate and weak. Despite the fact that such compromises must have been galling to King Edward—who surely held Godwin responsible for his brother Alfred's death—Edward had no choice but to make concessions to Godwin in order to secure his support in preparation for meeting the threat of an invasion from Scandinavia. The immediate price of Godwin's loyalty (such as it was) was that King Edward had to marry Godwin's daughter, Edith.

Cnut the Great, during his rule of England, had created a relatively few but large earldoms in England, with the result that, after his death, those earls engaged one another in bitter battles. They treated their titles and lands as theirs by hereditary right, and paid little attention to the king. Though the weakened tradition of central government still lingered enough to prevent them from ignoring King Edward altogether, they pushed their independence as far as they could. Yet if England was to be protected from foreign invasion, it was precisely those earls who needed to act together, with united purpose. Such unity was missing. Earl Godwin had risen steadily under Cnut. Now, as the earl of Wessex, he controlled both the Midlands and all the south of England. This he did either directly or indirectly through two of his many sons: his eldest, the abominable Sweyn, and Harold, his second.

They posed an intolerable challenge to King Edward's authority. Edward now did one of the few things he could have done, considering that he lacked any real supporters: he began importing men from Normandy whom he could trust. He considered Normandy, in fact, even more his home than England.

We can detect from many of King Edward's actions that he was building up strength and looking forward to the day when he could confront Godwin and dismantle the whole Godwin power matrix. Finally, in 1051, a fracas occurred between visiting men from the court of Boulogne, France, and the citizens of Dover. The king ordered Earl Godwin to punish the citizens, but Godwin refused, instead calling upon those feudal levies which were under his control.

The king called on the loyalty of the general populace, including those Normans who now resided in the kingdom, as well as the loyalty of those earls who, traditionally, were enemies of Godwin. In this very decisive contest of wills and popular support, King Edward won a bloodless victory. He immediately ordered Godwin, Harold, and Leofwine (another son) to appear before him and answer for their conduct. Godwin refused to come. All three of them were banished, therefore, and Godwin hastened to the court of Flanders, where he joined his sons, Sweyn (the oldest, who had previously been banished from England for his brutish and violent nature), Tostig, and Gyrth. Harold and Leofwine sailed to Ireland. From those two points of banishment the father and these five sons then conceived and carried out a brilliant plan to attack England.

King Edward "the Confessor" of England, only months after banishing the Godwin family, was defeated and had to accede to all their demands, reinstate them in the lands they'd previously held, and receive back Edith, Godwin's daughter, as his wife whom he had repudiated many years earlier. Godwin completed his power ploy by compelling Edward to send away many of the Normans who at his invitation had been assigned lands and offices in England.

Meanwhile, even before the first "showdown" between the king and Godwin, Edward had almost certainly made the decision, by 1051, to name Duke William of Normandy as his lawful heir. According to Douglas, the English king sent, by the newly appointed archbishop of Canterbury, Robert of Jumieges, a Norman himself, a message of his decision to make William of Normandy his heir.

Godwin later removed this archbishop, a prelate of high repute, from his position despite the fact that Robert of Jumieges had been duly consecrated, and had received his pallium from the pope himself. Godwin's act showed flagrant disregard for the Roman Church, and particularly for the pope's authority. In Godwin's career, marked by the boldest possible deeds of self-aggrandizement, his removal of Robert of Jumieges was surely the most high-handed of them all. It also reveals, in a curious way, the Nordic paganism which the Godwin family symbolized. Great rulers in the Latin West did, certainly, flout the authority of the church from time to time, sometimes even flagrantly. In the end, however, they always did penance, and made restitution, if only to retain the goodwill of their largely pious countrymen. Earl Godwin's action, of which he never repented, and the fact that over the ensuing years it did not cripple him politically, tells us much about the exceedingly weak ties between pre-Conquest England and the authority of the Western church, centered in Rome.

Robert of Jumieges was replaced by Stigand, whose reputation was despicable. Stigand, in accepting and retaining the position of archbishop of Canterbury solely on Earl Godwin's authority, was excommunicated. Indeed, the excommunication was repeated by no fewer than five succeeding popes. Stigand's reputation became so sullied that newly appointed prelates hesitated to be consecrated by him, though he was nominally their superior and primate of the whole church in England.

From 1052 on, Godwin and his family were so inextricably entrenched as the ultimate power in England, despite their having been anathematized by the Roman Church, that (so Conquest scholar Sir Frank Stenton stated) only warfare could possibly dislodge them. The hope that the succession might be achieved peacefully was utterly lost after the Godwin family's return from brief exile.

Duke William, meanwhile, was still fighting to control his duchy in Normandy, and the outcome of that struggle by no means clear.

CHAPTER 9

The Rightful Heir to the Throne

Earl Godwin died in 1053. His atrocious oldest son, Sweyn—a man so vicious that his own countrymen branded him a *nithing* (outcast)—had predeceased his father. Evidently, the banished Sweyn had undertaken a pilgrimage as an act of contrition but had died on the journey. Thus, the leadership of the Godwin family passed to the second son, Harold. Another death caused a further change in England, adding substantially to the already great power of the Godwin clan. Earl Siward of Northumbria died in 1055, and the earldom of Northumbria was bestowed on Harold's younger brother, Tostig.

From all accounts, King Edward steadily refused to have anything to do with Edith, his wife, whom Godwin had forced upon him. During the king's short-lived victory over the Godwin family, which had resulted in their brief exile, Edward had banished Edith from his household. After he'd been forced to take her back, it was abundantly clear that no male heir would result from their "union." In fact, King Edward's intention of naming Duke William of Normandy as his heir was evidently no secret among the English nobility.

By this time, about 1055–56, Duke William's reputation as a strong leader, and as a supporter of papal reform, had certainly reached England. The noblemen under Edward surely viewed with alarm the prospect of William of Normandy as their next king, for he was strong, and under Edward they had enjoyed great freedom of action.

Among some of them a plan was formed to "field another candidate," in the person of another Edward, a grandson of King Ethelred, who had been residing in Hungary. This Edward "the Exile" was invited to England in 1057, and arrived in great state, accompanied by his wife and three children. Not unlike the ill-fated Prince Alfred, this man, too, died suddenly and mysteriously before he could even meet King Edward. The suggestion of foul play is strong in the *Anglo-Saxon Chronicle*, which exclaims over Edward's death: "We do not know for what cause it was arranged that he might not see his relative, King Edward. Alas! that his life ended so quickly after his arrival in England was a cruel fate, and harmful to all this nation, a great misfortune for all this wretched nation." (*Anglo-Saxon Chronicle*, p 188)

Whether or not Earl Harold Godwinson had a hand in Edward the atheling's death, Harold does seem from this time on to have begun to think seriously about usurping the succession, himself. The thought was surely irresistible to Harold, considering the fact that the Godwin family now directly controlled most of England. In 1062, Harold, now at the summit of his power, began to be referred to in some of the chronicles of the time as the "under-king."

Duke William at this time was concentrating on building a strong ducal administration in Normandy. He brought unity and reform to the church, and moved forward with other works he had initiated: works such as the architectural masterpieces St. Etienne and La Trinité, the two monasteries and abbey churches in Caen. William also devoted himself to other crucial matters, such as regularizing the coinage system, dismantling castles that had been built in defiance of him, and placing his own ducal garrisons in the fortresses of lords whose loyalty he did not completely trust.

In 1065, it seems that King Edward the Confessor requested Harold Godwinson to cross the channel and confirm to William, Duke of Normandy, his appointment as Edward's successor.

Chronicler William of Jumieges wrote that King Edward ordered Harold to make the trip to Normandy specifically in order that Harold might publicly swear support for Duke William's succession. Others have suggested that Harold undertook the journey in order to secure the freedom of the Godwin family members—including Harold's youngest brother, Wulfnoth—who were already hostages at Duke William's court as insurance that Earl Harold would support William's succession. This was "standard procedure," as we might call it, and it is difficult to imagine that this suggestion as a motive for Harold's journey is correct. For on what grounds might Harold Godwinson have imagined that he could obtain the return of those hostages?

Historian David Bates doubts that King Edward had enough clout to order Harold off on such an errand as William of Jumieges suggests. Other historians, however, have cautioned that Edward, though stripped in certain areas of much power, was still a force to be reckoned with. Among other things, the king's choice of a successor, in those days before primogeniture had been strictly established, was the single most important factor in legitimizing anyone's claim to the throne. Since this is a controversial subject, however, and crucial to the legitimacy of William's invasion of England, we must admit that Harold may have considered refusing Edward's order. In the end, however—perhaps partly because his family members *were* hostages—Harold must have decided it would be unwise not to go. The fact that members of the Godwin family were already in Normandy, at William's court, as surety for the good behavior of Earls Harold and Tostig Godwinson, tells us that Harold had already gone a certain distance toward acknowledging Duke William's right to the throne.

Then, too, between functioning as the "power behind the throne" and actually laying claim to the throne himself, there yawned a wide chasm—particularly since Harold was not of royal blood. This point held paramount importance in those times. Even those from Scandinavia who had seized the throne of England were of the royal line of Denmark. Had Harold refused King Edward's order to visit Duke William and swear fealty to him as Edward's successor, he would have been challenging the reigning monarch's right to choose his own successor, and would, of course, have "tipped his hand" regarding his own ambitions to the throne. On the whole therefore, it would have been foolish for Harold to balk at King Edward's orders.

Nearly every contemporary chronicler recorded also that, in making the Channel crossing, Earl Harold's ship was blown off course and ended up making landfall on the shores of the county of Ponthieu, where, according to the "barbarous customs of that county," he was seized and thrown into the dungeon of one of the count's castles. When Duke William heard what had happened, he demanded, as the count's overlord, that Harold be released into his custody. Count Guy complied speedily, and the English earl was conducted with all dignity to the ducal seat at Rouen. It was there, before a large assembly of ecclesiastics and noblemen, that the earl swore his famous oath that he, Harold Godwinson, would support in battle, if necessary, Duke William's right to the throne of England.

Historians who, perhaps out of chauvinistic patriotism, have supported Harold as a true, full-blooded Anglo-Saxon, have been quick to seek excuses for the fact that he later broke his oath. They have cited the level of intimidation he must have felt. However, historian David Douglas expresses grave doubts that Earl Harold faced any such difficulty. Given that Harold might not yet have completely made up his mind to claim the throne of England, he would surely have wanted at least to be seen as supporting the duke's cause.

Furthermore, Harold was probably not able to grasp just how compromised his position became, as he enjoyed Duke William's lavish hospitality. This point deserves more emphasis than it is usually accorded. The Scandinavian-acculturated Harold, born to and trained by perhaps the greatest opportunist of the age, probably had not the slightest compunction about swearing an oath that he knew he might ultimately break. Perhaps he didn't even realize the seriousness of the oath. Or perhaps (more likely) he simply didn't care.

Harold Godwinson has been fictionalized as the "golden warrior," a pure-bred Anglo-Saxon (as if that meant anything, considering that the Anglo-Saxons, too, in their time had invaded

England). For one thing, contrary to tradition, Harold was as much Danish as he was Anglo-Saxon, and he had, in addition, descended from an entirely scurrilous line of selfish opportunists.

After swearing on the relics of many saints, in the presence of a large assembly of noblemen, to support in every way Duke William's succession to the throne of England, Earl Harold was given the arms of knighthood by William and thereby became William's vassal. Harold's knighthood added another layer, of course, to the fealty he owed to William as his liege lord. Duke William then invited Harold to accompany him on his military campaign against the count of Brittany, which was the last area of unrest that the duke wanted to settle before he turned his attention fully to England.

As, over the next weeks, they rode and fought together, Harold's role, in the mind of any medieval man observing him, was that of vassal and liegeman to Duke William—his lord and protector, who had so recently rescued him from the count of Ponthieu. It was one thing for Harold to repudiate an oath which he later claimed he'd been forced to swear, but this line of argument became quite unconvincing considering the fact that Harold subsequently for many weeks appeared by the duke's side and partook of the duke's magnanimity, received many honors from him, and even helped William in fighting his battles.

Harold, when he returned to England laden with rich gifts from Duke William, found a rebellion underway against his brother, Earl Tostig of Northumbria. Many people of consequence in Northumbria had denounced Tostig as a despoiler of his own land and people, and had risen against him, asking that another great nobleman, Morcar, be given the earldom. Harold sought to intercede, but failed in his diplomatic efforts, and Tostig, his younger brother, was forced to seek refuge at the court of Count Baldwin of Flanders. Knowing Tostig's ambitious nature, Harold must have been well aware that he now had a new enemy to reckon with.

CHAPTER 10

Signs and Portents

On January 5, 1066, King Edward the Confessor died after a long illness. With speed bordering on sacrilege, Harold moved to secure the throne of England for himself. He gathered a council of elders in the kingdom with a view to bestowing some semblance of legality to his accession, and promptly—the very day of King Edward's funeral—had himself crowned king. One of the chroniclers stated that William was genuinely outraged, though it could not have come to him as a complete surprise that Harold had, after all, betrayed his oath.

The duke instantly dispatched messengers to Harold, urging him to renounce his act of folly and be faithful to the oath he had pledged. Harold, however, not only disdained to listen: he even turned the English people against Duke William.

William's message of protest to Harold was, of course, merely *pro forma.* There could have been no doubt in William's mind that only through battle would the throne of England now become his, as King Edward had intended.

Virtually every chronicler wrote that King Edward, at the very end, changed his mind and nominated Harold as his successor. Harold was, it seems, hovering very close to the king in those last days. So also, evidently, were some of the nobles. The Bayeux Tapestry shows a great gathering around the dying Edward, suggesting some level of intimidation as well as of concern. The *Vita Edwardi,* written soon after the king's death, suggests something of the sort, for its author wrote, without referring specifically to the succession, that at the end "old" King Edward was "broken with age and knew not what he said."

We cannot offer a "blow by blow" account of how Duke William spent the opening months of 1066, but we know that he was meticulously preparing for the invasion of England. His preparation included a very well considered plan for persuading the barons under him that his strategy was feasible. Various chroniclers mentioned at least three large assemblies of magnates and ecclesiastics of high position, convened by Duke William to discuss the likelihood of success for such an invasion. It seems that some of his magnates were doubtful at first, but as William developed his plan all their reservations were resolved.

There is a tradition that one of William's closest men, William fitz Osbern, made a stirring speech that overcame every objection on the part of "stragglers." In fact, as David Douglas points out, the level of unanimity was already quite remarkable, and offered strong testimony to the respect and loyalty William had won from those fiercely independent, strong-minded men.

The duchy itself was to be left under the regency of William's wife, Matilda, and also of Robert Curthose (their oldest son), and of elderly Roger of Beaumont and Robert of Montgomery, close *familiares* of the duke. In those days William proclaimed Robert Curthose, now somewhere between twelve and fourteen years old, as his heir, and held a great oath-taking ceremony among the barons and the great churchmen of Normandy. Again, the fact that there was no rebellion or private warfare within Normandy during Duke William's absence is the strongest possible evidence of the level of cooperation and control he had achieved by 1066.

From the beginning, Duke William carefully sought acknowledgement of the righteousness of his cause from the leaders of Western Europe. Gilbert, archdeacon of Lisieux, was sent to Pope Alexander II, where he laid before the pontiff the duke's legal claims to the crown of England. It is interesting that no chronicler mentions whether or not the pope sent for Harold, or in any way demanded from him an official explanation. When the decisive contest occurred, all Western Europe knew that Duke William was fighting with the full support of the Holy Roman Church; he carried into battle the papal banner, sent to him by Pope Alexander II, for all to see.

For some months the duke had been engaged in putting out smaller diplomatic and military "fires" to ensure that Normandy's borders would be secure in his absence. Now William actively sought, and received, official support for his claim to the English throne from King Philip of France, who was still in his minority, as well as approval from King Henry IV, the Holy Roman Emperor. Duke William's thorough diplomatic preparations for the invasion of England were all spectacularly successful. Probably the care William took in communicating his position so thoroughly to all the right quarters resulted in a perception of England as having once more fallen in thralldom to barely Christianized Northmen, who had, to show their disdain for the true church, delivered its leadership into the hands of the excommunicate and simoniac Stigand.

With the blessing of the pope, and with the growing conviction within Europe that the taking of England was a holy war, there came a tremendous influx of soldiers from France, Brittany, Boulogne, Poitou, Anjou, and even Sicily. Douglas points out that no one in Europe would have perceived Duke William's proposed invasion of England as an act of aggression. Furthermore, the pope's blessing, joined to the groundswell of public opinion on the side of Duke William's invasion, forestalled in great measure any likelihood that some Western European country might offer support to Harold.

Nearly every contemporary chronicler takes note of the brilliant star that appeared in the night sky around the middle of April 1066, and continued for at least a week, as everyone agreed, to herald the approach of great events. The *Anglo-Saxon Chronicle* refers to it as the "haired star," which all men saw as portending a momentous happening. In fact, we know now that it was Haley's Comet.

Astonishingly, many contemporary chroniclers, some at great distances from Anglo-Norman events, linked the appearance of that comet to the succession crisis in England. All saw it as signaling the death of a great man, and the victory of another even greater man. The contemporary chronicler William of Jumieges added this thought to his comments on the appearance of the "haired star": "When beggars die, no comets are seen."

CHAPTER 11

His Divine Birthright

Duke William began to gather his ships and men on the
coast of Normandy, near the mouth of the river Dives, beginning about May of 1066. Some say that as early as August William's
fleet was all but ready for the voyage. If so, it was an astonishing
feat, for the majority of the larger ships were constructed on the
spot, expressly for the transportation of this enormous army.

About the time that the duke was collecting men and ships on
the coast, Harold's brother Tostig returned from exile at the head of
an army of Norsemen, and began to harry and plunder the north
of England. In short order Earl Edwin of Mercia led out an army
to confront them, inflicting terrible slaughter on them. Evidently
those who survived this confrontation with Edwin's army were
not strongly bonded to Tostig or to his cause, for they straightway
deserted him. Tostig himself fled to the court of Malcolm, king
of Scotland, to try rallying another army, either from Malcolm or
from Scandinavia. There remained a number of pretenders to the
English throne, who might be persuaded to try their luck during
this unsettled time.

Harold ruled England for eight months. The Anglo-Saxon
Chronicler wrote understatedly: "He experienced very little quiet
while he ruled the kingdom." Harold, no doubt under great tension,
kept his men and ships in the south of England in mixed dread and
hope that Duke William would arrive before Tostig could invade
with another army. Word came then that Norway's King Harold

Hardraada, another claimant to the throne of England—this one, through the line of Cnut the Great—was speedily assembling an enormous fleet and planned to join forces with Tostig, who was still at King Malcolm's court in Scotland.

One of the deciding factors in this war was the tremendous logistical problem which both William and Harold faced: the maintenance of an enormous army while awaiting actual battle. We are told—and this is of considerable importance—that Duke William strictly ordered his vast army, comprising men from many nations, to do absolutely no plundering in the local countryside. The fact that everyone, to a man, obeyed him is astonishing—indeed, almost unheard of. The duke was, however, a supremely practical man who well understood how to maintain discipline and high morale. Ordering an army not to plunder, but giving them nothing to eat, was obviously not an option.

He made generous provision both for his own knights and for those from other parts, and forbade them from taking their sustenance by force. Contemporaries stated that the peasants' flocks and herds remained unharmed throughout the province.

It seems that Duke William was concerned with setting a certain tone within the army and maintaining a somewhat higher standard of discipline and morality than was usual in such endeavors. For indeed, plunder in the eleventh century was considered a soldier's right—just as surely as were the few pennies he was paid daily for his services. Evidently, the duke had planned for every contingency, including the misfortune of a prevailing north wind, which continued for weeks and prevented him from sailing.

Harold, though he'd stationed his army within the bounds of his own earldom, was unable to provide for them, and was forced on September 8 to disband the Wessex *fyrd*, ordering his ships to return to London. Meanwhile, he himself, with his housecarls, also returned there.

Duke William must have received word very quickly that the southern coast of England was now, with the disbanding of Harold's army, completely clear. Tradition has it that William kept his gaze fixed on the weather vane on the church tower of St. Valery. All he needed was a change of wind.

Soon after Harold had been obliged to disband his English army, Harold Hardraada, king of Norway, sailed for England with three hundred ships, joining Tostig at the mouth of the river Tyne with the forces Tostig had been able to round up in Scotland. Sailing up the Humber, the Scandinavian army landed in Yorkshire and, with Tostig, marched on the city of York. Everyone in England had been expecting this great host, and Earls Edwin and Morcar quickly mobilized their armies to meet it outside the city walls. The fighting was long and sanguinary, but Tostig and the Norwegian king were the clear victors. The chroniclers wrote that the city of York then welcomed Harold Hardraada, who accepted their submission. Thus, Hardraada, the third man with ambitions to secure the throne of England, fresh from his first victory on English soil, felt that victory was all but certain.

When King Harold received the news of Edwin and Morcar's defeat, his first thought had to be, "Can I make it to the north of England and confront Tostig and Hardraada before the wind shifts, and William lands on my southern coast?" His second thought, then, must have been: "In any case, I have no choice but to risk it."

Harold and his housecarls swiftly collected his scattered army, and in only five days of forced marches arrived in the area of York, where the Norwegian army was still resting. There, King Harold attacked immediately, fighting the battle of Stamford Bridge. By the end of that terrible day, the victory was his, the field strewn with dead and dying. Among them lay both Tostig and Hardraada of Norway. Thus one contender for the throne of England had been eliminated, and the north of England was, for the time being, secure.

That battle was on September 25. Two days later, on September 27, the wind on the Channel finally shifted in Duke William's favor. That evening, William gave the order for his fleet to sail, with his own ship in the lead.

When William landed on the morning of September 28 at Pevensey, on the southern coast of England, he arrived virtually unopposed.

Tradition has it that William, who was the first to land, stumbled and fell to his knees. A gasp of dismay went through his troops at this unfavorable omen. But William turned the omen to good advantage. "I am so determined to conquer this land," he shouted, "that I have grasped it with both my hands!" His statement was received with a great shout of approval.

After a careful assessment of the surrounding countryside and shoreline, Duke William moved his army to the town of Hastings, which provided the best protection for his ships. Fortifications were constructed within the town, and soldiers were sent out to ravage the countryside—not so much because supplies were needed as to create a greater sense of urgency in Harold Godwinson's mind, and to provoke him to a swift response.

Duke William's accurate assessment of Harold's character contributed a great deal to his victory that day. In fact, many historians have pointed out that time was now on Harold's side, and that if he had held back for some weeks before engaging the Norman force, it would have caused William serious problems. However, the duke had taken Harold with him on his campaign in Brittany, partly (one assumes) with the purpose of assessing the man's character. Duke William now counted on the bold, precipitate nature he had observed in Harold to seek as soon as possible a decisive confrontation, even though it would have been greatly to his advantage to wait.

William had judged Harold rightly. By October 6, Harold, having heard that the Norman army was wreaking havoc on his own lands in Wessex, quickly force-marched to London those in his army who were capable of such exertion. Here, Harold paused to gather reinforcements. New troops were added, almost all of them foot soldiers, and most of them, evidently, by no means battle-hardened. To have waited a few days there for more experienced troops to arrive from the north would have been well advised, but Harold wanted to engage William as soon as possible.

On October 11 he left London with such reinforcements as he had gathered, and again force-marched them from London to the Sussex Downs—a distance of fifty-eight miles—in a little over forty-eight hours, arriving on the night of October 13 or 14. The march may have ended quite late in the day, since the chroniclers tell us that Duke William came upon them at 9:00 a.m., before they were fully drawn up in battle formation. This was rather late in the morning, considering Harold's avowed purpose that day.

Nevertheless, Harold was able to get his men into position before the battle began in earnest. He was, for some reason, able to take up a strategically advantageous position, forming a line along the top of a long ridge, while Duke William's men were arrayed in three contingents below. It is thought that Harold's "shield wall" stretched for three hundred yards along the summit of Senlac Ridge, as it is now called, in a very strong defensive position indeed. The fact that they were on the defensive, however, tells us that William essentially "outgeneraled" Harold from the beginning. Harold's entire strategy consisted of making his traditional shield wall as impenetrable and immovable as possible.

William's infantry made the first move; it charged up the ridge, discharging spears and arrows against the interlocked shields of Harold's army. The disadvantage of fighting uphill, however, was soon obvious as those missiles were deflected easily by the wall of shields. Next, heavily armed knights charged, mounted on horseback. They had no better luck. Gradually, however, as the fighting continued, and the Normans kept battering at the shield wall, Duke William introduced techniques and strategies that began to have more effect.

In the end, it was the "feigned flight" maneuver of mounted knights which tricked the inexperienced men behind Harold's shield wall into pursuing the supposedly "fleeing" enemy, who at a certain point turned suddenly on their pursuers, and cut them down.

It was perhaps during the first "feigned flight" maneuver that a rumor circulated among the duke's men that William had been killed. William instantly removed his helmet and galloped around among his men, shouting to them to look: He was still alive, and fully in command of his troops.

The duke himself then adjusted his archers' angle of aim to send their arrows soaring, more effectively, over the shield wall to targets behind it. The "feigned flight" stratagem was used at least three times, and each time successfully, at different points along Harold's long line. This strategy, combined with the high arc of arrows, undid or bypassed the shield wall on which depended Harold's entire strength.

Late in the day Harold himself fell from an arrow piercing one of his eyes and reaching the brain. Tradition has it that Harold's body was then set upon by some in the duke's army who intended simply to butcher it in a spirit of revenge. Duke William quickly intervened and put a stop to this savagery. (Harold's disfigured body was identified by his mistress from "certain marks" upon it.)

Casualties on both sides were heavy, and many of England's chief landholders were killed that day. Historians and military strategists have pointed to the Battle of Hastings as one of the first clear examples of the superiority of mounted knights over infantry. However, sifting through all the evidence, it becomes clear that William's victory must be attributed chiefly to his own superior leadership. His great refinement of planning, and the daring and creative way he met the usual problems connected with moving an army into hostile territory, played a role of enormous importance in his victory.

Above all, as historians almost unanimously agree, the Norman victory must be attributed in the end to the strong, creative character of Duke William: to his unyielding will; to his ability to inspire confidence in the men under him and impose a level of group discipline that until then, had been unknown. William also believed in the righteousness of his cause—a fact which is rarely offered as a reason for his success. In fact, most historians have simply assumed that it was only his ambition for power that brought William to England. William had no such ambition, however, and seems to this author never to have been motivated by personal desire of any kind. His entire purpose was dedicated to serving the will of God. Previously, as duke of Normandy, he had demonstrated again and again his devotion to spiritual principles.

There is a strong tradition in England that, following William's victory at Hastings, he sat up all night on the battlefield itself, praying for the souls of those soldiers on both sides who had been slain.

Harold Godwinson, by contrast, was by no means dedicated to spiritual principles, or to the well-being of those he led. Not only did he lack support from the church, but he was also, in the eyes of all, the forsworn vassal of Duke William, who had secured his deliverance from imprisonment, had knighted him, and had given him great honor only a year earlier. He could have had no confidence in the justice of his cause.

Harold Godwinson's own nature had driven him to impatience, whereas William, in stark contrast, never acted in a spirit of bravado, and even less so of fear. Every move he made or refrained from making that day was entirely appropriate to the moment, and supportive of his end, which was the throne of England—his by divine right.

CHAPTER 12

Establishing His Rule: "A Gracious Liege Lord"

The days immediately subsequent to William's victory at Hastings were choreographed just as carefully. William now sought the submission, with a minimum of bloodshed, of the surviving members of England's aristocracy. Until at least October 14, Duke William remained at Hastings. Doubtless his troops needed rest, and William may have reasonably hoped that some of the landholders in England, recognizing the significance of the battle that had just ended, would come and offer him feudal submission. Even in those first days, alas, we see a pattern that was to play itself out over and over again in the coming years: William, as the rightful king of England, would extend his hand in trust and friendship, only to be betrayed by self-interest, which was the underlying reality of those times and of that country. Not a single English nobleman still alive after those two major battles of early autumn of 1066 presented himself to swear fealty to William.

When his troops were sufficiently rested, William moved his army eastward, subduing key coastal fortresses. His army was once attacked. William had to demonstrate to the English the tactic that had become his hallmark in Normandy. He attacked Romney, nearby, with such ferocity that the neighboring and vitally important fortress town of Dover submitted to him without a fight, as did the cathedral city of Canterbury just north of Dover.

William fully understood the strategic and commercial importance of London. Its surrender was now the focus of all his energies. He cut a wide swath of devastation around the city, in effect isolating it. The two most powerful surviving earls, Edwin and Morcar, after learning of Harold Godwinson's death at Hastings, had been part of a confused and disunited council that was hastily convened in London to submit a candidate of their own for the crown. Predictably, the council ended in disagreement. Persons of high rank in London, perceiving themselves indeed isolated, surrendered speedily. Even as Duke William was making his terrible progress around the city, Stigand, the excommunicated archbishop of Canterbury and "fair-haired boy" of the Godwin family, came out from London, so chronicler William of Poitiers tells us, to transfer his loyalty to William. Ultimately, a larger and highly significant group, including Aldred, archbishop of York, Earls Edwin and Morcar, and others came out from the city to swear fealty to Duke William as their new overlord, and offering hostages as a guaranty of their good faith. William, for his part, swore to be to them a gracious liege lord.

One more step was needed in the process of bringing the crown of England to William's head: he needed acquiescence to his coronation from his own great men. The chronicler gives the impression that, while there was no serious opposition, the discussion could not simply be assumed as a foregone conclusion. A consensus was needed, with all the great men swearing to uphold whatever was agreed upon. Otherwise, William might have been confronted by a disaffected contingent within his own forces, in addition to the inevitable pockets of rebellion in England.

Whatever questions or objections were expressed concerning Duke William's accession to the throne of England, they evidently found no resonance among his own men. Duke William received their universal approval. On Christmas Day, 1066, in Westminster Abbey, William, duke of Normandy, was crowned the king of England.

Despite the cold English winter, there may have been a few who felt a new and warmer wind flow over the land. England, in turning away from her Danish, Scandinavian, and Germanic ties, would now be enlivened and shaped anew, partly by France and the

Mediterranean world, but even more so by an inner coherence and justice, which William brought, that were still unknown elsewhere.

Between 1067 and 1072, King William spent the greater part of his time in England, quelling inevitable pockets of rebellion in that still-unsettled kingdom. Contrary to long-accepted myth, there was never a unified, nationwide movement by the Anglo-Saxon population seeking to cast off the "Norman yoke." Indeed, England's notable characteristic in those days was its complete lack of unity. Noblemen frequently sought personal benefit in that disunity, trying to wrest greater power and wealth for themselves. Such men, however, acted on their own.

In the summer of 1068, three of Harold Godwinson's illegitimate sons landed with a small army from their base in Ireland. They planned to recapture the throne for their father's "dynasty." It is important to note that they were turned away from the area around Bristol by English thegns: not by Normans.

The legendary activities of Hereward "the Wake" in opposing the Norman invasion are an instructive example of several lawless elements in the country who, in order to forward their own interests, seized upon the many shifts in land tenure that arose out of the Conquest. Though Hereward the Wake has been glorified in song and legend for his imaginary fight for the freedom of Anglo-Saxon England, and portrayed as a sort of Robin Hood, he was simply, in fact, an outlaw.

Before the Norman Conquest, Hereward's own father had petitioned King Edward to banish his son as a violent troublemaker. In 1070, when King Sweyn invaded England, briefly occupying the Isle of Ely, Hereward the Wake seized this opportunity to reclaim land and power by throwing in his lot with the Danish king. Hereward's interests, however, were entirely selfish. As a former tenant of the venerable institution of nearby Peterborough Abbey, he demanded the return of the fief he had previously held of the abbey. When the abbot refused, Hereward and his men looted and sacked the monastery and church. His act of sacrilege was condemned universally.

Hereward continued now to hold out against King William, even after Sweyn and his Danish army had made peace and withdrawn. Hereward's resistance attracted the participation of a higher echelon of former Anglo-Danish leadership, now disaffected, including Morcar, the former earl of Northumbria. It is perhaps owing to the presence of a few well-known displaced noblemen like Morcar that the eighteen-day resistance at Ely took on the patina, later, of an Anglo-Saxon "last stand." The actual event, however, was nothing of the sort. Hereward, one of the more energetic and violent of the Ely holdouts, also managed to escape, when other leaders surrendered after negotiating terms that were pleasing to them. Most medieval scholars have marveled at how relatively quickly the character and motives of Hereward the Wake were completely recast into that of an Anglo-Saxon champion, when in plain fact his one "high profile" deed had been the sacking and burning of the centuries-old Peterborough Abbey, a deed he perpetrated solely for personal revenge. Edwin earl of Mercia escaped and was killed by his own men as he fled to Scotland. Truly history *is*, in many ways, "a lie agreed upon."

The true story of Hereward the Wake illustrates also that the dramatic events of 1066 reignited, rather than initiated, violent disputes and rivalries. Thus, it should be understood that King William not only had before him the task of quelling uprisings that were directly related to shifts in land and power, but also that of dealing with long-standing private grievances and local vendettas, which his "conquest" had stirred once more to life, causing great conflict throughout the kingdom.

Although the southeast and Midlands of England, within two years of the Battle of Hastings, had come largely under King William's control, the north was an entirely different story. In the spring of 1068, William had conducted a vigorous campaign into the northland, where the largely Scandinavian population was growing restive as rumors came that King Sweyn of Denmark was planning another invasion, which seemed imminent. Greater and lesser noblemen of the old order saw in Sweyn's invasion threat a golden opportunity to pursue their own ambitions.

It should be mentioned in passing that there was little sense anywhere in those days of what we know as patriotism. There wasn't even much sense of countries divided by languages. In Italy alone there were over two hundred distinct dialects. Sir Walter Scott's fanciful notion of fiercely loyal Anglo-Saxons pitted against scornful Normans was an anachronism. Loyalty to one's country began, in fact, with William the Conqueror, and achieved its first sense of consolidation under his son Henry. It may, indeed, have achieved its highest level as a virtue after the Battle of Agincourt, fought by Henry V of England.

King William's march to the north took him to the key area of York where, after some minor bargaining, the city's leaders submitted to him, swearing an oath of fealty to him as their lord and king. One of the Normans' greatest defensive and offensive "weapons," the motte and bailey castle, was immediately erected near the city. After its construction, William moved on to other areas that had yet to acknowledge him formally as their lawful king. He was equally effective elsewhere, receiving recognition, submission, and oaths of loyalty, which were his immediate goal. The success of his remarkable series of campaigns in the first nine months of 1068 was destined, however, to be short-lived.

CHAPTER 13

1069: A Kingdom Hangs in the Balance

Late in 1068 William sent a trusted nobleman, Robert de Commines, to the north, charging him with keeping order beyond the Tees River, which runs roughly between Yorkshire and Durham. Once in the city of Durham, however, Robert de Commines was attacked in the streets, and took refuge in the bishop's "palace," which was then burned to the ground with Robert inside it. News of this incident quickly traveled south to York (at the center of a large Scandinavian population), where it sparked a siege of the king's garrison. William acted with great speed. Marching north, he arrived to relieve his garrison long before any of the attackers had believed possible. The besiegers fled in disorder, and the king, at the beginning of 1069, took possession of York for a second time.

William then erected a second motte and bailey castle in an area closer to the troublesome city, and placed a man named Gospatric, a descendant of an older ruling family of the North, in charge of the earldom of Northumbria until such a time as he could establish more permanent, trustworthy leadership in this critical area. Since William, in the first few years after his accession, usually favored retaining, where possible, the native English nobility in positions of power, hoping they'd demonstrate good faith, it is equally possible that King William was testing the loyalty of another section of Northumbria's population.

In the summer of 1069, King Sweyn Estrithson launched his long-anticipated invasion of England. Right on the heels of William's incessant and vigorous campaigning in 1068, and after his second critical occupation of York in the early spring of 1069, William now found himself confronted with what would be the greatest challenge of his entire reign to his control of England. The strength of Sweyn's armada has been compared to that of Norway's King Harold Hardraada in 1066; it comprised about 250 ships, the largest of which probably carried one hundred men. These, moreover, were not levies, but trained warriors, including many of the highest rank in Denmark. All of them had been drawn by promises of great wealth and rich land.

The Danish fleet first appeared off the coast of Kent. Moving up the east coast, it attempted to land warriors, but these were repelled repeatedly until Sweyn's ships reached the north of England. There, his reception was very different, owing largely to the fact that the population itself was of recent Scandinavian descent. It was an area in which royal control had never been better than tenuous. Sweyn's great Danish fleet anchored unchallenged in the estuary of the Humber River, which flows between Yorkshire and Lincolnshire. Edgar the Atheling, grandson of Edmund Ironsides (of the Anglo-Saxon royal house of Wessex), who had sought refuge at the court of King Malcolm of Scotland, now moved south to join King Sweyn's forces. Also swelling this already formidable army were the same Gospatric whom King William had so recently entrusted with Northumbria, and Waltheof, a younger son of Siward, former earl of Northumbria.

Waltheof is remarkable in that he had already done homage to William the Conqueror and accepted him as his lord and king. King William, in his turn, had welcomed Waltheof into his court, where Waltheof enjoyed royal favor. In some discussions of Waltheof by contemporary chroniclers, one gets the impression that, for King William, this young nobleman symbolized his hope that Anglo-Saxons and Normans would be able to live together and rule England cooperatively for her greater good. Perhaps further disruption of the old order would not occur then. If Waltheof had remained loyal, he would have been greatly elevated—so the contemporary chroniclers assert—and also much enriched by King William. As it was, both Gospatric and Waltheof allied themselves with King Sweyn—in the hope, presumably, that one of them would be given the earldom of Northumbria. With King William, honors and land were bestowed more circumspectly on those who had proven themselves steadfast, over time, in their loyalty.

Waltheof's betrayal may have forced the king to accept at last that a cooperative relationship with Anglo-Saxon leaders would not be possible. William's subsequent campaigns in the north were ferocious, a fact that suggests not so much his keen disappointment as his clear awareness that the area could not be subdued in any other way. Immediately after his coronation in 1066, King William had allowed every Anglo-Saxon nobleman, ecclesiastic, and member of the previous royal household to keep his traditional post unless and until that man proved himself a traitor. Many, many betrayed him, until William finally lost hope of the Anglo-Saxons ever coming to appreciate their new king's vision for the kingdom's future. They could have willingly joined their energies with his to construct a great nation. Instead, selfishness, avarice, and ambition for personal power disappointed William again and again. With Waltheof's betrayal, William must finally have accepted the role of "conqueror," rather than that of visionary leader of a harmonious blend of Germanic, Celtic, and Scandinavian peoples. In no other way would he ever be able to rule England.

King Sweyn's Danish army, augmented by the forces of Waltheof and Gospatric, now marched on York. The two garrisons King William had put in place could not possibly hold the royal castles against such an onslaught. In an act of great bravery, William's garrisons marched out of their castles to set fire to the city of York itself, hoping to deprive the Scandinavian army of any supplies the city could offer them. After intense fighting, the garrisons, greatly outnumbered, were killed to a man.

Some of Sweyn's army now moved to fortify the island of Axholme in the Humber River estuary, while other contingents moved south across the river into the countryside of Lincolnshire to procure supplies. These supplies, evidently, were willingly provided by the villagers, amid great feasting (so the chroniclers relate). Thus there took shape, for the first time since Hastings, a very sizeable and coherent challenge to William's rule, led not by "native" Anglo-Saxons, but rather by the invading king of Denmark, who attracted to his army many of the disaffected, self-interested elements in England.

On top of these alarming events, which saw the threat of a large army moving unchecked into northeastern England, King Malcolm of Scotland, who had negotiated a peace treaty one year earlier with King William, decided now to back King Sweyn also.

King William now faced the very real possibility that the Scandinavians might again rule northern England, or even create a separate realm in northern England ruled by Edgar the Atheling and buttressed by the support of Malcolm and Sweyn. The campaign to stop this crisis required William's utmost force.

The king evidently did not misjudge the level of response that was needed: in all cases, his trusted commanders were successful in pacifying different areas of rebellion. It also appears that King William was careful to send relief to any location where the royal garrisons were under attack. His first goal, however, in moving northward with a large army was to intimidate the Danish army.

At a certain point in his movement northward, William heard that the Danish army was preparing to reoccupy the town of York. Upon receipt of this news, the king marched directly upon the city, which was hastily evacuated once again by the Danish army. Along King William's route, as he was nearing York, and after the nearly abandoned city had been retaken, he ordered the devastation of the surrounding countryside in what has become known as the "Harrying of the North."

There is no other act in all of William's career for which he has been so unreservedly condemned, both by the monk chroniclers of his times and by subsequent historians. Neither of those groups, however, had the knowledge and experience to judge such a difficult military decision, one made "in the field" by a great general facing the worst crisis of his entire reign. Sweyn's invasion, and the repeated treachery of the North, had thrown into sharp relief what would certainly have proved the undoing of Anglo-Norman England unless William took drastic action. William deeply believed that his rule of England, and the Conquest itself, had been by God's special will, and that it was his divinely ordained responsibility to rule the English people. In fact the devastation of the North, together with King William's brilliantly conceived westward march in the dead of winter across the Pennine Mountains, taking the town of Chester completely by surprise, caused the Danish army to accept a very modest bribe and sail away.

A final question: Can we see in Paramhansa Yogananda any likelihood that he might have handled such a crisis in a similar manner? He never had military problems to confront, of course, but Kriyananda says that, although Yogananda was divinely loving toward everybody, he also demonstrated a divine impersonality toward the entire illusion that is God's creation.

Kriyananda remembers his guru once, with appropriate gestures, speaking to him of God as "eating people." Death meant nothing to him, for he saw human life as eternal in God.

Once, when speaking of disciples who had left the ashram, Yogananda said, "I *made* them leave, by my will power. They weren't responding properly to the life we have here." This might, in one sense, have seemed heartless. Yet his entire life was dedicated to lifting people out of the mud of delusion. What he saw, in addition, was the many lives it takes a soul finally to realize that the only "way out" is first to realize God. Yogananda was impersonal in the sense that he knew spiritual victory comes only after one has uprooted to its depths all ego-consciousness and every attachment. God Himself loves us in our souls. He doesn't love our delusions.

CHAPTER 14

The New Forest: A Vision for the Future

Another controversial act of William's reign was his creation of the New Forest, a large area that he is said to have set apart for his own pleasure in hunting. In fact, what he did was extend the forest. Peasants (we are told), in order to make room for this New Forest, were uprooted from their homes. This seems to have been an arbitrary act on William's part, and unnecessary to the good governance of his kingdom.

Yet New Forest may well have been a consequence of William's far vision. Today, when people are increasingly conscious of the importance of ecology, they are beginning to realize how important forests are to the well-being of our planet.

In Greece, where at a certain point in its history all the trees were cut down, there is little or no rainfall. Trees attract rain, which is essential to crops and to human life.

The gradual destruction of the Amazon jungle is of great concern for the entire planet. Yet Brazil is a country with its own integral boundaries and national rights. Can other countries rightly interfere?

There is much that we don't know about the ecology of our planet, but William may have been acting far-sightedly in imposing New Forest on his people. Their resentment may have been due mostly to their ignorance of realities that, to us today, are beginning to come clear. Today, in fact, England is turning parts of New Forest into National Forest.

And we ourselves may yet have much to learn. There may be a closer connection between man and trees than anyone today realizes.

For example, there was a pine tree growing on Yogananda's property on Mt. Washington, in Los Angeles, California. The tree was dying, and one day Jean Haupt, one of the monks, cut it down. Yogananda remarked sadly, "He should not have done that. You'll see: cutting down that tree is a sign of the approaching end of my own life." It was not long, in fact, before Yogananda himself died.

Another time, in speaking to a group of monks, he indicated an avocado tree. "Another tree was here also," he said, "on the other side of the walkway. A *very* devoted disciple lived here then. I told a few people, 'One of these trees represents him. The other one represents me. One of them will die; whichever one it is will leave this path.' Well, his tree died, and he did leave. His problem was attachment to money. But he had been *very* devoted."

"Yogananda," so Kriyananda says, "used this story to warn us against the traps of delusion. But why did he make that reference to those two trees? Is there some kind of natural connection between trees and human beings?"

The Bhagavad Gita compares the human body to a tree: the legendary *ashvatta* tree, with its roots above and its branches below. The human body is indeed like an inverted tree. Its downward-spreading "branches" are the nervous system. Its "roots above" are the hair, which in the astral body emanates rays of energy from the brain.

How infinitely intricate is Nature! We cannot know whether the above suppositions are right concerning William's New Forest, but he may have been acting from deep insight into subtler realities of this planet.

William may not have been so fond of hunting as has been claimed. Not only did he have very little time for such "pleasures," but he is also said to have loved the deer. Yogananda tells of a pet deer he specially loved—so much so that, when the deer was very ill and he prayed for it to live, its soul appeared to him and asked him to release it from that body so that it might continue its upward evolution. As he writes in *Autobiography of a Yogi*:

"You are holding me back," the deer said to me in a dream. "Please let me go; let me go."

"All right," I answered in the dream.

I awoke immediately, and cried out, "Boys, the deer is dying!" The children rushed to my side.

I ran to the corner of the room where I had placed the pet. It made a last effort to rise, stumbled toward me, then dropped at my feet, dead.

CHAPTER 15

Archbishop Lanfranc and King William: A Harmony of Church and State

William the Conqueror's achievements in governing his new kingdom—his innovations as well as his brilliant adaptations of Anglo-Saxon institutions—may be seen in every aspect of England's administration: in its legal system, its diplomatic relations, its military strategy, its incentives to trade, and—perhaps most spectacularly—in the reform and flowering of monasticism, which began during William's reign and reached its peak under the rule of his youngest son, Henry I.

The single most important decision King William made with regard to the church in England was his choice, in 1070, of Lanfranc of Pavia for the position of archbishop of Canterbury, the *de facto* head of the Christian church in all England. Theirs became the most fruitful, harmonious, and universally beneficial partnership between monarch and primate in the High Medieval period.

A monk of Battle Abbey, writing during the reign of King Henry I, stated that men of their generation used to say, "No two figures were to be found together in one land as were King William and Lanfranc his archbishop." Before William the Conqueror and Archbishop Lanfranc, even Pope Gregory VII, who ultimately stood against virtually the whole Christian world in the overweening role he sought for the church of Rome, became silent when confronted by their combined authority.

Lanfranc, born around 1010, and thus approximately eighteen years William's senior, had trained as a lawyer in Pavia,

Italy. Around the age of twenty, he traveled into Burgundy and France, where he continued his studies, then settled in 1039 in the Avranches in Normandy, where he probably taught the traditional *trivium*, as it was called: grammar, logic, and rhetoric. According to the *Vita Lanfranci*, the young teacher's decision to enter holy orders came upon him quite suddenly. He was traveling to Rouen when he was set upon by a band of robbers who, after relieving him of what little money he had with him, tied him to a tree, where he remained the whole night. Like Saint Paul's experience of the resurrected Christ on the road to Damascus, Lanfranc's mystical experience that night changed him forever. Passers-by cut him loose the following morning after dawn, and Lanfranc asked only that he be directed to the smallest and humblest monastery in the area. Thus began his treasured three years of near-seclusion and silence at the new abbey of Bec.

Lanfranc's brief years of seclusion ended as the needs of Bec Abbey drew him first into teaching, and then into serving as the prior of Bec. Ultimately, his personal piety, his knowledge of canon law, and his abilities as a leader brought him to the attention of Duke William, who asked him to assume the role of abbot at Saint-Etienne in Caen, which the duke himself had founded. It was natural, therefore, that when the king removed Archbishop Stigand of Canterbury from office (which of course he did, despite the unscrupulous Stigand's submission to him), Lanfranc was brought from Normandy to serve at William's side as his archbishop.

Lanfranc, like William, was a great supporter of Gregorian reform in the church. Like William, however, he also stopped short of embracing the reform ideal at those points where reform would have limited the role of lay princes in selecting and investing prelates with the symbols of office, and sought in other ways also to curtail the power of princes in matters vital to their rule. Lanfranc expressed with great consistency his views on the role of the lay prince. In a letter to certain ecclesiastics in Ireland, he wrote:

"God bestows no greater mercy upon countries than when he advances lovers of peace and justice to the government of souls or bodies, and especially when he commits the kingdoms of this world to be ruled by good kings. For thence peace arises, discord is quietened, and the observance of the Christian religion is established."

Concerning William's rule in England, Lanfranc wrote to Pope Alexander II:

"I beseech you to ask the Divine Clemency that he should grant a long life to my lord the king of the English, that he should make peace for him against all who resist him, and that he should incline his heart to love of him and his holy church, always with spiritual devotion. For while he lives we have peace of a kind; but after his death we expect that we shall have neither peace nor anything that is good."

The monk Eadmer, biographer of Anselm of Bec, Lanfranc's successor as archbishop of Canterbury, observed that Lanfranc was "acceptable to the king before all other men," for the reason that in all things Lanfranc sought to make William devoted to God. In this regard the king apparently gave his archbishop complete latitude.

Once, during a ceremonial occasion when King William was wearing his crown and was royally bejeweled for the evening, the court jester pranced before the king, declaiming, "Behold! I see God! I see God!" Lanfranc, who was seated by the king's side, took William to task for allowing his jester to speak words that were, in his estimation, blasphemous. The king followed Lanfranc's guidance and had the jester flogged for his act.

William was always prepared to listen to Lanfranc's advice, including corrections he advised concerning lax morality or unnecessary cruelty within the kingdom. It was evidently on his archbishop's prompting, also, that the king took steps against the highly profitable slave trade with Ireland.

However, when Lanfranc disagreed with a decision that William had made—perhaps even a decision that involved a cleric—Lanfranc did not speak, or spoke with great diffidence, unless the king actively sought his opinion. It was not fear which prompted Lanfranc's reticence. In spheres that involved keeping the peace, order, or raising the money necessary for the kingdom's defense,

Lanfranc remained silent out of respect for the burdensome responsibilities King William carried. Others, knowing the high regard in which the king held Lanfranc, would urge Lanfranc to intervene, but Lanfranc's response to this well-meant advice reflected perfectly his own deep conviction: "Against the king's command I presume to ask nothing, and to order nothing."

Both Lanfranc and King William had the greatest respect for the integrity and righteousness with which each sought to act within his own sphere. King and archbishop, together, adhered to tradition and to law, rather than taking arbitrary action in any matter. Both men were able to find fresh solutions to the unprecedented difficulties to which the Conquest had given rise, while at the same time they made sure that their solutions were intelligible and logical extensions of past tradition, which could be understood and respected by those who would be the most affected. Lanfranc, as archbishop of Canterbury, modeled for cleric and nobleman alike an ideal expression of loyalty to the king—loyalty that put into action creatively and energetically, in Lanfranc's own arena of responsibility, William's vision for the kingdom, offering the king thoughtful solutions and spiritual support, and even, when superficial disagreements arose between them, acknowledging with his full and grateful cooperation the burden that the king carried alone.

CHAPTER 16

Domesday Book —
What Manner of Land and Men Has England?

Though England was changed forever by William's broad vision, the Conqueror was forced to spend most of his time in Normandy even after the Conquest, from a few years after it to the time of his death. On the continent, the Capetian dynasty of France was beginning energetically to increase its authority over its many vassal states. For King Philip I of France, one of the many challenges to his efforts to centralize his kingdom was the fact that the duke of Normandy (an important vassal state of France) was also the sovereign king of England. Curbing the power and independence of the Norman duke involved King Philip in constant alliance-building with Anjou and Flanders, while William, king of England and duke of Normandy, worked with equal vigor and with brilliant stratagems to break down these alliances.

After a few years' respite from continental conflict, while William stabilized his control of England, and, in fact, even while he was completing his desperate fight in the north of England in 1069, a rebellion broke out in Maine, on Normandy's eastern border, which, the following year, caused the collapse there of the Norman government. Thus began, for William, a new phase of nearly continuous warfare on the continent, where he had no choice but to fight France, Anjou, and Flanders, together and separately, on every one of Normandy's borders.

In addition to the superhuman effort needed to maintain the borders of the Anglo-Norman kingdom, King William also applied his seemingly inexhaustible energy to creating a new government in England, which meant both identifying and then infusing fresh life into those Anglo-Saxon institutions which could continue to serve the needs of his kingdom, as well as instituting administrative innovations of his own.

Among the Conqueror's greatest achievements was a vast kingdom-wide survey that came to be known as Domesday Book. The Domesday Inquest was followed in the same year, 1086, the penultimate year of King William's reign, with a great oath-taking. The nature of the Oath of Salisbury, too, was an innovation of William's, and may well have carried the additional symbolic weight of each oath-taker placing his own individual "seal" on the sworn testimony gathered in Domesday. Both the Domesday Inquest and the Oath of Salisbury were born from and reinforced crucial tenets that shaped all of King William's administrative, diplomatic, and military policies. Both events took place, as mentioned above, in 1086, and both were ostensibly products of the latest (and, as it turned out, the last) threat of a Scandinavian invasion into England.

Within England, the king had been forced to imprison his own half-brother, Odo, bishop of Bayeux, on charges of treason. William himself had elevated Odo to great power and wealth. However, as Douglas points out, Odo was perfectly capable, even from prison, of inciting rebellion against William among certain members of the aristocracy. On England's northern border, King Malcolm of Scotland had once again become hostile to William, and was a likely ally for King Cnut IV of Denmark and Count Robert of Flanders when spring weather permitted them to renew their planned attack on England from Scandinavia.

Looking at another aspect of King William's situation, toward the end of his life, the question of his successor must have been a great burden on William's mind. His oldest son Robert Curthose, now in his early thirties, had been named many years previously as the heir to the whole Anglo-Norman kingdom. The king's great men on more than one occasion had sworn oaths of fealty to

Robert. By the time William the Conqueror held his great court at
Gloucester at Christmas 1085, however, Robert had been in rebellion against his father for two and a half years, and, at the same
time, was openly in alliance with William's great adversary, King
Philip I of France. Even as King William labored ceaselessly to
preserve the integrity of the Anglo-Norman kingdom, the question
of a worthy, competent successor remained unresolved. William
knew that unless Curthose became reconciled to him, his own
death would inevitably lead to warfare, and would bring great suffering on the whole kingdom.

Such was the backdrop of the king's Christmas court at
Gloucester in 1085, and of his extraordinary plan to mount a kingdom-wide inquest into the nature of its people and the extent of
its resources. Both of these actions appear all the more remarkable
in context.

The king's Christmas court was one of four times during the
year when William's tenants-in-chief—those great lords who held
tracts of land directly from the king—and the royal family, as well
as highly placed ecclesiastics from all over the kingdom, as his most
important liegemen, came together. It was also a time when the
king took council with a larger group, as they conversed together
about any problems facing the whole kingdom.

Again, the *Anglo-Saxon Chronicle* is our source for the fact that it
was at the Conqueror's Christmas court of 1085 that the Domesday
survey was first conceived:

"After this, the king gave much thought, and engaged in very
deep conversations with his council, about the land of England,
and with what manner of men resided there. He then sent representatives all over England, into every shire, to ascertain how
many hundreds of 'hides' there were in the land, and what dues
the king ought to receive from the shire over 12 months." Even the
contemporary chroniclers misunderstood the reasons why King
William had initiated the Domesday survey; thus, the question, for
centuries to come, became the center of scholarly debate. However,
information as to how the survey was carried out has been pro-

vided for us by the bishop of Hereford in 1085, who must have been directly involved in the Inquest.

In fact, the methodology of the Inquest casts light on the several purposes of Domesday, when we add the further testimony of a document known as the "Ely Inquiry" (*Inquisitio Eliensis*). After an enumeration of the detail the survey sought to capture, the author of the Ely document notes:

"King William required his royal commissioners to gather testimony on the disposition of land and resources as it was pre-Conquest, as it was in 1066 or shortly thereafter, and as it was now, in 1086."

Many historians, while admiring the Domesday Inquest as a testament to the cohesion of Norman England and to the great power wielded by the ruler, dismiss the survey as having only one motivation: the king's desire to find more resources to tax. Such great labor and care, however, to establish, through the sworn testimony of so many people, the past history of every village, manor, fishery, fief, woodland, and pasture suggests a great deal more than avarice in seeking every possible asset to tax. As one historian observed: "[I]t would have been perfectly possible to reckon the tax due, and to increase liabilities where these were unnecessarily small, without creating the elaborate machinery of the Domesday Inquest."

What were King William's actual goals in launching the Domesday Inquest? Additional revenue was, certainly, an important short-range goal; in order to meet the threatened invasion of King Cnut of Denmark, the Conqueror had returned from Normandy recently with a large army, which consisted in part of mercenary soldiers who needed to be paid and fed. New ships, and the construction of additional defensive castles along England's east coast, also required money. Huge loans and extensive lines of credit were not an option for an eleventh century king. Even those chroniclers who lamented the collection of taxes would later praise King William because the country during his reign had been safe—safe from foreign invasion, safe from private warfare, and to a very great extent safe from thieves and highwaymen. Finding more revenue from as-yet-untaxed, or undertaxed, resources was, indeed, an important goal of the Inquest.

Nevertheless, William's deeper purpose deserves emphasis. David Douglas wrote that the most significant feature of the Domesday Inquest was its attempt to record the conditions in England as they were, not only in 1066 and 1086, but also as they were in the time King Edward the Confessor. Regarding himself as King Edward's successor, William wanted to record the conditions in England before the Conquest and to document and legalize the great changes brought during his realm.

Twenty years had passed since William's invasion of England, when he claimed the throne as successor to his kinsman, Edward. Land had been granted to various noblemen who had served William well, and whom he could trust. The various bishoprics, abbeys, and smaller churches also held land and other revenue-producing assets, and still other vast areas of land had been retained by the Conqueror as his demesne. The lands of those Anglo-Saxons and Danes who had died in battle up north at Stamford Bridge or at Hastings, or who had been imprisoned or executed later for repeated acts of treachery, had been redistributed as they fell into King William's hands. Royal commissioners such as Geoffrey of Coutances had been busy continuously with all manner of land disputes.

There was much that King William wanted to know. Had his own great men greedily taken over a neighboring fief as their own? Surely this was a great temptation, as part of an all-conquering wave of Norman warriors. Had an abbey been improperly deprived of some revenue-bearing lands? Had an over-zealous royal official in some area expanded the king's demesne inappropriately?

Apparently, the enormous amount of sworn testimony by two separate teams of royal investigators, one after the other sent into each shire, must in itself have had the effect of resolving innumerable points of contention concerning land, rights to waterways, bridge tolls, borders and boundaries, and much more. This, too, was surely part of the Conqueror's intention. The process of conferring great fiefs upon his own great men, in the first months following his coronation as king of England, must of necessity have been less exact than King William would have liked. The intervening twenty years had involved him unremittingly in the defense of Normandy, while litigation over land use had formed the backdrop to his administration in England.

It was completely characteristic of William the Conqueror to conceive of such a great endeavor as the Domesday Inquest, which would serve a multitude of needs. William needed to know much more about the land and peoples of England, in order better to defend it, administer it, promote trade, assess the number of free men versus slaves, the amount of forested land, and much, much more. William felt the need to place on a firm footing every arrangement concerning the disposition of land, so that his legacy would not involve further and endless litigation. He well knew that such disputes were being held in check for the present by his great personal authority, but a later ruler, with a less commanding presence, might soon find these *clamores* erupting into private warfare across the land. The stability of England depended on putting the post-Conquest distribution of land on a firm legal basis.

The Conqueror gave so much importance to the taking of this Inquest that he himself, so the chroniclers tell us, rode through the south of England, where it was first set into motion, his awe-inspiring presence reinforcing the authority of his royal commissioners.

We can imagine that, accompanying him, would have been his youngest but most capable son, Henry, upon whom the Conqueror (together with Lanfranc) conferred the belt of knighthood at Westminster during Pentecost, 1086. King William's second son, William Rufus, who was some years older than Henry, perhaps added royal authority to the Inquest as it proceeded to other parts of the kingdom.

King William's travels brought him to Salisbury for Lammas. His council and all the landholders who were of any account over all England, whosever man's they were, arrived, submitted to him, and pledged their loyalty to the king against all other men.

The most significant act of the reign of William the Conqueror was this "Oath of Salisbury," discussed briefly above. While it is inconceivable that every single landholder in England actually came to Salisbury, many came who held no lands directly of the king. Those great men who had been invested with land by the king himself were, in the feudal system, called his "tenants-in-chief." Far greater in number were those who, in exchange for serving as one of the knights whom a tenant-in-chief owed to the king in wartime, had been granted land within one of the great fiefs held by King William's tenants-in-chief—men like Odo, bishop of Bayeux; Robert count of Mortain; and William fitz Osbern—to name but a few.

Robert, count of Mortain, for example, when called upon to do so by King William, was obligated by virtue of the amount of land he held of the king to present himself for battle along with a previously agreed upon number of fully armed, mounted and trained knights. To show up with even one fewer than this number was unacceptable. To bring to battle knights who were poorly equipped was equally unacceptable. In order to meet these quotas of knights, the tenants-in-chief, encouraged by King William, bestowed varying numbers of hides of the land they had been granted on a knight in order that he might, from the productivity of that land, feed himself and his family and equip himself properly for battle: a not-inexpensive undertaking. Most of these knights, depending on the size of their holdings from the tenant-in-chief—now their feudal lord—in their turn also bestowed portions of their land on still-lesser tenants who would farm the knight's land as well as cultivating a portion which they held for their own maintenance. Thus the process of what is called "subinfeudation" had become well established by the end of the Conqueror's reign.

Traditionally, in the simple example provided here, the lesser tenant was the vassal of the knight; the knight was the vassal of the tenant-in-chief; and the tenant-in-chief was the vassal of the king. Add to this picture the idea that the knight in question might also hold another fief—a smaller number of hides of land, let us say, in the next shire—which had been granted him by a fellow knight who was himself a vassal of another tenant-in-chief of the king, and the picture becomes very complex indeed. What if, as a knight, one's immediate lord betrayed the king, making war on him? To whom, in such a situation, did a knight owe fealty? As the decades, then the centuries, went by, there are actually cases in which a lord held land of his own vassal!

Those who held land of the king did so not by their right of birth, but because they continued to fulfill the feudal duties that were required of landholders, and were personally loyal to the king. If a vassal's duty to his immediate liege lord conflicted with his duty to the king, first in importance under the Oath of Salisbury was his duty to the king. This was the central meaning of that oath, administered in 1086 to the great gathering of men who held any significant amount of land, whether directly of the king, or of one of his tenants-in-chief, or of another lord.

In England, a baron in rebellion against the king did not automatically have his own private army of sub-tenants to count on by virtue of their oath of fealty to him.

While in the rest of Europe the development of feudalism had the effect of weakening central authority, in England this tenet of William's, woven into the fabric of law and government administration, immeasurably strengthened the king's power, and enabled England to survive the disintegration of Medieval Europe.

When in the reign of his youngest son, King Henry I, Robert of Bellême, England's richest landholder, rebelled against Henry and ignored royal prohibitions against private warfare. Henry disseised him, and Bellême's vast lands in England reverted to the king. It is interesting to note that when Robert of Bellême was imprisoned years later by King Henry, and disseised also of his lands in Normandy, Robert's heir eventually petitioned Henry for the return of the traditional Bellême-Montgomery family holdings in Normandy, but never attempted to reclaim their lands in England.

Though not stated in so many words, William demonstrated time and again his profound conviction that a king was worthy of the royal power he wielded only if he made himself subservient to God. At William's deathbed, his disposition of England stated (paraphrased): "I dare not bequeath England, acquired with so much blood, to anyone but God Almighty, though I hope He will bless my son William Rufus in taking on its governance."

William was interred at his own request in the Abbaye-aux-hommes at Caen, which he himself had built. His tomb was left undisturbed until 1522, when, for reasons unknown, an exhumation was ordered by the Roman Catholic Church. The disinterring, according to the French author who (much later) published a history of the Abbey, was done with proper reverence. The body, states historian David Douglas, was found to be in a state of "good preservation." Indeed, so good was its condition that a color sketch was made of it on wood, showing his face and hair, and mounted on the wall above the spot where his body was "reverentially reinterred."

Had William been recognized as a saint, these facts would have been sufficient for his body to be declared "incorrupt."

CHAPTER 17

The Problem of Succession:
Who Will Provide the Vision?

To cherish high ideals is the first step
To high attainments.
As important is the second step:
To work with things,
Not as you think they ought to be,
But as they are.

    —*The Peace Treaty*, Act Two, Scene 3, Swami Kriyananda

In **the heat of** late summer, 1087, William I, king of England
and duke of Normandy, lay dying in a dark stone room in the
priory of Saint Gervais, outside Rouen. Tension hung in the air,
and darkened the vision of those gathered there. It was a tension
so palpable that there was no room even for grief. The fate of the
Anglo-Norman kingdom was now to be decided irrevocably.

Fatally injured by his stumbling horse, and (one assumes) in
great pain from an internal hemorrhage, William was nevertheless
completely clear in his mind, and brought all his formidable will
power to bear on the question of who would succeed him. It was
now September of that year; twenty-one years had passed since his
conquest of England.

Kings did not live or die in private; too many lives were intimately interwoven with their own. Even in his *extremis*, William
was surrounded by some of his inner circle: barons and bishops, all
of whom brought to this crucial moment the one-pointed focus of
men who felt they were standing on the verge of a precipice. Each

knew that his own future depended on William's decision in the matter of succession.

Much of the tension in the room was due to the fact that Robert, nicknamed "Curthose," the Conqueror's oldest son and previously designated heir, was even then in active rebellion against his father. Nine years earlier, Robert, urged on by sycophantic followers as young and restless as himself, had for the second time demanded for himself more real power to govern the duchy of Normandy. That was while his father was still alive and robust. Even now, Curthose and others of the second generation of the great Conquest families—sons of some of the men who were now in attendance on William—were conducting raids on Normandy's borders, urged on by Philip I, king of France, William's nemesis. Curthose was consorting, even now, with that same nemesis.

A very strong Norman tradition, however, held that the lands a ruler inherited from his father should pass intact to his oldest son. On the other hand, anything that a man had gained on his own, through conquest in his lifetime, could be disposed of as he wished.

At the heart of the Conqueror's genius for military strategy, and his brilliant administrative innovations, lay his ability to judge the character of men. William had chosen as leaders a group of men who were highly intelligent, intensely energetic, and, in their own right, very creative. This remarkable aristocracy had given its complete loyalty to William—in some cases, for many decades. The Conqueror himself had chosen his commanders in the invasion of England, the brilliant administrators for his kingdom, the highly important frontier military leaders, and the reform-minded, deeply committed monks and priests who now led the church in England and Normandy. William had shown time and again that he possessed penetrating insight into the minds and hearts of men.

It took no great insight, however, to know absolutely that Robert Curthose lacked the character to lead others and govern wisely. It must have been a grave disappointment to William, for clearly it had been his intention, at first, to confer on this son both England

and Normandy, and he had taken pains to train him in government and in diplomacy.

King William had demonstrated his willingness to take risks with people. After his victory in 1066, he had allowed the Anglo-Saxon earls of Mercia and Northumbria to retain their positions until they showed themselves fundamentally treacherous. Repeatedly, William had accepted fervent vows of loyalty from men who later betrayed him. In many cases he had done so despite his certain knowledge of how it would end. As England's new king, he had wanted to give the old Anglo-Saxon aristocracy and household officers of King Edward the Confessor every opportunity to prove themselves worthy of his confidence.

Likewise, the Conqueror had given his son Robert ample opportunity to prove himself worthy of a leadership position. Repeatedly, however, he had seen Robert's crippling limitations. He had forgiven the young man's first open rebellion, which had included an outrageous attempt to wrest for himself the seat of ducal administration, Rouen, by storm. Even more monstrous was the fact that, in a later pitched battle during Curthose's first period of rebellion, William himself had been nearly killed—some say by Curthose himself, who did not recognize his father dressed in battle armor.

After a relatively brief period of reconciliation, engineered by the Conqueror's great magnates, Robert Curthose had betrayed his father a second time, and his nearly incessant plundering along Normandy's frontiers was now in its fourth year.

Most damning of all was the fact that Robert's current activities were not only a betrayal of his father, personally, but also a betrayal of the integrity and independence of the Anglo-Norman kingdom. Through his alliance with Philip I of France, Curthose had been stupid and selfish enough to risk the sovereignty of the kingdom itself, for the goal of all of Philip I's military and political maneuvering was to bring Normandy, as a vassal state, under the control of France.

Ultimately, Curthose's self-indulgent breach with his father threatened everything that had been gained in 1066: the very throne of England. By dividing the Anglo-Norman aristocracy against itself, Robert's pique was steadily eroding the unity that had allowed a relatively few men to bring England into a new and vital relationship with the Latin and Mediterranean world.

William the Conqueror, as death approached, determined that Robert Curthose should have no part in ruling either Normandy or England. He perceived these two lands not as separate entities, but as one kingdom, united under a single ruler.

Now, however, William's great magnates and close companions, his *familiares* as the chroniclers called them, bore down on their dying lord with counter-arguments regarding the succession.

There was Norman tradition to be considered: Robert was the oldest son and so should at least, by right, have Normandy. Many argued also that they had taken oaths of fealty to Curthose as his father's successor, at King William's behest. Were they now to be forsworn?

If Robert were not given some part of the kingdom, then he would be in a strong and easily justifiable position to attempt to take it by force. Many would feel the righteousness of his claim, certainly to the duchy. If Curthose were forced to fight for the dukedom of Normandy, he would undoubtedly call on Philip I of France for assistance and, in so doing, would tighten the bonds of vassalage to the French king. This was not what the Conqueror wanted. William, a king in his own right, had refused as duke of Normandy to do homage to Philip of France.

There must have been a few present, also, who saw the unshakable unity between their ruler and his magnates as their greatest strength. They were now hoping to resurrect that unity despite the disruption that had been introduced by Curthose.

Then, too, there were the sons of these great families who had defected with Robert Curthose. Were they now to be thrust forever, with Curthose, into a kind of exile? Perhaps it was still possible to view Robert's actions as due to youthful high spirits, which might be properly channeled. Robert was about thirty-three years old at this time—certainly no longer a youth by any standard.

Of the important ecclesiastics in the room, at least one would have been present to hear the king's final confession, and to counsel him how to dispose of his lands and wealth in such a way as to assure him of heaven, thereupon administering extreme unction. This priest would have urged William to forgive Robert, and may have joined his voice to those of the barons present. A reinstatement of Robert as heir would be the mark of the father's complete forgiveness.

An enormous calamity was bearing down on these men, as vassals of the great lord who lay dying. It was surely difficult for any of them fully to comprehend the Conqueror's deepest reason for refusing to name Curthose his successor. It had nothing to do with paternal anger, no matter how justified such anger. It was, rather, that this son did not understand or share his father's vision for the future of the kingdom he had created.

Robert Curthose, though sporadically a good warrior, and at times a magnetic military leader, seemed uninterested in the skills of good government. Reckless in his distribution of largesse as he showed devotion to a superficial chivalric code of honor, Robert was more pleased with form than with creating stability, peace, and good government. Normandy, lacking a strong central authority, would quickly sink back again to petty warfare between avaricious noblemen. Curthose was ruled by sentiment and self-interest, while his father acted, as we have seen, to manifest a vast vision for the crucial role that England, in particular, would play in the ongoing future, even up to our own times.

The barons' barrage of reasonable arguments must have become more insistent, as the tensions grew over what loomed on the horizon. If the Conqueror's main objection to Curthose was his lack of judgment and his self-indulgence, then, the barons urged, there were surely men who could guide Robert. Counselors like themselves would make up for defects in Curthose's character.

The king's most fundamental objection to Robert, however, remained unanswered. Even with wise, seasoned advisors, who would provide the vision? The dying ruler felt deeply, also, that a strong and devotional monastic presence in England and Normandy would be necessary for the kingdom. The church, too, needed royal protection and leadership for a strong monastic presence to exist with a minimum of interference by an over-autocratic pope.

Extremely important, moreover, was enforcement of the idea that all land was held only at the king's pleasure. A key component of the Conqueror's vision had been the idea that each individual's loyalty was due first and foremost to the king, even if that person's immediate overlord set himself in rebellion against royal authority. This policy would, William saw, prevent the rise of local despots with petty, self-serving agendas. Such men had previously kept the countryside seething with private wars. Strengthening the royal authority would be the next step to bringing the country greater peace and stability, and an expanded awareness of national identity.

The Conqueror, during his twenty-one years on the throne of England, had concerned himself almost wholly with protecting the land militarily. Now the Anglo-Norman kingdom needed a ruler who could develop governance and law. This task required a clear-minded, strong visionary. Robert Curthose, as the Conqueror well knew, was far from being such a man.

The king also knew the hearts of those who were now with him, urging him to reconsider his decision to disinherit Robert Curthose. It was clear to the dying William that these powerful magnates were determined to support his oldest son; quite probably they would do so regardless of whom he named now as his successor. Such was the reality of the situation, and this wise, ever-practical leader of men made the best decision possible under the circumstances. His oldest son would have the "real power" he had always demanded of his father, and many of William's closest companions would support him. With the conquest of England essentially complete, some among the Conqueror's *familiares* felt, perhaps, that a less powerful central authority would be adequate—perhaps even welcome. Hard experience would now be their teacher, as they discovered for themselves Curthose's extreme ineptness.

In great pain, and (as one contemporary chronicler expressed it) "worn out by their importunities," William the Conqueror reluctantly agreed to name Robert Curthose as his successor to the duchy of Normandy. The oldest son, however, was to have *only* Normandy. The crown of England was, William decreed, to go to his second oldest son, William "Rufus" (the "red").

The brusque, iconoclastic Rufus, unlike his older brother, had at least remained loyal to his father, even if he didn't understand his ideals, and had been by his side during his father's constant warfare. Rufus was a fine, if flamboyant, warrior. This second son, now about twenty-six years old, had been at his father's side during the siege where his father had been fatally injured. He was now present in the room, along with the men who had been urging the Conqueror to make Robert Curthose his heir.

Those present greeted in silence King William's decision to name William Rufus as his heir to the throne of England. Their silence was surely occasioned in part by the tone of the dying man's voice. No doubt they understood immediately that this decision was not negotiable. William's mind was now firmly set.

In that silence, the king commanded a scribe to come forward with parchment, and ordered that a certain crown—one of several which he had had made according to his own designs—be brought. Rufus himself was ordered to ready himself for immediate departure to England. There wasn't a moment to lose, since news of the king's death, when it came, might run ahead of Rufus and cause chaos before the young man could take charge of the royal treasury at Winchester.

After some brief dictation by William, a letter of instruction addressed to Archbishop Lanfranc, regent of England in William's absence, was put into Rufus's hand. The letter, affixed with the seal of the Conqueror, instructed Lanfranc to crown William Rufus as king of England. The father knew his son well, and undoubtedly now offered him a few words of counsel on avoiding the pitfalls into which his character would tend inevitably to lead him. Rufus knelt for a final blessing, then left hurriedly.

It must have been a moment of great poignancy—and filled with a sense of finality. Some of those present would have felt, with Rufus on his way to claim the crown of England, that they now faced a painful but irrevocable choice. Both Curthose and Rufus would surely strive to reunite their father's Anglo-Norman kingdom. The barons themselves, as great landholders on both sides of the English Channel, would be required to swear fealty to Duke Robert Curthose for their Normandy fiefdoms, and to King William Rufus for their tenancies in England. They knew they could not offer unswerving loyalty to both lords—especially when conflict between the two was almost inevitable.

Though the great men present had urged the reinstatement of Curthose as William's heir, they must have been shocked to realize that William was actually willing to split the Anglo-Norman kingdom, rather than put all of it under Robert's control. With war inevitable between the two sons, did the Conqueror have some more long-range plan for resolving this issue?

As a matter of fact, he did. He knew what would happen, and felt safe in leaving matters in God's hands. Divine destiny was at work. Everything, in the end, would turn out well for all concerned.

CHAPTER 18

William's Death, Henry I, and the Birth of the English Nation

This division of the Anglo-Norman realm created a completely untenable situation. William surely realized that chaos would ensue. It may have seemed to some of those present that he was actually guaranteeing that chaos. But his vision was more far-reaching than anyone realized at the time.

As if in answer to this extreme dilemma, King William now summoned to his bedside the youngest of his three living sons, Henry, who was then eighteen years old, and whom William had only recently knighted. Henry had also been at his father's side at the siege of Mantes, which was quite possibly the lad's first experience of battle since his recent knighthood.

The young man now knelt by his father's bed. William Rufus had probably known, or at least anticipated, that their father would bestow at least some portion of his patrimony on himself, as his second son; he certainly also knew of William's deep displeasure with Curthose for his treachery, and shared their father's strong conviction that Robert was not fit to rule.

Henry, however, had no foreknowledge of what his father had in mind for him. It would have been normal for him at least to be bequeathed an earldom. As King William and Queen Matilda's youngest son, Henry couldn't have expected any great patrimony or role to play in the Anglo-Norman kingdom. Even so, he was rather shocked to receive no land at all, but only a grant of money.

"To you, Henry, I bequeath the great treasure of five thousand silver coins," the Conqueror said, smiling warmly on his youngest son, whose qualities and intelligence he had "lost no opportunity to encourage," as chronicler William of Malmesbury put it.

Though by nature calm and non-attached, Henry could not but be taken aback by this unusual bequest: no land at all; only money? No one spoke; all were waiting for Henry to say something.

"Father, what shall I do with this money, if I have no land to call my own?" Henry's voice was steady as he presented his reasonable question. Though bewildered by his father's bequest, he seemed ready to accept whatever the Conqueror wanted. In feudal Europe, however, even a significant fortune was no guarantee of ever having true wealth and power, for these came with land. Land alone, in those days, was true wealth.

The silence continued. Everyone strained to hear the king's reply. Only a few, however, could hear William's words when he spoke:

"Be patient, my son. For in time you shall have all that your brothers now have, and shall be greater than they." The father placed his hand in final benediction on Henry's bowed head. His words proved no empty prophecy. Years later, they were fulfilled to the letter.

As things turned out, Henry was repeatedly betrayed by both his brothers. Finally he was forced into exile, when Curthose and Rufus for a brief time became allies.

When circumstances, in August of 1100, made the Conqueror's youngest son the only rightful candidate for the throne of England, he had already experienced the peaks and valleys of ever-changing fortune, which often are the destiny of those who eventually achieve great worldly power. By the time he was crowned king of England, Henry, then thirty-two years old, no longer had any illusions about what it meant to exercise authority, to possess great wealth, and, inevitably, to receive every imaginable gradation of loyalty and treachery.

A thoughtful examination of Henry's life must lead to the firm conviction that, contrary to the conclusions of most historians, the youngest son of the Conqueror did not come to the throne of England or the rule of Normandy out of hunger for personal power. History shows, rather, that throughout Henry's life, all his decisions, and all the actions he undertook, expressed a single motivating desire, as had been the case also with his father: in Henry's case, the fulfillment of his father's vision for the Anglo-Norman kingdom. Henry focused what proved to be an extraordinarily firm will toward achieving that goal: the completion of William the Conqueror's legacy,

Henry succeeded gloriously. With the seed of nationhood deeply implanted and growing during his reign, the establishment of common law, and the beginnings of a national constitution all but inevitable, the course England was to follow through succeeding centuries was well established by the end of Henry's thirty-five year reign. Is it too fanciful to state that William and Henry's legacy even led, eventually, to unity between East and West through England's colonial empire? Indeed, from the reign of King Henry I onward, we glimpse the coalescing of that constellation of ideas concerning government and its relationship to the individual which gave birth, eventually, to the United States of America.

It is in Henry's astonishingly creative thirty-five-year reign, finally, that we feel the truth of what the great medieval historian Sir Richard Southern stated: "This is where the real history of England [as a nation] begins."

In this book it is our thesis that the Conqueror's vision anticipated the role that England, specifically, would play in bridging East and West, uniting the strengths of each to bring mankind to the present time when the general level of consciousness on our planet is rising toward greater unity and also greater subtlety and refinement: an age of energy which promises greatness for the future.

The number of books on the Norman Conquest of England, and especially on William the Conqueror, are legion. In every one of them, if the historian is honest and willing to risk making statements that express his own sincere assessment of William's character, there must come a moment when the writer seeks in vain for words to explain the stature of the man. Even writers who bring to the subject tremendous prejudice have ultimately had to admit that the 1066 Conquest of England, and its impact on Western Europe's subsequent development, could only have been accomplished by a degree of determination and a breadth of vision very rarely seen on earth.

Though this book may be read as a straightforward and, we hope, not uninteresting account of the lives of two great leaders of men and of nations, we propose to look closely at what might be called another layer of possibility: that the lives of William and Henry may have special significance for our planet, and for our own lives today.

Part Two

THE LIFE OF HENRY: HIS PRINCEHOOD

CHAPTER 19

The Winding Path of Reincarnation

For the many millions of people in this world who believe that our souls are born again and again to learn the lessons this world has to teach us, before we transcend its limitations, the lives of William the Conqueror and his son Henry, and their present-day incarnations, must hold extraordinary interest.

Most of us believe that God, Providence, a Higher Being—however one chooses to name the Supreme Power—intervenes in human affairs in ways both little and great. Many people also believe that God *wants* to help man in his quest for ever-higher experiences of love, joy, and understanding of who and what we are, in our souls. Thus, despite His seeming distance from us, we believe He is intimately involved in our lives. Spiritual masters have declared that God intervenes also in the great drama of history.

The Norman Conquest of England is nearly one thousand years removed from our day. It is more difficult, now, to feel the significance of that era. Yet it was a crucial moment in history, involving not only William and Henry, but a wholly remarkable group of people who acted as instruments of a higher power in human affairs.

Such a dramatic and pivotal event of the past as the Norman Conquest, which changed the very course of history, suggest the possibility that God "hand-picked" a special soul to play the challenging "role" of William the Conqueror, and that He sent high souls to help him with that mission.

93

Paramhansa Yogananda dumbfounded his disciples when he first declared that he himself, in a previous life, had been William the Conqueror. In that lifetime, quite as much as in his recent one, he also attracted highly advanced souls to help him with his mission. Lanfranc himself in our time, Yogananda declared, was Swami Sri Yukteswar, his own guru (spiritual teacher). To many of his disciples Yogananda said, "You were with me in that life." Some of them he told who, specifically, they had been.

A great master like Yogananda would naturally bring his disciples with him into every new incarnation. This fact would account for the many loyal and highly competent men around William. His great strength of will would also account for the extraordinary enmity he awakened in others who were not on his "wavelength."

Jesus Christ, too, inspired envy, leading to such enmity that, eventually, he was crucified. Great strength of character inspires great, if emotional, opposition. And if a person is without personal motives—as was the case with both Jesus and William—his character is bound to be misread by selfish minds, to whom it will appear as villainy. ("After all," thinks the normal person, himself ego-driven, "one must have *some* motive for doing anything. If someone doesn't admit his own motives frankly—as a businessman might say, '*Of course* I'm in it for the money!'—it must mean his motives are so shameful that he must hide them from others." Most people, in other words, tend to see themselves in others.)

Yogananda told some of his disciples who they had been in the past. Many had lived with him during his lifetime as William. Other lives he told them about also, in other contexts—perhaps lives not spent with him. I will briefly reveal here a few of those whom he himself named, and a few that his close disciple, Swami Kriyananda, has suggested as possibilities.

Robert Curthose, Yogananda said, in this life was Swami Dhirananda. Dhirananda betrayed his guru, as Curthose had betrayed his father. In both lives, this soul was in very truth Yogananda's Judas, for as Curthose he did his best to destroy his father, and later, as Dhirananda, he tried to undermine his guru's

work. Yet Dhirananda too—and therefore Curthose—was spiritually advanced. (Yogananda once, in speaking to Kriyananda about
Judas, said, "He was a prophet." When Kriyananda expressed
amazement, his guru answered, "He'd have had to be, to be one
of the twelve.") Yet despite Dhirananda's treachery Yogananda predicted that he would be liberated after another three incarnations.

Strange to say, highly advanced souls often display very notable faults—in this instance disloyalty tantamount to treachery.
As the sunlight, streaming through a stained-glass window, high-
lights colors which looked gray and colorless before the dawn,
so Dhirananda's faults, and those also of Curthose, were glaring.
Both men might have served their guru's work greatly. Yet, instead,
they chose to undermine it.

What about William Rufus? In this life, Yogananda said, he was a
wealthy merchant in New York City, Warren Vickerman. Vickerman
was loyal to Yogananda, even as William Rufus had been to his
father, but he was still too rough-hewn to live in close proximity to
the guru. Kriyananda met Vickerman in 1955 in New York; it is to
Kriyananda that these observations should be attributed.

What about others? Yogananda told Faye Wright (Daya Mata)
that she had been his daughter Agatha. Agatha, though little known
to English historians, is listed in Spanish annals as the daughter
whom William sent to Spain to be married to the heir to the throne
of Leon-Castille. (This subject will be discussed at greater length
later in this book.) An interesting sidelight is that Leon-Castille was
almost all that remained at that time of Christian Spain; the rest
had been conquered by the Moors. William, an important part of
whose role was to strengthen Christianity in Europe, later incarnated as a king of Spain to drive the Moors out of that country.

If Lanfranc in this life was Swami Sri Yukteswar, the guru of
Paramhansa Yogananda, who was St. Anselm, who followed
Lanfranc as archbishop of Canterbury? Kriyananda suggests
Anselm might have been James J. Lynn, Yogananda's most
advanced disciple, to whom the master gave the spiritual name,
Rajarshi Janakananda.

What about other disciples? There seems to be good reason to suppose that William's wife, Matilda, was Virginia Wright (Ananda Mata), Daya Mata's sister in this life. Both Matilda in that life and Virginia in this one showed motherly qualities, but Kriyananda says that Virginia (Ananda Mata) was for all that too personal in her affections. Matilda championed Robert Curthose, even after his betrayal of William. Ananda Mata, too, had shown excessively judgmental prejudice against those whom she thought had fallen spiritually, and was even untruthful—in attempting to protect what she believed in—in a legal deposition she gave under oath, during a massive lawsuit Self-Realization Fellowship (SRF) brought against Kriyananda in 1990. (SRF lost that suit on virtually every point.) The judge himself would not admit Ananda Mata's testimony, giving as his reason its blatant lack of truthfulness.

Kriyananda feels that there is good reason to believe that Dr. M.W. Lewis, Yogananda's first Kriya Yoga disciple in America, was William's half brother, Bishop Odo. Odo in that former life was a strange mixture of qualities; his downfall came about due to attachment to money and power. In this life, Dr. Lewis, though a faithful and devout disciple, had yet to overcome his attachment to money, a quality that was strong enough in him to disappoint Yogananda seriously more than once in his life. He also, in Kriyananda's eyes, showed an unnatural fondness for power—unnatural, that is to say, for a devotee of God.

Mernaloy Brown (Mrinalini Mata) may have been one of William's daughters, Cecily, who entered a convent as a nun. In the present lifetime, she displays very strong Roman Catholic tendencies.

Yogananda told quite a number of his men disciples that they had been with him during his lifetime as William. To Norman Paulsen he said, "You were my giant!" In this life, too, Norman was physically large and very strong. Also notable was his deep devotion to his Guru.

Jerry Torgerson, another large and strong man, though somewhat uncouth in his mannerisms, was told by Yogananda, "You were good. You used to fight for me." Jerry's saving grace was his deep devotion to his guru. Yogananda once said of him, "He has great love. That is what saves people."

Of other incarnations among the disciples, it may interest the reader to know that Yogananda said of Dr. Lewis's wife, Mildred, that she had been Queen Elizabeth I of England. Did he himself live on earth during that century? Who knows? Mrs. Lewis certainly was headstrong enough to have been that queen.

Yogananda also said that he himself had lived—as I have indicated—as a king and military leader in Spain, where he was deeply involved in driving the Moors out of the country. He never said who he had been then, but certain followers of his, having researched the matter carefully, say the facts suggest strongly that he was Fernando III "el Santo" (the Saint) of Castile and León (1198–1252), who played a significant role in driving the Moors out of Spain, and that Henry I of England later became Fernando's son, Alfonso X "el Sabio," the Wise (1221–1284), who was noted as a composer, astrologer-astronomer, spiritual poet, and founder (or crystallizer) of Castilian Spanish.

Yogananda also said that he himself had been Arjuna, of *Mahabharata* and Bhagavad Gita fame. He said that his chief disciple in this life, Rajarshi Janakananda (James J. Lynn), had been Arjuna's brother Nakula in that life, and that Florina Darling (Durga Mata) had been Nakula's mother, Madri.

The winding path of reincarnation is endlessly fascinating, though difficult to trace through history, and slow in the progress people make owing to the strong bonds of ego-attachment.

One strange omission from Yogananda's revelations concerning those who had been with him in his life as William was the present identity of his youngest son, Henry, who single-handedly completed the Conqueror's earthly mission. Henry must surely have returned to be with him in the present life. Yogananda, however, never announced that identity.

The "why" of not doing so is, on reflection, easy to understand. The same thing happened in Henry's life: had it been widely known that it was his destiny to fulfill their father's mission, his brothers might have killed him out of sheer jealousy. Certainly, as we shall see in our discussion of Henry's life, they did their best to rid themselves of him anyway. And had it been known, in the present life, what Kriyananda was destined to accomplish, the jealousy that flared up against him would have come to a blaze much sooner—perhaps stripping him of any shred of the credibility he gained before he was, in fact, thrown out of his guru's work by his fellow disciples.

Henry was born late in their father's life, presumably to ensure that there would be enough years for him to complete his father's mission. There was evidently a need, also, for a hiatus after William's life, that his mission might have time to "settle down" and its true purpose to become clear.

Robert Curthose and William Rufus lacked completely any understanding of their father's mission. They, like most rulers, lived only for their own power and glory. William certainly must have foreseen this destiny for his mission. Therefore he made that promise to Henry on his deathbed, quoted in the last chapter.

Robert would have been disastrous to that mission. Neither he nor William Rufus was even aware that it *was* a mission. At the same time, a hiatus was necessary—a pause not only in time, but also—perhaps amusingly—of incompetence. Had Henry's older brothers been more capable of carrying on their father's legacy, that legacy might have been "derailed" onto a barren field of dedicated mediocrity. The much worse reality of dedication to ordinary worldly power and self-aggrandizement made it possible for Henry to become all the more determined to give what he had to give, when the time arrived.

Henry's crowning as the king of England was quite unexpected, however. Though the benefits of his reign were very real, the unobtrusiveness of his dedication to completing his father's mission has led many historians to describe him as "the least-known king" of England, and—surprisingly—as someone who lacked any attractive qualities. Henry's near absence of personal motives—a fact which becomes apparent if his life is studied sensitively—has led historians to attribute to him only the darkest of motives, and such qualities as avarice, harshness, cruelty, and indifference to others' feelings. Strange to say, Henry's contemporaries saw none of these traits in him. Perhaps they, too, couldn't "figure him out"— owing to that same lack of personal motives which resulted in there being nothing in him to "figure out." His long reign of thirty-five years, however, was one of unprecedented peace and prosperity in England; his reign in Normandy also brought peace for a significant, though shorter, number of years. Historians who attribute this fact to anything but Henry's character are simply showing themselves to be like most people, incapable of attributing high motives to anyone.

C. Warren Hollister, who has given us the only full biography of Henry, paints a very different picture from the one commonly presented by historians. Hollister himself marveled at how his fellow scholars had managed to reach such negative conclusions, which, as I said, have been imposed on the very favorable impressions of Henry that his contemporaries held. It seems rather a case of Henry's seeming, centuries later, "too good to be true."

Whatever the case, Henry did in fact complete his father's mission, and for that fact deserves careful study, even if his own life was less colorful than those of many other rulers—Henry the Eighth, for example.

It would be natural for Yogananda not to say who, among his disciples, had been Henry. William was equally reticent in predicting that his youngest son would be his true successor. To do so would have spoiled Henry's chances. In Yogananda's life, had he revealed Henry's present identity and mission, the problems would have been the same: either this "heir" would have been confined in a narrow role, from which it would have been impossible to emerge, or (if he hadn't been driven out) he'd have been deliberately suppressed, owing—as the saying is—"to jealousy in high places." It is surely unthinkable, however, that Curthose should have come back as Dhirananda, and William Rufus as Warren Vickerman, and yet Henry, who alone completed William's mission, should have "sat out" Yogananda's present incarnation on the sidelines.

Later, I shall present many indications that point to Henry's having come again in this life as Swami Kriyananda. Kriyananda, alone among Yogananda's disciples, has furthered the master's work and taken it into the world, reaching literally millions of people. Kriyananda has written over a hundred books, showing the universality of the guru's teachings. He has founded eight cooperative spiritual communities so far, manifesting an ideal regarding which Yogananda expressed the most fervent zeal, but which his other disciples dismissed as something to be "swept under the carpet." Alone among the master's disciples, Kriyananda's entire ambition has been to spread his guru's mission throughout the world.

I shall discuss, as we go, the great similarities between Henry's life and character and those of Swami Kriyananda. First, however, let me present Henry's life.

Let me begin, therefore, by discussing Henry's early years, when his older brothers eclipsed him and in fact subjected him to constant humiliation and persecution.

CHAPTER 20

The Treacherous Road to the Throne of England

W hen word reached Robert Curthose of his father's death, he rushed to Rouen. Entering the capital unopposed, he laid claim to the duchy. When he learned further, however, that King William had bequeathed the crown of England to his younger brother William Rufus, it is said that Curthose spluttered with rage. At first, he refused to believe it. He and Rufus had never been friends. The first open break Curthose had had with his father had come on the heels of a violent quarrel between these two brothers, which involved their personal followers also. The Conqueror had been forced to intervene physically, and though he must have upbraided them both equally, it was Curthose who felt so humiliated that he angrily left his father's court that very night.

By early 1088, Duke Robert was assembling an army to invade England and claim the throne. So confident were he and the powerful men who backed him that these last caused an insurrection in England, supporting the duke, even before the invasion. The insurrection was to be joined shortly by the invasion force now assembling in Normandy, led by Curthose himself.

While the duke was building his ships, however, and drawing his army together on his side of the Channel, he—predictably, given his usual carelessness—ran out of money. Faced with this emergency, Curthose turned to his brother Henry, and requested a loan of three thousand pounds.

Henry had remained in Normandy after the Conqueror's death, and had personally seen his oldest brother's incompetence, as duke. He refused the loan. His position, however, was delicate, and became more so as hostilities between his two older brothers escalated to open warfare. Henry, even at that young age, displayed a gift for diplomacy. Thus, although refusing to make Curthose the requested loan, he was still able to hold his older brother's good will. Henry continued to live in Normandy.

Meanwhile, Curthose was getting urgent messages from England: the insurrection that had been mounted in his name was in urgent need of reinforcement from Normandy. The duke's preparations, however, could not proceed without a large infusion of money. Robert, therefore, now offered to sell Henry a countship in western Normandy in exchange for the three thousand pounds he so desperately needed.

Henry did accept this offer, and became count of the Cotentin. His lands included Avranches, Mont-Saint-Michel, the Hiemois in south-central Normandy, the Bessin, and even some lands in the Norman Vexin. The monk chronicler Orderic Vitalis states that Curthose sold Henry, in effect, nearly one third of Normandy for those three thousand pounds.

We may fairly safely assume that Henry accepted these terms in part to show what was needed in Normandy for it be ruled effectively. Curthose had shown utter incompetence as a ruler. His next-oldest brother, Rufus, though he demonstrated some leadership ability, showed no concern for the well-being of the people he ruled.

As Duke Robert resumed his haphazard preparations for the invasion of England, Henry lost no time in throwing all his energies into his new responsibilities as count of the Cotentin. This was the first test of his abilities as a leader. He soon showed an innate ability to create lasting relationships. His countship was his first step toward demonstrating what kind of leadership the furtherance of their father's mission needed.

Henry was, in fact, highly successful at drawing people to his vision. Not so surprisingly, years later those same *fideles* backed him against Curthose. Even before that—only months, in fact, after his purchase from Curthose of the countship of Cotentin and most of western Normandy—his oldest brother threw him into prison and seized back that land. Even in those few months, however, Henry had already developed the network of friendships and alliances that remained firmly loyal to him for the next forty-seven years.

Henry had been educated in a monastic setting, under the tutelage of the saintly Osmund, bishop of Salisbury, and had conceived a lively appreciation of the need for written records in administering an institution. As one historian remarked, Henry was the first ruler in a long time who was literate, and who used that skill to good purpose in his governance of the Anglo-Norman empire. He understood that governmental record-keeping, as well as the royal writ, was a highly effective tool in administration. Record-keeping under Henry would play a new role in controlling and stabilizing the kingdom.

With vast lands now under his stewardship, this period in Henry's life was highly creative. While Henry concentrated on creating a stable government in western Normandy, Robert Curthose "dallied away his days," as William of Jumieges wrote, "in ways ill-befitting a man." William Rufus, on finding that he lacked a significant number of Norman supporters, roused the Anglo-Saxon population to fight for him. Soon the pro-Curthose leaders of the insurrection (Bishop Odo and Robert, count of Mortain) were besieged in Pevensey castle by Rufus, who starved them out.

By mid-summer, the haphazard duke's preparations seemed finalized at last. Even then, however, Curthose did not set sail for England. Historians have wondered for centuries why Robert, with his whole fleet of ships ready and waiting, continued to stall. Perhaps he encountered difficulties with the weather: the Channel crossing could be treacherous even at the height of summer. In fact, he did send a portion of his fleet ahead of him, but William Rufus, who was monitoring the channel, sent a fleet to intercept it, and routed Robert's fleet—indeed, slaughtering nearly the whole invading force. Curthose had acted impatiently and unwisely. Perhaps he simply believed that "if a thing is worth doing, it's worth doing badly." At any rate, essentially he continued to procrastinate.

Thus, Curthose left his supporters in England "high and dry." They had depended on his speedy intervention. Now the insurrection collapsed, and three of England's greatest tenants-in-chief under the Conqueror—including Bishop Odo, who from then on nursed a deep animus toward William Rufus—were disseised of their English lands and exiled from the country. William Rufus was still king of England, though "by the skin of his teeth." In the end, however, we can attribute his victory to sheer luck—specifically, to the incompetence of his older brother.

A wiser king than Rufus would have sought immediately to mend the widening breach between himself and his most prominent barons. But William Rufus, too, had many faults, one of them being that he completely lacked the patience required for diplomacy, and never bothered to consider the importance of winning his major landholders to his side.

Rufus did reward with more land those few Norman barons who had allied themselves with him, but he failed to follow through with a long-term policy of showing those barons that he had their interests at heart—interests which would have been best served had they supported their king. King William II continued to alienate his chief landholders, meanwhile spending his days, instead, with a ragtag coterie of disreputable "buddies" whose comportment scandalized his subjects.

Nor did Rufus concern himself with drawing prominent people to his court: highly placed ecclesiastics, for example; representatives of the newly emerging cities; princes from Wales and Scotland. In short, his idea of kingship was very different from his father's. He felt no obligation to keep the peace, protect the church, provide justice through the courts (rather than by warfare), encourage trade, oversee the national monetary system, and fulfill all the duties of a true king. All these things Rufus ignored. Instead, he sought only to please himself.

He did understand, however, that the division his father had left in the Anglo-Norman kingdom could not endure. His defeat of those self-seeking supporters of Curthose was only the latest event that illustrated what had been obvious to him since their boyhood: that he would always be able to get the better of his older brother. In the evenings, Rufus, while drinking with his buddies, no doubt recounted stories from his youth to underscore the fact that he had nothing to fear from the foolish duke of Normandy. Rufus now hatched scheme after scheme, and swore great, blustering oaths that Curthose, on the other hand, would have plenty to fear from the king of England.

Sometime in the early autumn of 1088 Henry evidently undertook a brief visit to Rufus' court. It's highly likely that he took this opportunity, after the clear defeat of Curthose's supporters in England, to ask his brother the king for his maternal inheritance—those modest English lands bequeathed to him by Queen Matilda. Rufus probably kept Henry dangling for a time, but in the end refused to transfer Matilda's lands to his brother, though this had been her express wish.

C. Warren Hollister, in his detailed and insightful portrait of Henry, has conjectured that Bishop Odo led Curthose, who feared his uncle, to his next step, by convincing him that Henry and Robert of Bellême, now in possession of the Montgomery-Bellême lands, had conspired with William Rufus against the duke. (And why did Odo have this animus also toward Henry? Principally because Odo's bishopric lay surrounded by Henry's new land acquisition.) In this way, Odo managed with one move to eliminate two key players. (Kriyananda has stated he observed this same characteristic in Dr. Lewis: a tendency to belittle good individuals so as to raise himself in others' esteem.)

One can easily imagine that it took little evidence to persuade Curthose to arrest two men whose imprisonment and (in Henry's case) forfeiture of property would so greatly benefit the duke himself. As for Robert of Bellême, both Curthose and Odo concurred that his imprisonment would give Curthose the opportunity to halt the expanding power of the Montgomery-Bellême family.

It had been a slap to Curthose's ducal pride, and one he felt keenly, that immediately on hearing the news of the Conqueror's death, Robert of Bellême had driven the ducal garrisons out of key Bellême strongholds along the southeastern frontier of Normandy. William the Conqueror had established as his absolute right, as duke, to place trusted garrisons in those fortresses. His son, Duke Robert, had been unable thus far to enforce any such policy with the Bellême family.

Roger II of Montgomery, the Conqueror's close companion and *fidelis*, was well respected, but he had been married to the great heiress Mabel of Bellême, whose reputation was atrocious. The eldest son and heir of Roger and Mabel was this same Robert of Bellême, who had already gained notoriety for his cruelty and for the obvious enjoyment he took in torturing his prisoners. His treatment of them was remarkable for its savagery even in those days, when people were inured to all kinds of brutality. Bellême, intelligent, arrogant, and utterly self-serving, was destined in future to become a mortal enemy of King Henry when the king was striving to establish peace. Bellême lived only to build a base of personal power, usually by violence, and in absolute defiance of any fragile government that was coalescing in Normandy.

For this one moment in time, the fates of Henry and Bellême conjoined as they returned to Normandy on the same ship. Curthose arrested them both, accusing them, as I said, of colluding with William Rufus and of serving him as spies. Both men were handed over to Bishop Odo, the architect of this masterstroke, and sent for imprisonment to separate fortresses.

Odo may well have taken Henry to his own city of Bayeux, perhaps in order to monitor more closely Henry's interactions with Robert Curthose. Henry was also very persuasive, and— something Odo feared even more—might be able to arouse some brotherly feeling in the ever-sentimental Curthose. We may be sure that both Odo and Curthose would have taken the first opportunity to force Henry to relinquish those lands which Curthose had purchased from him for three thousand pounds. Henry no doubt resisted as long as he could, and with all his powers of persuasion insisted on his own innocence. However, he had nothing to bargain with. Moreover, if we judge his character by that of Swami Kriyananda, we may wonder whether he resorted to any power of persuasion at all. He may have simply accepted the false charges as the grace of God. As Kriyananda often says, quoting his guru, "What comes of itself, let it come." (Lest anyone see these words as advice to passivity, I should explain that they concern an attitude of very strong inner affirmation. Otherwise, human nature can incline toward very negative reactions.)

Even in the short time Henry had been count of the Cotentin, he had formed strong bonds with many of his vassals, and felt a deep sense of duty to them. Nevertheless, he was forced in the end to return all those lands to his feckless brother.

The trumped-up charges against him served to relieve Curthose and Odo of the need to return Henry's three thousand pounds, paid in cash for those lands. All this must have been, as chronicler Henry of Huntingdon noted, "very displeasing to God." God, however, delayed vengeance for now. Henry was still being readied for the work he had to do.

CHAPTER 21

1089: Henry's Imprisonment

From the end of the eleventh century onward, a growing body of government records was preserved—especially grants, writs, and official documents of all kinds. From this time period it is possible to learn a great deal about who was in attendance on the king (or the duke), from the list of important men who witnessed the charters.

In the spring of 1089, the names of a number of Henry's most important "great men" from western Normandy appear as witnessing several charters issued by Duke Robert. Dr. Hollister suggests that these friends and vassals of Henry had quite possibly come to petition Curthose's court for Henry's release from prison. Curthose had already secured what he wanted from Henry: the return of western Normandy to ducal control. To whatever extent Curthose had actually believed Odo's trumped up charges of collusion between Rufus and Henry, it no longer really mattered to him. He had what he'd wanted. Those who had come to request Henry's release were now, once again, the duke's most important vassals in western Normandy. Gifting some land to the bishopric of Bayeux, to soften possible protests from his uncle Odo, Curthose, sometime late in the winter or early spring of 1089, released Henry from confinement.

There are no official documents or comments from the chronicles of this period mentioning Henry's activities during the remainder of 1089 or the greater part of 1090. We may be sure he kept away from his brothers, having experienced quite enough of their "brotherly regard" for him.

It is of greater interest that Henry was welcomed back, it seems, to the Cotentin, Avranches, Bessin, and Mont Saint-Michel by those with whom he had worked so closely in the short time he had been "officially" their count. Evidently, the government and the justice Henry had provided for the area were so welcome to them that Henry continued, to all intents and purposes, to function unofficially even now as the count of the Cotentin.

Duke Robert had plenty to occupy his mind besides Henry's positive efforts to provide order in western Normandy. More ducal fortresses in strategic areas were slipping from Curthose's control. And there was also the matter of Robert of Bellême, who had begun to wreak havoc along the southern boundary in vengeance for his imprisonment.

Henry's older brothers expected loyal obedience from him, but showed him no reciprocal loyalty or even respect. That Robert wasn't worried about the respect shown Henry in the Cotenin and elsewhere was probably due mainly to his own belittling attitude toward his youngest brother. What (this, one imagines, was his line of thinking) could there be to worry about from that pip-squeak? Soon, of course, with Henry's saving of Rouen—a deed I'll describe in the next chapter—Robert began to realize that in Henry he had a force to reckon with. It was then that jealousy really stirred in his heart toward his "little" brother. At first, however, I imagine his motivation in imprisoning Henry was primarily to get his money back.

It may be a matter of interest that the way Swami Kriyananda was first treated by Daya Mata, the office head and later the president of Self-Realization Fellowship, bore some resemblance to Robert's treatment of Henry. When Kriyananda first showed interest in promoting and developing their guru's work, she tried to resist his efforts.

Yogananda had told him many times, "You have a great work to do." He never did so, however, before others; almost always it was when they were alone. Shortly after the master's passing, Kriyananda and one other monk came up with ideas for reorganizing the main office so that incoming letters might be answered more promptly. There was, however, much resistance to these ideas among the office force, and Daya herself joined the resisters. She backed down when Rajarshi Janakananda, the second president after Yogananda, declared, "These are good ideas. They should be implemented." As more and more creative ideas began to come from Kriyananda, however, Daya tried another tactic.

For years, in fact, she tried to divert him into less responsible activities. Later on I'll mention her effort to get him to accept a job in the printshop. For years she approved the designs he proposed, only to withdraw her approval after he'd carried them almost to completion, simply because people who were entrenched in the old ways expressed opposition.

In fact, although she too (like Robert Curthose) demanded loyalty, she often felt no obligation to reciprocate it. To her, this subordinate was a young "pipsqueak" (a word she often used). When she became jealous of Kriyananda, she treated him in much the same way as Curthose had treated Henry after Rouen—which is our next topic of discussion.

CHAPTER 22

The Saving of Rouen: The Players Show Their Hands

In the autumn of 1090 there occurred an event which one cannot help feeling was pivotal to the future of the Anglo-Norman realm, even though it has not been so identified by most historians. If one could place oneself in imagination in the streets of Rouen during late October of that year, surely one would feel that some "point of no return" was passed, as (once again) the main players showed their true character in a way that no one could possibly overlook.

King William Rufus, in his energetic recruitment of allies within Normandy, had come into contact, indirectly through his agents, with a very wealthy burgher of Rouen, the main city of Normandy and the seat of ducal government. This burgher's name was Conan; he was the leader of a large faction of townspeople who disliked Robert, and who supported Rufus in his bid for the duchy.

In this situation, another important element was introduced into the usual clashes between groups of aristocratic knights, all of whom had had similar military training in arms and a code of what might be called "chivalric ethics." Feudal society recognized three groups, each of which, in fulfilling its functions, contributed to the well-being of the others. There were those who fought, those who prayed, and those who did manual or mercantile labor. Conan was a burgher, not a knight.

The contemporary chroniclers Orderic Vitalis and William of Malmesbury have nothing good to say about Conan. Perhaps the reason is partly that both those monks were steeped in the feu-

111

dal perspective concerning what was appropriate for each social group. Tellingly, Orderic writes that Conan "arrogantly maintained against the duke a huge permanent household of knights and dependents." Both chroniclers suggest that Conan's pretensions to political power were rank *hubris*, an offense against the divine order of society, which led inevitably to his downfall.

Sometime in the summer of 1090, Conan entered into a secret pact with certain followers of King William Rufus to hand over to him the city of Rouen. In October, deeming the time ripe for an uprising, Conan sent messengers to Rufus loyalists in Upper Normandy, telling them to proceed towards Rouen where Conan, townsmen of his faction, and Rufus' followers would open the city's gates to them.

Curthose got wind of the plot in time to summon barons who lived near him and were still loyal to him—mainly those in southeastern Normandy. Incredibly, Curthose included in this ducal summons his brother Henry, and also Robert of Bellême, both of whom he had only recently released from prison. Probably Curthose got a good response from his barons because they smelled ransom money. Burghers might be mere commoners, but they did often have money—cash to pay exorbitant ransoms, which would be demanded by knights like Bellême. This practice was common in high medieval warfare. As to Henry's motives in helping his eldest brother in this crisis, this answer can be best arrived at after we examine his behavior during and after the conflict in Rouen.

Henry and his retinue were the first to arrive, joining Curthose early in November in his ducal citadel. Quite possibly this was the first meeting between the brothers since Henry's release from prison.

Fighting erupted in the city on November 3. Conan ordered that one city gate be opened to Rufus's approaching forces, and a second gate closed against Curthose's men approaching Rouen from another direction. Before either retinue could even enter the city, however, fighting already erupted in the streets among the townspeople, who could no longer tell who was on which side. The battle was chaotic and extremely bloody.

Unlike traditional combat between trained knights, governed as they were by certain rules which dictated that the combatants, under most circumstances, stop short of killing their noble opponents, this situation was a mêlée. One doubts whether even women and children were spared in that frenzy.

This slaughter of townsman by townsman had already gained strong momentum by the time the noise of the conflict reached Curthose and Henry in the ducal citadel. Orderic Vitalis tells us the brothers rushed out from the fortress. Curthose, "much alarmed" by the chaos he beheld, hastily quit the city for fear of being ignobly murdered by some commoner (for a duke, this would have been dishonor indeed). He fled to a priory some distance across the River Seine. His desertion left Henry as *de facto* commander of the ducal cause. By now, mounted knights on both sides had gained entrance to the city, and Henry did his best to rally those who were pro-Curthose.

Imagine, now, that sanguinary scene with its attendant cacophony: clashing swords, screaming wounded, shrieking women and children, bleating, mooing, barking, and baaing animals that lived close to their owners. All this confusion taking place within the tightly circumscribed walls of a medieval city. Perhaps, even from these few words, the reader will gain a better appreciation for the monumental task Henry undertook.

It was a hard-fought battle. After several hours of gruesome slaughter, the pro-Curthose group led by Henry gradually emerged victorious. The Rufus partisans fled to the woods outside the city, and hid there from Robert's supporters. Conan himself was captured and brought before Henry for judgment. Henry promptly ordered that Conan be taken to Rouen castle. Robert of Bellême and other aristocratic latecomers, intent on securing ransoms with which to swell their baronial coffers, now busied themselves with rounding up wealthy townspeople to fill their private prisons. Henry had quite another purpose in mind.

As he moved through the streets of Rouen, strewn with bodies of the dead and dying, his feeling towards Conan, the perpetrator of this horror, was one of outrage. It is interesting to note that Orderic Vitalis attributed the particularly gruesome slaughter, not to the skilled knights, but to the townsmen themselves, who had been butchering one another with abandon. Without Conan's money and leadership, this bloody mess would never have happened. Rouen, the principal city of Normandy and the duchy's seat of government, would not now have had corpses strewn about the streets, nor its citizenry suddenly transformed into a howling mob, had it not been for Conan's ambition.

What happened next must be imagined against the backdrop of this social tumult. Henry wasn't sitting quietly at his desk, thinking what he might do to calm the situation. He had been fighting a serious battle all day in the streets. Certainly he was agitated; his emotions could hardly have been otherwise.

Arriving at the ducal citadel of Rouen, Henry gave the order for Conan to be dragged up behind him to the top of the main tower, on reaching which he addressed Conan, sweeping an arm across the skyline before speaking:

"Admire, Conan, the beauty of the country you tried to conquer. Off to the south, behold the delightful hunting region, wooded and well stocked with game for the chase. See how the River Seine, full of fish, laps upon the walls of Rouen, and daily brings ships to the city laden with merchandise. On the other side, see the city itself, fair and populous, with its ramparts, churches, and stately buildings. All this, from earliest days, has rightly been the capital of Normandy."

Though of course Orderic Vitalis cannot have given us Henry's words *verbatim*, William of Malmesbury also attributes a very similar speech to Henry on this occasion. Those words paint a picture of Rouen and its surroundings as almost a Garden of Eden. Henry chastised Conan for forgetting that the real Ruler of all this bountiful land was God—not man with his puffed up sense of self-importance. Man creates wretchedness when he seeks to overthrow the Divine Order. Thus, Henry tells Conan, in attempting to overthrow those who had been ordained by God to rule this earthly kingdom Conan betrayed God Himself.

"Pale with dread," Conan pleaded for his life, offering Henry all his very considerable wealth, and promising to serve him personally for the remainder of his days. Henry responded tersely with an oath: "By my mother's soul, there shall be no ransom for a traitor—only the swift death he deserves."

Upon so declaring, Henry gave Conan a great push. The leader of the uprising fell from the castle tower to his death. Almost surely, many townspeople were gathered outside the castle, awaiting news of Henry's judgment of the traitor. Seeing this punishment for themselves was certainly a salutary lesson. In fact, for centuries thereafter the Rouen castle tower was known as "Conan's Leap."

Kriyananda has said that, on reading an account of this episode, he felt his own heart grow agitated, as though he himself had been at that scene.

Historians have condemned Henry's "cruelty" in carrying out this act. Yet what he did was entirely appropriate. It suggested, in the fall of this arrogant, ambitious man, the figurative fall of presumptuous ambition itself. The act was symbolic, and, as such, was well appreciated by his contemporaries. Henry's method of execution, moreover, was mercifully speedy and relatively painless compared to most medieval methods—and certainly compared to the modern electric chair. Many people have committed suicide by leaping from heights, but I know of no case where anyone deliberately killed himself by electrocution. Above all, however, Henry's deliberate choice of this method conveyed an unmistakable message. The wryly humorous phrase, "Conan's Leap," suggests an opinion widely held in those times, that it was Conan himself—not Henry—who had caused this disastrous end.

It seems indeed strange that so many historians have accused Henry of cruelty for this righteous, necessary, and (legally) correct act. As the victorious military leader, it was Henry's right to decide the fate of a rebel.

Clearly, Henry's overriding motivation—both in responding to Curthose's call for help and in the execution of Conan—was outrage on behalf of the duke of Normandy. Whatever Henry may have felt personally about Curthose's competency and sincerity in carrying out his duties as a duke was beside the point. Henry was responding to the fact that Conan, whose loyalty belonged to the duke, had betrayed his liege lord, and in a particularly culpable manner. The quality of loyalty ran deep in Henry's nature. He would have considered Conan's particular form of treachery to be a deep wrong.

Every twelfth century chronicler of the event, including Abbot Suger of St. Denis (biographer and chief adviser to King Louis VI of France) applauded this act of Henry's. (In fact, although Abbot Suger had no reason to support Henry, he admired him greatly.) William's youngest son had saved the city for the reigning duke. It was—so the chroniclers concluded—this same son, again, who had taken the appropriate action of vengeance on his brother's behalf.

Duke Robert, hiding in the priory of Notre Dame du Pré (across the River Seine) until he learned the outcome of the struggle, now returned to Rouen. At first he failed to realize the extent to which his flight from battle had further eroded his already greatly diminished authority over his barons. He ordered his men to deal mercifully with the wretched townspeople, but was utterly ignored. A few of his greatest barons openly continued to take prisoners for ransom. William of Breteuil, a great magnate who appeared on the scene of the battle very late, ransomed one of his prisoners for three thousand pounds—the same amount that Henry had paid Curthose for the whole countship of western Normandy in 1088. (An interesting point for those historians to consider who have accused Henry of avarice: Henry could have squeezed much more than those three thousand pounds out of Conan, the wealthiest merchant in Rouen. However, he didn't even consider this personal profit for himself.)

It was in the days immediately following the battle of Rouen, as Henry's brave deeds became recounted time and again, that Curthose began to realize how greatly his own prestige had fallen relative to that of his younger brother. Someone like Robert of Bellême, who had no love for Henry but actively despised Curthose, undoubtedly took every opportunity in the next few days of "mopping up," and of evening banqueting, to rub salt in the wounded ducal pride. None of the barons present had forgotten how Henry had recently been deprived of lands he had fairly come by, and how he had been imprisoned by Curthose on obviously rigged charges. Henry's defense of Rouen had demonstrated, beyond a shadow of a doubt, his innocence, and his dedication to Normandy as his father's legacy.

As for Henry himself, the relief he must have felt at having averted a coup in Rouen was soon replaced by uneasiness. He saw his brother's mood turn to dark jealousy. William of Malmesbury wrote with undisguised disapproval that the duke "immediately became ungrateful and, being a man of changeable disposition, compelled his deserving brother to leave the city."

Historian C. Warren Hollister suggests that Henry may quite reasonably have chosen this occasion of victory to ask Curthose to return to him his countship in western Normandy. Curthose was capable, as we've seen, of quixotic bursts of generosity, and Henry may have decided to give him an opportunity to show himself magnanimous. Instead, Curthose took the "low road"—perhaps even turning Henry's request against him with the dark hint that Henry's act of saving Rouen had been a mere device for personal aggrandizement.

However, since the chivalric code by which Curthose purported to live required him to be magnanimous in at least *some* direction, and to distribute largesse for the help he had received in saving Rouen, the duke once more made an astonishingly bad decision: He chose Robert of Bellême as the recipient of his gratitude. Curthose now threw ducal support behind Bellême in his efforts to expand his territory northward.

CHAPTER 23

A Brother's Jealousy

Across the Channel, in England, news of the battle of Rouen reached King William Rufus. He, too, may have been regaled with glowing accounts of Henry's decisive role. Already chafing impatiently over his so-far unsuccessful efforts from a distance to unseat Curthose, Rufus decided on a direct military move against the duke. Such a course of action was in fact better suited to a man of his hasty temperament.

In February 1091, King William Rufus himself landed in Normandy with a large army, bearing treasure to meet all expenses. Undoubtedly his army included also those barons in northeastern Normandy where Rufus had already begun to form a power base. In fact, so great was his show of force that Curthose decided it would be safer to bargain with him than to fight.

The treaty to which the two older brothers agreed was a masterpiece of bad faith and vindictiveness. Ironically, the negotiations took place in Rouen, which only three months earlier had been saved *for Curthose* by Henry. No copy of the treaty survives, but the Anglo-Saxon Chronicler no doubt saw a copy of it, or heard about it from someone with firsthand knowledge of it, for he recorded its main points, as follows:

a. The Normandy lands of those magnates who had already gone over to Rufus's side, along with those magnates' vassalage, were now to be recognized by Curthose as being under the control of Rufus.

b. Curthose's supporters in England who had been disseised of their lands as a result of their participation in the pro-Curthose rebellion of 1088 were to have their English lands returned to them. (At least two of the men who had lost their lands never had them reinstated. One of these was Bishop Odo.)

c. Curthose himself was to receive from Rufus a certain (unspecified) amount of land in England.

d. Rufus and Curthose each named the other as his heir to the throne of England and the duchy of Normandy, depending on which of them predeceased the other, and on whether or not either of them produced a son.

e. Rufus was to help Curthose regain those lands which had belonged to the duke of Normandy during their father's reign. (Though this agreement seems reasonable on the face of it, and the brothers may have also discussed a campaign to recover Maine, Hollister thinks this clause was directed mostly at Henry's *de facto* control of western Normandy.)

f. In exchange for the help of Rufus in recovering their father's lands, Curthose would gift Rufus the abbey of Mont-Saint-Michel and the city of Cherbourg—both of which were part of Henry's original 1088 purchase of a countship in western Normandy and in actual effect, at the time of this treaty, were under Henry's control.

King William II and Duke Robert then added a final point to the treaty; it was a clause which strikes one as entirely vicious and vindictive: The two older brothers agreed that Henry should be disinherited of everything, including his lands, as long as either of them should live.

It was surely Curthose who insisted on this clause. His jealously of Henry was heaped on top of everything else he had been feeling already: a nagging insecurity and wounded pride that Henry's leadership was so welcome in the Cotentin, regardless of whether or not he still bore the "official" title of count; and Henry's success in defending Rouen. Rufus, for his part, was probably waking up to the fact that Henry might soon become a force to be reckoned with—not as an aggressor against either brother's authority, but simply because of his own natural ability, and the universal respect he received. At this point, while Rufus himself was establishing his power in Normandy, he did not want another strong presence around whose flag some of the contentious barons might rally.

Now that Rufus possessed Mont-Saint-Michel and Cherbourg, Henry would no longer be able to function as the real power in the Cotentin or other parts of his countship, regardless of the loyalty the local lords had accorded him. Whichever older brother was the first to suggest this clause, both of them agreed unhesitatingly to the treaty's repressive last condition.

With the king of England "officially" involved now in Normandy, many of Henry's staunchest allies could no longer safely remain on his side. Most of them held lands in England as well as in western Normandy. If they showed support for Henry, they would risk divestment of both their English and Norman properties. Hugh of Avranches, one of Henry's closest friends, was also the English earl of Chester. It was surely with deep regret that he deserted Henry, but desert him he did. Some who were not cross-Channel landholders were overawed by the sheer size of the two armies of Rufus and Curthose.

There is no evidence that Henry ever held any personal animus—either at that time or later on—towards those in his network of allies who felt forced to abandon him. Nor is there any evidence that he became bitter against his own brothers. As we'll discuss later, Henry was remarkable all his life for his readiness to receive back as friends his former self-styled enemies, once they'd demonstrated even a slight change of heart. (Warren Hollister wrote of Henry, "He forgave even to the point of folly"!)

Nevertheless, in those trying days, faced with impossible odds, it must have taken a great effort of will for Henry to fend off a feeling of deep sorrow, as he saw one friend after another desert his cause and fight against him on the side of his treacherous brothers.

Why didn't Henry give up, on beholding even his friends desert him? His cause must have seemed utterly hopeless. There was a chance, of course, that a change of heart might occur in the quixotic, sentimental Curthose, and that Curthose would then persuade Rufus that they might, after all, spare Henry a few hectares of land. It is even likely that Henry *knew* that his brothers would quarrel again, ere long, denounce each other violently, and repudiate their recent treaty. Henry may have told himself that if he could only last long enough, his problems would blow over like a cloud. Perhaps things would smooth themselves out even before Curthose and Rufus managed to uproot him from the Cotentin altogether.

Henry was certain that resisting his brothers' determination to victimize him was a higher course of action than passive acquiescence to their joint bullying and repression. He therefore, after formally protesting the terms of his brothers' treaty, fortified the castles he held in the area, and retreated to the abbey of Mont-Saint-Michel on Normandy's western shore, from where he continued his resistance. The fortress Henry chose for his last stand was built on a huge, formidable rock which at high tide was surrounded by the sea. The monks welcomed Henry and his entourage. Under the terms of his brothers' new treaty, Mont-Saint-Michel was now controlled by Rufus, a fact that must have appalled the monks, who were surely at least somewhat aware of Rufus' treatment of the church in England.

Rufus and Curthose arrived with their respective armies, and settled on the shore in two separate encampments, with the intention of laying siege to Mont-Saint-Michel. A frontal assault on that great mass of rock was virtually impossible, but it was well known that the abbey's real vulnerability lay in its limited supply of fresh water. About six weeks into the siege, with the supply of fresh water for the whole abbey exhausted, Henry negotiated an honorable surrender with his brothers. They guaranteed him safe passage into exile—perhaps allowing him to keep what remained of his cash inheritance from their father.

After paying off the mercenary knights he'd hired, and thanking them for their assistance during his time of great need, Henry crossed the frontier into Brittany with five household members, and officially joined the many *juvenes*—landless aristocratic young men, reduced by penury to roaming about aimlessly. Orderic Vitalis portrayed Henry at this time as a wanderer seeking from knightly households hospitality for himself and his few companions.

Many other young men in his position would have abandoned their dreams and gone off to seek their fortunes elsewhere—perhaps on pilgrimage to Rome or Jerusalem. Henry, instead, stuck to Normandy like a burr. Even though exiled, he was evidently determined to remain in touch with the duchy's internal affairs. While his exile must have been a great challenge for him, he never lost sight of the fact that he was a son of William the Conqueror. Nor did he forget what his father had whispered to him on his deathbed. Those words were a charge he could not ignore, nor dismiss as unrelated to his destiny. How could he let fade from his mind his inner certainty that he still had a role to play in furthering his father's mission?

CHAPTER 24

An Unexpected Haven

Is any man a god, that you must bow to him,
And accept his decrees as commandments
Carved in stone?
You've been thwarted, Lord Crystar:
You've not been overthrown.

—*The Peace Treaty*, Act Two, Scene 3, Swami Kriyananda

It **was in April** 1091, that Henry honorably surrendered his position atop Mont-Saint-Michel, and, with his small company, began his period of exile.

Robert Curthose had already justified in his own mind the harsh treatment he and Rufus had meted out to their youngest brother. He chose not to acknowledge the deep jealousy he felt for Henry's victory at Rouen.

As for William Rufus, he was seldom bothered by a need for self-justification; his was not an introspective nature. He unabashedly followed a principle that might be expressed thus: "Get away with as much as you can, and play on other people's weaknesses or follies as often as you can." In his own bid for Normandy—toward which he saw that worthless piece of paper called a "treaty" as a mere flag waving in the breeze—Rufus was happy to have his excessively intelligent brother Henry removed from the picture.

King William remained for some months in Normandy with Curthose. He was then called back—Curthose accompanying him—to deal with a border dispute that had been created by Malcolm Canmore, king of Scotland. Duke Robert played some part in settling the dispute with Malcolm, but his main purpose in going to England was undoubtedly to receive from Rufus the English lands he had been promised in their treaty of 1091. Rufus used a variety of delaying tactics, very much as he had done earlier, when Henry sought the lands bequeathed to him by their mother. It should be noted that Rufus subsequently gave those lands to another person. (Amazingly, Henry never bemoaned this betrayal, and actually befriended the man for whose sake Rufus had disseised him.)

By Christmas 1091, when Curthose urgently and angrily pressed his brother for the land that had been promised him in their treaty, the king frankly admitted that he had no intention of ever giving Curthose any English land at all.

Realizing the extent to which Rufus had negotiated their treaty in bad faith, Curthose left Rufus's court in a blind rage. The short-lived peace between the two brothers was now shattered. No one was surprised, of course—no one, except Curthose. To everyone else, it was obvious that William Rufus didn't want peace: he wanted Normandy.

After Henry had wandered in exile for about a year, there came, in the summer of 1092, an extraordinary invitation from the citizens of the town of Domfront, whose citadel was westernmost in a string of fortresses held by the Montgomery-Bellême family. Orderic Vitalis and Robert of Torigny both wrote that the townspeople, thoroughly fed up with the "abusive rule" of Robert of Bellême, decided to invite Henry to be their lord.

Domfront is situated in the area where Henry had ruled officially (and, later, unofficially) as count of the Cotentin and the rest of western Normandy. The town and its fortress were strategically important in Normandy, and nearly impregnable. At the same time, they were not so "high profile" as to draw attention to Henry's presence until he'd become well established there.

Had someone remembered Henry's sound leadership in those years when he was count? Perhaps the former circle of friends he had cultivated so carefully in western Normandy had not, in actual-ity, turned away from him, even though the threat of being stripped of their lands had temporarily driven them away. Whatever the case, the invitation extended by Domfront came as a wholehearted offer on the part of the townspeople.

Orderic Vitalis wrote that Henry swore to the citizens that he would never, so long as he lived, allow the lordship of Domfront to pass to another; nor would he change any laws or customs without their agreement. True to his word, even after Henry became the most powerful ruler in Western Europe, and his *vicomtes* oversaw all the administrative affairs of that area of Normandy, he always kept that city under his personal protection.

For the next forty-three years until his death, Domfront flourished in every way. New construction began almost immediately, including a large stone keep to replace the original wooden one; the new one rose to an impressive height of eighty feet. The castle priory, and the Church of Notre Dame sur L'Eau below the city, were both rebuilt by Henry in a fine Norman Romanesque style of architecture, as was also the nearby abbey of Lonlay.

One French specialist in medieval architecture has described Henry's impact on Domfront's growth at that time as "*Spectaculaire!*", adding that in those years the city became "*un vaste chantier* (construction site)." While the image of such a site doesn't exactly suggest architectural beauty, it does speak volumes for the activity, growth, and economic vitality that came to Domfront with Henry as its lord.

Henry's continued presence in Domfront, and the growing network of west-Norman barons that coalesced around the prince, were all made possible by another essential change. The chroniclers tell us that King William Rufus at this time "acquiesced" to his younger brother's renewed influence in the Cotentin and Avranches regions.

Rufus, as king of England, always held the "trump card" of ultimate power over the disposition of the English possessions of Henry's most important vassals in western Normandy. It seems likely that, after Curthose's angry departure from England the previous Christmas, Rufus had been approached by some of Henry's old friends from the Cotentin-Avranches region, who tried to make a case for the supportive role which Henry could play in helping Rufus to win the duchy.

William Rufus and his household knights prepared to cross over to Normandy very early in 1094. Ostensibly the trip was so that he could appear before a panel of noblemen who would judge whether he had acted rightly in denying English land to Curthose, but in fact his motive was to conquer Normandy, for he went with an army and a substantial war chest.

Archbishop Anselm—of whom more later—sent word assuring the king that the venture had his blessings and also the prayers of everyone at Canterbury. As primate of all England, Archbishop Anselm, like Lanfranc before him, had made it clear that his prayers for God's grace on the king's endeavors had the highest priority, and he spared no effort in drawing the ecclesiastical community into his own deeply held conviction that "the king's prosperity is our prosperity, and his misfortune, our misfortune." The archbishop, who, like the king, received daily appeals for the succor of Normandy, also felt keenly the suffering of that leaderless duchy.

Anselm, however, felt it his duty to God and to his flock to protest against Rufus's abuses of the church. The archbishop believed with all his heart that a strong king, providing centralized leadership, was vitally important to good governance. Rufus's parents had been friends of Anselm, and Anselm for this reason was loyal to Rufus, and supportive of him as his earthly lord.

Unfortunately, Anselm's message of Godspeed to the king arrived nearly at the same time as an unwelcome response from Anselm concerning Canterbury's payment to the king of a certain geld which the archbishop was disputing. Rufus, in a rage over the geld, responded to Archbishop Anselm's blessings on his journey with a stream of abuse: "Tell him that from now on I will hate him more and more day by day. No longer will I recognize him as my father and archbishop; as to his blessings and prayers, I utterly abominate them and spew them from me!"

The king's intimates, like him, were not a particularly refined or pious group, though in those times religious feeling pervaded society in ways that we today can scarcely comprehend. At that moment the king's household and his knights, who were gathered on the shore prepared for what was often a perilous crossing, surely felt that Rufus had gone too far in refusing the benediction of the saintly Anselm, father of the church in England.

Historian Hollister conjectures that a growing sense of unease was spreading through the ranks of Rufus's army, as the story of the king's shocking retort to Archbishop Anselm was circulated, and as the military skirmishes with Curthose's men continued to be so demoralizingly indecisive throughout 1094. Perhaps Rufus's own men were beginning to feel that their efforts were cursed because of their leader's treatment of the saintly Anselm. Was righteousness on their side, they wondered?

If someone had dared to suggest a conciliatory message to Anselm, Rufus would have utterly refused to cater to such "superstition." Were these, he would have asked, battle-proven warriors? Or were they merely spineless monks, that they put such stock in a few mumbled words from a caped fellow like that irksome Anselm?

During these many months of desultory fighting between Rufus and Curthose, Henry kept well away from them both. At intervals he may have allowed himself the enjoyment of overseeing some of the building projects he'd begun at Domfront, but more important still, we may be sure he spent his time primarily in forging alliances and strengthening the fortifications throughout his lands. He must have been growingly certain that the prediction his father had made on his deathbed was shaping toward its necessary fulfillment.

CHAPTER 25

The Shifting Balance of Power

R oger of Beaumont, a loyal, dedicated vassal of William the Conqueror, had remained behind in Normandy in 1066 to act with Matilda as co-regent of the duchy. His oldest son, Robert count of Meulan, who was then twenty years old, had fought at Hastings as his illustrious family's representative. Robert of Meulan was intelligent, cool-headed, and circumspect, with an amazing ability to grasp quickly all the ramifications of any proposed course of action. He was also a man of piety and principle. His spiritual sentiments, however, were private and individual, and didn't include accepting unthinkingly the doctrines of the Roman Church. He was a philosophically subtle man, and a good judge of character. Like Archbishop Anselm, with whom he conducted very civil and civilized "battles" over a broad range of church-state issues, Robert of Meulan could remain people's friend even if they disagreed with him on fundamental issues.

After the death of William the Conqueror, and during the first years of Robert Curthose as duke, Robert of Meulan stayed for the most part in the duchy. His name appears fairly regularly as a witness to ducal charters. He may well have served as an advisor to Curthose. Beginning in 1093, his name begins appearing also on witness lists for William Rufus in England. At some point, Robert of Meulan's greater loyalty definitely shifted to the cause of Rufus. It was not in Count Robert's nature—nor was it part of his conscious policy—to openly sever relations with Curthose.

At the same time, the duke was aware that when the moment came for each baron to choose between his or Rufus's banner in a military confrontation, Curthose would no longer be able to count on Robert of Meulan, nor on the crucial string of fortresses held by Robert count of Meulan and the lord of the Beaumont in the important Risle River valley.

Sometime in the autumn of 1094, Rufus, unable to gain any real advantage in his campaign against Curthose, decided that he needed reinforcements, and sent ships to bring Prince Henry and Hugh of Avranches, earl of Chester, to his base of operations in Eu, in northeastern Normandy. By the time the ships reached Henry and Hugh in the Cotentin, however, Rufus had decided to return to England, leaving a few captains to continue a low level of harassment of Curthose. The king apparently still wanted Henry with him, for Henry and Hugh together boarded a ship that carried them to their new destination: Southampton.

The *Anglo-Saxon Chronicle* informs us that during this stay of some months at the court of Rufus, Henry evidently took an oath of fealty to him "against their brother," and in the spring of 1095, when he returned to his lands in Normandy, Henry was laden "with great treasures" from Rufus. Now it was Henry and his vassals who continued to wage war against Curthose in Normandy, doing him "much damage both in land and men," as the *Anglo-Saxon Chronicle* recorded. William Rufus remained in England, where in 1095 he faced a second baronial rebellion, including a well-formed plot to assassinate him. A spontaneous confession from one of the conspirators saved the king in the nick of time, and Rufus successfully crushed the rebellion.

It is interesting to note, here, an example of how William Rufus never learned to work cooperatively with his barons. Henry, by contrast, learned to work with his barons, and at least in England, once they realized it was in their interest to work also with him, had their complete support.

CHAPTER 26

Robert Curthose and William Rufus

Pope Urban II, in November 1095, made his first appeal for knights to recapture the Holy Land from the Muslims. Robert Curthose, with typical romanticism, decided to respond. Peace was arranged between King William Rufus and Duke Robert. In order to raise the considerable cash that Curthose would need to travel with his large entourage in the style befitting his station, Curthose further agreed essentially to pawn Normandy to Rufus for ten thousand silver marks. The terms of the agreement made it clear that this was not a sale, for if and when, by the grace of God, Curthose returned after an anticipated absence of three to five years, the duchy would revert to him as its rightful duke—after he'd repaid Rufus his ten thousand silver marks.

Could Duke Robert possibly have believed that his brother Rufus would honor the terms of their agreement—after an absence of several years—and return the duchy peaceably to him upon his return from Jerusalem? Pope Urban had promised that the church would throw the full weight of its authority behind protecting the lands and families left behind by those valiant knights who took up the Cross. One wonders, however, whether Curthose was not content for the most part to let his thoughts of the future remain vague, for at the moment they seemed relatively unimportant compared to the grand adventure he anticipated on this crusade.

Thus, Robert Curthose in the autumn of 1096, now about forty-four years old, set out with a large retinue to save his soul—as the pope had promised—and, perhaps, to restore his damaged reputation on earth as well.

Odo, bishop of Bayeux, half-brother of William the Conqueror, had actually been among those who were in the great field outside Clermont when Pope Urban II had delivered his galvanizing exhortation to the crusaders. After the Council of Clermont, Odo and two other Norman bishops who had been present at Clermont also officially promoted the Crusade within Normandy. Now Odo himself was beside Robert Curthose, seated proudly astride a richly appointed horse, part of the ducal retinue setting out for the Holy Land.

Odo must have had strangely mixed feelings about this journey. He surely deplored the ineptitude of Curthose, who was once again determining his uncle's fate. When Odo first heard his nephew's decision to take the Cross, he knew that his own fate was now being determined for him. As leader of the 1088 baronial insurgency against King William Rufus in England, and as the one who, in 1089, had engineered Henry's imprisonment and relinquishment to Curthose of his western Normandy lands, Bishop Odo knew he would not fare well under the leadership of these two nephews. They had ample reason to bear him ill will.

Yet a part of Odo was surely stimulated by thoughts of the unknown vistas awaiting the Crusaders. Perhaps he hoped that these new horizons would include some great position of power for a man of his acumen and energy. Like Curthose, Odo in recent years, ensconced at Bayeux, had felt dead-ended and confined. As the retinue began finally to move forward, Odo—one of the last of that strange breed who passed easily back and forth between the bishop's miter and full battle armor—was alternately swept by grim foreboding and a sense of anticipation. As it happened, having reached the age of about sixty-five years, he died en route to the Holy Land, and was buried in the cathedral of Palermo, Sicily.

From late in 1096 until August 1100, the accounts in contemporary chronicles are scarce concerning Henry's activities. We know that once Curthose had departed for the Holy Land, William Rufus formally conferred on Henry those lands in Normandy which he had in effect ruled since 1088. The chroniclers suggest that Count Henry was often by his brother's side during these four years. Hollister believes, however, that although Henry was often in attendance at his brother's court, he spent much time also in Normandy, conscientiously overseeing matters in those lands where he was at last recognized formally as lord.

Henry was certainly at the court of Rufus in May 1099, for what must have been a very grand affair. In that month the king's court assembled for the first time in William Rufus's awe-inspiring new palace at Westminster, where the king's favorite (and almost universally loathed), Ranulf Flambard, was installed as bishop of Durham. Amid exclamations of delight and admiration for the great size of the king's main hall, Rufus replied with typical bluster that it wasn't "half big enough for me!"

These were good years for William Rufus. Not only did he have Normandy in his hands at last, and with it the satisfaction of a reunited Anglo-Norman kingdom, but in Ranulf Flambard he had found a "right-hand man" as predatory as himself—someone willing to squeeze every last silver piece possible from the church, the barons, and the common people so as to fuel the further campaigns of consolidation and conquest that Rufus planned.

Contemporary chroniclers, nearly all of whom were monks, were distressed and outraged to a man at Rufus's treatment of the church, especially at the *carte blanche* he had bestowed on the detested Ranulf Flambard to strip vacant bishoprics and abbacies of their assets.

Relations between the king and Anselm, the archbishop of Canterbury, reached a critical impasse which drove Anselm to take extreme measures: The archbishop left England in 1097 in a self-imposed exile with the purpose of drawing Pope Urban II's attention to—and inviting his intervention in—a state of affairs within the church of England which Anselm saw as being in serious crisis. Even from his exile, which he spent mostly at Lyons, Anselm continued his protests via letter and messenger to both King William Rufus and the pope in Rome.

The depravity of William's royal court was a scandal throughout the kingdom, while the king's blatant impiety made some men tremble as they waited for God to strike the kingdom in divine punishment: punishment on themselves as well as on the whole kingdom. In 1093, when the saintly Gundulf, bishop of Rochester, admonished William Rufus to maintain his improved habits now that he'd recovered from his serious illness, Rufus (it is said) shouted back, "By the holy Face of Lucca, I will not repay God with good for the evil He has done me." Several chroniclers noted in bewilderment that, far from William Rufus suffering God's vengeance, even the Channel waters seemed to grow calm just before Rufus crossed!

Kriyananda, however, who had an opportunity to study Warren Vickerman (who Paramhansa Yogananda stated was the recent incarnation of William Rufus), found him a "diamond in the rough," but for all that, a diamond. Vickerman was, in his own way, deeply devoted to God, though almost fiercely skeptical of the bonafides of churchmen. He fitted the common saying: "His bark is worse than his bite." Vickerman's nature was warm and enthusiastic—blustering, yes: rather like those hirsute blusterers who like to puff out their long mustaches and make the long hairs fly out before them every time they expel their breath. Actually, Kriyananda says, he found Vickerman quite likeable, definitely given to bluster and (probably) to boasting, the sort who announced loudly to the whole world how he was going to treat someone who had offended him, but then probably wouldn't do much, if anything. To Kriyananda's surprise, Vickerman took an instant liking to him, and remarked to him several times, "I don't know what it is about you, but I feel as though you were my brother." This he said when he was perhaps sixty or more years old and Kriyananda was twenty-seven. This meeting, I might add, was the only one that Kriyananda ever had with Vickerman.

CHAPTER 27

The Death of Rufus

Word came to the king that Robert Curthose, after an absence of nearly four years, was on his way home from the First Crusade. The successes of the First Crusade had far exceeded anyone's wildest hopes. The hardships that Christ's soldiers had endured had already passed into legend, and the survivors among those noble warriors were perceived by many as special beings, transfigured by the purifying fires of battle and divine victory.

Duke Robert had acquitted himself well, both in the occupation of Antioch and in the battle for Jerusalem, and had thereby succeeded in bolstering his sagging reputation as a warrior. In addition, as the duke's retinue was passing on his return journey through the Norman-held lands of southern Italy, the again-impecunious Curthose had won the hand of a very wealthy heiress, of noble character, Sibylla d'Altavilla, contessa di Conversano. Duke Robert would have no difficulty, now, in repaying Rufus the ten thousand silver marks required of him by their agreement for Robert's repossession of the duchy of Normandy.

Orderic is the source of another vital piece of information: William Rufus, when he heard of Robert's imminent return to his duchy, had begun to assemble a large army, planning to do battle with Curthose over Normandy. William Rufus had not yet been able to unite his barons under his leadership to the extent needed for a decisive defeat of Curthose. Furthermore, Curthose now had the monetary resources to pay mercenaries. Most importantly,

Curthose was now a hero of the Crusade, which at present was Christianity's greatest glory. For William Rufus to fight this returning hero for a land that had been entrusted to him by the hero himself was to invite the severest papal censure.

It is doubtful whether Rufus was fully aware of all these implications. He was, for many other reasons as well, in the best of spirits on the afternoon of August 2, when he gathered with his usual group of intimates for a hunt in New Forest, the royal hunting preserve. In addition to Henry, many others also comprised the group. The hunting party dispersed in the forest, as it always did, in pursuit of game. Orderic and Malmesbury both wrote that it was Walter Tirel, a minor lord visiting from Normandy, who shot the arrow that by pure accident killed the king. Abbot Suger of St. Denis, on the other hand, in his life of King Louis VI of France, averred that he had heard Tirel himself, in circumstances where he had absolutely nothing to lose or gain from revealing the truth of the matter, deny that it was he who had shot that arrow. The fact (often cited) that Walter Tirel, upon determining that William Rufus was dead, rode for the coast and took the first ship to Normandy proves nothing. This would have been the only wise course for someone in his position: Tirel's mere word that it was not he, or that the death, like countless others that had occurred while hunting, was an accident, would not have saved Tirel from the retribution that some might have wanted to exact from him.

One of the attendants, blowing a huntsman's horn urgently and repeatedly, gathered the king's scattered intimates. One by one they galloped up in response to that summons, and were confronted by the spectacle of Rufus lying on the ground, shot through the chest with an arrow. The arrow had entered from the front, and Rufus had inadvertently hastened his own death by falling forward, driving the arrow's shaft deeper into his chest—probably into the heart, since he died almost immediately. William Rufus, the second son of the Conqueror, was only forty-one years old when his life so abruptly ended.

Although hunting accidents were an exceedingly common occurrence among medieval noblemen, the fact that this was a king, struck down in his prime, was explainable to the pious only as the avenging hand of God, who had delivered His church from the spoliation of this king who had no conscience.

After a brief exchange of shouted communications between the quaking royal huntsmen and the noble companions of William Rufus, which made it clear that it was, in fact, the king himself who now lay dead on the ground, the noblemen dispersed immediately. Just like those who had gathered around William the Conqueror, and had abandoned his body, so Rufus's intimates, too, galloped off to secure their own property.

It was left to the lowliest of the royal attendants to load the body onto a wooden peasant's cart, cover it with a rough, dirty cloth, and transport the king's remains, still dripping blood, to Westminster. According to the monk Orderic Vitalis, no church bells were rung for the dead king; no alms were distributed to the poor for the good of his soul. Senior churchmen declared that, because of his depraved life and the unrepentant way in which he had lived and died, they could offer him no final absolution for his sins. William Rufus was buried the next day, August 3, under the tower of the Old Minster. It seems to have been a "bare bones" ceremony. Many magnates attended, but none grieved.

In the New Forest that afternoon, "Every man for himself!" became clearly the unspoken motto of the king's intimates. Each one drew apart from the others and considered his own options.

Henry, on the other hand, gazed with sorrow on Rufus's lifeless remains. He was saddened that his brother had not made a better end. Henry, owing to his brother's parsimony, had no English property to secure. But even if he had been the owner of the largest fief in England, its protection would surely have been only a secondary concern at that moment. From what we know of Henry, he could only have been wholly and urgently concerned for the future of their father's kingdom.

For he saw instantly the various possible alternatives before him, and the likely results of each. Even while his mind played out these possibilities, he was already turning his horse away from the scene and galloping off in the direction he had fixed upon. Intuitively, as if his whole life had been a preparation for this crucial moment, the Conqueror's youngest son knew exactly what he must do now, and without a moment's delay.

Part Three

THE LIFE OF
KING HENRY I OF ENGLAND

CHAPTER 28

A New King

These good things, which all men rightly crave,
Cannot be found aimlessly, nor achieved
By any who stand resistant to new realities.
Life's blessings must be sought by dedication,
Cooperation, and clear vision.

—*The Peace Treaty*, Act One, Scene 1, Swami Kriyananda

In an absolute monarchy, the death of the king meant absolute anarchy. Leaderlessness invited lawlessness and a widespread return to vengeance, feuding, murder, and other time-dishonored methods for exacting false "justice" in the absence of just government. Such a country was far more vulnerable to invasion, and to the fall of strategically crucial royal castles into the hands of unscrupulous barons. Every day that England's throne remained vacant afforded more opportunities to various pretenders for the throne to make all the more potent their own bid for power, and to render the struggle for the crown, therefore, all the bloodier. For the sake of the kingdom, Henry had not a moment to lose.

It was the country's great good fortune that there were two other men hunting with Rufus and Henry that afternoon: men of clarity, intelligence, and decisive will. Within moments, Robert count of Meulan, and his younger brother, Henry earl of Warwick, joined Henry. No word was spoken. The three shared but one thought: to reach the royal treasury at Winchester as quickly as possible.

From the New Forest to Winchester was about seventy miles. Traveling light, they would have reached their destination on

Friday, August 3 at the earliest, or at the latest by Saturday, August 4. Orderic Vitalis wrote that William of Breteuil, son of William fitz Osbern—a *familiaris* of the Conqueror—who had also been with the hunting party, arrived at Winchester at nearly the same time. Henry at once, as the rightful next king of England, demanded the keys to the royal treasury and control of Winchester Castle. William of Breteuil, however, insisted to Henry and all those present that they had all sworn oaths of fealty to Robert Curthose. Duke Robert, he pointed out, was even then approaching Normandy in the last stages of his journey back from the Holy Land. Whatever his faults may once have been—so argued William of Breteuil—he was now a hero who had helped to free Jerusalem from the infidels. Henry, however, had never sworn any such oath. He had long been painfully aware of his oldest brother's incompetence as a ruler, of his traitorous nature, and of his almost pathetically human weaknesses. Henry would do much to ensure that Curthose never held the reins of the kingdom in his hands; he might even have questioned Robert's competence to hold the reins of a horse!

According to Orderic, Prince Henry drew his sword in the ensuing exchange, and declared he would not tolerate any delay that might permit another "to seize his father's scepter before him." Given the fact that Breteuil was a military leader, with respect for power and worldly importance, Henry's drawing his sword at that moment was probably the most effective gesture he could have made. It also allowed the Beaumont brothers to intervene as diplomats and peacemakers, a role they played surpassingly well. In short order the control of both the royal treasury and the castle were turned over to Henry.

Interestingly, Kriyananda today says that that scene is as real to him now as if he were actually living it in the body of Henry, confident of his right to get his father's mission "on track" at last.

Prince Henry, Robert of Meulan, and Henry of Warwick now went separately about the tasks connected with getting the news of the king's death to key magnates and royal household officials; dispatching couriers with the news of the death; distributing new orders from Henry to various parts of the kingdom; and arranging in all possible ways for a smooth transition of royal authority to Henry.

It was of urgent importance to locate a sufficiently high-ranking prelate to officiate at Henry's coronation. Anselm, archbishop of Canterbury and primate of all England, was in exile on the continent. The archbishop of York was ill and was also too far away. Fortunately, Maurice bishop of London lived relatively near by. When Maurice was located, he agreed to anoint Henry at Winchester as the new king of England.

The night before his coronation, Henry slept very little. Since Rufus's death two days earlier, he had searched his conscience for confirmation that it was God's will that he become the king of England. Intuitively, indeed, and also from his father's words to him, Henry knew such was his destiny.

William Rufus had set his will to reclaiming all the lands that had been part of their father's Anglo-Norman kingdom. It was, above all, this expression of filial devotion on the part of Rufus that had made it possible for Henry to maintain a supportive relationship with his brother, when in fact the two of them were temperamental opposites. The younger brother had long chafed, with feelings of helplessness bordering on despair, as he observed how poorly Rufus understood or even cared about the true well-being of the country, or the brilliantly innovative institutions their father had set into motion. Henry felt an inner attunement with their father's underlying purpose in the reforms he and Lanfranc had initiated: church reforms; reforms in the system of justice; the deeper purpose of the Domesday Inquest; the amazingly practical step William had taken in administering the Oath of Salisbury; the over-all unity he had created between England and Normandy. William's life had had a purpose far beyond that of creating a new-model kingdom. Its larger purpose was to usher in a new age; to inspire a new direction for all of Europe; to infuse new blood into and reform a weakening religious spirit; to resurrect law and bring order to the chaos of the preceding centuries; and, finally, to reform England—already a country uniquely positioned—by creating here a law-abiding government, free from the bloodbaths that had been the hallmark of Europe for centuries. A single lifespan was by no means sufficient to bring about such sweeping changes.

Henry, now thirty-two years old, was mature enough to complete William's significant reforms. Temperamentally, too, Henry's inclination was to think broadly, far beyond his immediate horizons. At one time in his life, indeed, he became interested in constructing a highway over the Alps in order to make it easier for people to travel from Switzerland to Italy. He was interested in the improvement of religious architecture everywhere. In his zeal for monastic reform he founded many monasteries, and sought to institute monastic reform far beyond the English and Norman boundaries, even donating toward the founding of several such communities in other countries.

It was Henry's very real appreciation for the enormous potential inherent in his father's vision for England which convinced him that it was God's will for him to assume the kingship. No one else had shown understanding of, or even interest in, the reforms William had sought.

Thus, Henry answered with deep conviction the arguments raised by William of Breteuil concerning Robert Curthose's right to the kingdom. Far from Henry's ever having pledged to support Robert, he knew that the Conqueror had grieved deeply to see the mess Robert was making of Normandy. Henry knew that his oldest brother would surely try to seize the throne. He knew also, however, that Curthose was totally unfit to be king of England, just as he had already shown himself totally unfit to rule Normandy.

Rumors were circulating that Duke Robert was now a greatly changed man: more mature and responsible in consequence of the searing experiences he had endured in the Holy Land. Curthose was also now married to a wealthy and refined young Italian noblewoman, who might soon give him yet another reason to create responsible government within Normandy: an heir. Leopards don't change their spots merely by bathing, however. Henry surely knew that the character of his still-living brother, however much changed by the Crusade, could not possibly have changed his basic nature so much as to have undergone a fundamental shift of character. In fact, as events showed, Curthose hadn't really changed even superficially. He was still the same arrogant, shiftless, disloyal, and incompetent braggart he had always been. Henry had suffered quite enough at the hands of this incompetent brother.

In the space of a very few days between the hunting accident and his coronation, Henry created a document, called his Coronation Charter, that would some day become the model for the Magna Carta, and would provide the underpinnings for a form of government that is still unique to England today. The Charter was published on the day of Henry's coronation. It detailed how he intended to rule. He promised to correct prevailing injustices; to give the people of England a king who would not act arbitrarily, but would concern himself with their welfare; to provide good, evenhanded governance; and to create just laws.

With an ease born of years of deep reflection on a king's duty to his people, and following the example that had been set by his father, William the Conqueror, Henry created a document that promised a government radically different from that under which England had suffered under William Rufus.

In the charter dictated by Henry to a royal scribe, he gave back to the nobility certain rights which Rufus had usurped. Henry promised, moreover, to protect and uphold the rights of the people and of the church. Specifically, he promised to appoint new candidates to bishoprics and abbacies as soon as they became vacant, rather than hold their assets in trust while siphoning off their income. Henry promised peace to the land even as his father had done, and a return to "the good laws of King Edward the Confessor." Again, like his father, Henry strongly emphasized continuity with pre-Conquest English law. He promised to resurrect the Anglo-Saxon court system for hearing pleas and delivering judgments.

And (an important and also unprecedented proviso) he promised to bind himself to his own laws. He himself would be subservient to the law.

Henry I's Coronation Charter is a brief document: only four-teen points in all, written in clear and simple language. Its impact, however, was and has continued to be enormous. Previously, many kings of England had taken the traditional three-part oath at their coronation—"to keep the peace, to prohibit all rapaciousness and iniquities, and to maintain just laws as well as any king before me has done." They may have added something brief that was perti-nent to specific needs of their times. For the first time in England's history, however, Henry, apart from writing a much more complete charter, took the additional step of ordering many written copies of his Coronation Charter to be made, affixed with the royal seal, and sent to all the shires of England—both to the sheriff and the main tenant-in-chief. He ordered that it be read out loud at all appropri-ate public gatherings.

Chronicler Eadmer (assistant and biographer to Archbishop Anselm) wrote that Henry requested also that the Charter be read aloud during the three-fold-oath portion of the coronation cere-mony. The new king insisted on confirming publicly—"by sacred oath" and in the hearing of everybody—his solemn promise to abide by the statements he had made.

Henry's Coronation Charter was later invoked by his successors, Kings Stephen and Henry II, as their way of acknowledging public-ly the rights of free English men and women to protection from any unjust demands on the part of the crown. Most importantly, those who drafted the Magna Carta in 1215 cited, and indeed quoted from verbatim, Henry's Coronation Charter as the basis of their own document. As I have said but want here to underline, Henry's Coronation Charter stood apart from, and above, the king himself: he made himself answerable to it.

It is saddening to see the cynicism with which several historians have treated this monumental achievement of Henry's. Too many of them treat the events and the people they study like pieces and gambits in a chess game. One wonders whether their chief interest is not to draw snickers from students in the classroom. I have read tossed-off comments such as, "Of course Henry didn't keep his commitments"; or, "He kept only as many of them as suited his personal ambition." Some historians, accustomed to the campaign promises made by modern seekers of political office, have written as if Henry felt that he needed to win over the populous to his side, and that no other motive could possibly have prompted him to write such a charter in the first place.

Think about it: all this dour speculation, after the oppressive regime under which England had suffered! One marvels at the want of understanding of human nature on the part of intelligent people! Their own comprehension of human nature must have been skin deep. Therefore I commented that they often seemed to approach life as though it were a game of chess.

CHAPTER 29

Fulfilling a Father's Prediction

On Sunday, August 5, 1100, Henry was crowned at as grand a ceremony as could be arranged in such haste. The coronation ceremony included two elements which had been introduced by William the Conqueror: Two bishops, one speaking French and the other English, asking the assembled congregation if they accepted Henry as their new king. In answer, there was a resounding acclamation.

The second element, which also was a part of William the Conqueror's coronation ceremony, was the singing of the *Laudes Regia*, an import from the ceremony used in Normandy by William I, praying for God's blessings on the country and for the descent of divine grace on the ruler and on all he did for his people.

Though we do not know for certain, it seems likely that, of the several crowns which William the Conqueror had had made for himself, Henry wore the one which the Conqueror, on his deathbed, had given to William Rufus before sending him off to England to take charge of the royal treasury. This particular crown, designed by the Conqueror, was of gold, shaped like an arc, and embedded with twelve large pearls.

One of Henry's strongest claims to the throne of England was the fact that he alone, of all his brothers, had been born "in the purple"—that is to say, born in England to a reigning king and queen. Both William and Matilda, by the time of Henry's birth (around

September 1068), had been anointed with holy oil and consecrated as England's lawful monarchs.

In Henry, England again had a king who was fluent in the native language—though his daily speech was French—and who had been born on her soil. Within the Coronation Charter, some of the onerous laws that had been necessary after the Conquest were lifted; their purpose had been to protect the relatively few occupying Normans from violence—laws such as the *murdrum* fine.

From the very beginning of his reign, Henry affirmed what, during his thirty-five years as king, actually became a reality: England was no longer an occupied land, divided into conquerors and conquered. The state of watchful readiness that had isolated groups of Normans, and the periodic clashes between small rebel groups and their Norman overlords: all this was now over. By 1135, when King Henry died, several contemporary chroniclers averred that throughout most of the land, Norman, Anglo-Saxon, Breton, Dane, and Swede were so commingled—intermixed and intermarried—that, except in the topmost echelons of the aristocracy, most individuals' ethnic background could no longer be distinguished.

Just fifteen years earlier, William the Conqueror had been preparing for yet another invasion from Denmark. Now the Viking invasions had ceased, thanks to the Conqueror's strong defensive measures. King William I had reinforced and augmented England's laws and the already-existing system of justice, and everyone had taken note that these laws applied as much to Normans as to Scandinavians and Anglo-Saxons. Henry intuitively understood that many of those struggles were now over. The land and its people were ready for a new unity and, God willing, for peace.

Very soon after his coronation, Henry sent a letter to Anselm, archbishop of Canterbury, who was living on the continent, at Lyons, in self-imposed exile, and in the warmest possible terms invited him to return to England and resume his duties at Canterbury, as well as to serve at King Henry's side just as Lanfranc had done with William the Conqueror. Henry wrote, in part:

"I ask you now as a father, [together] with all the people of England, to come as quickly as you can to give your advice to me, your son. Indeed, I entrust myself and the people of the whole kingdom of England to your counsel and to the counsel of those who ought to advise me with you. And I pray that you not be displeased that I received consecration as king in your absence, for, had it been possible, I would more willingly have received it from you than from any other. . . ."

Implicit in Henry's letter to Anselm was the new king's expressed willingness to cooperate fully with his archbishop, in precisely those matters which had caused the rift to develop between Anselm and William Rufus. Of greatest importance, as far as Archbishop Anselm was concerned, was Henry's commitment to filling the vacant ecclesiastical posts as soon as possible, and his willingness to let Anselm convene within England synods of reform.

Archbishop Anselm had already heard of William Rufus's death "from two swiftly traveling monks," and King Henry's present courier encountered the archbishop already en route to England.

The new king also ordered the arrest and imprisonment of the man who still symbolized the worst abuses of William Rufus's reign: Ranulf Flambard, bishop of Durham. Thus it happened that Flambard had the dubious distinction of being the first prisoner ever to be kept in the Tower of London, which had been built by the Conqueror soon after his coronation in 1066. The Tower's first prisoner lived, however, in grand style, keeping his own valet and butler, and being supplied every evening with catered dinners.

Henry's two actions—the recalling of Archbishop Anselm to England, and the arrest of Ranulf Flambard—spoke volumes to the English people. It reassured them that the coronation of their new king had indeed ushered in a new era that would bring comfort and reassurance to all who craved peace and justice, even if it repressed the selfish ambitions of the unrighteous.

Henry acted with respect for the former king's household, reassuring those in key positions (which in this period nearly always went to noblemen of high rank) that he intended for there to be as much continuity as possible between the household of Rufus and his own. Given the great differences in temperament between Henry and his brother, the men who held those positions surely would not have been Henry's first choice. This was not the moment, however, to make sweeping changes in his household.

As a matter of absolute necessity, moreover, Henry's greatest care, during the first months of his reign, was to win the support of his great tenants-in-chief.

CHAPTER 30

Bishops, Queens, and Pawns

I n September 1100, slightly more than a month after Henry's coronation, Robert Curthose arrived back in Normandy after his four-year absence in the Holy Land. He re-entered the duchy unopposed, and now, with the death of Rufus, found himself relieved of the necessity for repaying even a penny of the ten thousand pounds he had owed William Rufus. When Robert heard the news, however, of his brother Henry's coronation, he was livid with anger. (So much for those rumors about his changed character!) He denounced Henry as a usurper of his rights, and threatened an immediate invasion of England. Typically, there followed many months during which time he simply "rested on the oars" of his threat.

On September 23, 1100, Anselm, now about sixty-six years old, landed at Dover and was speedily conveyed in great honor to King Henry's court at Salisbury. Henry, following the tradition established by the Conqueror, had immediately insisted on holding his first great court, which included a crown-wearing. His courts coincided with the great liturgical feasts: Michaelmas (September 29), Christmas, Easter, and Pentecost. Archbishop Anselm's reentry into England could scarcely have been more dramatic, since it was to Henry's great Michaelmas court and crown-wearing at Salisbury that he was conveyed. Eadmer, who traveled with Anselm, wrote that the whole countryside was in a state of rejoicing at Anselm's return.

No one was more delighted to see Anselm than King Henry. Besides his official letter inviting Anselm to return, Henry had instructed his messengers to relay to Anselm that much business was being delayed in the kingdom, awaiting the archbishop's counsel and approval. Now, at their meeting, King Henry again apologized for having allowed another bishop to place the crown on his head. The archbishop replied that he fully understood, and accepted the king's explanation and apology.

The great celebratory mood of the people assembled there was heartfelt; the kingdom was finally reunited, with the addition of its spiritual father, Archbishop Anselm, whom everybody considered to embody divine wisdom and the love of Christ gathering all sinners in His embrace.

Then came the moment when, in order to seal the relationship formally between king and primate as it had stood for centuries, Henry asked Anselm to render him the traditional homage and receive from his hand the office of archbishop and the lands of Canterbury, which William Rufus had confiscated from him. To Henry's utter astonishment, Anselm answered firmly that he neither could nor would agree to receive the symbols of office from the king; nor could he render the king homage.

King Henry was dumbstruck by this completely unexpected response. Nothing had prepared him for a radical departure from what had always, up to now, been a smoothly functioning formality. In the few moments before the archbishop spoke again, the king must have thought Anselm was even going to protest his own accession to the throne. After all, Anselm had received the symbols of office from William Rufus, under far less congenial circumstances, and had rendered that king homage. Nor had Anselm raised any objection to the fact that Rufus, as king, continued to invest prelates, just as William the Conqueror had done, and also every previous king of England.

The archbishop now offered a simple explanation for his new position concerning investiture and royal homage. During his two-year exile, Anselm had attended the 1099 Easter Synod of Pope

Urban II in Rome. At the close of that session, Urban II, with the same sense for the dramatic that he'd demonstrated when announcing the First Crusade in 1095, "rose to his full height" and declared it as the church's uncompromising policy that the practice of lay rulers investing clergy with the symbols of office was now forbidden. On no account was a member of the clergy to render homage to any lay person.

These two issues had for fully fifteen years been part and parcel of the Gregorian reform movement; they were already the focus of bitter power struggles on the continent. What was completely new in the pope's Easter Synod speech in 1099 was that Urban II proceeded to declare a series of anathemas. Nothing less than excommunication would now be the punishment for any lay person who invested prelates, as well as for any prelate who received his office from a lay person, or who rendered homage to a lay person.

Anselm next provided King Henry and those there assembled with a vital clue to his difficulty in this matter. He emphasized that he had heard the pope's pronouncement *with his own ears*. As a monk, and therefore under a vow of holy obedience, he was bound by that pronouncement.

Eadmer, Anselm's companion and biographer, wrote that the archbishop concluded by saying that if the king could but agree to these decrees, then "it will be well between us and bring lasting peace; but if not, I cannot see that my remaining in England would be either profitable or honorable."

Capturing the moment well, as one who had actually been on the scene, Eadmer wrote that, for Henry, "It seemed to him a terrible thing to lose the investiture of churches and homage of prelates, as if he were losing half of his sovereignty." Indeed, at the time of the Domesday Inquest in 1086, the church in England held control of fully twenty-five percent of the land in England. To Henry, clerical investitures and homage was *indeed* "a terrible thing to lose."

To appreciate the complex backdrop against which this pivotal exchange took place, we must remember also that some of those present were barons unfriendly to Henry. No doubt these men relished what seemed to them a blow to the new king's alliance-building efforts, and one that he would not possibly be able to deflect.

He quickly recovered from the shock of Anselm's refusal, and now listened intently to the archbishop's explanation of his new position on investitures and clerical homage. The king, like Robert of Meulan (who was by his side), did not fail to catch the detail which to others might have seemed unimportant: The archbishop had heard the papal decree *with his own ears.* Robert of Meulan, who, with Anselm, had been Rufus's chief negotiator, knew the archbishop well and understood that what mattered most to him were three things: 1) to establish the primacy of the see of Canterbury over the whole church in England; 2) to reform the church, especially with regard to simony and clerical celibacy; and 3) through his leadership, to minister to the spiritual needs of the English people—or, in Anselm's own words, "to encourage the ardor of Christianity in England."

It had been intensely painful to Anselm to impose on himself this three-year period of exile, but he had found it necessary. And why so? Under William I, there had been seventeen general church councils in Normandy, and six in England. Under William Rufus, there had been *no* such councils. When Anselm, after years of trying, had broached the subject to him again in 1094, Rufus had replied, "I will deal with these things when I think fit—not at your pleasure, but at mine. Enough! Say no more about it."

Anselm had hoped to move Pope Urban II to persuade Rufus to allow him, Anselm, to convene primatial councils, and to cease spoliating the church in England. However, the pope had not been so strong with William Rufus as Anselm had hoped. As soon as Anselm heard about Rufus's death, he had eagerly returned to England and to his duties as archbishop of Canterbury. A second exile now would have been for him a soul-searing experience, though he felt obligated to threaten that possibility. Both Henry and Robert of Meulan certainly understood these undercurrents.

Henry now understood the terrain on which he and Anselm had to operate. Anselm wanted very much to return to Canterbury and resume his responsibilities for the English church, which he regarded as his sacred trust from God. The king, for his part, needed time to absorb these new developments—during which time Anselm would remain in England in relative harmony with Henry, and in active support of Henry's claim over that of Curthose to the nation's throne. Henry also, it should be added, was concerned for the spiritual well-being of his people.

To those gathered in Salisbury for King Henry's crown wearing, and for the Michaelmas court—the first great court to be convened by the new king—the confrontation between Henry and Anselm very dramatically revealed the vast difference between Henry (the "lion of justice," as he was later dubbed) and Rufus (the "wolf of injustice," as we might now name him). Henry was caught completely off guard, and seemed diplomatically cornered by the very issue that was tearing the Holy Roman Empire apart. He responded, however, calmly and respectfully, in a way that conveyed his desire to cooperate with his archbishop as much as possible. At the same time, those barons who had gathered at Salisbury realized, perhaps with grudging admiration, that Henry had not yielded one inch on the underlying issues.

King Henry proposed to Anselm that he remain in England, and told him he would restore to him the lands of Canterbury, while the church in England would remain as it was—in other words, Henry would agree not to invest any more prelates—until Easter of the following year, 1101. Meanwhile, he suggested that both he and Anselm would send emissaries to the pope, asking him to "restore England to its former practices."

Anselm said he doubted that the pope would give his consent, but he accepted the king's proposal. Eadmer wrote that Anselm then happily returned "in peace" to his beloved Canterbury. A crisis, as everyone well understood it, had been averted by the new king's diplomacy.

After Anselm's installation as archbishop of Canterbury under William Rufus, he had publicly lamented the fact that he felt like an old mare yoked to a wild young bull. Holding up as his model the completely sympathetic, cooperative relationship that had existed between William the Conqueror and Lanfranc, Anselm had resigned himself to the impossibility of holding even basic communication with Rufus. Now, for the first time, he began to hope that, with Henry as king, something positive would result.

In November 1100, a few months after his coronation, King Henry took another extremely important, even a healing, step for the country. He married a young noblewoman of the Anglo-Saxon royal house of Wessex, Edith Matilda, daughter of Malcolm Canmore king of Scotland and his wife Margaret, a granddaughter of Edmund Ironsides, king of England in 1016. Henry was thirty-one years old at the time; his bride was twenty.

From the moment of Edith's birth she had had strong connections with the family of William the Conqueror. Robert Curthose was in Scotland on his father's business in 1080 when Edith Matilda was baptized, and he became the girl's godfather. William the Conqueror's wife, Queen Matilda, had become her godmother.

Both William of Malmesbury and Orderic Vitalis suggest that, before their marriage, there had been a long-standing "attachment" (the monk William's word) between Henry and Edith Matilda, and that Henry, "appreciating the high birth of the maiden whose perfection of character he had long adored, chose her as his bride." Evidently Henry's liking for Edith Matilda was more than reciprocated, for it was she who battled to overcome the objection people now raised to her marrying at all. In the post-Conquest era of England, many young women had taken refuge in convents until new order was established by William the Conqueror

Anselm, and Lanfranc before him, had both taken the stance that a woman who had lived within the walls of a convent for reasons of safety should not be considered as having bound herself to a life of renunciation. Such women were free to leave the convent and marry. If, however, a young woman for whatever reason during her time in the convent had worn the veil and habit of a nun, even if she didn't take the vows of a religious, marriage was no longer permitted for her.

The objection raised in the case of Edith Matilda was that she, too, had been found on more than one occasion, and by unexpected visitors, to have donned the veil of a nun. One of these occasions occurred when King William Rufus showed up with a group of his intimates, demanding to see the Scottish princess. The abbess on that occasion, alarmed because she felt that Rufus might do "anything that popped into his head," placed a nun's veil over Edith to protect her. The story states reliably that when Rufus saw Edith Matilda veiled, he abruptly turned away and left the convent, thereby confirming the abbess' suspicions regarding his intentions. Historians have suggested that William Rufus himself entertained the idea of marriage to Edith Matilda. After all, though Rufus preferred male companions, marriage was the only way he could produce an heir.

The fact that the abbess, in sudden alarm, had hastily veiled Edith Matilda did not signify that the young girl had willingly adopted the nun's veil.

After Henry's proposal to her, and her acceptance, Edith Matilda herself took the initiative of deflecting the objections she knew would be raised. She emphasized that she had been sent to the convent at Romsey, and then to Wilton, only for her education; that it had never been her own or her parents' intention that she take monastic vows.

In November 1100, King Henry and Edith Matilda were married on the steps of Westminster Church by Archbishop Anselm. Anselm took the additional precaution of explaining to the great gathering the care that had been taken to determine Edith Matilda's non-commitment to any vows. He said she was therefore not in any way bound to the convent, and was perfectly free to enter the married state.

Every nobleman present that day, listening to Archbishop Anselm's lengthy "disclaimer," understood just what was at stake. Unless this issue could be settled beyond any cavil, the legitimacy of the marriage itself, and therefore of any children born from it, might be challenged even decades later, with disastrous consequences for the dynasty and for the kingdom's peace.

The ceremony that day was not only a marriage, but also the coronation of Edith Matilda as the new queen of England. The king's Coronation Charter had announced Henry's intention of reinstating "the good laws of King Edward the Confessor." Additionally, the whole spirit of the Charter emphasized the dawn of a new era for England. King Henry's marriage to a princess of the bloodline of the revered Wessex (Anglo-Saxon) royal dynasty was a further confirmation that the king meant to make his Coronation Charter England's new reality.

There was a further significance to this marriage: King Edward the Confessor was said to have uttered a prophecy on his deathbed that a green tree would be split down the middle of its trunk and the severed piece carried the space of three furlongs from the stock, after which the tree would be joined once more to the trunk, and would again produce leaves and fruit. Only then, Edward had said, would England's ills end. Henry's marriage to Matilda, in fusing the lines of the West Saxon kings and Norman dukes in the third post-Conquest generation, was thus seen as a fulfillment of the Confessor's prophecy.

At Christmas, King Henry and Queen Edith Matilda held a great court and crown-wearing in the tradition of William the Conqueror. Noblemen in attendance on the king in the twelfth century and earlier were not polite, obsequious participants like their eighteenth century courtier counterparts. From rougher elements there was undoubtedly a certain amount of suppressed laughter, hardly short of open derision. The king ignored them. Throughout his reign, one reason for his success was his ability to know what was important, and to focus entirely on that.

At this first Christmas court, Henry and Edith Matilda had also to endure unfortunate slights—almost like schoolboy hazing—before they became well established as rulers. The Clare and Giffard families, recently united by marriage, were present. Former favorites of William Rufus, they retained the coarse nature of those former courts. Harking back to Queen Edith Matilda's Anglo-Saxon lineage, a member of these two families dubbed

Henry and Edith Matilda, "Godric and Godiva"—in other words, Anglo-Saxon "rubes"—and in other ways also ridiculed the royal couple quite openly.

Some of those who had received training with Henry for the knighthood now resurrected old jests about Henry's love of reading and study, which had earned him the teasing nickname, "Stagfoot." The idea had been that Henry, unlike his contemporaries, had actually studied the art of hunting—not only by observation, but also through books. Thus—so the jest went—he could even tell the number of tines on a deer's antlers by simply observing the animal's footprint. Such buffoonery, of course, only revealed the jesters themselves to be little more than rustic louts. At the same time, their antics suggest to us the low consciousness with which Henry had to deal, as he patiently waited for these throwbacks to the former reign to be gradually won over or replaced by people of higher caliber.

Kriyananda, too, in this life had to put up with a very strange assortment of people before he was able to winnow out those really capable of living together in the spiritual community of Ananda.

The chroniclers reporting the mockery Henry endured made it clear that he, while fully aware of the ridicule, had the grace to go along with the jibes good-humoredly when he couldn't ignore them altogether. The king didn't express anger, nor did he allow himself to be in any way affected by others' crudeness. He remained calm, as he had done under the demeaning insults and humiliations of his own brothers.

In all these ways his character finds a clear reflection in the life of Swami Kriyananda, who—unbelievably to those who know him—has had to endure much mockery and humiliation, and yet has always done so calmly and with grace. On one occasion a man spent a whole hour excoriating him for his numerous faults. Kriyananda, at the end, only thanked the man for having tried to help him. As to the remarks themselves, he said nothing. Only after the man had left did he sit down and write what people now consider one of his most beautiful songs:

I Live Without Fear

Though green summer fade,
And winter draw near,
My Lord, in Your presence
I live without fear.

Through tempest, through snows,
Through turbulent tide,
The touch of Your hand
Is my strength, and my guide.

I ask for no riches
That death can destroy.
I crave only Thee:
Your love and your joy!
(repeat)

The dancers will pass;
The singing must end:
I welcome the darkness
With You for my Friend!

It must be partly because of Henry's calm self-control that so many historians—in recent times, especially—have described him as lacking in human feeling—cold, contemptuous of others, and calculating. That Henry was warm-hearted, friendly, blessed with a good (and kindly) sense of humor, and deeply concerned for the welfare of others is simply beyond what those historians have experienced of life. Perhaps if Henry had been a monk, withdrawn from normal life and living in a cloister, those historians, though shaking their heads in wonder, might have accepted grudgingly that this man was perhaps motivated by some higher understanding. But Henry was a *king*, for God's sake! Ordinary men would say, "There must be something fishy about such aloofness!" Thus it is that a number of historians have totally ignored reports from those times that showed Henry to have had a warm and compassionate nature, motivated little, if at all, by self-interest.

It might help here to recount a story about Henry I that came to light years after his death.

Walter Map, who had first been a courtier under Henry I (and later served in the same capacity under Henry II), was keenly observant as a boy. He wrote many years after the death of the first Henry, whom he greatly admired, of an incident that demonstrated Henry's magnanimity conclusively.

It was Henry's custom to ask that a cup of wine be set aside for him, in case he awoke during the night and wanted it as an aid to sleep. Henry was a man of great self-control, and abominated drunkenness. Rarely, therefore, did he ask for the wine, even though one cup could not have affected him mentally. One evening, he asked the steward to bring him his cup. The steward shamefacedly (and perhaps trembling) confessed that he had drunk all of it himself. Worse still, he said, the cellars were locked and could not be opened until the following morning.

Walter Map wrote that not only did the king graciously forgive the steward this lapse, but he instructed him, "From now on, set aside two cups of wine every night—one for me, and the other for you."

Among the many possible ways that Henry might have responded in this case, wasn't this the kindest? Scholars who offer harsh judgments about Henry's character never relate this story, though it is well known. Yet they've had no reason to distrust Walter Map's veracity. Map is, in fact, one of the very few who could relate what it was actually like, participating at King Henry's court. Other contemporary sources confirm Map's estimate of the king.

One cannot but feel that historians have deliberately omitted this story and any reference to it, because the kindness and humility it shows don't "square" with their own (perhaps self-projected?) image of the man.

In comparing Henry with Kriyananda, everyone who has had any close dealings with Kriyananda must agree that this story about King Henry shows Kriyananda's character as they themselves know it.

King Henry's biographer, Warren Hollister, said that Henry was too refined and intelligent to have had an easy rapport with most of the young men with whom he had trained for knighthood. Though Henry was affable, reacted good-naturedly to barbs received, and offered his friendship unstintingly to others, by no means everyone could understand him. Henry baffled his peers by never losing his temper, never becoming angry, never hating anyone, and never entering into bitter rivalries. Many of his contemporaries, seeing him so different from themselves and from everyone else they knew, held him in some awe. This fact, surely, is the only conceivable explanation for why historians (especially more recently) have assigned dark motives to Henry. I myself, however, who have known Kriyananda for well over thirty years, can say without hesitation that I have observed all these remarkable qualities in him. I have never seen or known him to be angry, or to hold a grudge even toward those who did their best to destroy him, or who had hurt him deeply. He himself has sometimes remarked, "I don't understand the emotion of hatred."

In any case, during the High Middle Ages, and especially among the powerful and pragmatic Norman barons, a new king did not gain the respect of his magnates merely by wearing a crown. With the exception of those in western Normandy who had already lived and thrived under Henry's rule, England's great tenants-in-chief were waiting to see what manner of man was their new king.

CHAPTER 31

Battles and Alliances

Duke Robert, having returned from the Holy Land to Normandy in September 1100, found the duchy in a bad state. It is of this period—which ought to have coincided with his supposed transformation—that Orderic Vitalis was most condemning of the duke's behavior. Orderic wrote that on his favorites Robert lavished castles, lands, and money, and surrounded himself with "harlots and buffoons," who would even steal his clothes when, after too much drinking, he passed out at night. (One wonders what his new bride must have thought of these antics.)

Curthose had already sent a letter to Pope Paschal II, the successor to Urban II, protesting Henry's "seizure" of the English throne. The chroniclers tell us that Robert was planning in some vague way to move against Henry. Many of Henry's most powerful tenants-in-chief wanted to back Curthose against Henry, for they feared the prospect of being dominated by a strong ruler. (Their support of Curthose amounted, in other words, to a vote for anarchy.)

Duke Robert, however, felt also that the hardships he'd endured in the Holy Land entitled him to a little rest and self-indulgence. It was when Ranulf Flambard, as we shall see, escaped the Tower of London, and fired Robert with the hope that England might indeed be his, that things changed.

Ranulf Flambard, when it came to practicing deceit, was in a class by himself. While he was imprisoned in the Tower of

London, he fared better than one might have expected. By no means in "durance vile," he enjoyed his usual sumptuous evening banquet catered by his household staff. One evening, Flambard had a sturdy length of rope smuggled in to him inside a wine cask.

Toasting his jailers, who, after some time, passed out drunk, Ranulf lowered the rope and climbed down to a rendezvous with a group of friends who awaited him at bottom. These men, all cronies of his, had brought him a horse and in addition (we are told), a significant amount of money and treasure. Their only mistake lay in not providing a long enough rope. The rotund Flambard hung dangling at the end of it. When he released his hold on it, however, the drop was only a few feet to the ground. No bones were broken: he was safe. Flambard then, on horseback, made good his escape. He crossed the Channel, and on arriving in Normandy, speedily made his way to the court of Duke Robert Curthose.

It would be interesting to know whether or not the bleary-eyed duke experienced a little *déja vu* when he saw Bishop Ranulf enter the court. Though Ranulf Flambard's manner was obsequious rather than intimidating, he too was a near-despot like the fearful Bishop Odo, who saw in the ever-vacillating duke of Normandy his likeliest path to regained power.

Undoubtedly Ranulf got straight to the point, making it compelling enough to penetrate through whatever fogs swirled in the duke's alcohol-muddled brain:

"With me by your side, my lord," he declaimed, "I promise you'll be king of England within a year!"

Ranulf Flambard was a highly capable man, and worked tirelessly in the "great cause" of furthering his own career. Several points about his unfolding strategy are, however, puzzling. First, why, once he was safely ensconced at the duke's court, did he so intensely urge an invasion of England, the country from which he had only just escaped? He was a wanted man there. There can be one answer: that backing Robert was the one way he could become acceptable again. All he needed was get the "somnolent duke" (as one chronicler described Curthose) onto the island's throne, and

Flambard himself would be "sitting pretty." Chaotic Normandy did not hold the same promise for Rufus' former chief agent.

Flambard made the misjudgment, however, that Bishop Odo had made before: leaning on the same weak reed for support. He might as well have sought a rubber hose for a cane.

Ranulf Flambard knew that, for success in his plans, time was of the essence. Too soon for his ambitions, England's new king would have forged enough alliances to repel any attack his oldest brother could launch. In a few more years, Henry would be ready not only to repel an attack, but to lead a successful invasion into Normandy.

Meanwhile, Curthose was squandering the dowry he'd received from the lovely Sibylla. Soon there would be no way he'd be able to fund an armada. It took all of Flambard's enormous energy to rouse Curthose to action.

Beginning early in the spring of 1101, Duke Robert, under the renegade bishop's prompting, began to assemble a great fleet of ships at Le Tréport, on the northern coast of Normandy.

To make a longish story somewhat short—or, to borrow from Western cowboy movies: "Meanwhile, back at the ranch . . ." King Henry had good reason to expect that many men in England would defect from his own cause when Curthose landed. For not a few of his magnates feared that, once the kingdom was truly secured, Henry would become as arbitrary and autocratic as Rufus. Henry "threatened" them with a rule of law. Robert, on the other hand, offered them free indulgence in their every whim.

By the end of June, Duke Robert's preparations had been nearly completed. At this time King Henry wrote to all his magnates, reaffirming the promises of his Coronation Charter. He asked them once again to swear to defend England against all comers— "especially," he added, "against my brother."

Shortly after issuing this letter, King Henry judged the time ripe to call upon his entire feudal host. He required every landholder, including land-holding churchmen, to appear with the full *servicium debitum* assigned to them as tenants. If one was tenant-in-chief over lands for which the knights' fee was thirty, then to show up with only twenty-nine knights was unacceptable. King Henry ordered out another group of men also, based on the Anglo-Saxon *fyrd*. Thus, quite a large number of English foot soldiers, too, were ready for battle.

King Henry's army camped near Pevensey, where his father had landed in 1066. This was the closest and most direct landing place from Le Tréport on the coast of Normandy, where Curthose had amassed his armada. Additionally, Pevensey was close to the castle of William, count of Mortain and earl of Cornwall, who would (as Dr. Hollister points out) be certain to defect to Curthose at the first possible moment. It was vital that Henry keep an eye on the count, and also on his strategically important lands in Cornwall.

Despite the recent rounds of oath-taking, and though all the men had been ordered to appear, many of Henry's tenants-in-chief simply stayed home. Neither did they send the knights they owed the king, as tenants-in-chief, to Henry. Other men did appear, but with a marked lack of enthusiasm—ready to slip away, it seemed, at the first word of Duke Robert's arrival on English soil. This was only one of the many times in Henry's life when he seemed to be staring defeat in the face, deserted on all sides. But he had already displayed a remarkable talent for survival.

The chroniclers allude to the significant Anglo-Saxon support given to the king. It is reasonable to suppose that the response to his call to the *fyrd* had been successful. As for the magnates, however, nearly all of the greatest landholders allied themselves with Curthose. Indeed, Robert's army was so vastly more powerful than Henry's—in wealth, in the number of knights the magnates were able to field, and in other resources that Robert had at his command—that Henry's cause seemed all but hopeless.

Eadmer, Anselm's biographer, painted a vivid picture: an army encampment where few of the great barons could be relied on to hold their ground once the enemy appeared. King Henry moved through the camp, talking with everyone. He devoted special attention to the wavering magnates, trying to fire them with zeal for his cause. Those whose loyalty seemed particularly wavering he brought to Anselm, himself at the head of the Canterbury contingent, who talked earnestly with each of them, speaking from his own conviction of the righteousness of Henry's cause.

In a moving vignette of the activity in the encampment, the chronicles state that King Henry busied himself with training as many foot soldiers as possible. He went to special lengths to teach them the techniques of warfare, and probably, thereby, saved many lives in future battles. His teaching included how to meet a cavalry charge by mounted knights; how the soldiers should hold their shields; how they should return an enemy's sword strokes. To understand the extraordinary nature of Henry's efforts in this respect, we must remember that the untrained foot soldiers called up in a general levy were low class churls, whom their commanders often treated as the medieval equivalent of "cannon fodder." It was expected that a significant percentage of them would be killed; their officers simply shrugged their shoulders over this problem, and did nothing to alleviate it.

Henry busied himself not only with the Anglo-Saxon foot soldiers, but "frequently," according to contemporary chronicles, moved about through the ranks, encouraging as many as he could.

Henry had taken the precaution of positioning a royal fleet in the Channel. Ranulf Flambard, however, who was guiding Duke Robert's invasion of England, succeeded in bribing several of Henry's ship captains. Thus, a few of the royal fleet, whom Henry had placed as "look outs," ended up piloting the invasion fleet safely past Pevensey, where the king was encamped, and landing it at Portsmouth. There, on July 20, 1101, the Norman army disembarked—safely, and unopposed.

Curthose, after landing, was in a strong position: only twenty to thirty miles south of the royal treasury at Winchester. Henry himself was seventy to eighty miles southeast of this key strategic prize.

For Henry it must have been a serious blow to find that everything he had set in place to receive forewarning of the landing had been sabotaged. It is another proof of his mettle that Henry didn't waste time in repining at the perfidy of the bribed ship captains.

He moved his army swiftly north toward Winchester—in a wide arc which actually took his forces a little above Winchester, before turning and marching in a southwesterly direction. This was his strategy for keeping his own forces between Curthose's army and the city of London even while he moved toward Winchester to protect the royal treasury.

Orderic Vitalis wrote that the pro-Curthose baronial triumvirate of Bellême, Mortain, and Warenne (the three wealthiest landholders in England) met the duke at Portsmouth, then moved together with his troops to camp at Winchester. Curthose then, at the urging of those great barons, sent King Henry a message to either fight or abdicate. Dr. Hollister points out that such an ultimatum was in no way characteristic of Ranulf Flambard; it suggests, therefore, that the triumvirate mentioned had now replaced the bishop of Durham as the duke's main counselors.

At about this time, Archbishop Anselm sent a letter to Duke Robert threatening excommunication. Even were Curthose to defeat Henry in military action, Anselm's power as archbishop of Canterbury to issue this excommunication, and also to determine Flambard's fate as a bishop, was a force to be reckoned with. Flambard, as the architect up to this point of Duke Robert's invasion, knew that Anselm would not look on him with favor. He realized, now, that his only chance of regaining his bishopric was by making his retention of it a part of any treaty signed by Curthose and Henry. Ranulf Flambard, in other words, may well have had a moment of awakening when he realized he was about to make war on the two people who controlled his own future in the church: King Henry and Archbishop Anselm.

In any case, the two armies met near Alton, not far from where Curthose was encamped. In medieval warfare, all-out war was such a horrifying proposition that negotiation was almost always attempted first. Evidently the real negotiating was quickly taken over by the brothers themselves. One account stated that when they met, and after they'd exchanged a few words, they kissed one another on the cheek. It may be that the meeting was somehow deeply moving to sentimental Robert Curthose; it is difficult, otherwise, to explain how very much he simply gave away during the negotiations.

In this Treaty of Alton, Duke Robert relinquished his claim to the throne of England in favor of Henry. (This claim had been the entire purpose of his last six months of effort and expense.) One historian has called the Alton agreement "the most ill-considered step in the whole of Robert's long career of folly." One wonders whether Henry didn't make Robert aware of just how much of a burden he'd insisted on assuming.

In the complex mix of issues that were raised during these events, Archbishop Anselm's threat of excommunication if Robert didn't come to terms with King Henry must have carried special weight. Even if the pope's promise of absolution from all sins for crusaders was not the main reason Curthose took up the cross, that promise was in the very air he breathed during the hardships he endured during those years. Would a knight of the First Crusade jeopardize his hard-won salvation? How much did Curthose really want to be king of England? His proven inability to rule even Normandy, of which he himself was aware, was an important incentive toward his seeking escape in the crusade.

Henry, for his part, agreed to pay Curthose three thousand marks every year for as long as the duke lived. The king also agreed to relinquish his lands in western Normandy, with the one exception of the town of Domfront, which he had sworn never to abandon.

Another clause in the Treaty of Alton called for the restoration of lands to any baron who had been disseised of those lands for supporting either Henry's or Curthose's cause, an unusual clause since the only person who qualified for it was Ranulf Flambard, bishop of Durham.

The Treaty of Alton called, further, for the brothers to take united action in recovering their father's lands and, between them, to punish the "wicked sowers of discord." Hollister points out that King Henry must have remained keenly aware of the way the treaty was worded, to ensure that he had plenty of latitude to do what he knew would be needed: ridding England of chronically disloyal and bellicose barons. Thus the clause concerning punishing the "wicked sowers of discord" between the brothers was, for him, a welcome addition.

Archbishop Anselm must have been closely involved in these negotiations, for it was only by his order that Ranulf Flambard could have been reinstated to the bishopric of Durham—as indeed he was. Anselm even went a step further: he issued a special charter absolving Flambard *in absentia* of his conviction for simony and "other high crimes." The special treatment Ranulf Flambard received supports Dr. Hollister's reconstruction of Flambard's switch to the role of secret negotiator with King Henry to arrange that he himself would be restored to the bishopric of Durham.

Anselm's willingness to reinstate Flambard, who was a very embodiment of everything Anselm was trying to expunge from the church, is truly remarkable. The only conclusion to be drawn from this seemingly excessive leniency is that Anselm, a practical man, felt that, in Henry, the country and the church had a king worth nearly every compromise in areas of lesser importance. Everything Anselm hoped to accomplish for the church of England would be possible only against a backdrop of peace and order. He would sacrifice much to ensure that Henry remained on the throne of England.

Judging from the low-profile, but gratifyingly constructive, presence of Ranulf Flambard through the coming years, King Henry and Anselm together must have made it clear to him that, as bishop of Durham, his former ways would no longer be tolerated. Flambard died in 1128, at a ripe old age. During his remaining years he oversaw the remodeling and new construction of Durham Cathedral, which included in the nave and choir the first known example in England of pointed ribbed vaults as a way of carrying the building's weight. Durham Cathedral is an architectural wonder, manifested largely through the tireless energy of Ranulf Flambard. (Ribbed vaulting appeared first in Normandy in William the Conqueror and Queen Matilda's abbeys, St. Etienne and La Trinité.)

As historian Sally Vaughn points out, King Henry and Archbishop Anselm together, in averting the crisis of 1101, had fielded an army and saved Henry's crown—an effort that included the following measures: applying every diplomatic means possible; motivating those barons who were wavering; and shaping the concluding treaty. Such close cooperation between monarch and primate was rare in history; the only other collaboration easily recalled to mind occurred between William the Conqueror and Lanfranc.

Now, alas, there occurred another clash between the king and his archbishop—though this one must rather be viewed as a clash between the principles of kingship held by Henry, and Anselm's vow of obedience to the pope. Neither Henry nor Anselm ever looked upon their diplomatic maneuverings in a personal light.

Soon after they'd concluded the Treaty of Alton, and while Curthose was still at Henry's court, the envoys whom king and primate had each sent to Pope Paschal II, asking that England be restored to its "former usages," had returned from their mission. Instead of letters for both king and archbishop, the envoys carried only one letter, addressed to King Henry. For Anselm, this apparent rebuff by the pope was surely disconcerting.

As expected, the pope had not budged an inch on allowing the king to invest prelates. Because Anselm was hearing this second hand, however, through the pope's letter to the king, the archbishop's position was undercut.

Henry moved immediately to capitalize on the advantage he'd gained. Knowing by now—as he certainly must have—that Anselm's heart was not in the investitures issue, the king may have reasoned that an application of royal pressure now might allow his archbishop, even as an obedient son of the church, to find a loophole in Paschal's omission to address him directly.

Henry conveyed word to Anselm that he must either submit on the issues of investiture and homage, or else leave the country—a nearly exact reversal of the roles they'd played when Anselm had threatened to leave the country unless the king gave up the investiture of prelates. Henry restated his position: "I am not willing to lose the usages of my predecessors, nor to tolerate anyone in my kingdom who is not my man."

It is important to understand that Anselm did not personally consider investiture to be much more than a formal ritual—a papal ban on something which, in practice (so Anselm suspected), would often be supported by the king's own archbishops. For Henry, the act of investing prelates was part of the sacred duties and responsibilities of the king, and a rule that his father had followed as his unchallenged right. He would never allow English land, and the responsibilities and duties of the crown, to pass to churchmen unless they first did homage to him as king. This investiture issue was important especially considering (as I said earlier) that the church-related fiefs amounted to fully one fourth of the total area of England. The act of investiture was the moment when a prelate, on receiving the symbols of his new office from the monarch's own hands, acknowledged that all land and privileges were the king's to bestow, withhold, or withdraw. It was, to Henry, a sacred exchange between king and vassal.

Even more galling to Anselm, two of the churchmen present represented the pope, though they claimed not to be papal legates. Pope Paschal had also failed to respond to a second epistle from Anselm asking that he himself be allowed to represent the pope in all matters concerning the church in England. Not only had Paschal seemed to ignore Anselm's letter, but Anselm now found himself confronted with two papal representatives. Whether Paschal had acted intentionally or not, Anselm began to feel that perhaps some veiled insult was intended here.

Considering investiture to be a secondary issue, Anselm seems to have had trouble understanding the reason for Henry's deep feeling in the matter. However, the archbishop actually felt the same way concerning anything that challenged the rights and privileges connected with the see of Canterbury. Additionally, Anselm, like Lanfranc before him, felt that he, as primate of England, should be appointed the *ex-officio* papal legate within the country. It was the view of both Lanfranc and Anselm that the "vast and perilous

extent of seas and kingdoms," in the words of Eadmer, made it too
difficult for a papal legate from Rome to operate in England in the
best interests of either the papacy or the church. Local ecclesiastical
affairs ought to be overseen by local prelates, and not by someone
from far away, appointed by the pope.

These issues were Anselm's top priorities in his relationship with
both king and pope; investitures was not of great moment to him.
It is important to note that King Henry backed Archbishop Anselm
completely on the three issues that really mattered to Anselm:
1) recognition of the archbishop of Canterbury as primate of all
the church of England; 2) insistence that the pope's authority in
England was best represented by the archbishop of Canterbury,
not by legatine envoys from Rome; and 3) freedom to call ecclesiastical councils within England for the legislation of church reforms.

Now Archbishop Anselm, standing before King Henry at his
September 1101 court, politely but firmly refused to leave England.
He then returned to Canterbury to await further developments.
Since King Henry did not want Anselm to go any more than
Anselm did, the matter for the time being rested there.

It was late spring 1102 when Pope Paschal finally responded to
Anselm. His response was very nearly a boilerplate letter reaffirming
the papacy's position vis-à-vis investiture, and stating, "Lay princes
must be altogether excluded from ecclesiastical elections." It is interesting that Anselm simply chose to ignore this particular tenet of
orthodox Gregorian reform, which would by definition forbid King
Henry from having a hand in choosing those prelates who would
hold significant lands of the crown. The pope's message certainly did
not mesh with Anselm's own views, which had been those also of his
predecessor, Lanfranc. Both men saw the king and primate as resem-
bling two plow horses yoked together, pulling the plow that shaped
the kingdom temporally as well as spiritually. The king, in Anselm's
view, needed a strong hand in shaping the church and in choosing
its leaders, owing to the temporal power wielded by these men. In
fact, as the years went by, and for the rest of Henry's reign, no archbishop tried to interfere with the king's choice of prelates; Henry, for

his part, usually consulted with church leaders about anyone he was considering for a high church office.

With the resolution of Robert Curthose's claim to the throne of England, King Henry's strength as a leader increased in power as he moved vigorously against the chronic troublemakers in the kingdom.

Individually, the English landholders were no strangers to Henry. He had grown up with many of them; fought beside them (and, in some cases, against them); trained with some of them for knighthood; heard his father discuss them and their families; knew of decades of oaths and promises kept and broken, patterns of kinship, and a great deal more. Of those who had arrayed themselves with Curthose against him, Henry could easily tell who would never cooperate with him under any circumstances.

King Henry's action against his intransigent barons took place over many months. In no case did it suggest reprisal for opposing Henry during Duke Robert's bid for the throne.

Since Robert Curthose himself was still in England, where, probably, he remained until sometime in early December 1101, the duke himself was present when Henry disseised William II of Warenne of his lands. Curthose had shown himself extremely sensitive to any act that might be taken as a reprisal against those who had sided with him. Clearly, he was satisfied that William of Warenne's forfeiture in September 1101 was for causes connected with private warfare, which William had been constantly waging against his neighbors, rather than for his support of Curthose's cause some months earlier.

With the throne of England secure, King Henry now strictly enforced, as had William the Conqueror, the long-established ban on wars against one's neighbors. Over the next two years, Ivo of Grandmesnil was fined heavily by Henry, and Robert de Lacy was disseised—in both cases for inflicting violence on their neighbors' lands, destroying their crops, burning, plundering, and (in at least one case) building a castle without royal permission, an act that had been forbidden since the time of the Conqueror.

Henry, in his Coronation Charter, had promised to enforce "the king's peace" throughout the land. He now demonstrated that he fully intended to carry out that promise. His Coronation Charter had not, in other words, been a campaign "sop" offered to a war-weary nation with the purpose of winning needed support. The new king now oversaw the steady, consistent enforcement of laws that prohibited baronial bullying. Wisely, Henry treated first-time offenders differently from chronic ones. Otherwise, however, he applied the law even-handedly.

In 1102 King Henry confronted Robert of Bellême, the baron who, more than any other, continued to act as though he were a law unto himself. This would be no easy task. Robert of Bellême controlled thirty-four castles in England alone, mostly in Shrewsbury and eastern Wales, and his two brothers, Arnulf of Montgomery and Roger "the Poitevin," were his willing allies.

Beginning in the autumn of 1101, the king had his agents watch Robert of Bellême very closely. By Easter 1102, Henry was in a position to confront Robert with a catalogue of no fewer than forty-five offenses. Orderic Vitalis expressed them as having been "committed against the king and his brother Duke Robert," carefully reflecting the fact that the act of bringing these charges was in complete compliance with the Treaty of Alton. Confronted with these unanswerable charges, Robert of Bellême asked the king for permission to withdraw and consult with his advisers. Instead, he seized that opportunity to escape.

Although the contemporary chroniclers again offer us a somewhat confused account of Henry's campaign against Robert of Bellême, what emerges clearly is that he built a careful case against this malefactor, publicly declared him an outlaw, and once again summoned him to court to answer the charges against him. Only after proper procedural steps did Henry call up the entire feudal levy, as well as the old Anglo-Saxon *fyrd*: one foot soldier for every five hides of land. Robert of Bellême's only allies were his two brothers, whom Henry had also summoned to answer charges concerning their own violations of the king's peace. It was probably Henry's "iron-clad case" against Robert, as well as the earl's repellent personal history of torture and brutality, that now isolated him.

Arundel Castle, Robert's stronghold in Shropshire, was Henry's first military objective in April 1102. After overseeing the construction of siege towers, the king left a siege army in place at Arundel and moved the rest of his army to another Bellême fortress at Tickhill. The garrison of Tickhill surrendered as soon as they saw Henry's army, and acknowledged the king as "their natural lord." Arundel held out until July, the garrison commander following the usual procedure of requesting reinforcements from their lord, and, when these were not forthcoming, seeking his permission to surrender.

After the surrender of Arundel, King Henry disbanded his army and let them return to their homes; it was time for them to tend their crops. Thus, the king kept only enough men through the summer months to make sure that the three brothers, all of whom were under siege, would not be able to conduct raids with a view to restocking their dwindling provisions.

Henry also sent messengers to Robert Curthose, reminding him of their agreement to take joint action against traitors. In response Duke Robert undertook a siege of the Bellême fortress at Vignats in Normandy. The siege failed, owing to Curthose's usual low-energy approach, and also to treachery within the duke's own ranks. Indeed, the Bellême garrison at Vignats went on a rampage of reprisal through the surrounding countryside. Once again Normandy suffered because of Duke Robert's ineptitude.

Most interestingly, there emerges from this period an amazing portrait of King Henry; it owes greatly to the researches of C. Warren Hollister. Because contemporary chroniclers supply a plethora of conflicting information on the sequence of events in the campaign against Bellême, Hollister made a study of the royal charters signed by the king during this period. A charter always notes the place as well as the date when it was issued. A pattern of the king's movements begins to emerge for the period from April to September, 1102.

What comes sharply into focus is the picture of a highly energetic monarch constantly on the move, overseeing a military campaign with many *foci*, at the head of his army when it counted
most, and developing its strategy. At the same time, in those intervals when he was attending to other matters, King Henry was
himself besieged by administrative business, which followed him
doggedly everywhere.

In mid-August Henry again called up the feudal levy and *fyrd*,
and made short work of taking Bellême's castle Bridgnorth before
moving on to Shrewsbury. Orderic Vitalis, narrating this part of
the royal campaign, interjects an anecdote that illuminates another
aspect of King Henry's nature. It seems that, between Bridgnorth
and Shrewsbury, there was a section of road that narrowed significantly as it passed through a dense wood. This part of the road was
known locally as "Hovelhege" or "the evil path," because brigands
and cutthroats of all descriptions had used it for decades as the
ideal spot from which to attack travelers.

The king, hearing these stories, ordered his army to clear the
trees from both sides of the road, widening it considerably to provide safe passage for "all travelers ever afterwards."

It was at his castle at Shrewsbury that Robert of Bellême had
fortified himself. However, the chroniclers tell us that when Robert
saw King Henry's army approaching, and recognized that further
resistance was futile, he immediately surrendered Shrewsbury
Castle, personally handed over the keys to the king, and acknowledged the forfeiture of his English lands. He was escorted to the
coast, where he took ship for Normandy, to the welcome laxness
of the overlord there.

Orderic Vitalis wrote: "All England rejoiced as the cruel tyrant
went into exile." King Henry, as usual, sought immediately to close
and heal the wound left by the removal of so entrenched and powerful a tenant-in-chief.

Typical of Henry's effective and, it might even be said, kind
way of working with men is the case of William Pantulf, one of
Robert of Bellême's most important vassals. Henry managed to

win Pantulf to the royal cause and immediately gave him, as a mark of trust, the stewardship of Stafford castle in east Wales, including the task of bringing peace and order to the countryside around that castle. The king's trust in William Pantulf proved to be thoroughly justified. In succeeding years William Pantulf was able to persuade some of the troublesome Welsh lords to ally themselves with the king. He himself never thereafter wavered in his loyalty and duty to Henry.

As the second year of his reign came to a close, King Henry had not only faced down his brother's claim to England, but had rid the kingdom of its most violent, lawless barons.

CHAPTER 32

The Divine Role of Kings

By **this time it** was becoming widely felt once again, as had been the case with William the Conqueror, that the king's actions had divine sanction. Though it is very difficult to know how much weight to give this aspect of medieval society, it was true of that time that most people thought that the success of their crops, the absence of sickness, freedom from the fear of invasion, success in war, prosperity in commerce, and many other blessings came to them at least in part by the king's ability to attract divine grace through his reverence for God and the righteousness of his deeds.

William Rufus, because of the way he treated the church, his blasphemy, and his immoral personal lifestyle had caused great uneasiness in the country. People were convinced that their king was not living under the sanction of God's will and grace. It was not only the monk chroniclers who perceived Rufus's accidental death as a divine curse. The impression was general.

By contrast, King Henry had effected the return of the universally revered Anselm, and virtually the whole country knew that the archbishop himself had encamped with Canterbury's knights and all the king's army at Pevensey in the summer of 1101, urging all to do their utmost to support King Henry. The people felt that the affairs of state were once more being handled in a way that was pleasing to God. Henry had also given the country its first queen in seventeen years—a queen from the bloodline of the royal house of Wessex. King Henry and Queen Edith Matilda represented a new unity, and also, in their progeny, a propitious blending of royal blood, both new and ancient.

King Henry's campaign against Robert of Bellême was, for the remainder of Henry's long reign, his last battle on English soil. While the rest of Western Europe was riven by private wars; papal armies clashed with the anti-pope; the Holy Roman Empire embroiled itself in bloody internal struggles for power; and Christian Crusaders fought the infidel in the Holy Land, England enjoyed the gift of thirty-three years of unbroken peace.

This period, beginning in 1102, allowed the English people to devote themselves to matters other than fending off invaders and replanting crops that had been destroyed by vengeful neighbors. The period coincides perfectly with what historians have called the Twelfth Century Renaissance. Sir Kenneth Clark dubbed it "The Great Thaw."

It was a time period when man made greater leaps forward than would ordinarily seem possible—a time of outstanding energy, and strength of will and intellect. We can see it in the impressive architecture of Durham Cathedral and the east end of Canterbury. From the midst of small clusters of wooden houses, the rise of these "orderly mountains of stone," as Kenneth Clark expressed it, happened in a single lifetime—achievements that imply wealth, technical skill, and the political stability to push through such long-term projects.

With England enjoying a stability and peace that it had not known since Roman times, King Henry set about to recreate something else that had been lost during the reign of Rufus: a unity between his *curiales* on the one hand (those who surrounded the king and advised him in national affairs), and his tenants-in-chief on the other (those great landholders who served as extensions of the royal authority and made it possible for that authority to be extended to every part of the realm). Under William the Conqueror, that group of men had to a very great degree fulfilled both these functions. Under King William Rufus, his *curiales*—daily advisors and intimates—had not generally been great landholders. The landholders had attended court very infrequently, to the great detriment of good government, and with the result that, in the thirteen years of Rufus's reign, there were two baronial uprisings.

King Henry I was now determined that only those who were great landholders, and who had shown themselves loyal to the king, should be his friends and *curiales*. Additionally, Henry set about making great landholders of those who had already demonstrated both loyalty to him, and sound counsel.

In the early twelfth century, as in William the Conqueror's time, the stability and peace of the kingdom depended on these close, personal ties.

CHAPTER 33

Henry's "New Men"

King Henry was now free at last to turn his attention to uniting a loyal, highly capable group of men under him to help him with the governance of his kingdom: capable administrators and wise personal advisors.

Orderic Vitalis wrote in a much-quoted passage that the king's advisors and administrators were men whom Henry himself had "raised from the dust." More recent historians have drawn the conclusion from this statement that Henry only wanted supporters who owed him everything. In fact, however, Henry worked with all sorts of men, creating a broad, highly skilled, and dedicated group of royal servants, men who acted as a harmonious, tightly knit, visionary group. They worked closely with the king, and usually traveled with him on his peregrinations around the kingdom as well as, later on, across the Channel. Both C. Warren Hollister and Judith Green explain in great detail, however, that Henry's men were drawn almost entirely from the upper echelons of an aristocracy that had not yet become rigidly stratified.

Rather than approaching the matter of who were the king's closest men solely from a statistical perspective—how many royal charters each attested, for example, and how many knights' fees of land each held—let us look first at men whom Henry did raise from low positions, and who served him in crucial ways.

Prominent among them was Roger, the "poor priest of Avranches," and the only member of the king's closest circle of whom it may safely be said that Henry did, in fact, raise him "from the dust." As we noted above, it is thought that Henry met Roger of Avranches in 1088–1090, when nineteen-year-old Henry, as the new count of the Cotentin, had the task of creating a countship in western Normandy, where none had existed before.

From about the year 1110, Henry gave Roger, in whom he placed great faith, an executive role in the royal treasury. Both Roger and the tax collection systems had to make speed that year to gather the enormous geld levied for the ten thousand mark dowry of Henry's daughter, Princess Matilda. Under Roger's long leadership (1110–1138), the exchequer—including accounting, collecting taxes, assessing gelds, and creating a high-quality coinage—became coherent and efficient.

Probably Roger, who became bishop of Salisbury under Henry, also played a part in the great increase of judicial activity in the 1120s. A man of enormous energy, Roger conscientiously discharged his diocesan duties even when serving as regent during King Henry's absences in Normandy.

These are the bare facts about a pivotal individual in Henry's life and reign. Some of the other dynamics between King Henry and Roger bishop of Salisbury tell us even more about how Henry viewed the questions of leadership and loyalty. In 1114, and again in 1123, during both of which years it was necessary to appoint a new archbishop of Canterbury, Roger of Salisbury, and Robert Bloet bishop of Lincoln, headed contingents that opposed the idea of naming a monk rather than a secular clerk to the archbishopric. Significantly, this meant on both occasions that they placed themselves in opposition to the king's own thinking on the matter.

In 1114, when a vacancy occurred in Canterbury (owing to the death of Anselm), Henry proposed to fill the vacancy with Faritius, a learned Italian monk, who was then abbot of Abingdon, the king's personal physician, and one of the most highly regarded scholars in Western Europe. Bishops Roger and Robert, however, asserted that the post could not be filled by one whose hands had been contaminated by handling the urine of women. The king replied mildly that he would leave the choice to them, provided that it was acceptable to the monks and the people of Canterbury. (Swami Kriyananda, it may be mentioned here, has often yielded to those under him, in the name of a greater priority: that of harmony.)

Thus, the "witty and easy-going" Ralph d'Escures was elected to the Canterbury archbishopric. Despite his reputation for affability, once installed as archbishop he took up the cause of Canterbury's primacy against York with a zeal that, in its public expression, often looked like petulance. One cannot help feeling that Henry's choice of Faritius would have served the kingdom better. However, nothing served everyone so well, or created greater loyalty to Henry, as his willingness to compromise on points that were, ultimately, of secondary importance.

Henry's thirty-five years on the throne of England have been absurdly characterized as a kind of reign of terror, with the king himself harshly repressive of everyone around him. A few historians have actually stated that the reason Henry created his own "new men" out of talented but non-aristocratic and impoverished "nobodies" was to exact unthinking obedience from people who owed him everything, as king.

In any case, the known facts of King Henry's court present a completely different picture. In the example I've just given, we see that the quintessential "new man," Roger of Salisbury, disagreed openly with the king. Moreover, these were not disagreements on petty matters—such as, perhaps, the right stipend for a scullery maid—but involved decisions that for years to come would affect the entire kingdom.

What were the consequences to Bishop Roger of his dissension? He never fell out of the king's favor; nor did he suffer any demotion. In fact, the king continued to express his friendship and support for Bishop Roger until his own death.

This is only one example of Henry's leadership, showing that he encouraged individual initiative, supported the well-being of all in his service, and frequently demonstrated his loyalty to others who had shown themselves loyal to him.

Bishop Roger, once the "poor priest of Avranches," represented within Henry's *curiales* a very small group of men who had come with absolutely no pedigree.

In the end we must surely agree with Hollister's insight that a regime designed to *prevent* the rise of new men would not be very successful or attractive. Henry's rule, by contrast, was as successful and as attractive as any in history.

William II of Warenne, from the greatest of the Conquest families, was someone who seems to have made a nuisance of himself in Normandy at the court of Curthose. He complained incessantly to the duke that, in the duke's cause, he had lost his family's enormous holdings in England, and had been left with nothing to show for it. (In fact we must recall that Henry disseised William in 1101 for conducting private warfare.) He must have been either movingly eloquent in his appeal, or perhaps he simply caught Curthose in a compliant state of inebriation. Ultimately, in any case, the duke responded to William's importunities and made another of his impulsive, self-destructive decisions. Almost alone, Curthose—in the company only of William of Warenne and a handful of others—crossed the Channel in the summer of 1103, and arrived completely unannounced to plead his vassal's cause with his brother, Henry.

When Henry learned of Curthose's uninvited landing, almost alone, on England's shores, he was (according to the chroniclers) "distressed." In fact, however, it seems much more likely that he was simply amazed that even foolhardy Robert would place himself in such an extraordinarily disadvantageous position. Henry at once understood the advantages that might be gained from this situation. It is impossible to imagine him being angry with Robert for this almost pathetically ill-considered act. Henry sent his brother quite a different message, however, through Robert of Meulan, who led a small contingent of the king's *familiares* to talk with Curthose.

The count of Meulan must have found high entertainment in the incongruities of the situation. The last time he'd seen Curthose arrive on the English coast, the duke had come at the head of a large invading force to claim the throne for himself. Now here stood this same duke, virtually cap in hand, accompanied by William II of Warenne and a handful of other intimates who could only have been acutely embarrassed to be coming on such a fool's errand.

Robert of Meulan, however, pretended grimness. He warned Duke Robert of Henry's terrible anger on hearing that his brother had dared to come there uninvited. The king—so continued Robert of Meulan—was considering throwing Duke Robert into prison: such (he said) was the intensity of his fury. This threat, the chroniclers related, plunged Curthose into a state of intense fear. Robert of Meulan, tongue firmly in cheek, went on to assure Curthose that he would intercede personally with the king on the duke's behalf, and do his best to soften the royal rage.

The chroniclers wrote that Duke Robert was then conducted to Henry's court, where he hid his apprehension behind a mask of easy insouciance. The king met his brother pleasantly—probably because he perceived no need for further intimidation. After some discussion, King Henry agreed to reinvest William II of Warenne with the earldom of Surrey, provided that William promised to be absolutely loyal, now, to King Henry. Duke Robert then placed William's hands between Henry's. Thus was accomplished the formal transfer of William's allegiance from Curthose to King Henry.

King Henry required another concession from his brother. Queen Edith Matilda, he said, as Duke Robert's goddaughter, asked if the duke would, out of love for her, relinquish his annual three-thousand-mark payment from King Henry and England. This was, of course, the central prize Duke Robert had gained by formally renouncing his claim to England's throne in the Treaty of Alton. Robert's profligacy left him perennially broke. However, in these compromised circumstances, which he'd created for himself, there was nothing he could do but agree to this request.

Orderic Vitalis concludes the story by observing that William of Warenne "served the king faithfully for the remaining thirty-three years they both lived." William was evidently not at Henry's court very frequently after their reconciliation, but clearly the king was steadily drawing him in, for by the time of the battle of Tinchebray, Normandy, in 1106, King Henry appointed William of Warenne as a field commander. Again, according to Orderic's account, William of Warenne's younger brother, Rainald, who had inherited the Warenne family's lands in Flanders and was an avid supporter of Robert Curthose, had been captured by Henry's men in a skirmish before Tinchebray. Orderic tells us that Henry released William's brother Rainald just before the battle, an act which pleased William very much, and inspired him to urge the troops under his command to fight valiantly for their noble king.

When, in 1119, Normandy was threatened by a strong coalition of its neighbors, William of Warenne remained firm in his loyalty to King Henry. He is quoted in the *Hyde Chronicle* as saying to King Henry, "There is no one who can persuade me to treason. I and my kinsmen here and now place ourselves in mortal opposition to the king of France, and are totally faithful to you. I will support this undertaking, with my men, in the first rank of your army and will myself sustain the full burden of battle."

King Henry had patiently coaxed William of Warenne along a winding path from those first days of his reign when William had frequently ridiculed the new king, to a place among the king's most trusted cross-Channel advisors and *familiares*. Others have pointed to William of Warenne's evolution from rebellious baron to dedicated royalist. I myself perceive an even subtler transformation in Earl William—from an attitude of barefaced self-interest to one of willing self-sacrifice for a greater good, which included maintaining the peace and supporting all the ideals expressed by Henry during his kingship.

One man whom historians have cited to show Henry's coldness toward *familiares* of his who had fallen out of his favor was Robert Bloet, bishop of Lincoln. The bishop in old age had lost two lawsuits in royal court, and had grumbled against Henry about what he considered the unfair outcome. In fact, as Warren Hollister discovered on researching the matter, the cases had been trivial, and the grumbling was probably due to the bishop's senility. A monk had heard him complain and had decided to make a case of it. Henry himself, however, did much to soften the judgment against his friend Robert. Robert, on the other hand, far from losing favor with Henry, was riding with the king and one other man at the time of Robert's death. Robert suddenly cried out, "My lord King, I am dying!" King Henry leaped from his horse and caught his old friend as he fell, carried him to a nearby huntsman's lodge, and stayed with him over the next hours until Robert Bloet died.

The above accounts go on to relate more about some of those who were close to Henry, and who were members of his *curiales* and *familiares*. A close study of the known details of Henry's reign reveals many more instances of his finely-tuned skills as a leader, including his extraordinary patience in creating a close loyal following. Again, one can only marvel at the historians who have depicted Henry as a cold man whom anyone with a warm heart would have done his best to avoid. They seem, as I have said, more like intellectual chess players than flesh-and-blood human beings.

Even those historians who describe Henry as an essentially repugnant person have acknowledged that he created a rational and effective government. Dr. Hollister challenged two of his contemporaries, to whom Henry's government seemed only a "machine," to ponder what it takes to create a system that is *human*, and that functions harmoniously:

"A successful king," wrote Hollister, "must above all else be capable of dealing with his subjects skillfully. Administrative machine-building is a kind of political science, whereas good personal relationships are a political art. In this sense, Henry I was not only a scientist, but an artist."

Some historians have suggested that the anarchy of Stephen's reign, which followed Henry's, was the natural result of Henry's so-called repressive regime. They imply that a kind of seething cauldron of baronial rage boiled beneath the surface, kept in check only by Henry's iron-fisted control and by the general fear of reprisals against anyone who "stepped out of line." Considering the vast array of personalities involved, however, and the varying motivations that Henry's leadership accommodated and regularly rewarded, it seems obvious that Stephen's anarchic reign was in fact a consequence of England's sudden loss of a strong, clear-headed, and decisive leader. King Stephen soon showed himself quixotic and vacillating; the aristocracy deeply felt the lack of effective leadership. Henry had, alas, been unable to provide a good successor. As Dr. Hollister observes, the Anglo-Norman magnates, accustomed as they were to effective, centralized royal authority, found themselves, after Henry's death, drifting without a rudder on a heaving sea of uncertainties.

Even while Henry was expending great energy in building mutually supportive relationships with his tenants-in-chief, the investiture issue demanded further attention. Just after Duke Robert and his entourage finally departed for Normandy (in late 1101), Henry invited Anselm to his court to seek a resolution to their shared dilemma with Pope Paschal. Henry and Robert of Meulan proposed that both king and archbishop again send personal envoys to Pope Paschal, making essentially the same request: for a reconsideration of his position on investiture as it pertained to England. They wanted the kingdom to be allowed to retain its "former usages." This time, however, the envoys were very high ranking prelates (two bishops and an archbishop), and Henry and Robert of Meulan proposed to include a list of consequences if the pope did not accede to this request: 1) a withholding of Peter's Pence (a geld sent annually to the pope); 2) the withdrawal of England's backing from Pope Paschal—a compelling threat in view of the anti-pope's power in those times; and 3) Archbishop Anselm would once again be sent into exile.

It was obvious to Anselm that all three of these threats were directed solely at maximizing the pressure on Pope Paschal II, for Anselm readily agreed to the proposal. Furthermore, Anselm wrote a letter of his own to the pope, "laying it on thick" so to speak: "They would expel me from the kingdom rather than obey this decree, *and* they would leave the Roman Church."

The distinguished group of prelates, representing both Anselm and the king, returned in the spring of 1102 to England, bearing Paschal's answers. Predictably, Paschal did not budge an inch on investitures. However, and significantly, he did not repeat his ban on prelates doing homage to lay persons. The great student of medieval times, R.W. Southern, wrote that Paschal never again mentioned the issue of homage, and that this was the beginning of the compromise that was ultimately adopted—though it would not be Paschal himself who proposed it.

Archbishop Anselm had asked once again for legatine authority (the power to represent the pope) within England, and requested also that no papal legates be sent there. In Paschal's response to the archbishop, this long-standing wish of Anselm's was fulfilled.

At this point in the envoys' report, another one of those "events" occurred which hopelessly muddy the waters of diplomacy: the two bishops and the archbishop who had represented the king before Pope Paschal now swore to Henry that the pope had told them confidentially that, if King Henry "behaved as a good Christian prince," Paschal would permit him to continue to invest prelates without any consequences. Anselm's envoys vehemently denied that Paschal had said any such thing, to which the king's envoys replied that Paschal had meant it for their ears only.

King Henry may or may not have believed his envoys: they were, after all, dedicated royalists. There has been endless speculation on this subject, with even an official church publication called *Councils and Synods* weighing in with a church view of the matter, stating that the king's envoys were not lying outright, but had misconstrued something Paschal may have said concerning the pope's willingness to consider some level of compromise on the prelate homage issue. It seems highly unlikely that King Henry and Robert of Meulan would have helped to concoct any plan that would bear so little fruit, and that carried so great a potential for embarrassment, since the lie could be exposed by simply consulting the pope again.

Henry, however, not one to miss opportunities, immediately made the best of the conflicting stories brought by the envoys to gain certain short-term concessions from Anselm. The king asked Anselm to recognize and accept that this was indeed what Paschal had said. Though the archbishop was in a sense in a worse position than before, the confusion did delay his own exile while he wrote again to the pope, requesting clarification. Hollister stated that Anselm, in this letter, came as close as he ever did to outright pleading with the pope to drop the ban on lay investiture as far as England was concerned. This side-eddy into which he had been drawn by his vow of obedience would likely force Anselm to abandon the reform of the church in England, and his fight for a unified English church under Canterbury's primacy—issues which the archbishop considered his real work. Exile, for Anselm, at this stage of his life, was painful to contemplate.

Henry and Anselm now made two important concessions to each other which expressed their deep mutual respect and support—despite the surface friction that had been produced by their respective positions. Anselm agreed to allow Henry to invest prelates "for the time being," without fear of excommunication—though Anselm would not consecrate prelates that had been invested by the king. And Henry agreed to let Anselm call the first great primatial reform council in England since the days of William the Conqueror and Lanfranc.

This first council, convened in September 1102, produced a great deal of church legislation. Simony was again condemned and monastic discipline was tightened. New mechanisms were put in place which would more effectively protect parish churches from the inroads of unscrupulous laymen. The clergy were required to dress and behave appropriately (for example, priests were not to wear multicolored clothing or fancy shoes, attend drinking parties, or imbibe alcohol to excess). The most controversial canons were those which enforced clerical celibacy. Lanfranc's synod of 1076 had ordered that no priest thereafter could marry, but that those priests who were already married might keep their wives.

Anselm's council of 1102 went farther: it prohibited clerical marriage altogether, and required all married clergy to abandon either their wives or their vocations.

The archbishop proceeded to act immediately on some of the newly adopted canons, so that everyone would understand that he was serious about enforcing them. Anselm deposed nine abbots and abbots-elect on the spot for simony; six of them had purchased their offices from King William Rufus. This great primatial council included not only a large number of bishops and abbots, but also many lay magnates who had attended at Anselm's invitation. Thus, as Eadmer wrote, the decisions of the council were understood as having been ratified by both the clergy and the laity of the kingdom.

The great cloud over the investiture issue, however, which remained unresolved, rolled back in upon them. By March 1103, both Anselm and Henry had received responses from Pope Paschal hotly denying the statements of King Henry's envoys, Archbishop Gerard of York and the two other bishops, that Paschal had privately indicated his readiness to "wink" at Henry's investing prelates provided the king proved cooperative with him in all other ways.

Both king and archbishop knew that they were running out of options. Remarkably, both men decided to act as if neither of them had yet opened and read the letters from Paschal. In this way they could continue to operate in the more comfortable area provided them by the prelates' false story. At last, however, the inevitable moment arrived: Anselm suggested they open and read together their respective letters from Paschal. King Henry refused, saying: "What business have I with the pope about the things that are mine? If anyone wishes to rob me of them, he is my enemy."

Historian Vaughn expresses well the archbishop's terrible dilemma: he was "caught between two grinding stones." In addition, the issue was coming to a final head at an impossibly bad time for both men. Following Anselm's primatial council, and the removal of nine abbots for simony, many vacant abbacies needed to be filled.

When Anselm read his letter from Pope Paschal, he found that there were three more bishoprics to fill, for the pope had ordered Anselm to excommunicate those bishops who had created the fiction that the pope was prepared to turn a blind eye to Henry's investiture of prelates.

Pope Paschal's opposition to Henry, moreover, through Anselm, was occurring just when the new king was deeply focused on building a loyal baronage and administration. The conferring of high church office was one of the most important ways in which the king could reward those who had served him well—especially as the royal demesne lands, from which the king had been able to grant land, were shrinking.

King Henry now pleaded with Archbishop Anselm to go to Rome personally and lay the king's case before Paschal. The archbishop agreed, though with understandable reluctance. It was a dangerous and arduous journey, and Anselm was now approaching his seventieth birthday.

William Warelwast, a devoted royal servant who traveled nearly continuously on diplomatic missions for the king, accompanied Anselm to Rome. There, not surprisingly, they encountered once again the pope's adamant refusal to allow King Henry to invest English prelates. On the return journey from Rome, Warelwast carried out the second part of his instructions from King Henry (as reported by Eadmer). The king's most trusted envoy said to Anselm:

"What [King Henry] says is that if you return to him on the understanding that you will treat him in all respects as your predecessors are known to have treated his predecessors, he'll be glad to approve of your returning to England, and will welcome you."

"Is that all you will say?" asked Anselm.

"To you, a word is enough. There is no need to say anything more of this matter," responded William Warelwast diplomatically.

"I hear what you say, and I take your meaning," said Anselm. With this exchange in November 1103, began Anselm's second period of exile from England. He turned aside to begin an extended stay at the home of a friend, the archbishop of Lyons. Over the entire period of Anselm's exile the king wrote him many letters, urging him to return to England so that they might work together for the country's welfare, as William the Conqueror and Lanfranc had done.

Meanwhile, Henry made great strides in creating loyalty around him. Eustace count of Boulogne, who had been disseised by William Rufus for his part in the baronial uprising of 1088, was reinstated by Henry, and remained loyal to the king for the rest of his life. The king further expressed his faith in Eustace by giving to him in marriage Mary, the younger sister of Queen Edith Matilda.

Ivo of Grandmesnil, who at the time of Curthose's invasion in 1101 had withheld his support from Henry, had subsequently run afoul of the king by waging private wars. His lands now passed, at his own request and with the king's hearty concurrence, to Robert count of Meulan. This seems to have been one step, for Ivo, towards turning over a new leaf. Through the intercession of Robert of Meulan, Ivo was at last reconciled as the king's vassal; he now undertook his second journey to the Holy Land.

Years earlier, Ivo had fled in fear from the siege of Antioch. Now, he was intent above all on salvaging his reputation, and on obtaining remission of his sins as a Crusader. He never returned, and his lands passed permanently to Robert of Meulan. Henry added other holdings to Ivo's, making Count Robert a very wealthy man, indeed.

William count of Mortain and earl of Cornwall was, after his uncle Robert of Bellême (now disseised), the second largest landholder in England. Before and as part of the Treaty of Alton in 1101, William of Mortain had demanded of Henry that he be given their uncle Odo's earldom of Kent. Had Henry done so, Hollister points out, the count of Mortain would have had an annual income of 4,500 pounds a year (315,000 pounds a year, using R.W. Southern's multiplier of 70 to arrive at the modern-day equivalent), and, as Hollister put it, would potentially have loomed over England like a new Harold Godwinson.

Somehow the king had managed to delay giving the count a definite answer, and also kept him from rushing to the aid of his uncle

Robert of Bellême in 1102, when Henry was fighting to dislodge Bellême from England. Though chronicler William of Malmesbury referred to the count of Mortain's "shameless arrogance," the king may have felt that the young man might still be won over to the royal cause. From the evidence, one feels that Henry worked with William of Mortain very carefully and with great diplomacy. The hand of Mary of Scotland, the queen's sister, was offered to him (obviously, this was before her match with Eustace of Boulogne). William of Mortain refused contemptuously, pointing out that Mary was landless. Dividing the loyalties of the uncle, Robert of Bellême, from those of his nephew William, would have lightened the task of taking over Normandy from Duke Robert, and though Mortain was hotheaded, disdainful, and violent, he was less so than his uncle.

Henry took a completely different approach in Mortain's case. He began a series of legal actions against the earl of Cornwall concerning neighboring lands that Mortain had misappropriated. One can imagine the fury of William of Mortain, a bold and proud warrior, on finding himself on the utterly unfamiliar battlefield of legal procedure, his "enemy" now being cold words written on parchment. In this field he was impotent. By 1104, Mortain was in such a rage over issues that allowed him no field of action but the council chamber that at last, of his own volition, he left England permanently and was divested by the king of all his English lands.

The Clare family, who, with the allied Giffard clan, had scoffed openly at the new king and queen during one of Henry's first great crown wearings, were gradually won over by Henry's kindness to them. In 1110, the king bestowed on Gilbert of Clare the lordship of Ceredigion in Wales, and shortly thereafter bestowed grants of lands also on Gilbert's two younger brothers, Walter and Robert. The Clare family became from then on Henry's staunch supporters. It was the younger brother, Roger of Clare, who saved Henry's life in the battle of Brémule in 1119, when the raging William Crispin struck at the king's head with his sword. Roger quickly moved to the king's aid, struck William Crispin from his horse, and then, in the spirit of chivalry, threw himself upon William Crispin to save him from the wrath of some of Henry's more single-minded knights.

Richard de Redvers and Ranulf le Meschin were Henry's *familiares* from his days as count of the Cotentin in Normandy. Over the years of his reign, the king rewarded them greatly for their steadfastness, enriching each of them with lands in both England and Normandy.

As the citizens of Domfront could attest, Henry was a man of his word. He strove always to keep his promises, to honor old loyalties, and to reward people for services rendered him—especially those who had supported him when his prospects were dim. Henry also had in his care the child heir of his long-time *fidelis*, Hugh earl of Chester, who died shortly after the Treaty of Alton.

Broadly stated, the evidence points incontrovertibly to the conclusion that Henry I of England sought always, first, to win over those magnates whose loyalties were still in doubt. In every case he began by offering them the hand of friendship. He also made it crystal clear that those barons who cooperated with him and supported his vision for England would prosper greatly. Only Robert of Bellême and his brothers were disseised and forcibly exiled. King Henry worked very differently with Bellême's nephew, William of Mortain, using a tactic that seems inspired.

Henry, like his father, found that offering an instructive example of the consequences of right and wrong behavior saved much trouble and bloodshed in the end. After making an example of Robert of Bellême, who had shown himself the most powerful and bellicose landholder in England, the king had no need to declare war on other recalcitrant barons. Further object lessons were not needed. Following Bellême's defeat, Henry's methods soon changed to a show of legal acumen—which was how he won against Mortain. His justice sent a second and equally clear message to the magnates: "Might—including the king's might—will not make right. England will not be ruled by self-interest and the arbitrary whims of an elite few, but by just laws, applied equally to everyone."

Not only did warfare on English soil cease for the remaining thirty-three years of Henry's reign, but there were no more forcible disseisements after that of Robert of Bellême and his brothers. In 1103, King Henry did take from William de Mandeville three of his many estates, possibly—some historians have guessed—in delayed punishment for having allowed Ranulf Flambard to escape from the Tower of London in 1101. King Henry must have had solid evidence, perhaps built up over the intervening two years, that de Mandeville had either been bribed by Ranulf, or had been criminally careless in his duty.

The ways that Henry worked with his barons can only be ascertained, ultimately, by identifying those who were his most wealthy men, then piecing together both narrative and documented evidence concerning their careers as well as the rewards they received from the king; by the number of times each witnessed royal charters and writs (evidence of how frequently they attended the king in person); and by the advancement of their family members. By far the most exhaustive attempt to name and categorize those who held any significant amount of land (magnates) under Henry I is that of William Corbett in his *Cambridge Medieval History*. However, once again Hollister has shone the light of clarifying simplicity, without losing any meaningful categories, on information that is, otherwise, nearly unintelligible.

By using such markers as knights fees (the number of knights a landholder owed the king when the feudal levy was called up), danegeld exemptions (at two shillings on the hide), and a number of other lesser factors, Hollister divides the significant landholders in England into four categories. At the top are what he calls "super-magnates": Robert earl of Gloucester, Stephen of Blois, and Roger bishop of Salisbury. Each of these much-favored men owed 300 knights fees on the lands they held of the king in England.

Next come eight Class A magnates, each of whom holds lands owing 100–200 knights fees.

Class B landholders comprised about a dozen laymen, each of them owing 60–90 knights fees on their lands.

Finally there were about thirty lay landholders who were classified as "C," owing 30–60 knights to the feudal levy.

While a few of these last, who comprised the top tier of the aristocracy, held no significant lands in Normandy, most of them did so. Many were also connected together through a web of intermarriages and other ties of kinship which to us seem hopelessly complex, but which were probably factored in easily by King Henry as he worked with each of them.

Looking closely at the eleven "supermagnates" and Class A magnates, Hollister offers compelling evidence that many of the generalizations which have been made about Henry's relationships with his barons are simply not true. As an additional answer not only to contemporary chroniclers, who stated that Henry "raised men from the dust," and the corollary statement that his reign saw the great families that had been established in England after the Conquest uprooted and disseised, the evidence shows that, quite the contrary, seven of the eleven of Henry's wealthiest men came from the greater or lesser baronage under William the Conqueror. Moreover, before we decry (if we are so inclined) the loss of the "old guard," Hollister reminds us that the Conqueror himself had worked with "new men." Henry I's reign is only one, or at the very most three, generations away from the establishment of a so-called family "dynasty." It is very easy to imagine that William the Conqueror himself would have handled the situations in much the same way Henry did, for in similar matters he actually did so. Many of the Norman families who had loyally supported the Conqueror's father, Duke Robert I, were gone by the end of the baronial rebellions in Normandy during William's minority, swept away by the widespread and swift changes that occurred during those uncertain times.

Other historians, as I've stated already, have described a repressed and fearful baronage, its membership submitted to constant change while Henry kept on removing troublemakers. The statistical evidence, however, carefully assembled by Hollister and Corbett, tells an entirely different story. From the Treaty of Alton in 1101 and following the removal of Bellême, until the end of Henry's reign in 1135, *none of the eleven wealthiest magnates in England* opposed the king on either side of the channel. In other words, there was enormous stability within Henry's aristocracy.

Keng Henry I was, as I said, able to keep the peace in England for a phenomenal thirty-three years—and this in an age when life, by present-day standards, was inconceivably brutal and when social brigands of every description were commonly encountered everywhere. He made this peace possible because he, like his father, skillfully created a baronage that was highly loyal to him. The "Pipe Roll" of 1130 gives incontrovertible evidence that Henry secured the dedication of his barons not by force, but by kindness, forgiveness, and humility, as well as by *being* loyal, first, to others. Furthermore, Henry drew his barons into a greater involvement with government than had ever been the case before: They attended primatial church reform councils, witnessed charters, attended Henry at court, went to war with him in Scotland, Wales and Normandy, heard and adjudicated legal cases, performed the functions of sheriff, went on diplomatic missions for the king, relaxed with him at his hunting lodge, and much more. As Henry's reign progressed, the tasks of a *curiales* were performed more and more often by one of the king's "great men"—a blending of roles that had been prominent under William the Conqueror.

The Conqueror, in settling England with a Norman aristocracy of his own choosing, had had an opportunity that no future English monarch would be able to enjoy. His youngest son Henry had to build a loyal baronage out of those who were already in place, and sought to do so with a minimum of disruption. Henry's leadership may truly be described as an art form, with human beings as his medium of expression. It was not through luck, brute force, or the application of an unchanging formula that Henry created loyal barons. In his ability to discern which barons could be won over, and by what means; by rewarding generously all who rendered true service without impoverishing the king's demesne and without creating any baronial "giants"; by his ability to draw

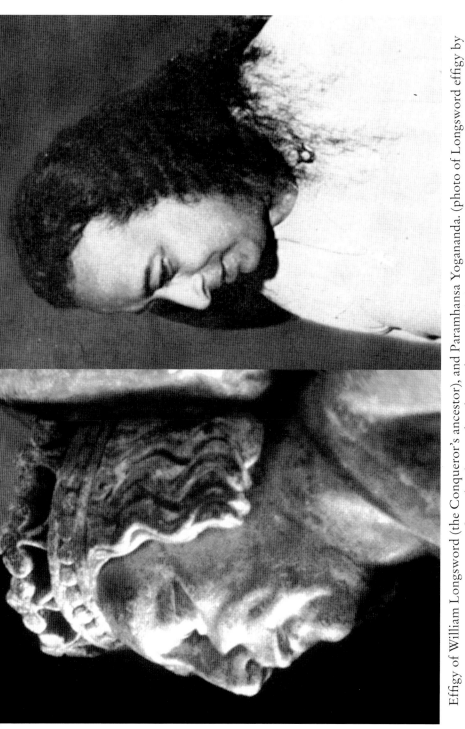

Effigy of William Longsword (the Conqueror's ancestor), and Paramhansa Yogananda. (photo of Longsword effigy by Swami Kriyananda; photo of Yogananda by Unknown)

Swami Kriyananda a young man of nineteen, and an image of Henry I of England. (Swami Kriyananda (J. Donald Walters) at nineteen, from *The New Path*; Henry I depiction from Cassell's *History of England* {1902})

Statue of William the Great, Falaise Square *(photo by Richard Salva).*

Falaise Castle: where William was born *(photo by Richard Salva).*

William the Conqueror's castle in Caen *(photo by Richard Salva).*

Avranches, where Lanfranc taught
(*photo of ruins of Avranches Castle by Ranjit Scutti*).

above: Bec Abbey, where Lanfranc served as prior *(photo of St. Nicholas Tower, Bec Abbey by Richard Salva).*

right: St. Stephen's Church and the Monastery for Men, Caen, built by William (Lanfranc, abbot) *(photo by Richard Salva).*

above: The island Abbey of Mont-Saint-Michel *(photo by Richard Salva).*

right: William the Great *(from the Bayeux Tapestry).*

inset: William knighting Harold *(photo by Matthew Sloan from a reproduction of the Bayeux Tapestry).*

WILLELM:
HAROL,

The ruins of Hastings Castle *(photo by Matthew Sloan)*.

Battle of Hastings *(from the Bayeux Tapestry)*: William raises his helm to show his men that he is uninjured.

Battle Abbey, built by William to commemorate the fallen: outer walls and interior *(photos by Matthew Sloan)*.

above: Tower of London: White Tower, built by William *(photo by Barbara Bingham)*

right: St. John's Chapel in the White Tower: where William worshipped
(photo by Michael Kooiman)

above: William's tomb, St. Stephen's, Caen *(photo by Ranjit Scutti).*

left: The Seal of Henry I *(Public Records Office, London).*

St. Gervais church, Rouen: where William died *(photo by Richard Salva)*.

Ely Cathedral, west tower *(photo by Tom–)*.

above: Interior of a Norman church *(photo by Ranjit Scutti).*

left: The sinking of the White Ship *(British Library).*

men who could share in the vision he held up for the kingdom: in all these ways, and in many more besides, we must conclude that King Henry I practiced the art of leadership with the most consummate skill. His secret of success, however, was not artful; it was based on deep sincerity.

In order really to appreciate and accept the reality of his skill, one might look at the present-day example of Swami Kriyananda, who forged a community out of a motley group composed mostly of young Americans, many of whom had been rebellious "hippies," and not a few of whom were outspokenly independent. He succeeded in doing so in ways that paralleled amazingly the behavior of Henry: through kindness, patience, humility, firm adherence to principle, and unstinting generosity, acceptance, and forgiveness.

Another quality Kriyananda showed, which he had in common with Henry, was a practical knowledge of human nature. One time, in the early days of Ananda, several people came to him offering high recommendations for a new member who, at twenty-nine, was already "skilled" in a wide range of activities.

"He's only twenty-nine?" Kriyananda asked. "By that age, he can't be an expert in such a wide range of ways. This is bluff." Indeed it proved so to be.

Another man who came asked someone, "How does one get ahead in this organization?" Kriyananda gave him no chance. He sought people who weren't seeking self-importance, but rather who shared his own spirit of service. That man soon left, aware that to "get ahead in this organization" he would have to become humble.

I'll explore these matters further in a later chapter. For now, however, let me say that I, too, might have found Henry "too good to be true" had I not had the good fortune, over many years, to observe the same virtues actively practiced by Swami Kriyananda.

CHAPTER 34

Invasion of Normandy: Reuniting His Father's Kingdom

Henry insisted that Duke Robert honor the Treaty of Alton by declaring war on Robert of Bellême. Bellême, scion of the Montgomery family, having been expelled from England, was now back in Normandy, continuing to wreak havoc. It could not have been a happy moment for Curthose when he realized that Henry's decisive action against Bellême meant that this bellicose baron would now become his full-time problem in Normandy.

In pressuring Duke Robert to take action against Bellême, King Henry was affirming that part of the Treaty of Alton which meant the most to him—namely, those provisions which called for the brothers to work cooperatively for the well-being of the Anglo-Norman kingdom. The dark specter of magnates alternately extorting favors first from Henry, then from Duke Robert, in exchange for their loyal (but temporary) support, with each change motivated by a desire for some short-term gain, loomed large in Henry's mind.

Curthose did, as we know, rouse himself in 1102 to besiege the Bellême fortress of Vignats. His offensive had to be abandoned, however, when one of the duke's barons, Robert of Montfort, decided to withdraw his knights. Since most of Robert of Bellême's neighbors had supported Curthose in that siege, the failed offensive had catastrophic results for central Normandy. Robert of Bellême, determined on revenge, went on a rampage, plundering and devastating neighbors' lands well into 1103.

For King Henry, this collapse of Curthose's offensive may have been the last straw: the point at which Henry determined to win Normandy and reunite his father's kingdom whatever the cost. From now on a new urgency is apparent in Henry's efforts to build Norman alliances.

Even by the harsh standards of those times, Bellême's conduct in warfare, and especially his treatment of the prisoners he'd taken in battle, horrified his contemporaries. What they found most repugnant was his gratuitous torture of prisoners, and the fact, against all chivalric codes, that he sometimes held them, as his fancy took him, without possibility of ransom, simply starving them to death.

The duke himself could no longer ignore Bellême's continuing devastation of central Normandy. In the summer of 1103, his forces rode out to meet Robert of Bellême in battle. Again, however, they were almost immediately defeated. Bellême took many prisoners, and triumphantly occupied the duke's fortress of Exmes. Curthose had to concede virtually all of Bellême's demands in what, for him, was a deeply humiliating treaty.

King Henry, as he continued to build strong alliances in Normandy, won over Gilbert of Laigle, whose lands in southeastern Normandy were of strategic importance, by granting him part of the honor of Cornwall forfeited by William of Mortain. When Ralph of Tosny and Conches came to England to claim his father's lands, Henry welcomed him very warmly, and even arranged a marriage for Ralph with a great heiress.

It was obvious where matters were headed. Though King Henry took Duke Robert formally to task for not adhering to the agreements in the Treaty of Alton—especially for failing to stand with him against their mutual enemies (Robert of Bellême being only the most recent example), the real issue had to do with the general chaos and lawlessness that continued to be the prevailing reality wherever Curthose "ruled." A long succession of ecclesiastics and minor aristocrats kept arriving in England from Normandy to plead with Henry to right the many wrongs in their duchy.

It became clear to Duke Robert that Henry would soon intervene in Normandy; he therefore cast about for allies. The crisis came to a head in 1104, when Curthose, on discovering how very few allies he had left among the Norman barons, was more or less forced to enter into an alliance with none other than—Robert of Bellême!

William count of Mortain having departed England in a rage, now allied himself with Curthose and with Mortain's own uncle, Robert of Bellême. William of Mortain was in a good position, from his strongholds, to lead attacks on Norman fortresses belonging to King Henry and to Richard earl of Chester and count of Avranches, the very young son of Henry's great *fidelis* Hugh of Avranches. The king's proprietary involvement with these fortresses dated back to his days as count of the Cotentin, the people of which had considered Henry their overlord ever since. Furthermore, Earl Richard had been placed in Henry's care by his dying father, and was now only ten or eleven years old. The king therefore felt an obligation to protect Earl Richard's interests in Normandy.

The evidence shows that these attacks on his and on young Earl Richard's Normandy holdings were the immediate cause of the king's decision to cross over to Normandy with a great show of force. Henry, unlike Curthose, determined to show immediately that his authority was not to be challenged, nor his Norman holdings attacked or damaged by anyone.

Thus it was that, in August 1104, King Henry arrived in Normandy with many of his great men, and drew more noblemen to his banner as he proceeded unopposed and "in great state" (according to Orderic Vitalis), to Domfront and other strongholds under his command.

Next, according to Orderic Vitalis, King Henry and Duke Robert came together for what the duke may have thought was going to be an informal discussion between the two brothers, only to find himself confronted with what amounted very nearly to a formal arraignment. Henry began with the charge that Duke Robert had betrayed the Treaty of Alton by making his own private agreement with Robert of Bellême.

King Henry's 1104 crossing to Normandy, including the well-orchestrated and highly public confrontation with Curthose, was a masterpiece of diplomacy and public relations. In Orderic's report of the meeting, King Henry is shown making a very strong speech that carries a ring of authenticity. He denounced his brother for having abandoned Normandy to thieves and robbers, thereby betraying one of the most important duties of a ruler. It was useless, the king continued, for Duke Robert to hold the position of prince, since, instead of protecting the church and the people and striving for their good, he had allowed this entire trust to be plundered. King Henry was very clearly preparing the ground for the more drastic action he was already determined to pursue.

According to Orderic, Curthose was flustered (as he may well have been!) and fearful lest he be forced to relinquish the duchy then and there to his brother. He turned to his "resident parasites" (Orderic's colorful phrase)—the men, that is to say, in his own entourage—and asked for their advice. When nothing of substance emerged, Duke Robert, in desperation, offered to transfer to King Henry the fealty of William, count of Evreux. This complete non-sequitur was certainly an offering of value to Henry, but it suggests also that Duke Robert had lost all ability to face and deal with reality.

Orderic (in paraphrase) quotes a little speech by the count of Evreux, at first protesting the idea that his loyalty could be transferred, "like a farm animal." The count ended, however, by saying: "Both are sons of my lord, the king [William the Conqueror], and I revere them both. I will do homage, however, to only one, and I will serve him as my lawful lord." Curthose then placed the hands of the count between Henry's two hands, making William of Evreux the vassal, now, of King Henry.

When King Henry returned to England later in 1104, he had won the loyalty of all but two of the fourteen or fifteen wealthiest barons in Normandy. Furthermore, he had demonstrated that no one could tamper freely with his own holdings, nor with those of his *fideles*, in Normandy. He had also laid the groundwork for more serious action, which had become inevitable, publicly proclaiming the rationale for what was now, obviously, his next step: a planned invasion of Normandy.

Back in England, in December 1104, Henry received papal envoys, who brought the pope's next salvo in the continuing battle over investiture. Evidently, the pope had also a well-developed "public relations" campaign in hand. A year earlier, King Henry's tireless ambassador, William Warelwast, had brought to Henry a letter which made it clear where Pope Paschal intended to take matters if the king did not submit on investitures: "Consider, my dearest son, whether it redounds to your credit that the most learned and religious of all the English bishops, Anselm, bishop of Canterbury, is afraid on this account to stay at your side or live in your kingdom. What will those think of you who, until now, have heard such good things of you? What will they say when this matter is published abroad?"

Anselm himself was experienced in the power of propaganda. His first letter to Henry from exile laid out a clear exposition of the investiture issue, interspersed with sincere expressions of affection for the king. The archbishop-in-exile portrayed himself—truthfully, impersonally, and articulately—as a dutiful son of the church, bound by monastic vows of obedience. At the same time, Anselm noted that Pope Paschal II, in insisting that the king relinquish investitures, was only following the well-trod path of his predecessors in the Vatican. What King Henry did not know about this letter from Anselm was that copies had been sent to Gundulf, bishop of Rochester, as well as to the prior of Canterbury, with detailed instructions from Anselm to make the letter—and the issue itself—public.

With a full-scale campaign now in hand to conquer Normandy and thus reunite his father's kingdom, Henry was in a very delicate position. On the one hand, he had to unseat his older brother from a post which not only the Norman aristocracy, but all of Europe (including the church in Rome), viewed as belonging to Curthose by right. On the other hand, because Curthose had been utterly derelict, this powerful objection was not insurmountable. Yet it was absolutely critical that Henry receive the support of Rome. Even though the pope knew that King Henry would bring order to the duchy, and would effectively promote the church, this was, to Rome, a less crucial matter than the question of investitures. The pope was willing to use King Henry's urgent need for papal approval on Normandy to gain leverage on investitures. Both men knew that Henry needed to be perceived as championing the church in Normandy if he was to succeed in rescuing it from the lawlessness Duke Robert had created by abdicating his duty.

Now, in December 1104, a letter came from Pope Paschal making it abundantly clear that the church meant to intertwine the investitures issue as closely as possible with King Henry's drive to reunite his father's kingdom. The pope, after addressing the investitures issue in ways that by now had become tiresomely familiar, ended ominously with the words: "Whoever desires not the grace of Christ will feel the sword of Christ."

Meanwhile, the king's rebuttal to Anselm's publicized statement on the church's view of investitures was very effective; it had been disseminated in such a way as to have the greatest impact. Henry continued, in his letter, to insist on his position as the church's protector and benefactor, who, for thanks, was being asked by an exceedingly stubborn prelate to relinquish ancient kingly rights that had belonged to his royal predecessors. Later, Henry's court was able to augment this fundamental position by charging that Anselm, owing to his continued stubbornness in upholding the church's unlawful demands, was abandoning his sacred duties as primate of England's church, and leaving England a prey to wickedness of all kinds.

This line of argument proved so effective that even Anselm's intimates at Canterbury took up the same cry in letters to him. One prelate wrote him, "Even the king himself now declares that never in this country has wickedness been so brazen as it now is. Without any doubt all these things reflect upon one person, and that, your holiness, is you. *You* are responsible." Anselm replied to his querulous flock that they must take a longer view, and not react so hastily to current conditions.

Another complicating element was the king's need for money to support his intended full-scale invasion of Normandy. Every source of revenue had to be used to the fullest, including not only a very inconvenient special geld, levied on all of England, but the full use of the income from the many vacant bishoprics and abbacies. Unlike his brother King Rufus, Henry had earnestly sought to fill these vacancies, and had been stymied by the investiture controversy. However, there now were vacancies, despite Henry's best efforts to fill them. These vacancies existed in some of the wealthiest bishoprics and abbacies in the land. The king did, in fact, exercise his undisputed right to their revenues, after making full allowance—quite contrary to the practice of Rufus—for the dependents of each institution, and (again in contrast to Rufus) carefully husbanding the assets of those properties.

Anselm did not question the king's right to such revenues, but he did take exception to Henry's claim on Canterbury's revenues on the grounds that he, as archbishop, had been forced into exile without the benefit of due legal process. Implicit in his written protest to the king (with copies sent to others within the kingdom) was the threat of his publicly branding Henry as having abused the church and ignored ecclesiastical "due process."

As for Henry, we may be sure from the way he'd conducted Anselm's exile in 1103 that he had foreseen this pitfall, but that he had evidently decided this was a lesser evil. Any kind of legal process would, in the short run, have been far more upsetting. Anselm's protest, via letter from exile, against the king's use of Canterbury revenues was far less potent than the spectacle of Anselm presenting himself in some highly public setting as a martyr to royal policy.

This gradual escalation in the "public relations war" between king and archbishop is fascinating, but not distressing, for neither of them ever attacked the other's character. Each did charge the other, however, with relinquishing a part of his God-given duty, respectively as monarch and as primate. Though they clearly disagreed with certain decisions that had been made, they understood and respected each other. In reading parts of their correspondence during these months, it is impossible to feel that any real animus existed between the two of them.

As the war of words continued, both the pope and Anselm began to make it clear in their letters to Henry that they would first mete out punishment to the king's "evil advisors." Accordingly, in March 1105, the pope excommunicated Robert count of Meulan, a few other royal counselors, and all the prelates whom King Henry had thus far invested. Robert of Meulan was specially anathematized for his role in advising the king not to cooperate with the pope on investitures. Another rumble of distant thunder accompanied the pope's statement that any action against the king himself would be postponed until Henry's envoys, who were at that time attending the Lenten synod in Rome, had arrived and could be heard.

From this point on, the observer feels that a race is being run for huge stakes. King Henry obviously hoped to achieve his conquest of Normandy before the sword of public excommunication could strike him, for he couldn't possibly take on the role of righteous savior of the duchy as an excommunicate himself. Henry was equally determined, however, on the one hand not to relinquish his right to invest prelates, and on the other to demand homage from the churchmen in his own kingdom. The king now bent his formidable energies toward moving up the timing of his full-scale invasion of Normandy.

Everyone who had ever had any dealings with King Henry, or who had observed his governance in western Normandy or in England, knew that he took his duties, as he perceived them, very seriously. Anyone who had traveled in Normandy had seen with his own eyes the devastation of the land. The situation there had become desperate. To handle that situation, the king now laid the groundwork carefully with the counts of Anjou, Maine, and Brittany, as well as with King Philip of France and Philip's heir, Louis. He persuaded these rulers either to remain neutral in the conflict to come, or to help resolve those internal problems which most impacted them as Normandy's closest neighbors. Thus, Helias, count of Maine, decided to fight on the side of King Henry, and persuaded Geoffrey Martel, count of Anjou, to do the same.

In securing the neutrality, at least, of these neighboring states, Henry's diplomatic achievement may be described as almost miraculous, especially considering that King Philip of France was also, in a valid sense, the liege lord of Duke Robert Curthose. We don't know how Henry and his diplomatic team were able to persuade these neighboring states to refrain from involving themselves, but one suspects that a great deal of money changed hands. For it was crucial— even if a great financial strain on England—to keep Normandy's neighbors from allying themselves with Robert Curthose.

Besides the pope's excommunication of Robert of Meulan in March of 1105, and the compressed timeline within which Henry had to act before receiving the same repressive treatment himself, another event occurred early in 1105 that caused him to launch his invasion immediately. It was relatively minor, but was something that Henry could not ignore. Robert fitz Hamon, the king's great friend and *curialis*, who held lands in Normandy and England, was taken prisoner by two of Curthose's commanders and imprisoned in Bayeux. Thus, Henry's full-scale invasion to reclaim Normandy, meticulously planned in every detail, was launched in April 1105.

The king was in an ideal position to land unopposed, since most of western Normandy was already under his control. We don't know the strength of his army when it landed on the Cotentin peninsula, but many more men would soon join him as he marched through Normandy. Serlo, the bishop of Sées, who had fled to King Henry's court in England after Robert of Bellême had burned his cathedral church, had re-crossed the Channel with the royal fleet, and now conducted Easter service for the king and his barons in the little town of Carentan.

The irrepressible Orderic Vitalis is our source for this highly colorful account of that Easter service. The church evidently served also as a haven of safety for the villagers, for it was littered with boxes, farm implements, clothing, and all manner of items which the local people had hoped to keep from pillage. (At this time, seats were often not provided for church services.) It is not difficult to visualize the royal entourage picking their way through the litter, a few of then—including King Henry—finding seats here and there on wooden boxes. Most of the great magnates were left standing in the midst of this confusion, jammed together with their swords and personal accoutrements intertwined. This, however, was Bishop Serlo's moment and he didn't limit himself to a few brief statements.

What he delivered instead was an impassioned oration urging those there assembled to rescue Normandy from the disorder prevailing everywhere. He decried especially the burning of churches and monasteries—sometimes with their congregations or community inside them. He dwelt at length on Duke Robert's folly:

"Indeed the jesters and harlots who constantly keep his company steal his clothes at night, while he lies snoring in drunken sleep, and guffaw while boasting that they have robbed the duke. When the head is sick, the whole body is afflicted; when the ruler is foolish, the whole province is in danger [of chaos], and the wretched people suffer utter deprivation."

Serlo exhorted King Henry to conduct his campaign "not out of lust for earthly power, but to defend your very homeland."

According to Orderic, King Henry responded, "I will rise up and work for peace in the name of the Lord, and will devote my utmost endeavors to procure, with your help, the tranquility of the Church of God."

Serlo, after pleading with the barons to come as true deliverers and not as conquerors, reminded them that they were entering a wounded land, which had been abandoned to lawlessness for nearly two decades.

The bishop then seemingly digressed, observing that many in that illustrious gathering wore their hair long, in an effeminate style. This practice could have no other effect, he said, than to rob them of man's particular strength. He went on to quote St. Paul: "If a man have long hair, it is a shame unto him." (I Cor. 11:14) Furthermore, Serlo declared, the knights' long beards made them look like "lascivious billy-goats"—indeed, more like Saracens than like Christians. He concluded by whipping out a pair of scissors, whereupon he declared his readiness to shear anyone in that prestigious flock who was willing to be shorn.

Henry gave his immediate acquiescence, and Bishop Serlo began by cutting the king's hair. Next came Robert count of Meulan. Ultimately, all the men gathered there had their hair shorn. Whether this or any part of Serlo's Easter Sunday "pageant" was staged, it *was* well conceived. Like ceremonial bathing before receiving knighthood, or like a novice monk receiving his tonsure, that Easter morning haircut set these men apart, as if ritually cleansed, and feeling more fit for their mission to save Normandy.

Merely the sight of King Henry's army approaching Bayeux sufficed to persuade Gunter d'Aunay, Duke Robert's *fidelis*, to release his prisoner, Robert fitz Hamon, whom Henry had come to rescue. Once Robert fitz Hamon was safely among the king's men, Henry demanded that Gunter turn over Bayeux to him. Gunter refused. The king therefore laid siege to Bayeux. His army then set fire to the town; a high wind that day drove the flames forward, quickly destroying everything before it. Most of the town was destroyed, including the cathedral Bishop Odo had built. (Later, King Henry rebuilt the Bayeux cathedral, at his own expense, and the rebuilt cathedral seems to have been just as grand as the one that was destroyed in 1105.) Duke Robert's garrison fled the town—into the "embrace" of the king's army.

The burning of Bayeux, as an object lesson, was not lost on the citizenry of Caen, which was King Henry's next objective. Even as the army moved swiftly toward the city, a contingent of representatives came out from Caen to meet Henry, and agreed to surrender the city to him on his terms. It is reasonable to conclude that the king had deliberately made Bayeux a sobering example. The citizens of Caen, having surrendered the town, expelled Curthose's castellan and ducal garrison from the castle.

Henry's army now moved on to the intimidating stone fortress of Falaise, about twenty miles southeast of Caen. This castle, whose stone keep was rebuilt in about 1123 by King Henry (it is still stand-ing today), sits on a jutting rock promontory—the same formidable outcropping that confronted the king's army now, in 1105.

At Falaise, King Henry encountered an unforeseen difficulty. Helias, count of Maine, abruptly withdrew his troops, and Henry had no option but to drop his plans for taking the citadel by storm.

A few historians have expressed the view that Henry's withdraw-al was quixotic. Indeed, the withdrawal of Helias could not have been completely crippling to Henry, who had come to Normandy with plenty of money—enough to augment his forces with mer-cenaries. What those historians have suggested, however, is that his behavior at this point was as vacillating as his older brother's. Even Hollister wavered at this point in his very real admiration for Henry. To me, however, the matter seems perfectly simple. It only requires an acceptance of what I, knowing Swami Kriyananda as I do, have seen in him again and again: a firm commitment to doing God's will at all times, and a readiness to drop everything, regard-less of the consequences to himself, if he had any reason to doubt whether what he was doing was pleasing to God. Henry's values, as I believe an overview of his life shows, were centered in pleas-ing above all God alone. From this point of view, there was a very good reason for his withdrawal from Falaise, virtually in the teeth of victory. It lay, I suggest, in Henry's own deep piety. Helias had withdrawn from the field out of fear of excommunication, or per-haps the excommunication of Robert count of Meulan had caused him to doubt the righteousness of the king's cause. Henry was now threatened also, by Anselm, with the same punishment if he didn't relent on the question of investitures. He very simply decided that, faced as he now was with such an open declaration of God's disfa-vor, nothing mattered to him so much as keeping open his own line of communication with God. This didn't mean that he dropped the idea of conquering Normandy. It simply meant that he felt a need to wait for further "inner instructions."

Anselm knew that King Henry was well on his way to taking the duchy, and that if he accomplished this victory before the pope made good on his threat of excommunication, the church would have lost every shred of leverage it had with the king. In 1101 also, when Henry, as the newly crowned king of England, had faced his brother's invading armada, the pope had tried to use the fragility of Henry's situation to extract his submission on the question of investitures. At that time, the pope's message had arrived too late. As far as Anselm could see, in the present crisis the pope was going to be too late again; Henry counted on it. Anselm, deeply frustrated, decided to take matters into his own hands. He now traveled north from Lyons toward Normandy, threatening personally, if necessary, to excommunicate King Henry. Anselm evidently felt very strongly the rightness of this step, for he himself, in taking this action without the pope's permission, was violating canon law.

King Henry, having abandoned the siege of Falaise, sought in mid-May 1105 to parlay with Duke Robert. For two days the brothers conducted peace negotiations at the village of Cintheaux in Calvados. In the end, of course, they parted without having reached any agreement.

We have seen that when Henry strongly felt the rightness of what he undertook, he was not to be deterred until circumstances actually forced him to stop and wait for a more propitious moment. His steadfastness to what he believed had been evident when he was a very young man in the Cotentin, at the time when his two older brothers had signed their peace treaty disinheriting him. It was true when they cornered and besieged him atop Mont-Saint-Michel. Henry's cause at that time had, as he well knew, been quite hopeless. Even earlier in his career, at the battle for Rouen, Henry had stayed to fight when Duke Robert fled the city, there being no doubt in Henry's mind that saving the ducal capital was a necessity. When, in 1101, Robert Curthose's invasion force bribed King Henry's Channel commanders to guide them to a safe landing at Portsmouth within striking distance of the royal treasury at Winchester, Henry moved with all swiftness—again, against all odds—to intercept Curthose.

This was King Henry's characteristic response to any setback, provided he continued to feel convinced of the rightness of his stand. The fact that he halted the siege of Falaise and negotiated with Duke Robert, forces the conclusion that, given the compromises that now loomed so large before him, Henry hesitated for a time before pursuing his ultimate goal: the conquest of Normandy.

Interestingly, as I've already observed, those who know Swami Kriyananda have observed the same trait in him—indeed, we have seen it even more pronounced in him. Despite his noteworthy determination in pursuing goals he considers worthwhile, if anyone can convince him that he is mistaken he will, as the expression has it, "turn on a dime" and never look back.

C. Warren Hollister is undoubtedly right in suggesting that Helias, count of Maine withdrew at the height of the siege of Falaise because of some communication he had received concerning Archbishop Anselm's announced intention of excommunicating Henry. It is also possible that he'd learned for the first time at Falaise that Robert, count of Meulan, King Henry's closest advisor, had already been excommunicated—something that would have disturbed the pious Helias very deeply. This same reasoning, however, applies also to Henry.

When the brothers' negotiations failed, Henry had no choice but to ask himself which course was right: whether to relinquish investitures and secure peace and order in Normandy, or to insist on his royal rights in relation to the church in England.

While he was wrestling with his conscience on this decision, help came from his sister Adela countess of Blois. This lady, considered by many to have been one of the most astute politicians of her day, had somehow got wind of Archbishop Anselm's threat of excommunication for her royal brother. Her envoy intercepted Anselm as he was traveling from Lyons, and entreated him most earnestly to attend the countess. Adela was Anselm's spiritual daughter, and the messenger stated that she was quite ill. The archbishop undoubtedly saw this entreaty for what it was, and welcomed the opportunity to confer with Adela concerning her favorite brother.

He of course found Countess Adela "much recovered," since her illness had been a useful contrivance. The archbishop confirmed to Adela his intention of excommunicating Henry. She in turn conveyed this information to Henry, and asked him to consider it deeply.

In response to his sister's urgent message, Henry sent word to her that he was prepared to compromise with Anselm on many points "for the sake of peace." A meeting was accordingly arranged between Archbishop Anselm and King Henry at the castle of Laigle in southeastern Normandy. It was in this small corner of the duchy that this enormously important meeting occurred between two leading figures of the twelfth century. There they hammered out a compromise on the investiture/lay homage issue for England—an issue that, elsewhere in Europe, was causing rivers of blood to flow.

Henry and Anselm's discussion seems to have included very few other men; perhaps portions of that meeting were only between the two of them. We must therefore piece together from subsequent correspondence, and from Eadmer's account, what was decided.

The king agreed to restore Canterbury's lands in full to Anselm, as well as to pay the "back rents" which Henry had appropriated as his royal right. Anselm agreed to return to England, and agreed also "to restore to communion" Robert count of Meulan.

Because Anselm was so greatly overstepping his authority in negotiating the investitures and homage issues with King Henry, it is difficult to discern precisely what the two men discussed at Laigle. Only the pope had the right to negotiate issues like these. Thus (so Vaughn writes), Eadmer, in his chronicling of the discussion, sought to protect Anselm by purposefully "glossing over" the role he played in negotiating the final agreement with Henry.

In fact, Henry and Anselm reached an agreement that would become a model for settling this issue in much of Western Europe. The king—so the compromise stated—would relinquish his right to invest prelates with the ring and staff of office. This would become the right of the archbishop. Prelates would continue to offer homage to the king, however, for the lands and other mundane rights and benefits that they held in connection with their high ecclesiastical office. Undoubtedly both of these astute leaders had noted that the pope's recent letters had not mentioned the issue of clerical homage to a lay prince.

Anselm immediately shifted his energy into communicating to the pope the facts of the Laigle meeting, but only insofar as it pertained to Canterbury, stating also that he had lifted the ban of excommunication from Robert of Meulan. Furthermore, the archbishop wrote his holiness only that he (the pope) would soon hear from King Henry directly on what he (Anselm) hoped were compromise proposals on investitures. Thus, Anselm, in this and in subsequent correspondence with the pope, managed to keep himself in the background—a mere observer of matters which, he repeatedly affirmed, were strictly between the king and the pope. More frankly, in a letter to Robert of Meulan following the Laigle meeting, the archbishop wrote that it was a compromise "so badly needed and so clearly right."

Pope Paschal's relief must have been very great when he realized that the compromises Henry proposed to make on the investiture/homage issue would allow him, as pope, again to support the English king. Frank Barlow observed that Paschal "was unwilling to make the first example of Henry [by excommunicating him], whose piety had aroused strong hopes in reforming circles, but he found it hard to go back on his avowed policy."

There were still crucial steps to be taken before this proposed compromise could be put into place. Both Henry and Anselm certainly hoped they had interpreted correctly the fact that Paschal had omitted any mention of the lay homage issue in all correspondence for over two years. Would the pope be willing to relinquish the homage issue to gain Henry's acquiescence in the matter of investitures?

In August 1105, King Henry returned to England. Until the investiture compromise was ratified by the pope, Anselm refused to return to England. It is very interesting that the king evidently continued to hope he could bring about Anselm's return (and the public restoration of good relations between primate and king), and return to his campaign in Normandy without relinquishing investitures. Though he immediately set about restoring Canterbury's revenues, he delayed somewhat in sending his envoys to Paschal with the compromise proposal, and implored Anselm all the while, through a barrage of letters, to return to England immediately. Clearly, Henry was not yet resigned to the loss of his regal right and duty to invest prelates with the symbols of office, and was tenaciously exploring every possibility of salvaging this right, even while he continued his campaign to win Normandy. Though some historians have seen duplicity in Henry's delay in sending his envoys to Rome, surely the king was only keeping the door open for a last minute, divinely engineered reprieve from the looming loss of what, to him, was his God-ordained duty as a king. Here again, as too often, historians have overlooked important human realities. To call Henry "duplicitous" in view of the fact that "diplomacy" would not only be a kinder, but also a more accurate and perfectly legitimate word, suggests surprising prejudice coming from scholars whose metier demands that they be objective.

Astonishingly, in December 1105 Robert of Bellême visited Henry's Christmas court in England. Historians have guessed that Robert came to ask for the return of his English lands—possibly offering in return to abandon Duke Robert's cause for Henry's. Despite the fact that Bellême's withdrawal from the duke's shrinking coalition would have made the conquest of Normandy a "walk over," Henry refused this offer; evidently he didn't "pour honey" on his refusal, either. The Anglo-Saxon Chronicler tells us that Robert of Bellême departed the kingdom "in a hostile fashion"; we ourselves would rather use the term, "in a fury."

In Henry's refusal to compromise his principles for the sake of an easier victory, we see a strong similarity to Swami Kriyananda, who often has risked utter failure rather than compromise what he knows is right.

In February 1106, Curthose himself arrived to ask Henry for the return of his cities of Bayeux and Caen, as well as the other lands in the Cotentin and western Normandy that Henry had won in the previous spring's campaign. What Curthose added, if anything, to his request to make it in any way compelling to his brother, we are not told. From one of Anselm's letters we learn that Henry simply answered, "No," though the letter goes on to note that the king felt the time for compromise had passed. Duke Robert departed, exceedingly angry, and perhaps more than ever on fire to resist his brother's campaign for Normandy.

In early May, the tireless royal envoy, William Warelwast, returned from Rome with Pope Paschal's agreement in hand to the Laigle compromise. A very happy King Henry, keenly aware that the military campaign season was already upon him, immediately sent William Warelwast back over the Channel to bring Anselm back to England. Clearly, the king felt that a public reconciliation was now required to reinvigorate the sense of divine blessing on his Normandy enterprise.

Warelwast arrived at Bec, however, to find the archbishop too ill to travel. Henry, deciding he could wait no longer, crossed to Normandy in July 1106, and went first to Bec where Anselm, though he continued ill, was able to perform High Mass for Henry and his barons. Publicly, before a very impressive assemblage, King Henry made solemn promises to Anselm concerning his intentions to honor the Laigle agreement. The king capped this highly charged reconciliation by appointing the archbishop regent of all England during his absence. After more than a year's delay, the king was at last free again to do what he knew was needed for Normandy.

The contemporary chroniclers tell us that on the eve of battle, King Henry sent a legation to Curthose. Orderic said the king's envoys delivered this message for Henry: "I have not come here, my brother, out of cupidity for any worldly lordship, nor do I aim at depriving you of the rights of your duchy; but in response to the tearful petitions of the poor whom I wish to help, and for the well-being of the Church of God, which, like a pilot-less ship in stormy seas, is in deep peril. In truth, you occupy the land like a barren tree, and offer no fruit of justice to our Creator." Henry backed up his statement that he did not intend to strip Curthose of his rights in connection with the duchy, for then and there, through his envoys, the king offered Duke Robert half of the income from the duchy for the remainder of his life. Curthose refused this offer, no doubt seeing his refusal as a matter of honor.

On September 28, 1106, the two armies faced each other before the castle of Tinchebray. William of Malmesbury noted that it was exactly forty years to the day since William the Conqueror had landed at Pevensey on England's southern coast. Orderic wrote that the deeply revered hermit, Vital of Savigny—presumably at the last minute—came between the two armies and pleaded with the brothers to make peace with one another. Of course, every possibility for peace had already been explored and abandoned, and Vital's entreaties were without avail.

The battle began. We don't know how successful Duke Robert's first charge of mounted knights was, but soon the entire throng of warriors was locked in close combat—so close, in fact, that both defensive and offensive movement was all but impossible.

Suddenly, two of Henry's contingents—one led by Helias count of Maine, (again fully supporting Henry's cause), and the second by Alan duke of Brittany—burst out from their positions just out of sight of Curthose's army, and made a devastating attack on the flank of Duke Robert's infantry. Robert of Bellême, who was in charge of the rear of the ducal forces, was thrown into a panic, and, turning, fled with his troops, causing the complete collapse of Curthose's army. Duke Robert himself was captured, and the Breton contingent captured William of Mortain.

The noblemen who were part of Curthose's army were, of course, taken prisoner; none were killed, and nearly all of them were subsequently set free by King Henry. The exceptions were Robert Curthose, Robert I of Stuteville, and William count of Mortain, who became the second to occupy "guest rooms" in the Tower of London.

There was nothing haphazard about Henry's decision regarding whom to imprison and whom to release. He knew nearly all of these men well. Robert of Bellême, who had fled the battlefield, could not be taken prisoner, but was stripped by King Henry of those ducal lands which he had recently extorted from Robert Curthose in return for his support.

What is most interesting is the extent to which Duke Robert cooperated with his younger brother, now that he was Henry's prisoner. He provided Henry with key information as to what orders he had given the garrison at the main ducal fortress of Falaise, and suggested a strategy for ensuring that Robert of Bellême, who was still moving about freely, did not gain control of Falaise before Henry could reach the fortress. It was Curthose himself who ordered the Falaise garrison to surrender and to transfer their fealty to King Henry.

What was going on in Robert Curthose's mind at this point? It doesn't appear that he was anxious concerning what kind of treatment Henry would mete out to him, or what would happen to his small son and heir, William Clito. Yet, unless Robert lacked all imagination, he must have known that Henry had very few options now for how to deal with his oldest brother.

Duke Robert was imprisoned—in very luxurious style, it must be added—in three or four English fortresses successively until his death in 1134 at an age between eighty and eighty-four years—an astonishingly long life in the twelfth century. The fact that he lived so many years speaks volumes in itself concerning the quality of his imprisonment. The suggestion that King Henry had his brother's eyes put out came much later, and is flatly contradicted by contemporary testimony. We know, for example, that he spent his last years at Cardiff Castle in Wales, and attended dinners where entertainment was provided by Welsh bards, and Curthose himself, it seems, decided to learn the Welsh language, in which he eventually became a poet of some ability.

The allegation that William count of Mortain, was similarly mutilated must be completely discounted for many reasons: 1) It was completely out of character for Henry, particularly since the count of Mortain was not guilty of treachery. Mortain had relin-

quished his lands in England in 1104, technically of his own free
will, and at that point had announced his alliance with Curthose.
Unlike many others, Mortain was unwavering in his commitment
to Curthose; 2) Blinding a noble prisoner of William of Mortain's
status would have been a complete breach of knightly etiquette,
and would have made Henry vulnerable to endless criticism; 3)
The public records show William of Mortain receiving an annual
income twice that of a knight of the times, with additional generous
stipends for the count's personal servants. Henry evidently treated
Mortain just as he treated his other noble prisoners, which were
few in number, and none of whom was mutilated; and 4) There is
strong evidence that, after King Henry's death, William of Mortain
was released from prison and became a monk at Bermondsey
Abbey, the annals of which contain no mention of his blindness.

Whether or not Robert Curthose seriously contemplated the possibility of being imprisoned for the rest of his life, his almost upbeat
behavior in the days following his defeat at Tinchebray suggests
that, on some level, he was relieved. His governing of the duchy
had always been a travesty, and there are indications that he was
not only aware of this fact, but also knew how much suffering had
resulted from his misrule. The code of honor of the day, and perhaps the momentum created from the years he had fought against
his father William the Conqueror for the control of Normandy,
made it impossible for Curthose simply to hand over the reins to
Henry. Then, too, as Orderic Vitalis frequently reminded his readers, the duke had attracted quite an aggressive and vocal group of
"parasites," who poured into his ears day and night all the reasons
why nothing was his fault, and all would come out right in the
end. Since King Henry's easy victories at Bayeux and Caen in the
summer of 1105, Curthose undoubtedly had been exceedingly anxious about the day of reckoning, which, obviously, was approaching
rapidly, when Henry would return at the head of an army for their
ultimate contest. Duke Robert may well have been relieved that the
days of awful suspense were over. He had fought "to the end," and
thus could claim a defeat that preserved his honor.

At Falaise, King Henry for the first time met his nephew, Robert's only legitimate child, William Clito, now just three years old. (His mother, Duchess Sibylla, had died shortly after giving him birth.) Orderic wrote that the child was brought "trembling with fear" before his royal uncle, and that Henry compassionately soothed and tried to reassure him. The chroniclers wrote that the king, fearing that he would be blamed for any harm befalling the boy while in his care, decided to entrust Clito to Helias of Saint-Saen, to whom Curthose had married one of his illegitimate daughters. Helias of Saint-Saen—not to be confused with Helias count of Maine (King Henry's great ally in his Normandy campaign)—was a man of good character, and completely devoted to Robert Curthose, as he became subsequently to the duke's son. Unfortunately, Helias of Saint-Saen became equally devoted to Clito's claims to the duchy of Normandy.

To the historians who have branded Henry I cruel and brutal, the king's treatment of the pro-Curthose noblemen he captured at Tinchebray is an eloquent answer. Hollister put it well: "If anything, . . . Henry's treatment of his captives in 1106 was kind to the point of foolhardiness."

There is an interesting similarity, here, to Swami Kriyananda. He, too, has shown kindness and forgiveness "to the point of foolhardiness" to others. However, Kriyananda used to say that, like Henry, when he had once given up on someone, it was forever. In this respect, I have noticed a change in Kriyananda over the years, for I've observed that now he always keeps the door open to those on whom he once would have given up entirely. His love, which has always been evident, has developed an impersonal quality which makes it unconditional.

It was in King Henry's nature to place his trust in generosity and compassion, hoping thereby to elicit a similar reaction from others. In his treatment of Robert of Bellême, William of Mortain, William Crispin, and many other self-defined "arch enemies," Henry showed that he was prepared to win them, first, as friends by extending his hand to them in friendship.

At this time (after Henry's victory at Tinchebray), it must have seemed as though a new dawn had broken for the Conqueror's Anglo-Norman kingdom. Not only was the positive new work of bringing order and peace to the war-torn duchy about to begin in earnest, but the neighboring principalities—Maine, Anjou, France, Flanders—were not actively opposing the reuniting of William the Conqueror's cross-Channel kingdom. The combination of events and personalities that were to prove so nearly fatal to the reunited kingdom were not yet obvious. In this atmosphere of positive upliftment, King Henry may have trusted to the fact that the highly prosperous, orderly kingdom he was determined to create would, in its positive momentum, be able to overwhelm and dissolve those violent and divisive energies which barons like Bellême represented. With very few barons of Bellême's stripe left in the land, Henry may reasonably have imagined that anyone who still harbored animosities and petty personal ambitions would have little fertile soil in which to develop self-serving schemes.

King Henry wrote to Anselm, after Tinchebray, that the victory was not his, but was "the gift of God who so disposed it." Anselm's response to the king reveals his heartfelt friendship and real joy on finding that Henry was ready to give the glory to God alone.

Today also, Kriyananda states after every undertaking, whether large or small, "God did it; not I. Without Him, I could do nothing."

CHAPTER 35

Peace Through Justice

King Henry (**so wrote** the chronicler William of Malmesbury) "preferred to contend by council rather than by the sword." Historian Warren Hollister goes farther in stating that Henry actually *disliked* war. In this respect, Henry was definitely unlike the normal warrior king of his day. If anyone doubts the validity of Hollister's opinion in this matter (considering all the fighting Henry did in his lifetime), he need only recall those kings who actually gloried in battle. They were legion. Henry became, in time, the most powerful king in Western Europe. Usually, ruling monarchs did their best to extend their territories. Henry fought only to reclaim what had belonged to his father, that had since been lost owing mostly to his brothers' bad management.

In this respect also, Kriyananda's nature has never been to attack. As a boy, he got into some of the usual boyhood scraps, but he never initiated one. In most cases he won. Two that he lost were against bullies much larger than he (one of them weighed 230 pounds to his 107). He wouldn't run away, however, and never wept, protested, or shouted for help. The dignified reserve he displayed toward those bullies afterward caused them to keep their distance from him from then on. Probably his stoic indifference under attack had struck them with awe, making them feel that, with this boy, they were out of their depth. As he put it, in one case, "I wasn't afraid."

As an adult also, he has always preferred to "contend by council." I have never seen him angry. When his senior sister disciples—karmic equivalents as one might describe them, to his older brothers in William's time—tried to destroy him with a twelve-year, fifty million dollar lawsuit (almost all of which they lost), they hired the third-largest legal firm in the world; Kriyananda hired a sole practitioner who was without even a secretary. He sought this man's help because he respected his integrity. Kriyananda's strategy throughout the twelve-year battle was to find solutions that would be of benefit to *both* sides.

Warfare and conflict, then, were not natural to Henry's temperament. He always addressed issues calmly and clearly. He knew, however, when to stop being a diplomat and take up arms. As many historians have noted, Henry, when it mattered most, was always at the head of his army. (In the present life, too, Kriyananda has been at the forefront of most of Ananda's "battles." In 2008 he stopped over in Italy on his way back from America to India, just so he could tell the judge in a suit against Ananda, "I know we are innocent, but if you find the slightest blame in us, the blame belongs on my own shoulders." The judge was inspired by this statement to dismiss the case.)

Up to this point in Henry's career he had never lost a battle. Remarkably, Tinchebray, a resounding victory with a minimum of bloodshed because of the strategies Henry employed, was also his very first experience of actual, pitched battle. Owing to his expert generalship, this crucial battle lasted hardly one hour.

Once the boundaries of the Anglo-Norman kingdom had been reestablished in conformity with its borders at the time of William the Conqueror's death, King Henry sought no further conquests. This is a fact, and impossible to square with the charges of "ambition," "avarice," and "ruthless suppression" that have been leveled at him by over-bookish historians.

The fact that King Henry preferred diplomacy and negotiation to combat made him well suited to build a new system of governmental justice, which he raised upon those Anglo-Saxon institutions which had worked well in the past, and on the framework William the Conqueror had started to put into place. New laws were needed; existing laws needed reexamination and clarification. Good laws and a smoothly working system of justice would be meaningless without a strong central government to enforce them. Finally, this government and its arm of law enforcement would, in its turn, require consistent funding.

King Henry, unlike either of his brothers, was deeply interested by temperament in creating a government that would completely replace violence and would introduce, for the settling of all disputes, the majesty of the law. Himself highly creative, with an astonishingly wide range of interests, Henry clearly recognized that the kingdom could flourish truly only in an era of peace. He envisioned many prospering endeavors, and many works of beauty.

King Henry, like his father, very consciously and deliberately set about also to create a spiritual foundation for the peace he hoped to establish. This serious, conscious effort has been too often overlooked. In addition to all that might be accomplished by an effective central government, Henry did his best to instill in his kingdom a strong, godly presence, spearheaded by spiritually minded men and women who wanted sincerely to live by Christian precepts.

Several historians have called the reign of King Henry I the "Golden Age of Monasticism" in England. New religious orders, such as the Cistercians and the Augustinian Canons, were first established in England during his reign, and were funded by him and his aristocracy. Small, deeply devoted enclaves of meditatively inclined hermits received strong encouragement from the king, who often bestowed little plots of land on these pious men so that they might live in greater security.

The Cluniacs, who by the time of Henry's accession were well established in England, and other orders also that followed the Rule of St. Benedict, built their monasteries in isolated rural settings. Some of the new orders that were established during Henry's reign worked among the people, and built their communities of monks and nuns in the towns that were emerging everywhere.

These new religious orders, settling in and near larger centers of population, were encouraged by Henry, as a means of helping to inspire the populace, and of discouraging the less desirable aspects of urban life.

These new orders were in keeping with the deep belief King Henry and Archbishop Anselm shared: that, by their mutual cooperation, both church and state would the more readily benefit the people of England and Normandy. Pious Christians made good citizens, and when the population enjoyed the fruits of peace, its members would be better able to turn their attention to the things of the Spirit. In these respects, perhaps especially, we see a great change from the times of William Rufus, who showed himself almost hostile to religion.

Judith Green makes the astonishing statement that Henry's first priorities after the victory at Tinchebray, which were the securing of Normandy's borders and the reinstatement of order, were accomplished within only a few months! How, one marvels, was King Henry able to achieve so quickly what Robert Curthose had not been able to accomplish during his nineteen-year reign?

After Falaise, King Henry, accompanied by Robert Curthose, entered the ducal seat of Rouen, whose townspeople, so the chroniclers tell us, welcomed him with rejoicing and offers of fealty. It is interesting to contemplate that this may have been the first time Henry had entered Rouen since the horrible bloodbath of October 1090. To those who remembered that terrible day, as well as to those who had heard the story told and retold over the intervening years, Henry must have assumed almost mythic proportions. No matter on which side a townsman had fought sixteen years earlier, young Henry's role on that occasion was acclaimed as wholly admirable.

In October, King Henry called a great council of Norman magnates at Lisieux. There he laid out the new principles which, he said, would now apply to those who held land in Normandy. Orderic relates that the king decreed "by royal authority" that peace was to be strictly maintained, and that plundering and robbery would be as strictly suppressed. Henry also declared that all properties that the churches had held at the time of William the Conqueror's death were to be returned to them. Other lands that had been seized, or that had in any other way changed hands since the Conqueror's death, were to be returned to their previous, lawful owners. King Henry included very specifically in this decree those lands which Duke Robert had "rashly" granted from the ducal demesne, as well as other barons' land that the duke may have gifted to some of his favorites. In short, King Henry returned Normandy to its 1087 state, as if Robert Curthose had never ruled there as duke.

Thus, with a stroke of the pen the king communicated that no one would own land simply because it had been granted him by Duke Robert. It would be up to those now who had received land for legitimate reasons to prove their right to it in a court of law. Undoubtedly, there were cases in which Duke Robert's gift of land had been reasonable. In such cases, the recipients came to possess their land permanently.

King Henry was also making an indirect comment on what he considered ducal or royal authority. Again, his nullifying of land grants was consistent with the position King Henry had taken *vis-à-vis* Robert's right to lead the duchy. If Duke Robert, by his own actions, had vacated the right to rule, the responsibility and the sense of stewardship with which he had distributed land must also be called into question.

The same debate was also taking place elsewhere in many other parts of Western Europe. The question was: Under what circumstances is it right to remove an anointed prince? Henry had certainly answered that question where it concerned Robert Curthose, to the satisfaction of his own conscience.

Over the next months, Henry's activities consisted largely of judicial hearings, over which he presided himself, as well as full councils of his magnates and leading prelates in Normandy. Between the all-Normandy councils we may be sure that there were many smaller hearings, which also involved Henry as he worked tirelessly to adjudicate disputes, identify trouble spots, clarify old laws and create new ones, and set a new tone for the entire duchy.

Striking among Orderic's accounts is how many magnates and prelates were listed as participating in those gatherings. Clearly, Henry was not only creating channels of just and solid administration: he was also giving his fledgling *curia* in the duchy a "crash course" in how to conduct themselves and the affairs of the kingdom. The ducal court system, which had been active under William the Conqueror, once again now began to function smoothly.

Normandy underwent an internal transformation. It began again to enjoy the order and peace that William the Conqueror had established. Henry's post-Curthose Normandy won the undying admiration of Abbot Suger of Saint-Denis—a monk, brilliant architect, man of prodigious energy, and advisor to and biographer of King Louis VI. In many ways Suger epitomized—in his talents, enthusiasm, and supreme self-confidence—the spirit of the Twelfth-Century Renaissance. Though Suger represented Saint-Denis, a non-Norman abbey, he found justice in Henry's court when lands donated to Saint-Denis, but lost in the Curthose anarchy, were restored.

The year 1108 stands out as one which King Henry dedicated almost entirely to instituting a wide variety of reforms. Eadmer tells us that at his Whitsuntide (Pentecost) court that year, the king turned his attention again to other aspects of reform within the church. Most of the discussion centered around the continuing effort to enforce the ban on clerical marriage, promulgated by Archbishop Anselm's all-England ecclesiastical council of 1102. Six years later it became apparent—and surprised no one—that many priests were simply ignoring this decree. Anselm and Henry, together, were determined that the church should be led by real renunciates. They now set about creating a series of harsher penalties for priests who continued to cohabit with women. The penalties included a gamut of punishments from the loss of benefits to excommunication. No one could miss the point that both men took this matter very seriously.

Eadmer takes special note of the fact that the king spoke with deep concern about the perfunctory, purely mechanical way in which many priests were conducting their church services. We know that Henry's contemporaries viewed him as a man of deep piety, though this core aspect of his nature may today be seen mostly by inference. The point raised by King Henry in the Whitsuntide council is significant because there is no way to interpret the king's concern cynically as part of some political ploy, or as anything but a clear expression of Henry's truly devotional nature.

Sometime during 1108, King Henry tackled the ongoing problem of provisioning the growing number of people who were a part of his household or were temporarily in attendance at his court. He wanted to ensure their good behavior as they traveled with him around the kingdom. Great difficulties had arisen during the reign of William Rufus, when the courtiers who went with him committed every manner of atrocity. Eadmer gives us this searing account:

"Because there was no discipline to restrain them, they laid waste all the territory through which the king passed. . . . When they could not consume all the provisions they found in the homes that they invaded, many of them, intoxicated by their own wickedness, made the inhabitants take the remaining provisions to market and sell them for the benefit of the invaders; or else they set fire to the goods and burned them up; or, if it was drink, they washed their horses feet with it and then poured the rest on the ground. It is shocking to contemplate the cruelties they inflicted on the fathers of families, the indecencies to their wives and daughters. As a result, whenever it became known that that king was coming, the inhabitants would all flee from their homes, intent on doing the best they could for themselves and their families by hiding in the woods, or by seeking refuge elsewhere."

Very early in his reign even King Henry had had to endure the ridicule of rowdy courtiers: callously independent men, warriors, accustomed to being the undisputed authorities in whatever locality where they ruled. By 1108, however, Henry became widely recognized, as Hollister points out, as a true king: one who had faced down a full-scale invasion of England; expelled rebel barons (the widely feared Robert of Bellême being a notable example);

conquered Normandy; and, by wise patronage, won the loyalty of the most powerful magnates of the Anglo-Norman kingdom. The members of Henry's *curia* had come to understand that this was not a man who would brook bad behavior.

The rules King Henry put into place called for strong measures against any member of his court who stole, plundered, or raped. The penalty might include blinding, or castration. Those times were such, remember, that even saintly Archbishop Anselm had counseled King Henry in one of his letters to rule in such a way "that the good will praise you, and the bad will fear you." Half measures would have been worse than useless.

One can imagine that the king had long been waiting for the time when he could establish certain standards of behavior among his own household and *curia*. Before setting in place the strict code of behavior that he instituted in 1108, however, he had to convince his *curia* that he was able to carry out whatever threat he made. Evidently, Henry had not misjudged the moment, for we hear of no such punishments ever being actually inflicted to keep his courtiers in line.

At the same time that Henry instituted these severe punishments for misbehavior, he also wisely established fixed allowances, for both his household staff and the magnates who were in attendance at his court. It would indeed have been unreasonable to expect people in power, given no other way of providing for themselves, to refrain from plundering the countryside. These lists of allowances—the bread and wine; the number of candles for each of the five departments in the king's household—the buttery, the chamber, the chapel, the hall, and the constabulary—have survived in a document called the *Constitutio domus regis*. Everyone in the household is specifically provided for, from the master chamberlain down to the watchmen, tent-keepers, and the laundress (the only woman on the staff). The king also established appropriate allotments for the noblemen in attendance, since their presence was something he wanted to encourage.

Three other steps were also taken that are worth mentioning, for they testify to Henry's care for even small details:

1) The practice of requisitioning goods from the local villages came under strict regulations, which were also carefully outlined.

2) Fixed prices were instituted for purchases by the royal household, and were widely published, inviting tradesmen who wished to sell at that price. This rule prevented the court, in its turn, from being "gouged."

3) The king adopted the practice of announcing his court's itinerary far in advance, including the number of days he would stay in each place. This announcement was not only for the sake of farmers and merchants who wanted to sell to the court, but also for any would-be petitioner, local landholder, and other person who had business connected with the court.

One of the most interesting commentators on the court of King Henry I is someone referred to earlier, Walter Map, who later became a clerk in the household of Henry's grandson, King Henry II. Walter Map, along with Geoffrey Gaimar—a poet who wrote in the vernacular—are two of the very few non-monastic commentators on the affairs of this period. Walter Map, in his *Courtier's Trifles* (as its Latin title is usually translated) looks back nostalgically to the reign of Henry I, and bemoans the loss of that court's ordered dignity, which he said formed a sharp contrast to the tumultuous and impulsive nature (and court) of Henry I's grandson. King Henry I's household, and the conduct of his *curia*, reflected to a great extent the manner of man Henry was, personally. Walter Map seemed to be longing for the "good old days" as he dipped his quill in ink to write: "Nothing was done without preparation, or without previous arrangement, or in a hurry; everything was managed as befitted a king, and with proper control. A veritable market followed the king wherever he moved his court—so fixed were his journeyings and his welcome stays."

From 1108 to the end of Henry's reign, no mention is made by any chronicler of rowdiness or abuse on the part of his courtiers.

In April 1109 King Henry suffered the loss of his great friend and advisor, Archbishop Anselm. Anselm's health had been delicate since 1106—though his spirit was always strong until nearly the end, when he had had to be carried into Canterbury Cathedral to celebrate mass. In Anselm's last letter to Robert count of Meulan, whom he now addressed as "my lord and friend, dearest Robert," he promised that he would fight to the last breath in his body for the primacy of Canterbury within the kingdom. And so he did. After deposing Thomas, the archbishop-elect of York, for refusing to submit a written profession of obedience to Canterbury, Anselm's very last letter warned of dire consequences to any English prelate who took it upon himself to consecrate Thomas II as archbishop of York without that written profession.

Posthumously, Anselm, who had been authorized by the pope to "order things as he would" within the English church, won this contest with York. King Henry presided while Thomas II submitted his written profession of obedience to Canterbury. Hugh the Chanter, a highly partisan chronicler for the York monastic community, wrote that Ranulf Flambard, bishop of Durham—the only dependency of York—had (very much in character) offered King Henry at the last moment one thousand silver marks if he would release Thomas from writing his profession. The Chanter of York tells us sourly that the king was "unmoved."

Anselm's end, as Eadmer describes it, was beautiful and peaceful. In his last hours, in the spirit of true renunciation, the archbishop asked that his body be laid on a piece of sackcloth on the bare floor, and scattered with ashes. He was buried in Canterbury Cathedral next to his beloved teacher, Lanfranc, where both men have lain undisturbed to this day. Anselm was canonized in the fifteenth century, and was recognized in the eighteenth century as a Doctor of the Church.

The death of Anselm must in many ways have been difficult for King Henry. The archbishop had understood the king's spiritual nature, probably in a way no one else did. His passing also signaled the end of the close partnership between the king and the archbishop of Canterbury—a partnership that closely resembled that of William the Conqueror and Archbishop Lanfranc. King Henry would never again experience a working relationship that allowed him such intimate, like-minded, and creative cooperation between the spiritual and temporal spheres of the kingdom.

King Henry seems to have been far ahead of his time in appreciating the value of military and political intelligence as an aid to diplomacy, to shortening wars, and to avoiding assassination. He had also mastered the use of diversionary tactics, such as creating "events" to keep his enemies occupied on other fronts. Henry's intelligence network and mastery of diversionary tactics involved—in addition to his own highly creative diplomacy—the creating of alliances through the careful selection of spouses for his children. It also involved—something that Kriyananda has always firmly eschewed—flat-out bribery. Over the next two decades, Henry saved the kingdom much bloodshed by his astounding ability to set in motion diplomatic and military strategies aimed at securing peace.

In these ways it must be said that Kriyananda is very different from Henry. Perhaps he has learned to rely more on God. At any rate, he has never shown any interest in ferreting out secrets, and has left people free to follow their own conscience in full independence to be and do what they willed. Moreover, as I said, he has never bribed anyone, not even with flattery. One of his notable characteristics is to let come what will, without forcing his will on anybody—even if their "will" is to harm him. One reason, perhaps, that both he and Henry have sometimes been considered unfeeling (in truth, what they were was unemotional) is that neither of them ever justified, explained, or sought excuses for their mistakes. Kriyananda's distaste for bribery of any kind may be a deeply felt reaction to his having had to resort to it in his life as Henry.

Once, when Kriyananda was invited to stay in the home of one of the wealthiest women in America, he deliberately expressed his milder opinion on feminism—an issue about which she, as he knew,

felt strongly. He didn't try to be offensive, but on the other hand he
didn't try to hide his much more balanced opinion that men and
women are completely equal. She, wanting a more "campaigning"
attitude from him, withdrew her support from him in consequence.
His attitude, however, was, "I'd rather she knew now than later."
In the communities he himself founded, men and women (I should
point out) enjoy complete equality, with leadership positions going
as much to women as to men. This even-handed position is all the
more remarkable, considering the further fact that, in the problems
he faced with his fellow disciples, it was the women who caused
him all his suffering, which in fact was considerable.

He has steadfastly refused to go out of his way to persuade
doubters to his views, even though it has meant building his work
more slowly.

As for Henry, he didn't hesitate to do battle, when necessary. At
the same time, he put tremendous energy into those diplomatic and
intelligence advantages which would lessen the need for bloodshed.

A passage in William of Malmesbury's chronicle expresses well,
supposedly in King Henry's own words, Henry's deep concern
for the lives of those who were loyal to him. Adela, Henry's sister,
urged her son Theobald, count of Blois, to ally himself with his
uncle Henry rather than with Louis VI of France. Perceiving Louis'
intentions to make war on King Henry, Theobald of Blois did
transfer his support to his uncle, taking a number of his minor barons with him. (From this time, Theobald of Blois never wavered in
his loyalty to King Henry.) King Louis, enraged, retaliated by sending raiding parties into Normandy. King Henry initially chose to
ignore those raids. When his hotheaded household knights urged
him to engage Louis in battle, King Henry answered them, "You
should not wonder if I avoid lavishing the blood of those who, by
repeated trials, have proved themselves faithful to me. They are
the adopted of my kingdom, the foster-children of my affection.
For this reason I am anxious to be a good and moderate father to
them, and to check the impetuosity of those whom I see to be so
ready to die for me."

William of Malmesbury concluded the story by relating that the king, perceiving that his knights could not understand his reluctance, and that they seemed inclined to interpret it as cowardice, led a contingent out personally to meet the raiders.

This incident suggests that there might well have been times when the king thought it politic to lead his restless knights out to reinforce castles, or to patrol borders, when, as he well knew, the right way to end the current hostilities was by envoys, or by arranged marriages, or by giving bribes of money to an overeager enemy prince.

On this same subject, Orderic Vitalis wrote that Henry, through his intelligence system, was "so thoroughly familiar with secret plots against him as to astonish the plotters, and swept away his enemies' designs like cobwebs, without shedding any of his own men's blood."

Henry spent Candlemas of one year at the abbey of Saint-Evroul, where Orderic Vitalis was a monk. Orderic tells how warmly Henry was welcomed into the monastic fraternity during his stay.

After some time, as Orderic Vitalis wrote:

"Henry returned victorious to England, after making peace with all his neighbors, and for five years he governed the kingdom and the duchy in great tranquility on opposite sides of the Channel, and his friends devoutly offered praise to the Lord God of hosts who orders all things mightily and well. Amen."

Since 1108 to 1113 full-blown warfare had been a threat to Normandy, from the time of French King Louis VI's ultimatum to Henry to render him homage as his vassal and surrender certain key border castles. All-out war had been averted by Henry's skillful combination of diplomacy, marriage alliances, and limited use of military force. Except for some very minor skirmishes along the border, the people of Normandy enjoyed peace throughout this volatile period. Monastics and priests had continued their devotions unmolested. Peasant farmers had continued to plant and harvest crops without helplessly watching them burned before their eyes, and thus without the specter of famine rising from those

smoky flames. Tradesmen, artisans, and merchants had been able
to continue their metiers, a fact that was already beginning to transform Western Europe. Peace had continued for these five years,
and appeared to be set in place for another five years: all this was
because of King Henry's tirelessly creative efforts to build alliances.

Though Normandy, from everything we know, was always
"volcanic," private warfare within the duchy had all but ceased.
Still to come, later in Henry's reign, was the development of the
sophisticated system of itinerant royal justices to augment local systems for dispensing justice. In the first years following his victory at
Tinchebray, Henry himself undoubtedly presided personally over
the resolution of many disputes whenever he was in Normandy.

The phrase "court of last resort" became both a fact (in describ-
ing King Henry's personal involvement in the dispensation of justice), and also a phrase that symbolized his constant insistence on
taking personal responsibility for whatever took place in his realm.

In this practice there is a close similarity between Henry and
Kriyananda. As an example, merely (I have touched on this point
before): A legal case was introduced into the courts that threatened
the very survival of the Ananda community which Kriyananda
had founded in Italy. Kriyananda himself was away in India at
the time, and was therefore not able to appear in the Italian court.
The case dragged on for five years. Several of Ananda's leaders
had to spend a few days in prison. When nothing could be proved
against them, however, they were released. The opportunity finally
presented itself for Kriyananda to appear before an Italian judge.
There was to be a hearing at a time when Kriyananda could pass
by way of Italy on his return to India from America. He went first
to Italy, therefore. Appearing in court, he told the judge, "I know
that the charges against us are completely false, and that the community is wholly without blame in this matter. Nevertheless, if any
blame is affixed to us, it must be to me alone. I myself am personally responsible for everything this community does. I alone, therefore, must be held culpable."

Implicit in his statement was the promise to return to Italy, and even to be imprisoned there if necessary, should that need arise. Fortunately, the judge ruled after two days that there had never been a valid case against Ananda in the first place. The charges therefore, being false, were dropped altogether.

Back to Henry: Historian Judith Green notes that a great mine of evidence exists concerning Henry's reign: the Pipe Roll of 1130, and thousands of royal charters which attest to the fact that the king, up to his very last days, made himself available to hear cases in which some difficulty had been encountered in reaching a resolution. His care for the maintenance of peace in the kingdom is manifest in his involvement in cases where people had been found guilty of breaking the Truce, or Peace, of God: times, that is, when there was a moratorium on war and on all acts of violence. For those who violated the "Truce of God" and had been sentenced to trial by battle, King Henry ordered that those battles take place at his court. In so doing, states Judith Green, "Henry himself was taking direct responsibility for making the Truce [of God] work."

In an early twelfth century passage from Geoffrey of Monmouth's *History of the Kings of Britain*, which we'll title (as others have done), "The Prophecies of Merlin," King Henry I is referred to for the first time as "the lion of justice, at whose roar the dragons trembled." Whatever else a contemporary chronicler chose to emphasize in discussing Henry's reign, every single commentator returned at last to the peace which the king established throughout the land by his adherence to justice. Even the Anglo-Saxon Chronicler, who tended to understate his remarks, wrote: "He [Henry] was a good man, and was held in great awe. In his days no man dared to wrong another. He made peace for man and beast."

CHAPTER 36

Losses and Betrayals

Henry had never been one who merely hoped for the best, when he could play a part in making it so. We may be sure that even though the political skies were momentarily clear that summer of 1113, the king took every precaution behind the scenes to keep himself well-informed about events on the continent, through his precocious intelligence system.

Piecing together the chroniclers' accounts, it seems that the fighting, before 1118, was confined entirely to the border areas of Normandy. In 1118, however—the year which Green calls the hardest of Henry's reign—pockets of baronial rebellion, encouraged by France, Anjou, and Flanders, began to erupt more centrally. Bad turned to worse in that terrible year for Henry, both personally and politically. In May, Queen Edith Matilda died. The following month another death occurred: Robert count of Meulan, who, in the role of wise advisor and accomplished military leader, had unwaveringly served first King William I, then King William Rufus, and finally King Henry.

It is not clear whether any illness preceded the queen's death. In any event, King Henry would not have been able to return to England for her funeral. His overriding priority, of which the queen herself would have completely approved, was the safeguarding of Normandy. Alas, Edith Matilda had also been Henry's highly capable and utterly reliable regent ever since the death of Anselm in 1109. To find another regent of her sagacity, experience, and attunement, possessed of his own vision for the kingdom, was going to be very difficult indeed.

Robert count of Meulan had, some short time before his death, retired to the monastery of Preaux (certainly with the king's blessing), there to live out his last days as a monk.

Besides the loss of his most trusted and experienced advisor, Henry must have felt that something else more intangible was lost with the passing of Robert of Meulan. Robert, as a very young knight, had fought for William the Conqueror at the Battle of Hastings, representing the Beaumont family. He had been with King Henry when Curthose's invasion force landed in 1101 to challenge Henry for the crown of England. He had fought in the vanguard at Tinchebray. Diplomatically, Robert of Meulan had been instrumental in helping King Henry to guide the course of the investiture controversy with Anselm, with its varied strategies and delays—all of which had made it possible for King Henry, in the end, to retain the right to require homage from newly invested prelates.

Within King Henry's current circle of *familiares*, Robert of Meulan had been the only one, besides Henry, who had served William the Conqueror directly, and who, with his subtle and sensitive mind, had understood something of the great man and his vision for the Anglo-Norman kingdom. This was a painful loss indeed for Henry! Now, as the crisis in Normandy worsened, Henry must have sorely missed Robert of Meulan's advice, and his proven capabilities as a military leader. Even more hurtful to Henry was that fact that, with Robert's death, the Beaumont "nexus," usually unshakably royalist, began to wobble in their commitment to the king.

Treachery surrounded the king. Predictably, those whom Orderic had aptly described as "passively frozen in their treachery," now believed that Henry's star was in the descendant.

Firmly determined to bring Normandy back under his control as a vassal state, King Louis VI of France, a man who reveled in subterfuge, scored a major victory in taking the ducal fortress of Les Andelys on the Seine. He accomplished this conquest by instructing his troops, so Orderic Vitalis wrote, to shout an

English battle cry as they approached Les Andelys. The gatekeepers, obviously not expecting subterfuge, admitted Louis' troops. Once inside, however, they suddenly changed their cry to the French, "Montjoie!" Outnumbering the garrison, they quickly took control of the important fortress. The garrison, which included Henry's brave and honorable natural son, Richard, had to flee for their lives.

King Louis was, in fact, the catalyst for stirring up a baronial revolt in Normandy during these years against King Henry. Louis' tireless agent was his kinsman Amaury de Montfort, who had his own ambitions to control certain important fiefs in Normandy.

For Henry, worse was yet to come. In February 1119, word reached him that Eustace of Breteuil and his wife Juliana, Henry's own natural daughter, were on the verge of joining the rebellion. There are points in the monk chroniclers' narrations of these events where we can almost feel Henry's pain, as a man, in enduring yet another betrayal. Breteuil was one of the wealthiest honors in Normandy, and the only reason that Eustace, the illegitimate son of the previous count, held Breteuil now was because King Henry had thrown his weight behind Eustace's bid. As a further mark of his friendship and favor, the king had given Eustace his own natural daughter, Juliana, in marriage. The young couple owed everything to King Henry, and this news that they were on the verge of betrayal was deeply painful to him.

Eustace of Breteuil, even before throwing in his lot with the rebels, had already made it shamefully clear that his loyalty to Henry was conditional. Eustace seized this moment to pressure King Henry into granting him the castle of Ivry, claiming that it was his by right. According to Hollister, the claim was doubtful, and Henry surely marveled that Eustace, whose right to anything he now held had been denied by everyone except Henry, could now speak so boldly about his "right" to the castle. Complicating matters for the king, Ivry castle was also claimed by Ralph of Gael, the current lord in residence, who, unlike Eustace, unconditionally supported the king.

Whatever Henry may have felt about the merits of Eustace and Juliana's friendship toward him, the king could not afford to alienate either claimant. He reassured all three—Eustace, Juliana, and Ralph of Gael—that everything would be settled to the satisfaction of each, and, as was usual in this kind of situation, hostages were exchanged. This hostage exchange was particularly important to King Henry, because it ensured that Eustace and Juliana would not, in the meantime, defect to the rebel camp. The young son of Ralph Harnec, the constable of Ivry and vassal of Ralph of Gael, Henry's loyal supporter, was placed in the care of Eustace and Juliana, while their two daughters, King Henry's own granddaughters, were handed over to Ralph Harnec at Ivry.

Orderic Vitalis is our source of information on the tragedy that now unfolded, a tale horrifying even by the standards of those brutal times. According to Orderic, Amaury de Montfort, King Henry's "premier enemy," had for some months now been closely involved with Eustace and Juliana, and it was Amaury, in fact, who had incited the couple to demand castle Ivry of Henry. It was also Amaury, so wrote Orderic, who now urged Eustace to blind the hostage in his care, the young son of Ralph Harnec, Ivry's constable.

As a tactic, though unspeakably dark and twisted, it made some sense. Now, no matter what Henry did or did not do, he would inevitably incur the wrath of either Ralph of Gael or Eustace and Juliana. The rules of hostage exchange absolutely demanded that a similar mutilation be inflicted on Eustace and Juliana's daughters. The question arises immediately: How could Eustace and Juliana have been persuaded to blind Ralph Harnec's son, knowing full well, as they certainly did, the rules of hostage exchange? The answer must be that Amaury once again used his famous "silver tongue" to convince the couple that Henry would never allow the blinding of his own granddaughters. (Intriguingly, this further suggests that those who knew King Henry more intimately, as Eustace and Juliana did, evidently considered him tenderhearted, or at least incapable of ordering the mutilation of his own granddaughters, even though the rules of warfare of the day left him no alternative.)

Now Eustace, acting on Amaury's advice, and continuing to exhibit the worst possible judgment, sent Ralph Harnec's son back to him, blinded and bleeding. When the distraught father brought his young son to King Henry, Orderic wrote that the king was deeply moved by the sight. We must not imagine, however, that what happened then was due to Henry's own feeling of outrage. He simply couldn't deny Ralph Harnec's right to do what tradition absolutely demanded in this situation. Ralph, as father of the mutilated boy, was distraught and desired revenge. It was Ralph, not Henry, who blinded Henry's granddaughters and cut off the tips of their noses. Henry has been vilified for centuries for this deed, which he didn't perform but was unable to prevent. If we put ourselves in his shoes, however, we must see how very little choice he had. The king had in fact no choice at all but to honor the universally accepted rules governing the exchange of hostages. The historian Judith Green has suggested that Henry allowed the blinding of the girls because otherwise a vengeful Ralph Harnec and his lord, Ralph of Gael, could have contributed to a further spiraling out of control of the rebellion in southeastern Normandy. Actually, however, the consequences to the king and, by extension, to England and Normandy could well have been even greater had he forbidden Ralph Harnec from exacting his revenge.

The code governing the exchange of hostages, which was an accepted part of any particularly delicate negotiation, was firmly fixed. Had Henry forbidden the mutilation of his granddaughters by Ralph Harnec, his promises from then on, as king and as military leader, would forever have been held suspect. For a monarch whose life consisted of treaties, negotiations, and agreements on which the welfare of an entire kingdom rested, the repercussions of denying Ralph Harnec his rights in this matter would have haunted Henry and the entire Anglo-Norman kingdom for the remaining years of his reign.

Amaury had committed a despicable act which had now had its desired effect: Eustace and Juliana (Henry's natural daughter) prepared immediately to defend the castles within the honor of Breteuil, with Juliana herself in command of the main citadel. The townspeople of Breteuil, however, fearing that the town itself would be destroyed by Henry's assault, sent messengers to the king offering to open the gates to him and his army. King Henry, giving strict orders to his troops to take no plunder at Breteuil, proceeded to lay siege to the citadel.

From Orderic Vitalis we get the impression that the siege had not been very long underway before Juliana, her knights daunted by the king's army and in awe of the king himself, announced that she wished to negotiate with her father. Henry entered the citadel, and Juliana approached her father. As she did so, however, Juliana suddenly produced a crossbow and fired directly at Henry. The bolt missed him, though we don't know by how much. The fact that she used a crossbow makes it clear that her intention was truly murderous, for the bolt from a crossbow could pierce solid armor even from a distance. King Henry was certainly shocked, and perhaps unnerved, knowing full well how lethal the bolt would have been. He turned immediately and left the citadel, destroying the drawbridge behind him.

Juliana's knights must have watched with intense alarm this bungled attempt to murder her own powerful father. It placed her liegemen in a dangerous position. King Henry kept Juliana a prisoner in Breteuil citadel for some days, where he may have hoped she would cool down and understand the role she herself had played in the blinding of her daughters. In the end, Juliana left the castle by the only route open to her, leaping from the castle wall into the icy waters of the moat, with the February winds brushing her bare bottom as she fell. (People in those days wore no underwear.) King Henry allowed her to escape and join her husband Eustace, who had fortified himself at Pacy. He left them both to meditate on the tragic choices they had made.

Meanwhile, the king decided to transfer the honor of Breteuil to Ralph of Gael, who was deeply loyal to Henry, with a kinsman's claim to the county.

In the end, King Henry dealt very leniently with Eustace and Juliana. Though he stripped them of the wealthy county of Breteuil, he allowed them to keep the honor of Pacy, within Breteuil, where they continued to draw about three hundred silver marks annually from lands they held in England. Hollister notes that, though they had acted with extreme dishonor, the king in a sense forgave them by allowing them to keep these three hundred silver marks as an income, allowing them to "live in style" for the rest of their days.

The Hyde chronicler described a "great despondency" which now overwhelmed the king, owing to the many betrayals he had suffered on all sides. In another case, a trusted member of his own household had tried to murder him. Hollister sympathizes with the extremely stressful situation Henry faced as he saw key strategic fortresses fall into enemy hands—partly or wholly because of the betrayal of men he had trusted and even promoted.

Historians who express lack of sympathy for Henry are probably influenced by the democratic "dogma" that when people are widely in agreement, they can't all be wrong. If so many people opposed Henry—such must have been their thinking—there must have been some justice on their side. Overlooked, however, are several facts: Those people *were* traitors, by nature; they were wholly self-interested. The real majority, moreover—the populace—suffered greatly at their hands. Henry was trying to bring order to the duchy to alleviate the general suffering.

In the middle of a seething sea of betrayals, King Henry, it was said, adopted the practice of having the position of his bed changed frequently, and of always keeping a sword and shield nearby, even while he slept. Hollister answers those to whom this strategy has seemed an indication of Henry's imbalance and paranoia by pointing out, with perfect common sense, that, considering the circumstances, most people would have considered Henry's precautions "eminently sensible."

The fact that Henry did not submit to fear or despondency can perhaps be accounted for only by what every contemporary chronicler notably says about him: that he was a man of great faith in God.

Henry also believed strongly in the rightness of his efforts to set a central government in place in Normandy, which could, without being dictatorial, provide a framework of law and justice, and the authority needed to challenge and eliminate private warfare. The proof that it was within Henry's power to achieve this stability in Normandy may be seen in the fact that he had already bestowed seventeen years of unbroken peace on England, where a whole generation now reaching adulthood had experienced no war, raiding, or plundering of the land. Normandy, too, for nearly twelve years after Henry's assumption of control of the duchy, had had its first taste of peace since the Conqueror's death.

Henry now began to make peace overtures in several directions, showing himself ever willing to compromise, except in cases where the peace of the kingdom might be undermined.

King Henry seems now, however, to have been more starkly isolated in what he had set himself to do. His sense of isolation was caused in part by the deaths of Queen Matilda and Robert count of Meulan. Partly it was due to the countless betrayals he had endured on the part of many to whom he had given the hand of friendship. He must have wondered how much he could expect of anyone. Anselm and Lanfranc had loved the image of the two plow horses, representing the church and monarchy, pulling together in tandem for the progress of the kingdom and its people. King Henry, it seems, though still "in harness," now had to pull the great weight of the Anglo-Norman kingdom alone. The burden weighed on him more heavily than ever before.

CHAPTER 37

The White Ship Tragedy

King Louis VI of France, having exhausted every military option for bringing the duchy of Normandy under his control, now turned for support to a usually reliable ally of France: the pope. Louis's agenda included not only establishing his suzerainty over the duchy, but also installing William Clito, Curthose's heir, as the duke of Normandy.

The French king showed up, accordingly, with the eighteen-year-old Clito beside him, at a very important church council in Rheims in October 1119. In fact King Louis had every reason to believe that the new pope, Calixtus II, who had been born to the comital family of Burgundy, would be more responsive than most popes to the French king's appeals, including his charges against King Henry I. Ever since Emperor Henry V of Germany had driven Pope Calixtus II from Rome, installing in his place the anti-pope Maurice of Braga (Gregory VIII), the exiled Calixtus had taken refuge at the court of Louis VI and Queen Adelaide, the pope's niece.

The Council of Rheims was slated to cover a number of vitally important items, and King Henry of England gave permission for Anglo-Norman prelates to attend. The one restriction he imposed on them was that they were not to present for resolution any matter that was strictly internal to the church of England or the Norman duchy. Ralph d'Escures, archbishop of Canterbury, was not able to attend because of illness, but he begged King Henry to ensure somehow that Thurstan, archbishop-elect of York, didn't receive consecration as archbishop directly from the hands of Pope Calixtus II. Henry himself strongly opposed such a consecration, not only because it represented undue papal interference in affairs internal to the Anglo-Norman kingdom, but also because it would cut the ground out from under Canterbury's claim to primacy within England, a claim which Henry supported, lest England's church be divided against itself. The right to consecrate Thurstan as archbishop of York belonged, in King Henry's view, to Ralph archbishop of Canterbury, and to no one else. In any event, before the Council of Rheims even got underway, Pope Calixtus II did bestow the church's blessing on Thurstan as archbishop of York—without referring to King Henry, and without Thurstan's written profession of obedience to Canterbury.

When the Council of Rheims took up the issue of the Anglo-Norman-Franco war, King Louis VI, with William Clito at his side, stood and detailed exhaustively his grievances against King Henry.

The Anglo-Norman perspective was never even heard. While historian Judith Green sees the Council of Rheims as a diplomatic failure for King Henry, Warren Hollister does not. After all, the pope's "bottom line" commandment—that both sides observe the Truce of God—suited King Henry very well. At this point he controlled all the strategically important fortresses. A cessation of hostilities could work only in his favor. Most significant was the fact that in such a highly charged, pro-French atmosphere, Pope Calixtus II made no specific condemnation of any aspect of King Henry's actions. King Henry, after all, supported the true pope against the anti-pope, whom Henry V of Germany had installed in Rome.

Furthermore, Henry was the most effective, most wealthy, and most powerful reform-minded monarch in all of Western Europe. We may be sure that the pope had no wish to anger him, regardless of his own present indebtedness to King Louis VI of France.

Because of Henry's dogged efforts between 1118 and 1120, both diplomatically and militarily, to end foreign interference and put down, one by one, each baronial uprising, the rebel barons in Normandy now sought, almost without exception, to be restored to Henry's good graces. Shortly after the Council of Rheims, Amaury de Montfort, whom Henry had been besieging cease-lessly at Amaury's citadel in Evreux, at last sought to make peace, with Theobald count of Blois acting as mediator. Henry had been clear from the beginning with regard to what was required to main-tain peace; his terms had not changed: Amaury could succeed to the countship of Evreux, and to its lands, but not to the citadel of Evreux, which was to be garrisoned by Henry's own men. Amaury de Montfort had evidently been sufficiently humbled by now to accept these terms "with great satisfaction," according to a rather remarkable comment by Orderic.

In these days near Aumale, as negotiations concluded with Stephen of Aumale, William Clito requested a private interview with his uncle, King Henry. Clito pleaded that his father, Robert Curthose, be released, swearing that if Henry would release him, Curthose and Clito, father and son, would both go to Jerusalem and never trouble Henry again so long as they lived. The king, however, had just suffered through two harrowing years of broken oaths, and two assassination attempts. (There had been another besides Juliana's; I have omitted to describe it here, feeling that the main point—betrayal by intimates—had been sufficiently made.) In those days, especially, Henry must have been acutely aware of the unreliability of human nature, even when sincere and honorable individuals are involved. Refusing absolutely to release Curthose, Henry instead, and very earnestly, offered Clito significant lands in England, and, more important, promised that he himself would train Clito in the "art of government," and would treat his young nephew "like his own son." According to Orderic Vitalis, William Clito refused, and departed the court weeping, accompanied by his most faithful knights and by the devoted Helias of Saint-Saen, in whose care Henry himself had placed the three-year-old Clito.

A touch of this sadness lingers even today in Swami Kriyananda, who, though basically sunny and enthusiastic by nature, seems deeply aware of humanity's unreliability. The impression is sub-tle and few people notice it, but it lingers slightly, and may be responsible for the hint of sadness that appears in some of his music compositions. Only God's love, he seems to feel, can be fully depended upon.

Meanwhile, King Henry learned that Pope Calixtus II had, indeed, consecrated Thurstan as archbishop of York in 1119 at the Council of Rheims. Though there may be some question as to whether Thurstan had formally promised Henry that he would not allow this to happen, we can fairly safely assume from the anger King Henry now displayed that Thurstan had made that promise, and had now broken it. Henry sent word to Thurstan that he was no longer welcome in Normandy and in England—unless and until he made a written profession of obedience to Canterbury. Accordingly, the now exiled archbishop of York accompanied Pope Calixtus' entourage as it departed Rheims and traveled through France.

Several chroniclers tell us that King Henry, like his father William the Conqueror, abhorred drunkenness—not only in himself, but in those around him. When Henry prepared to return to England in November 1120, however, the mood of celebration was high, now that the great threats to Normandy had been met and overcome. Henry's young noblemen gathered in Barfleur in a separate ship, the constraints of the king's presence removed, and we can imagine the numerous toasts that were offered.

King Henry's only legitimate son and heir, William Adelin, was joined by two of Henry's natural children, Richard and Matilda countess of Perche. The valiant royal favorite Ralph the Red and Henry's ward, Richard earl of Chester, also boarded with this gay throng. All of them were young, and had proved beyond any doubt their mettle and their loyalty. Each could be sure that the king would show his gratitude in a very concrete manner upon their return to England, by bestowing wealth and honor on them. There were many reasons for the very high spirits the young noblemen and knights exhibited that day.

Orderic Vitalis wrote that on November 25, a man named Thomas fitz Stephen approached the king and offered him one mark of gold (6 pounds, according to Judith Green) in order to repossess a fief which his father had held of William the Conqueror in 1086. Stephen, it seems, was the "master steersman" of the ship that had carried the Conqueror to England in 1066, and there is, in fact, a Stephen, who held the title of "steersman," mentioned in Domesday. This Thomas fitz Stephen had recently refurbished a vessel—the White Ship, he called it—which was completely and appropriately outfitted for royal service if it pleased the king to sail in it. Henry thanked Thomas, but explained that he had already chosen a ship for the crossing. He would be glad, however, to entrust his sons, William Adelin and Richard, as well as many other noble youths, to the care of Thomas.

Fifty rowers, according to Orderic, constituted part of the crew. The ship must, therefore, have been fairly large. These crewmen were evidently delighted at the prospect of being surrounded by a more youthful and less staid and awe-inspiring group of passengers than those who accompanied the king himself. They also anticipated a liberal sharing of wine from these already-tipsy young people. They were not to be disappointed. When the crew asked William Adelin for wine, the young prince shared it unhesitatingly, and in abundance.

Orderic wrote that about three hundred people boarded initially, but that a few of the more prudent passengers, deciding to go by another ship, disembarked. The young men aboard the White Ship had become quite rowdy, and their condition was only likely to get worse. Among those who disembarked was the king's nephew, Stephen of Blois, whom fate decreed as Henry's successor to the throne of England. Stephen declared with considerable irritation that the noise the young men were making was too much for him. Priests came to bless the departing ship, but the drunken marine guards (and probably also a few of the aristocratic youths) jeered at them, and with mock-threatening antics frightened them away.

Since the White Ship carried some part of the royal treasure, but little else as cargo, the drunken young men decided that there was a sporting chance of catching up with the king's ship, which had already left the harbor for the open sea. Thomas, the steersman, agreed to this idea, and the oarsmen, now also tipsy and ready to enter into the spirit of the chase, worked their oars vigorously. The White Ship, however, soon struck a large rock, which was a well-known hazard in the harbor, though by no means the only rock in the harbor that at high tide became shallowly submerged. The oarsmen were evidently attempting to push the boat off the rock, when suddenly she capsized. The single lifeboat was launched, and William Adelin was bundled into it. He was quickly rowed away from the foundering ship.

Henry's heir to the Anglo-Norman kingdom would have lived, had he not heard his half sister, Matilda countess of Perche, calling to him piteously and begging him not to leave her. William Adelin ordered the rowers to return to the White Ship for his sister. When his lifeboat came close again to the doomed ship, many others attempted to clamber aboard, causing the lifeboat, also, to capsize. The sole survivor related that Otheur fitz Count, natural son of Hugh of Avranches, and William Adelin's longtime tutor, in a final gesture of protectiveness and loyalty, flung his arms around the young prince, and they drowned together.

The story has it that at some point the steersman Thomas surfaced and asked the fate of William Adelin. When the few who still clung to the floating wreckage told him what had happened, Thomas, knowing the degree to which it was his irresponsibility that had caused the tragedy, chose death by drowning rather than facing the king's grief and wrath.

There was only one survivor of the wreck: a butcher, who clung all night to a spar, and was rescued by fishermen the next morning. Only the natural oils of his thick sheepskin garment, and his considerable body fat, saved him from the cold of the November sea water. After this well-padded butcher had been plucked from the water, and the tragic tale was revealed in full, a search began along the shore for the bodies of the three hundred passengers and crew lost with the White Ship. The passengers had included some of the most promising youth of the next Anglo-Norman generation. Though the body of Richard earl of

Chester was recovered days later, many miles from the wreck, the bodies of Prince William Adelin, Richard, and Matilda countess of Perche, all three of them Henry's children, were never found. Since the White Ship did not sink completely, snagged as it was on the great rock which had damaged it, the vessel was ultimately hauled to shore and the portion of the royal treasury aboard her was recovered nearly intact.

Meanwhile, the king's ship reached England safely, and Henry kept asking for news of the White Ship. We don't know exactly when or how the news of the disaster reached England, but most of the court evidently knew of it before Henry did. No one dared to tell him, however. One of the chroniclers relates that the courtiers, all of whom, without exception, had lost loved ones in the wreck, wept bitterly in private, but managed for hours to preserve a semblance of normality before the king.

Finally, Count Theobald of Blois suggested that a young boy be sent to the king with news of the disaster. This was done—with the child falling at the king's feet, sobbing, and relaying haltingly the traumatic tale. It was said that Henry fell to the floor, overwhelmed by grief, and had to be helped from the chamber.

The king had lost two sons—one of them his heir, and the other a courageous, loyal warrior, whose nobility of spirit had been one of Henry's few steady lights during the last two years of treachery. Henry had also lost a natural daughter, Matilda, countess of Perche; a niece, Matilda of Blois, daughter of Henry's sister Countess Adela; as well as two of his most dearly loved captains. He had additionally lost close members of his royal household, including William Bigod and Robert Mauduit. Orderic Vitalis leaves us with the impression that, although Henry grieved deeply for his children and for all who had been lost, he spoke most often of his two captains, recalling their many acts of selfless courage, and weeping while he did so.

(It is interesting that Kriyananda, in this life, has never felt the normal desire for offspring. Indeed, the thought seems to awaken in him a certain sense of repudiation. Even when people address him as their spiritual father, he says he must make a special effort not to reject that role, mentally.)

The loss of the White Ship, involving as it did well over two hundred of the young aristocracy and some of most crucial members of the king's household, was both a personal and a national tragedy. The entire Anglo-Norman aristocracy was stricken, and all were grieved and deeply demoralized. No one in the twelfth century would have contemplated such a sweeping devastation without asking the question, "Why? Why are we being punished in this way? How have we displeased God?" One can readily imagine the unhealthy atmosphere of blame, directed both inwardly and outwardly. King Henry, who always considered it his duty to inspire, motivate, and create harmony among those around him, must have felt everyone's grief very keenly.

Historian Frank Barlow expresses the awe that many writers through the centuries have expressed in contemplating the spirit with which King Henry met this disaster:

"It was an almost annihilating blow; and that Henry recovered, planned anew, indomitably pursued his new aims, and appeared to regain control reveals the true qualities of the man."

We are not told much about how King Henry and his *curia* observed Christmas in 1120. The holy season must have taken on a much more somber and contemplative air than ever before. It may have been during this time that the king conceived of the forward-looking religious foundation which became Reading Abbey. He dedicated Reading to his father, his brother King William II, "to all my predecessors and successors," and to his queen, Edith Matilda, who had died when Henry was so embroiled in fighting for Normandy's survival that he'd scarcely had time to mourn her.

Reading Abbey has always been seen, in any case, as an outlet for the king's grief.

Dedicated by King Henry to the Virgin Mary, and to St. John the Evangelist, the abbey was a unique and completely new expression of renunciation. The foundation modeled a new kind of relatively independent monastics—a community which was to manage collectively those lands and manors which financially supported their monastic service. In addition, the monks of Reading would make group decisions concerning their own leadership.

The monks, rather than living apart from their fellow men, would serve the public selflessly and continuously, thereby meeting (as Henry's charter for Reading stated it) an urgent social need: offering shelter to the poor, to pilgrims, and to all travelers. The monastery would offer food, warmth, and shelter, as well as all manner of compassionate care. Situated at a point where all passed who were traveling from London to the south of England, Reading Abbey's location, which Henry himself chose, was perfectly adapted to the fulfillment of its mission. While other monasteries endeavored to serve travelers in much the same way, they were often located in out-of-the-way places. The abbot and monks of Reading, however, were in a position to fulfill their assignment of serving every traveler, and took this mission very seriously.

William of Malmesbury praised the foundation of Reading in these words: "[At Reading, King Henry] placed monks of the Cluniac order, who are at this day a noble pattern of holiness and an example of unwearied and delightful hospitality. Here may be seen what is peculiar to this place, for guests, arriving at every hour, consume more than the inmates themselves. . . . They will, as I hope, endeavor by the grace of God to continue in virtue; and I blush not to commend men of such holiness, and admire that excellence in others which I possess not myself."

King Henry drew the members of the founding community from the Cluniac mother house, and chose as Reading's first abbot his good friend, Hugh of Amiens, a monk of Cluny and most recently the prior of Lewes. King Henry and Abbot Hugh most likely collaborated on the creation of the charter for Reading. Unlike any other religious foundation in England, the abbot and monks were to hold Reading's property in common, and could in no way divide it. When the position of abbot fell vacant, a new one was to be chosen by a vote of the monks—never by the king, nor even by a church superior. When Reading lacked an abbot, the property was to be administered collectively by the brethren, rather than by a royal agent as usually happened. No child oblates were allowed—only adults could enter Reading, of their own free will.

In founding Reading Abbey, King Henry followed closely the pattern set by William the Conqueror in creating Battle Abbey, which honored both Norman and Anglo-Saxon warriors, including Harold Godwinson, who had fallen at Hastings. Both were Cluniac foundations, richly endowed with income-producing lands, manors, fairs, tolls, etc., and both were free from all manner of taxes and gelds.

The archaeological evidence suggests that the abbey church, completed in 1125, was about the same size as St. Paul's Basilica in London. King Henry also sought holy relics for Reading, that the abbey itself might become a pilgrimage destination. Its most famous relic was the hand of St. James, brought back to England from Germany by the king's daughter, the Empress Maud. By the middle of the twelfth century it is estimated that about two hundred monks resided at Reading, and that they daily served the same number of guests, both pilgrims and the poor.

From our vantage point, serving the traveler might not seem so divine a calling, but in the twelfth century, when travel was perilous, physically trying, and filthy, Reading Abbey offered, quite literally, a life-saving service. It must have contributed in other ways also that we can scarcely imagine, to opening up routes of trade and communication between London and mid-England with the southernmost shires. The monks of Reading Abbey, following King Henry's original charter, aided all manner of needy people for the next four hundred years—until 1539, when its service was abruptly suspended, as Reading became one of the many victims of King Henry VIII's Dissolution of the Monasteries Act. This monastery seems to have drawn highly dedicated men to lead its monastic congregation until the end. The last abbot, Hugh Faringdon, refused to surrender his trust to Henry VIII's men, and was hanged, a martyr. For the abbey had, of course, been taken easily by armed might.

Even before the catastrophe of the White Ship, arrangements may have already been underway for King Henry's marriage to Adeliza, daughter of Godfrey VII, count of Louvain and duke of Lower Lorraine. If so, these negotiations were now considerably speeded up. In January 1121, about two months after his loss of William Adelin and so many kinsmen and friends, Henry and Adeliza were married with the hearty approval of the king's barons and church leaders. Though her birth date is not known for certain, Adeliza was probably about eighteen years old at the time, reportedly a great beauty, and, by all accounts, very devoted to her new husband. She was considered to be a descendant of Charlemagne, and therefore a worthy consort for the ruler of the Anglo-Norman realm. In addition, Adeliza brought with her to the marriage some Flemish allies for her new husband—allies who would prove important in the next few years.

From the moment when the first terrible shock of the White Ship disaster had passed, King Henry, who was now in the twenty-third year of his reign, did everything he could to forestall the political chain reaction that was now fated to begin.

CHAPTER 38

Holding the Reins During Rebellion

"**O**rderic," wrote Hollister, "describes the fifty-five year-old monarch [King Henry at the siege of Pont-Audemer in 1123] as hurrying to and fro like a young knight, energetically helping with anything that needed doing, encouraging everyone, smiling and joking, even instructing his carpenters in the construction of a wooden siege tower."

This brief but vivid portrait of King Henry in action runs directly counter to the image of those "chess player" historians, to whom the past seems more a sequence of events than a drama concerning flesh-and-blood human beings. Such persons have described a grim monarch presiding over what one of them actually called "a calculated reign of terror." Orderic Vitalis, however, was writing at the very time of these events. His monastery was situated near the scene of the action, and he had met King Henry personally.

It is also worth noting that this description of King Henry at Pont-Audemer, pitching in with humor and creative zeal to help with difficult tasks, took place in the earlier, less certain days when he was combating an outbreak of rebellion. The king's good spirits at that time were not due to the successful outcome of some decisive battle, with the concomitant release of tension. The evidence suggests that Henry's energy, enthusiasm, and comradely spirit were, in fact, intrinsic to his nature.

The siege of Pont-Audemer to which Orderic refers occurred during the second serious baronial uprising that Henry faced during his reign. Like the first one (1118–1120), this outbreak in 1123 was fomented by the activities of King Louis VI of France and his tireless kinsman and agent, Amaury de Montfort. Amaury had been forgiven by King Henry for his role in the 1118–1120 rebellion, and had been gracious reinstated as count of Evreux, in Normandy. Now, as count, Amaury became "irritated," so Orderic tells us, by the strength of the ducal government. Using his famed powers of persuasion and his network of powerful kinsmen, which included the king of France himself, Amaury drew a number of Normandy's barons into a plot, with promises of help from France and Anjou.

This second baronial insurrection again involved painful betrayals to Henry, for the three young barons most closely allied with Amaury against Henry had all been raised from childhood at Henry's court, as his protégés. Their leader was none other than Waleran of Beaumont, son and heir of Henry's great familiaris, Robert of Meulan, now deceased. Like Amaury, their only discernable motive in rebelling was restless resentment of Henry's effective centralized government of Normandy.

Since his accession to the throne, Henry had poured enormous amounts of energy into stabilizing the currency, trying to ensure that every coin met strict standards. This was a very serious problem in those days. A dishonest minter could destroy the whole economy, and with it the country. Henry tried every incentive possible to prevent debasement of the coinage. In 1124, faced with the mutiny and desertion of mercenary soldiers during this crisis, Henry had to resort to drastic measures. He now ordered that every minter in England who was proved guilty of adding tin to his coins was to be castrated and have his right hand cut off. Roger bishop of Salisbury, who was acting as regent for King Henry, had the task of carrying out the orders.

These were drastic measures, but King Henry was widely praised for initiating them. Every contemporary chronicler either praised King Henry for his threat to punish the minters, or stated, more neutrally, that it was a completely reasonable decision. The terse,

ever to-the-point Anglo-Saxon Chronicler wrote, "It was very just-
ly done, for they [the minters] had ruined the whole country with
their false dealing." Eadmer, Anselm of Bec's biographer, praised
King Henry for enacting all his strong laws with their concomitant
punishments, adding that Henry's strong measures against "evildo-
ers" had won strong approval from the saintly Anselm.

In fact, many people of those times would have considered the
punishment lenient. Under old Anglo-Saxon law—"the good laws
of King Edward the Confessor," which Henry had promised in
his Coronation Charter to restore—debasement of the kingdom's
currency was considered a particularly heinous act of treason, and
called for the outright execution of every false minter. This much,
then, is certain: for King Henry to have ordered any punishment
short of mutilation or execution for the minters would have been
perceived throughout the kingdom as pitiful weakness on his part.
In fact, he took the most merciful course available to him, and
nothing more is heard for the remainder of his reign about any
problems to do with the coinage. That was, as we have said before,
a brutal age; violent and greedy men responded only to threats
of the harshest punishment. Those who have excoriated Henry
for this or any other decision should stop to consider what his
alternatives were—including the alternative of not acting at all.
A psychiatric counseling session with a twelfth century minter concerning the psychic scars he might have received as a child that
now prompted him to steal was definitely not an option.

In the spring of 1124, an important series of events began the
breakup of this newest rebellion in Normandy. King Henry's forces had for some time been besieging Waleran's castle of Vatteville,
though it seems their activities were limited to preventing provisions from flowing into the castle, and to keeping any of its garrison
from leaving. The royalist troops, under the command of Walter of
Valiquerville, had built a siege castle from which they could keep
watch in relative safety, sallying forth as necessary to prevent any
movement in or out of Vatteville. In March 1125 Count Waleran
and his three noble brothers-in-law, including Hugh of Montfort

and nearly all the rebel barons, with Amaury de Montfort at their head, set out to relieve the Vatteville garrison.

The rebel magnates attacked the royalist siege castle, taking its garrison completely by surprise. With amazing skill and ingenuity, their first move was to snatch its commander, Walter of Valiquerville, from the ramparts of the siege castle by means of a long iron hook. He became their prisoner, and the rest of the king's garrison were overwhelmed by the sheer numbers of those who fell upon them. Orderic Vitalis related that Waleran now entered the nearby homes and churches and requisitioned (Orderic actually wrote "stole") food and other supplies for the very hungry Vatteville castle garrison that he and the other rebel magnates had just rescued. Then, "raging like a wild boar," Waleran rode with his men through the forest of Brotonne and "took as prisoners many of the peasants he found there cutting wood in the thickets, and crippled them by cutting off their feet." Orderic Vitalis wrote that Waleran did this because the peasants had come to the king's aid against him.

However, these rebel "covert operators" who, with Waleran and Amaury at their head, had relieved the besieged garrison at Vatteville were themselves being kept under observation by another covert group: King Henry's scouts. The attack on the royalist garrison that manned the siege castle at Vatteville had been witnessed by Henry's men, who now reported the position and activity of these rebels to Ranulf of Chester, commander of the royal garrison at the nearby castle of Evreux.

From the scouts' report, Ranulf could predict with nearly complete certainty what route the rebel magnates would take on their return from Vatteville to Beaumont castle. Ranulf also knew that it was possible for a royalist force to be in position to launch a surprise attack, if it could move quickly enough to seize this golden opportunity. He sent messengers at top speed to three of the closest royalist castellans: Henry of la Pommeraye at Pont-Authou, Odo Borleng at Bernay, and William of Harcourt, who, according to Hollister, was actually a vassal of the Beaumont family but had refused to follow Waleran in rebellion against King Henry. These three commanders must have been experienced members of the king's military household, for they acted immediately, with a unity and discipline born of experience.

Ranulf could not leave his post at Evreux's citadel, so recently seized back from Amaury, but the three royal castellans he had contacted came together, with at least three hundred knights just as Ranulf had urged, and set up an ambush for the rebels as they passed through Rougemontier. The speed with which all of this occurred is astonishing, given the times. Hollister points out that the rebel troops had moved against Vatteville, overwhelming, on the night of March 25, the siege castle which the king's troops had put in place. On March 26, the very next day, Odo Borleng, Henry of La Pommeraye, and William of Harcourt with their knight retinues were already assembled at the ambush point at Rougemontier. According to Orderic Vitalis, the king's castellans and their three hundred knights arrived in time, ahead of the rebel magnates, and arranged themselves in a well-planned formation. Odo proposed that "one section of our men dismount for battle and fight on foot, while the rest remain mounted ready for the fray." Archers were positioned off to the sides of the central group, with orders to aim for the horses of the mounted knights. This was not an ambush in the sense that the royalist troops would shoot with arrows from a safe distance or leap out upon them from behind bushes.

When the rebels first appeared on the road emerging from the forest, wrote Orderic, some of the royalist forces—certainly not its captains—quailed at the thought of engaging such great lords in battle. Usually, when these men fought it was while accompanying the king or some other great lord, riding at their head—someone of noble rank, that is to say, on the same level with those whom they faced across the battlefield this day. In the present case, not one of the king's men was even nearly the social equal of the approaching rebel noblemen.

Odo Borleng, hearing his men protest that they couldn't fight such great noblemen, exhorted them to stand firm, and reminded them that these were the very persons who had been devastating Normandy without fear of reprisal. Now they themselves, he pointed out, were at last in a position to stop the barons' arrogant rebellion against their king. "Be steadfast and fight bravely," Odo urged, "for if we fail in our courage, how shall we ever dare to enter the king's presence again? We shall deserve to forfeit both our wages and our honor, and never be entitled, so I think, to eat the king's bread."

Matthew Strickland, a specialist in medieval military tactics, cites this as one of the twelfth-century battles that went forward against the advice of the more seasoned men present. Amaury de Montfort, the most senior of the rebels, seeing the very strong defensive position that had been assumed by the king's captains, counseled those with him to avoid battle. According to chronicler Robert of Torigny, Amaury noted that a portion of the royalist force had dismounted; this signaled the fact that they would not surrender, but were prepared to fight to the death.

Waleran count of Meulan, however, would have nothing to do with caution. Still intoxicated by their coup at Vatteville, the count surveyed the king's men arrayed against them. Perhaps also he sensed the intimidation some of them felt. Waleran contemptuously declared that there was no reason to hold back—that the soldiers before them were nothing but "country bumpkins." Orderic relates that then, against Amaury's counsel, Waleran and about forty knights, all of them on horseback, charged the front ranks of the royalist foot soldiers. Before the young count could even come within striking distance, his horse was killed under him by the highly skilled archers flanking the dismounted royalist knights. Thus, Waleran became the first prisoner of battle. He was followed closely by his two noble brothers-in-law. Virtually all the knights in that first wave of forty were taken prisoner.

This is only one example of the bubbling cauldron of problems, crises, betrayals, sieges—it all seems almost literally like a boiling cauldron, with objects rising to the surface, sinking, rising again—that Henry had to face.

In the context of this book, those troubles seem less relevant to us than the question: Was it really Swami Kriyananda, in that former life, who was so embroiled in those difficulties? If so, what do they say about his character? Is what happened on the battlefield in that life even relevant to his life today?

The fact that Henry faced whatever had to be done, and *did* it: this, to us, is the relevancy of this part of his life. Kriyananda, too, has had to face many challenges, though not on the battlefield. The temptation to turn away from them and seek an easier path was certainly present—both in himself, and from the counsel of others. Many argued with him, "Surely, all these difficulties suggest that God doesn't want you to go in this direction. He is saying, 'I want you to follow another path.'" Kriyananda was not obstinate. He felt that he was indeed following what God and his guru wanted him to do, however. In the end, his amazing success fully justified him.

Such also was the case with Henry. That he finally brought peace, upliftment, and a more deeply religious spirit to both Normandy and England was, finally, its own justification.

An anonymous monk of Bec wrote in the monastery chronicle about the surrender of another castle, the one at Brionne, during this same baronial uprising in 1124. Since Bec is very close to Brionne, this monk seems to have been actually present during at least part of the building of the siege towers, and was almost certainly present at the Brionne garrison's surrender to King Henry. So far from being in the mood to have the garrison's commander blinded, as chronicler Robert of Torigny falsely reported, the Bec monk-author stated that the king was in a "quiet, tranquil mood," and was accompanied by three bishops, including John bishop of Lisieux, who often acted as the king's regent in Normandy, and also by the saintly Boso, newly elected abbot of Bec. Abbot Boso had been a student of Anselm's, and had been invited by that archbishop to come to England to help him with the writing of his philosophical masterpiece, *Cur Deus homo*.

R.W. Southern observed that Boso, more than any other student of Anselm's, showed the greatest aptitude and love for theological inquiry. We know that a deep friendship developed subsequently between King Henry and Abbot Boso, whom the king deeply admired for his great spirituality and keen intelligence. Ironically, the siege of Brionne may have been the starting point of this friendship, since it provided the king and the abbot sustained contact with one another during those days.

CHAPTER 39

Three Decades of Peace

The genius of great leadership is usually underappreciated, especially when that skill is applied to averting disaster rather than building something new and bold. While the other countries of Europe were enduring highly unsettled and ineffectual government, locally administered against a backdrop of nearly continuous warfare, Normandy, from 1125 onward, enjoyed ten years of unbroken peace, and England was nearing the end of its third decade of peace. Trade flourished, and there was effective administration of law—all this against a backdrop of economic stability. Henry of Huntingdon casually noted what was, in truth, a phenomenal achievement when he wrote that King Henry, "[now,] when everything was at peace in France, Flanders, Normandy, Britttany, Maine and Anjou, returned joyfully to England."

As King Henry crossed the Channel to England in July of 1129, his heart and mind must have been soaring in gratitude to God that Normandy and its neighbors had been spared the horrors of siege, battle, plunder, and pillage during the recent crisis.

I have deliberately omitted here to discuss his daughter, the Empress Maud, and also to say more about William Clito, the son of Robert Curthose, leaving out also the whole issue of Henry's royal succession and a seemingly endless succession of battles, sieges, and betrayals. All these give almost the impression, in the end, of a cork bobbing about on the surface of an ocean. This book has not been intended to be so much a biography of Henry or of William the Conqueror as a comparison between those two lives and what I know about Paramhansa Yogananda, first; and, second, what I firmly believe to be Henry's present incarnation as Swami Kriyananda.

I have deliberately included, in order to be fair, stories that seem to support views held by unrelenting critics of Henry, such as the time he didn't prevent his own granddaughters from being blinded. I have also explained others of his more questionable actions, and have shown that, given the times he lived in and his own position in those times, he simply had no choice but to act as he did.

We now approach the final chapter of Henry's life. As his ship got underway for England, having averted his latest crisis, Henry may well have allowed himself the rare enjoyment of reflecting on some of the creative projects he'd put into motion in his life, and others that kept coming to him continually: his idea, for instance, for a road over the Alps, and how such a road might be engineered; the zoo he was developing at Woodstock; the dozens of building projects that were then underway, sponsored either wholly or in great part by himself. There was also the time he had spent on the design and aesthetics of those buildings which included some of the earliest monumental stone buildings in England and Normandy.

Though he had little leisure to pursue these interests, he was a man whose curiosity ranged over many fields. (This same trait in Swami Kriyananda brought him increasingly hostile criticism from his monastic superiors, as a young man.) As we mentioned above, Henry had earned the scornful sobriquet, "Stagfoot," from his peers, jesting at his supposed ability to tell how many tines a stag had on its antlers by examining its footprints in damp soil. In later centuries Henry was also given the sobriquet "Beauclerc" for his exceptional learning at a time when few people were literate. (Kriyananda, too, has astonished many with his knowledge of languages, customs, and fund of knowledge on innumerable and diverse matters.) One of Henry's abilities, on which people remarked early in his life, was his interest in every detail of what went on around him. These details, the chroniclers wrote, formed a vast corpus of material that Henry, as one contemporary chronicler expressed it, "retained in his tenacious memory." Beyond his obvious genius for shaping and centralizing government, we know that during his lifetime he actively involved himself in architecture, road-building, zoology, new approaches to monastic organization, new systems for irrigation and the delivery of water, and even astronomy. (Kriyananda, when he was thirteen, wanted to be an astronomer.) We sense, in all the portraits of Henry by his contemporaries, that nothing was outside the king's interest or his ever-questioning mind.

It is interesting to note that his movements in the later years of his life reveal that he often sought out the company of monks. His movements through Normandy in the autumn of 1130 were for the most part connected with various monastic foundations, both large and small, and with strengthening the spiritual presence of the church in Normandy. First, the royal entourage traveled down the valley of the Risle River to visit the abbey of Bec. Boso, its abbot, was widely considered a saint, and was a close friend of Henry's. The king was welcomed with genuine warmth by the entire fellowship. The monastery had prospered greatly for many years because of Henry's unstinting support, and under the leadership of several saintly abbots.

The monastery at Bec, shaped in its early years by both Lanfranc and Anselm, received more support of every kind from King Henry than any other monastic community in Normandy. Clearly, the king cared deeply about this community, and appreciated the profoundly beneficial effect it had on the kingdom. Dr. Hollister notes that we know of at least four visits the king made to Bec. Quite possibly there were many others. Unlike some among the highest-level aristocrats, who waited until death was virtually sounding its knell at their very door before "throwing money" at religious works, in the hope of buying an otherwise undeserved salvation, Henry showed deep interest throughout his life in the many monastic foundations in Normandy and England. He was also acquainted with, and deeply interested in, the Rule observed in each monastery, and showed real concern for the spiritual health of its brethren.

Henry's love and reverence for Boso of Bec were deep. When the archbishop of Rouen asked King Henry to order Abbot Boso to make a written profession of obedience to him at Rouen, the king simply refused. Instead, he wrote to the archbishop that he did give him permission, however, to *try* forcing such a profession out of Boso, adding that he didn't think the archbishop would like the answer he was certain to receive. The king also intervened very forcefully when the townspeople around the abbey of Bec decided to intimidate Abbot Boso and his monks with physical violence, in the hope of gaining certain personal advantages over the well-endowed monastery. As a result, King Henry ordered that, henceforth, no one in the vicinity of the abbey could carry a sword, nor bear arms within the town. Anyone who did so would suffer the king's wrath and severe punishment. (Statements threatening "severe punishment" were *pro forma* in those days. Their virtue was that they accomplished their purpose.)

There is an amusing corollary, here, to the life of Kriyananda. A group of local children were playing at a building site on a corner of the monastery where he lived. Concerned lest their antics get out of hand, Kriyananda strode down to tell them the site was "out of bounds." As he started down the slope in their direction, he changed the tone of his voice from its customary warmth, demanding in a harsh tone (though inwardly he smiled), "*What are you doing down there!?*" One of the boys exclaimed nervously as they were running away: "God, what a *wicked* voice!"

Henry, while in Rouen, also gave a final gift to Cluny. This donation was in itself very forward-looking, since the charter which accompanied the grant called for an annual gift to Cluny, in perpetuity, and was clearly intended to maintain in good repair particularly the new nave, which King Henry had largely funded after the original vault, funded by Alfonso VI of Leon-Castile, collapsed. In many respects this last royal charter for Cluny anticipated what is familiar to us today as an endowment fund.

Henry spent another month in Rouen, during which he was deeply involved in administrative work (much of which he himself had initiated, and much of which concerned the well-being of the church and monasteries in Normandy). He crossed to England in August 1131.

Though much of the charter evidence for 1132 has been lost, it seems that King Henry remained throughout that year in England, which was now ending its third decade of unbroken peace. The king undoubtedly rejoiced that he was now afforded the opportunity to undertake some administrative innovations; review the efficacy of some of the judicial reforms of his reign; confirm the continuingly uniform quality of the coinage; gather information on how the people of the kingdom were faring; and observe the growth of the towns and the flourishing of all manner of trade.

Perhaps Henry also visited Reading Abbey, his major religious foundation, to see how well the abbey was fulfilling its charter to succor and aid all manner of travelers.

Though Henry has been rightly credited with instituting "administrative kingship," it would be very wrong to imagine him sitting at the top of a kind of medieval "flow chart," uninvolved with the details. King Henry was intensely "hands on," and continually astonished others with his knowledge of the relative minutiae of every aspect of the kingdom's affairs.

A number of historians have remarked that, before Henry's August 1133 crossing, he energetically, as always, disposed of an enormous amount of business. While, for whatever reason, there is a paucity of charters (representing the royal decisions taken) for 1132, a small mountain of royal documents dated in 1133 testifies to King Henry's intense activity in the first seven months of that year.

During that time, King Henry filled church vacancies; created a new bishopric; approved the foundation of Missenden Abbey; granted lands and privileges to about two dozen abbeys, bishoprics, and monastic foundations; resolved church disputes; and attended to a great number of administrative matters.

As usual, the king was constantly on the move—Dunstable, Woodstock, London, Windsor, Oxford, Winchester—accompanied by his household and *familiares*, making "the king's justice" more accessible to all. Judith Green notes that there is evidence that Henry made a visit to eastern England sometime in 1132, and at this time may have visited the shrine at Bury St. Edmunds, thereby fulfilling a vow which John of Worcester tells us the king made on a life-threatening Channel crossing in August 1131.

In early August 1133, King Henry, the most pressing matters in England disposed of, felt free to cross over to Normandy again. When, in 1066, his father's great fleet had sailed from Normandy to England, to do battle with the usurper, Harold Godwinson, Duke William's crossing had coincided with the sighting of a great comet—a particularly brilliant manifestation of Haley's Comet, as has since been verified. Significantly, Henry's departure from England—his last, as it turned out—was marked by both an earthquake and an eclipse of the sun. John of Worcester gives the most vivid account of the portentous solar eclipse. The king, his entourage, the ship's crew, and all the great men of England who had come to see Henry off were standing on the shore waiting for a favorable wind. The demands on the king's attention were ceaseless. Even here, on the windblown shore, Henry may well have been engaged in some administrative business. Suddenly, an enormous cloud appeared, seemingly out of nowhere. It grew so dark that, although it was midday, Henry's men had to use candles to go about their business. All eyes were fixed on the skies. They saw the sun shining like a new moon, and gradually changing its shape from wider to narrower. Judith Green suggests that we take these reports with a grain of salt, asking us to consider whether or not a medieval man who had lost three children in a shipwreck was likely to undertake to cross the Channel if all these signs had been occurring.

However, the fact remains that a solar eclipse on August 2, 1133, was observed by virtually all of Europe, including accounts from Salzburg and Prague, and is well substantiated. Moreover, there was in fact an earthquake on or about August 4, with its epicenter within or near England. Nevertheless, King Henry's ship pulled away from England's southern shores for the last time—so writes William of Malmesbury—on August 5, the thirty-third anniversary of Henry's coronation. Just as his father William the Conqueror had had to interpret for his men as a highly positive portent the dramatic appearance of Haley's Comet, while he prepared for the conquest of England in 1066, so King Henry undoubtedly had to soothe and reassure everyone to board ship as he cast off immediately for Normandy.

In fact, all the chroniclers refer to the portents and omens that surrounded Henry's final crossing. Wulfric of Haselbury (Somerset), an Anglo-Saxon priest who later become a hermit, on hearing of the king's plans to return to Normandy, prophesied: "He will go, but he will not come back." Evidently King Henry had had some contact with Wulfric the Hermit in his role as healer, and when this prognostication reached Henry's ears, he took it very seriously, sending messengers to ascertain that it had, indeed, been Wulfric who had made this prophesy. The hermit did not budge, but replied rather to the effect that, because his prophesy was impersonal and did not concern himself, he placed much confidence in it as a strong intuition.

Thus, amid a plethora of dark omens, the king set sail for Normandy. William of Malmesbury states, "The very elements accompanied with their sorrow the last crossing of so great a prince."

King Henry traveled directly to Rouen, where, as in England, he met many administrative, judicial, and diplomatic demands.

In February of 1134, an envoy from England brought the news to King Henry that his older brother, Robert Curthose, had died, at the age of slightly more than eighty years.

During this year, we know that King Henry enjoyed an interlude with a small group of monks whom he had taken under his protection, and who now lived in the forest near Lyons-la-Forêt. Warren Hollister and Amanda Frost draw on several sources to flesh out King Henry's touching relationship with this small group of devotional monastics. Evidently they were not connected with any of the established religious orders—such independence was not uncommon—and had come together by ones and twos to live in great austerity. Around 1130, the brothers had lost their patron, and, casting about for what they could do, they wrote to King Henry for permission to travel beyond Normandy and seek a new patron.

The king, so the sources relate, responded that they must on no account leave the duchy. He urged them to find a secluded site to their liking near their present location, and promised, if at all possible, to grant them this site permanently. The king considered deeply devoted monks and nuns as the greatest treasure of the kingdom, and sought urgently to keep them within Normandy. The small group duly began their search, and found a "*secretissima* valley" in the forest of Lyons that was already inhabited by three anchorites, well established in their practices. Already well-known to the king, the three hermits, "whom [Henry] loved very much," agreed to accept the homeless monks into their "most hidden" valley and their austere way of life. King Henry delightedly gave the newly formed group some land to be held by their fellowship in perpetuity, with the right to use the forest freely. Ultimately, he arranged for and financed the building of an abbey for them.

King Henry may have made the journey in April of 1134 to Lyons-la-Forêt, to assure himself that the brothers' new building project was progressing as planned. However, it seems more likely that he only sought spiritual refreshment in the brothers' company, and the simplicity of their surroundings at what now bore the name Abbey of Mortemer. Although the new order of Cistercians was already established in England, with the support of King Henry, Mortemer was to be the first Cistercian foundation in Normandy, when the monks there, after the king's death, offered their abbey to the new order.

Orderic Vitalis tells us that from August to November of 1135, King Henry, who during these four months probably celebrated his sixty-seventh birthday, personally directed the bolstering of the Normandy-Maine frontier's defenses. In what must have been increasingly wet, chilly weather, the king, so Orderic wrote, "prowled" the district of Sées, personally taking charge of the reinforcement of the defenses of Alençon and Almenesches. Henry also oversaw the enlargement of the castle of Argentan, and, more specifically, confirmed for himself that his recent disseisement of William Talvas, the son of Robert of Bellême and a man of comparable bellicosity, had been thoroughly enforced. The king took the further precaution of placing royal troops in those castles which, before that, had been garrisoned by local lords.

Henry had only a few months left to live, but he certainly was not perceived as tottering toward the grave. Except at Christmas, 1132, we know of no other illness in the king's long and arduous life. Moreover, judging by the enormous amount of administrative activity he undertook during the new year of 1133, that illness was not protracted. Moreover, during the whole of autumn of 1135, Henry had been constantly on the move—on horseback, of course—personally directing the fortification of castles in the Sées district, apparently with all his usual verve, until the tasks that he had set himself and his men were finally completed.

CHAPTER 40

The Passing of King Henry I

In late November 1135, with wintry weather coming in, the king arrived at his castle at Lyons-la-Forêt—a destination he may have chosen for its nearness to the new Abbey of Mortemer, and the dedicated monks he "loved very much." Orderic wrote, regarding his arrival at the castle, that he was weary from all his refortification efforts on the southern frontier. Nevertheless, the king made arrangements to go hunting the next day, giving orders to his huntsmen to be prepared.

It was during that first night, after his arrival at Lyons, that the king fell ill. In a slightly different report, William of Malmesbury wrote that Henry took sick while his party was out hunting the next day. Only Henry of Huntingdon, writing some years later, suggested that the king had overindulged in a "surfeit of lampreys," as the famous phrase has come down to us. This story, however, coming as late as it did, is probably no more than a (mildly humorous) fiction. Did King Henry die from overindulgence in this forbidden dish? Dr. Clifford Brewer (*The Death of Kings*, p. 34) writes that it is possible that the lampreys, if infected with salmonella, could have proved fatal, but he believes that something like a duodenal perforation is more likely. Brewer explains that salmonella is usually fatal only to children or frail, older people. The king, though advanced in years for the expected longevity during the twelfth century, was robust.

Orderic Vitalis, in his account, is primarily concerned with conveying the fact that King Henry left his body in a manner to which every Christian prince should aspire. In the beginning of the illness, the king confessed his sins—first of all to his own chaplains, and then, when it became apparent to Henry himself that he was dying, he sent for Hugh, archbishop of Rouen, who was not far away.

Henry probably fell ill sometime during Monday night. From Tuesday to the next Sunday, his condition declined steadily. When Henry's old friend Hugh archbishop of Rouen arrived, probably on Thursday, Henry again confessed his sins, worshiped the crucifix, and formally renounced all evil desires. During the last three days of his life, he made his confession daily, and received absolution three times from Archbishop Hugh. When Robert earl of Gloucester, his ever-faithful natural son, arrived at his father's bedside, Henry ordered him to take a large sum of money from the Normandy treasury and distribute it to his household staff, and then pay his stipendiary soldiers.

Much that King Henry did in those last days closely mirrored the final acts of his father, William the Conqueror. Henry arranged to pay off all his debts, distribute alms to the poor, reinvest with their lands those whom he had disseised, and agreed to receive back into the kingdom those whom he had exiled. Although it presented some great logistical difficulties, King Henry asked that he be buried at his foundation, Reading Abbey.

As death approached, King Henry implored all who were gathered about him to make the preservation of peace and the care of the poor their central concern. Clear-minded to the end, Henry died after nightfall on Sunday, December 1, 1135. Archbishop Hugh was constantly by his side, and wrote soon afterward to Pope Innocent II concerning Henry's final days, relaying the king's deeply felt acts of penitence, his confessions, and his distribution of alms. Peter the Venerable, the revered abbot of Cluny and close friend of King Henry, wrote to the king's favorite sister, Adela, what he had learned about Henry's passing from Hugh's letter to Innocent II. Archbishop Hugh of Rouen, as the king's confessor, confidant, and long-time friend, knew Henry's heart and character stripped of the burden he carried as monarch of a large kingdom during turbulent times. It is significant, especially in view of the terrible misconceptions that have gained force over the centuries regarding Henry's nature and motives, that Archbishop Hugh's letter to Pope Innocent II concludes with the words: "So he died in peace. God grant him peace, for peace he loved."

Henry's final recorded command as king, father, liege lord, and friend, to the *familiares* gathered around his bed, was that they guard the peace and protect the poor. This was not, for him, a platitude mouthed in the hope of making a good end. Henry, as William the Conqueror's son, had fought during his long reign for many things that he considered to be his father's legacy. When the end came, however, Henry did not exhort those gathered to "Keep the Anglo-Norman kingdom united!" Nor did he say, "Persevere in the administration of law and justice at all costs!" He didn't even say, "Protect the church!" All of these worthy objectives were, it is revealed by his deathbed deliverances, secondary to the overarching ideal Henry had cherished for his father's kingdom: peace— peace, in which architecture and the arts could flower, crops could be harvested, monasticism refined and given a vital new expression, domestic and international trade could flourish, cities with their constructive exchange of ideas could mature, and law and the courts of law could replace savage vengeance and warfare for the settling of disputes.

What Henry treasured most about peace can, perhaps, be best understood by taking note of whose company he sought during his all-too-brief periods of peace in his own life. Throughout his life, his companions of choice were austerely inclined hermits and monastics, as well as those holy men, starting with Lanfranc, who had been at least briefly his tutor, then Archbishop Anselm, Boso of Bec, Peter the Venerable of Cluny, the little band of monks at Mortemer, and others whom he revered. Even the relatively noble character of the *familiares* with whom the king chose to surround himself tells us what Henry valued most. It is expressed in the words: "peace he loved." King Henry, viewed by all his contemporaries as a man of deep faith in God, treasured peace and a well-ordered society because these good things provided a necessary foundation for the refinement of human nature and, ultimately, because they gave man the freedom to contemplate the truth of the soul.

Archbishop Hugh and Bishop Audoin of Evreux, perhaps thinking of the dishonorable and sacrilegious treatment that had been meted out to the bodies of both William the Conqueror and William Rufus, pressed five of King Henry's closest noblemen to take an oath together that they would accompany the body to the coast of Normandy, and see it safely to England and to Reading Abbey for burial. These intimates of King Henry swore, further, that none of them would abandon the body unless by joint agreement.

The day after King Henry's death, so Orderic wrote, a huge procession accompanied King Henry's body to Rouen, where it was at least partially embalmed in no less a place than Archbishop Hugh's own chamber. The journey of the king's body continued as far as Caen, still surrounded—in death as in life—by a host of knights, retainers, officials, and monks. In Caen, Henry's corpse rested for about three weeks at Saint Etienne, William the Conqueror's own foundation and chosen place of burial. It was not until after Christmas 1135 that the conditions of wind and sea in the Channel were judged to be safe enough to attempt a crossing with the body.

Finally, on January 2, 1136, King Henry was at last interred with great honor in Reading Abbey, as he had requested.

Historian R.H.C. Davis remarks that, for all those who knew that Henry lay dying at the insignificant hunting lodge of Lyons-la-Forêt, waiting for the great king's last breath must have been like "waiting for the Bomb."

The legacy of William the Conqueror and of his youngest son Henry was nearly smothered under the ashes of Stephen of Blois' ensuing anarchic nineteen years of misrule. There remained, however, beneath the charred remains, a few live embers. Such a sustained power could not be the product of human ambition, nor even of human genius. A mere puff of the great, raw energy of young Henry II brought the legacy of William the Conqueror and King Henry I back to life almost overnight. There was a return to strong central government, with well-articulated institutions ready to serve any king who could command the necessary obedience to them. The real work had been accomplished already: England was now unalterably aligned with Roman Christendom, swung toward it by the power of God through the Conqueror, and through his youngest son's devotion to his father's vision. Much more than that, many evils had been destroyed, and love of virtue had been reawakened in human hearts.

Let us now consider more closely: What was the vision and purpose of William the Conqueror's life, and King Henry I's crucial role in fulfilling that purpose? And what does it tell us about their more recent incarnations?

Part Four

THEIR REINCARNATIONS

CHAPTER 41

"I Come to Destroy Evil and Establish Virtue"

"The Norman Conquest of England has, in its nature and in its results, no exact parallel in history . . . largely owing to the character and position of the man who wrought it. That the history of England for the last eight hundred years has been as it has is due largely to the personal character of a single man. . . .

"That we are what we are to this day largely comes from the fact that there was a moment when our national destiny might be said to hang on the will of a single man, and that that man was William, surnamed at different stages of his life and memory the Bastard, the Conqueror, and the Great."

—E.A. Freeman[*]

From **now on in** this book I shall refer to William, wherever possible, as William the Great. It is much truer than calling him "the Conqueror."

Our exploration of all the ramifications of Paramhansa Yogananda's statement that, in a previous lifetime, he had been William (whether the Conqueror or the Great), has brought us to the final and all-absorbing question: "Why?" Why would a soul, who has won freedom from any need to reincarnate at all, elect to return to earth as a warrior king? What was at stake in twelfth century Europe, and in England in particular, that caused a Self-realized master to don once again the heavy cloak of a physical body—this time, as William the Great?

I have already quoted a passage, above, from the Bhagavad Gita, India's best-loved scripture: "O Bharata! Whenever virtue

* *William the Conqueror*, BiblioBazaar, 2006, p. 10.

declines and vice is in the ascendant, I incarnate Myself on earth (as an *avatar*). Appearing from age to age in visible form, I come to destroy evil and establish virtue." (4:7,8)

Saints as a rule attack no one—though there have been a few notable exceptions: for example, the tirades of St. Jerome. Normally, when one thinks of saints, one remembers men like St. Francis of Assisi, or women like St. Teresa of Avila. These people were still struggling to escape the meshes of *maya* (delusion) themselves. They needed to be careful, therefore, not to judge anyone, and, like Mahatma Gandhi, to perfect in themselves the quality of harmless-ness (*ahimsa*). An *avatar*, or divine incarnation, often comes in quite a different role. It is his actual *job* to destroy evil (not, be it noted, to destroy evil-doers, whose souls they often save), and to work mightily toward re-establishing virtue.

An *avatar* is a liberated soul sent by God—not a direct mani-festation of God Himself, for Yogananda said that God never acts directly in Creation. What the liberated soul has achieved is the destiny of every soul: final liberation from ego-consciousness, and from all bondage to past karmas (actions) in the attainment of complete oneness with God. When John Smith becomes one with God, only God will remain. John Smith will not be obliterated, however. In omniscience (so Yogananda explained this subtle but important teaching), the *memory* of John Smith, and of all his incar-nations, remains indelible. Thus, that memory can be reawakened: God can return to earth again through that particular soul. In this case, God is not forcing John Smith to reincarnate. That particular soul has retained the "desireless desire" to help others. Thus, in Yogananda's case, as he wrote in his poem "God's Boatman": "Oh, I will return again and again, if need be a trillion times, as long as one stray brother is weeping by the wayside."

Most souls, when they attain final liberation, have no wish to return to this "vale of tears" for any reason at all. They can and do return in subtle ways, however, to answer prayers—for healing, for example, or for guidance. People often find it easier to appeal to a particular person, whom they can visualize, than to pray to Infinite

God. God Himself is both vast and impersonal, and at the same time also intimate and deeply interested in each human being—according to how "He" is visualized. Souls that have become liberated in Him can respond to the prayers people direct to them.

Very few such souls, however, have retained that "desireless desire" to return physically to earth for the purpose of helping others, as *avatars*. It is due to their own willingness to return here that the Divine reactivates that portion of the Infinite Memory.

When Jesus Christ responded to the accusation of certain Jews—self-appointed "defenders" of their faith—who said he had blasphemed in stating, "I and my Father are one," he retorted, "Is it not written in your law, I said, Ye are gods?"

Jesus was an *avatar*. So also, in India, was Krishna. So also was Rama. So also were Buddha, Swami Shankara, Ramanuja, and a number of other great divine manifestations. Most of their followers would be aghast to hear that their own particular saviors were not unique. Paramhansa Yogananda, however—an *avatar* himself—stated that all souls come from God, and all are completely equal, in Him, even if they are still wandering in delusion. As the Jews say, "Hear O Israel, the Lord our God, the Lord is one." In truth, there is nothing in existence save that one, Divine Consciousness.

Frequently, the role of *avatars* is not only to inspire, but also to correct. It is in this light that William the Great's life must be understood. Swami Kriyananda, Yogananda's disciple, is not on that spiritual level, but the guru chose him to complete his divine mission.

We've already studied in some detail the lives of William and Henry, pointing out the wisdom and *righteousness* of their decisions, and showing how universally beneficial were the roles they played. We have shown that their lives were wholly noble, though they lived in times that demanded great bloodshed. What they created were new conditions in which religion, trade, the arts, and the recovery of classical learning could once more begin to have a salutary effect on people everywhere.

Historian E.A. Freeman, whom I quoted above, is not alone in his acknowledgement that what we are today was shaped in large part by the Norman Conquest, and that the effects of that conquest may be attributed to the "personal character of a single man," William. Nearly every historian would agree that, on that day in 1066, a completely new course was set for England. If William the Great was in fact a true spiritual master also, we must conclude that what motivated him to invade England, and his subsequent actions and policies, had nothing to do with fighting for his right to the throne. We are led back perforce, then, to the same question: What *was* at stake that autumn day at Hastings? What hung in the balance that was so important that a soul of Paramhansa Yogananda's high spiritual stature would play such a seemingly incongruous role as a conqueror?

Although a chronological narrative of the lives of William and Henry gives us a sense of the men themselves, it is difficult through such an account alone to gain a broader perspective on the overarching vision they held for the kingdom. To gain a truer perspective, we need to compare England on the eve of the Battle of Hastings to what England had become by 1135, the year of King Henry's death. Within that relatively short span of nearly seventy years, William the Great and King Henry I not only changed England, but set a new course for the whole Western world.

I have already shown the general impact of the Conquest, a point on which there is nearly universal agreement: the cultural and political orientation of England, deflecting it from a more-or-less pagan Scandinavian influence toward the more truly Christian culture of southern Europe. This reorientation toward a wholly new stream of influence is profoundly significant. It is important, therefore, to understand how overwhelmingly Scandinavian England had become prior to 1066, and the extent to which that Nordic influence represented a departure from the purer stream of Roman Christianity. At the same time, we must always bear in mind that this improvement was only relative, not absolute. For, as Yogananda said in the twentieth century: "Jesus was crucified once, but his *teachings* have been crucified every day for the past two thousand years!" His meaning was, of course, that the pope, too, despite the modern claim to the contrary, was far from "infallible."

Only recently has there been a lessening of sentimental nostalgia for what people have viewed as the pure "Englishness" of pre-Conquest England. Some people still mourn the loss, in 1066, of that imaginary Anglo-Saxon kingdom, and consider the Norman "conquest" to have caused the death of all that was "the true England." This sentiment resembles the nostalgia that has surrounded King Arthur. That probably mythical king of post-Roman Britain, if he lived at all, could only have been a Briton, a race which later was banished largely to Wales, as wave after wave of invading Angles, Saxons, Danes, Norwegians, and Swedes invaded the island.

The Angles and Saxons were the first to invade England (after the Romans, who later departed). They were not left long in peace to enjoy England's felicitous climate and rich soil—blessings bestowed by the warm Gulf Stream. Near the beginning of the ninth century, the Vikings began with new ferocity to attack the English coast. Initially, these ruthless bands sought only plunder. Before long, however, they began to claim land for themselves. In time, the population of the north and the east of England became heavily Nordic. Historians, backed by recent archeological evidence, including bone analysis, are in fundamental agreement on the nature of England's population, culture, and orientation on the eve of the Norman Conquest in 1066.

The country was saturated with Danish culture. A good deal of England was still under Danish law at that time. Many people spoke Scandinavian languages as much as they did what was then the native tongue of England—which of course, with its essentially Germanic origins, and no French, differed greatly from the language we know today. In fact, we nowadays call that language "Old English," the language of *Beowulf*; it would not be understood today.

The language that has evolved from the Norman Conquest, with its admixture of French, has become virtually the *lingua franca* of the whole world. This is only one of the ways in which William's "conquest" has impacted world civilization.

The church in northern Europe at that time, though Christian, was heavily mixed with paganism, and paid little attention to the clearest fountain of Christianity in existence at those times: the Roman Church.

The question remains, of course: Was the Scandinavian influence all that bad? No, of course not—not in itself, that is. There were disadvantages, of course. For one thing, the country knew no unity in those days. For another, there was little faith in God.

One of the most concise portraits of pre-Conquest England comes from Winston Churchill, who wrote in his *History of the English-Speaking Peoples*: "The condition of England at the close of the reign of Edward the Confessor was one of widespread political weakness. . . . The great earls were becoming independent in the provinces. . . .

"The King lived largely upon his private estates, and governed as best he could through his household. The remaining powers of the monarchy were, in practice, severely restricted by a little group of Anglo-Danish notables. The main basis of support for the English kings had always been this select Council, never more than sixty, who in a vague manner regarded themselves as the representatives of the whole country. It was in fact a committee of courtiers, the greater thanes, and ecclesiastics. But at this time this assembly of 'wise men' in no way embodied the life of the nation. It weakened the royal executive without adding any strength of its own. Its character and quality suffered in the general decay. It tended to fall into the hands of the great families. As the central power declined, a host of local chieftains disputed and intrigued in every county, pursuing private and family aims and knowing no interest but their own. Feuds and disturbances were rife. The people, too, were hampered not only by the many conflicting petty authorities, but by the deep division of custom between the

Saxon and Danish districts. Absurd anomalies and contradictions obstructed the administration of justice. . . . The island had come to count for little on the Continent, and had lost the thread of its own progress."

There was at this time, in fact, a stagnant or "stuck" quality all over Europe. After the collapse of the Roman Empire, and a briefly "smoothish" period under the rule of Charlemagne (d. 814), Latin Europe had sunk back nearly to its pre-Carolingian state of political chaos. The religion of Islam prevailed throughout most of the Iberian Peninsula. The Moors had come very close, in fact, to conquering even more of Europe. Their victorious progress was stopped and turned back by Charles Martel's army at Poitiers, southwest of Paris, in 732.

It is interesting to contemplate what might have been the course of events, had the newly land-hungry peoples of Scandinavia been able fully to conquer England—the most agriculturally hospitable land in the northern orbit. Many historians have observed, for example, that the relationship between the Germanic states and Rome was always uneasy, and full of mutual misunderstandings and mistrust. It is not too great a mental leap to imagine that the Germanic states—those in turmoil as they resisted the Holy Roman Emperor's central authority—might well have been pulled into the orbit of this prosperous, vital, muscle-flexing group from the northern kingdoms. It is easy to imagine the German and Saxon duchies and countries happily detaching themselves from the older culture of Rome and the Mediterranean world, and promoting a very much looser form of Christianity, admixed with paganism.

Even at the beginning of William's era, the Holy Roman Emperor (and therefore *de facto* king of Germany) was in open conflict with the pope. Had the Norman Conquest not brought England into a new relationship with the church in Rome, and thereby reconfigured alliances throughout Europe, it is not inconceivable that the German Emperor, along with the Germanic and Saxon states, might have pulled free, established an antipope (which, in fact, the Emperor eventually did) as the center of a third Christian world comprised of Scandinavia, Germany, England, Scotland, Ireland, and (perhaps) other northeastern European kingdoms. The Roman papacy, which in 1066 was a positive force for unifying post-Roman Europe, would have been isolated. The powerful Roman Church represented the recovery of classical knowledge, and the purest flow then extant for the religion of Jesus Christ. That stream would have shrunk to a trickle.

Only a very few kingdoms would have been open to the revivifying light that was beginning to pour through the Catholic church into the kingdoms of France and Normandy, especially through the monasteries. Lest the reader think I am a proselytizing Roman Catholic, I should add that I am not even a member of that church, though I try to be "catholic" (that is to say, universal) in my perception of truth. Nevertheless, at that time in history it may be said that Rome was "at the helm" in promulgating Christ's teachings.

Much—in fact, very much—hinged upon England's orientation. Though it was tucked off in a corner where one might not have thought her influence to be crucially important to Europe's development, it had the advantage of being a separate island: close enough to Europe to have strong ties with it, yet removed enough to enable it to develop a new spirit, not so closely involved with the great mix of existing influences on the continent.

The development of a new culture, one more harmoniously integrated than even the Roman Christian world, could perhaps only be accomplished in this island setting at a time when the world was barely emerging from the depths of a dark age. Literacy was now on the rise. People were seeking better ways of living, as may be seen from the numerous monasteries that were beginning to appear at this time. Brigandage was slowly coming under control; it was safer to travel, and merchandise, therefore, could pass more easily from country to country.

Jesus Christ, in launching a new expression of devotion to God, had urged people to form little Christian communities. It is true that one doesn't find any direct teachings of his on this subject in the Gospels, but we can infer this point clearly from what is later recorded in the Acts of the Apostles. The apostle Paul concerned himself almost wholly with founding small communities of Christians. England may be said to have presented a similar opportunity: a separate island, open to integral development socially, intellectually, and spiritually.

Interestingly, Paramhansa Yogananda also, in sermon after sermon, urged his listeners to create separate, self-sustaining communities, where a new consciousness and a new way of life might be developed. Again, though he was not able to bring this idea to fruition during his lifetime, his disciple Swami Kriyananda has succeeded in doing so.

The year 2009 marks the fortieth anniversary of the founding, by Kriyananda, of the first Ananda community. In these forty years it has flowered into eight communities on three continents, with a total residency of about one thousand members, and seems to be well on its way to becoming a worldwide movement.

David Douglas, in his great biography of the Conqueror, stated: "No aspect of the career of William the Conqueror is of more interest—or of more importance—than the part he played in the history of the western Church between 1066 and 1087." The church itself was in a state of upheaval. Some of the most forceful personalities ever to occupy the throne of Saint Peter, beginning with Pope Gregory VII, served as popes during the reigns of William and Henry. Spiritually speaking, Gregory's influence was both beneficial and far reaching, and these two kings allied themselves with him, contributing to his legacy. Both kings also, however, had to contend with Gregory's excessive ambition for the church, through which he clearly wanted to set up a theocracy, controlling all of Europe, with the pope's authority in every matter above that of all secular princes. In this ambition, Pope Gregory more than met his match in William and his archbishop of Canterbury, Lanfranc, as did subsequent Gregorian-reform popes in Henry and Anselm.

From the present vantage point, it is apparent that William supported church reform in ways that strengthened the church *spiritually*, but that he steadfastly resisted those aspects of the reform which called for increased power of the church in secular matters. Thus, in both Normandy and England, William encouraged all manner of religious establishments; ordered the convening of church councils throughout the kingdom; promoted the Gregorian reformers' insistence on clerical celibacy; established ecclesiastical courts so that the church could effectively correct its own errant brethren; forbade the purchase of church offices (simony); and, perhaps most importantly, was himself an unwavering model of Christian ideals, in both public and private life.

All of these policies of the Conqueror were perfectly in keeping with Gregorian Reform as it related to strengthening the church and the spiritual life of individuals. At the same time, the great king was adamant that papal legates not be allowed into England or Normandy; that he himself would be responsible for the collection of Peter's Pence (the tithe sent annually to the pope from the churches); and that all matters pertaining to the church within the Anglo-Norman kingdom would be decided internally by those churchmen who were closest to the situation. It is important to note that, whereas both William and Henry promoted the centralization of power at a time when fragmentation had brought disharmony, they opposed it when centralization meant control from a distance, particularly when "distance" meant a place so remote as not rightly to comprehend local situations and conditions.

In fact both William and Henry played a much more important role than Douglas indicates: They built a whole new society, organized along lines that would encourage a more upward, and Godward, flow. We find greater clarification of this aspect in the missions of Yogananda and Kriyananda (Kriyananda's being only to complete the mission of his guru, Paramhansa Yogananda).

Yogananda, in the worldwide organization he founded, formed two sister organizations: one in India (Yogoda Satsanga Society), and the other in America (Self-Realization Fellowship). He told his disciple, Faye Wright (Daya Mata), who later became president of both organizations, "India will organize itself."

To his disciple Donald Walters (Kriyananda), whom he placed in charge of the monks and gave the job of organizing them, he said, "Don't make too many rules: it destroys the spirit." Yogananda tried as much as possible to manifest on a social plane the ancient dictum: "God is center everywhere; circumference, nowhere." He named his organizations themselves after that principle: *Self-realization*. This term would in time, he said, become accepted as the underlying goal of all religions.

Time has brought a greater unfoldment of awareness since William and Henry's day, but already in the eleventh century William wanted to bring England not only under the wholesome influence of Roman Christianity, which was a truer reflection of the spirit of Christ, but also to develop England's own integrity, that the religious spirit might flower *from within* individuals, and not be a mere plaster coating over the outer edifice of religion. Hence, all of William and Lanfranc's decisions reveal a policy that adamantly rejected an excessive increase in the power of the papacy to make decisions within the Anglo-Norman kingdom. It was particularly to the pope's policies on uplifting the standard of personal morality and spirituality that King William gave his unstinting support. And King Henry's intentions were the same in every detail as those of his father.

What interested both men, in other words, was *personal* piety, over institutional reform.

England, as an island and therefore somewhat separate from Europe, could be developed more easily in new ways than any nation on the continent, surrounded as those were by other influences. Thus, William and Henry found it possible to develop a land with traditions that might outlast some of the disintegrating influences of time. William's insistence on each person's loyalty to the king above all, instead of to one's immediate overlord, ensured England against the disruptions that kept continental countries in constant turmoil owing to baronial uprisings. Both men, though concerned for the harmony and happiness of their people, were also very adamant in their efforts to prevent people, wherever possible, from pursuing paths that would lead to their own destruction. The goals of this father-and-son team, as we may term it, were long-range, and often didn't concern people's short-term fulfillments. Here, too, one can understand how the ego-centered individual might consider them tyrannical: one might say, figuratively, that they denied people candy in order to keep them healthy.

We can understand both men best if we keep in mind that their main interest had to be the same as what it was in their recent lives as Yogananda and Kriyananda: to help people toward understanding the true purpose of life: oneness with God. In their recent lives they have been able to emphasize that man's true fulfillment can be realized only on a soul level. As Krishna says in the great Indian scripture, the Bhagavad Gita: "O Arjuna! Get away from My ocean of suffering and misery!" Most human beings seek other kinds of fulfillment, and naturally think more in terms of perfecting society outwardly than of developing man inwardly. These two souls, however, cannot in their four lives have had such a compromised ideal. For society can never be perfected. As long as human nature is imperfect, society will be imperfect. No system of government can raise people higher than they themselves want to rise. The best any system can do is make it possible for the cream, so to speak, to rise to the top: for those with the highest ideals not to be thwarted in their aspirations, and for those with low intentions to be less free to impose their darkness on others.

These could more easily be instilled in a separate island state than in countries surrounded by peoples with different self-definitions. They could of course be instilled even better in even smaller communities: hence their interest in monasteries. In their recent two lives, they have devoted great energy to creating small, self-sustaining "colonies," as Yogananda himself referred to them, where people could live in society but also be somewhat apart from it—places where they could live integrated lives, and where all human activities—material, physical, mental, spiritual—could be directed harmoniously toward life's highest goal: God union.

Both men also set themselves against the disruptive tendency of barons to seek only their own selfish ends. William set the tone—as Krishna had said—of "destroying evil"; Henry followed his father's lead. Both did much during their reigns to "establish virtue." In both important senses, their mission was essentially a divine one, and its benefits accrued not only to England, but to society everywhere.

An *avatar* does not really have a normal human personality, in the sense that people usually understand the word. For to them a personality might be described as a "bundle of self-definitions." William had no such "bundle" to carry; he was burdened by not the slightest self-definition. Nothing separated him from others, or from God. He was simply an outward expression of the Divine Spirit—individual, yes, but inwardly free, and as such an ever-pure manifestation of Eternal Bliss.

Kriyananda once, thinking of his guru's incarnation as William, asked him, "Is a liberated soul always conscious of his oneness with God?" The guru answered, "One never loses his sense of inner freedom."

Henry was more than the son of William's body: he was, and had been for many incarnations, a dedicated (and, we must assume, advanced) disciple, born to help him with his mission, as well as to perfect those ideals in himself.

Historians see—in William's case, quite understandably—the towering rages in which he sometimes seemed to indulge, and they quite naturally ask, "So how can you say that he had no personality?" The answer is implied in a story Kriyananda told from recollecting the years he spent with his guru.

One day an older monk, Jean Haupt, was with the master in his interview room. A nun was present also, seated at the opposite end of the room. Yogananda was scolding her for some reason. "You'd have thought the roof would fly off, the way he was shouting!" Gene said later. "He was striding back and forth to emphasize his displeasure. Each time he turned his back to her, however, he winked at me humorously, then turned back again fiercely to resume his scolding."

To Kriyananda the guru said, "I like to work only with love. I just *wilt* when I have to speak in other ways." However, Yogananda well knew that gentleness would not always accomplish what he wanted, which was for people to take seriously what he was trying to teach them.

Kriyananda has said, "Though I lived with Yogananda, and saw him frequently, I could never remember clearly what he looked like. His features changed constantly, reflecting the situations and attitudes around him. When I wanted to recall his face, I always had to look at, or to visualize, a photograph of him. No two photographs of him, moreover, were ever exactly alike."

Yogananda's freedom from the usual "bundle of self-definitions" was due to his complete victory over ego-consciousness. "Looking into his eyes," Kriyananda has said, "was like looking into infinity. There were no personal reactions there, no likes or dislikes, no attachments. He was completely free of any slightest personal motivation."

Of course, there must be enough ego-consciousness to keep the body functioning. One day Kriyananda was walking with his guru around the compound of Yogananda's desert retreat, and had to support the master to keep him from falling. "It is difficult," the guru said, "to keep this one body, particularly, in motion. I am in all bodies." Such is the consciousness of an enlightened being. As Yogananda wrote in his poem, "Samadhi": "I, the cosmic sea, watch the little ego floating in me."

The individual soul does, however, manifest certain basic soul-characteristics, which are much deeper than the ever-changing personality. This basic nature persists through all one's incarnations, and stamps the soul's individuality on all its outward expressions. Thus, though souls may, in their evolution, become thieves, warriors, or merchants, they always express their own unique manifestation of God, who, one may say, has a special song to sing through each soul—even as His expression is unique in every snowflake.

Thus, Yogananda's soul was of a conquering nature. The spirit he sought to inspire in others was one of joyful *self*-conquest. This attitude was very different from that of many other saints—all of whom, however, had to achieve self-mastery by one means or another if they would know God. Saint Simeon, so called the "New Theologian" (he lived over a thousand years ago!) wrote that each saint is different, and should not be judged by the standards of other saints except in the love all of them feel for God.

People who describe Jesus Christ as "meek and mild" forget the force with which he drove the money-changers from the temple, and how fiercely he addressed the hypocritical Pharisees, calling them "sons of your father, the devil."

Most people like their saints to be "soft and cuddly"—recalling to mind a phrase by the British humorist P.G. Wodehouse, who described someone as "looking like a saintly but timid codfish." Every saint, however, has divine power. Each of them shows it in his own way, but all true saints have had that power.

Therese Neumann of Konnersreuth, Germany, as a young maiden, would drive the local swains fiercely off the premises with a pitchfork if any of them came around to court her! (Yogananda said she had been Mary Magdalene in a past incarnation. One suspects that in this life, she felt she had had it with men!) No saint could find God without a fiery will, though he may keep it hidden.

Thus, to understand William we must look not to his outer actions, which were necessary, but to that nature which we know in this incarnation as Yogananda, particularly as it has been explained in books by Kriyananda. Yogananda could be fierce, yes, when the occasion demanded it. But his inner nature, which he often revealed, was unconditionally blissful and loving. He wanted nothing, personally, and gave to all unstintingly.

What about Yogananda's worldly mission? It too was, in a sense, one of conquest: to win the West to new ideas that seem certain, eventually, to transform all of society. Ultimately, however, both he and William saw that transformation in the highest, spiritual terms.

His disciple Kriyananda has written many books to show how his guru's teachings relate to, and resolve, every problem of modern life. Kriyananda's own mission has been, like Henry's, to complete what his guru started.

Yogananda "destroyed evil" in the sense that he showed the countless fallacies of which modern Christians and Hindus have been guilty, and helped them to see how to correct those evils. His explanations of scripture are certain in themselves to change mankind's entire outlook on religion.

Ultimately, however—as I said—Yogananda's mission, like William's, was to bring souls to God.

And why did Yogananda reveal to people that he had been William the Great? I think it was to help them realize the vast impact his own mission was destined to have on the world. William the Conqueror has been described as having had a greater impact on the world than anyone else in the last one thousand years. In one way or another, William's life gave a new direction to history itself. And Yogananda's life is destined, as he himself often declared, to have a similar impact. Most of his disciples wanted to keep his work small and "cozy"—as something they felt themselves able to control. Only Kriyananda has understood its enormous power to change all of society. His more than one hundred books have shown many of the ways in which Yogananda's teachings resolve countless dilemmas of modern thought: from meaninglessness to scientific materialism to purposeless evolution to the delusion that a perfect society will produce perfect people.

All four lives have served the purpose, finally, of helping to return religion to its rightful place in society: at the head of the train of human progress in all areas, as its locomotive, rather than as a dead weight with antiquated notions, half-hearted energy, and pallid faith. Yogananda brought back to spirituality the enthusiasm, energy, and intensity that comes with high adventure and eager exploration. Gone forever, for those who allowed themselves to be swept up by that wave, the dispirited sighing of colorless hymns, followed by listening passively to dry homilies of which the main purpose seems to be to encourage people not to stray too far from the path of righteousness—as if they expect people to ask themselves, "How bad can I be and get away with it?"

Knowledge of these men's past incarnations can help us to develop greater energy, enthusiasm, and intensity in our own lives: to give us a sense of purpose and high destiny, and not merely to treat religion as a side issue—a respite, perhaps, from more serious matters, and a relief from life's daily "treadmill."

CHAPTER 42

Yogananda's Mission in the Present Age

A **further question needs to** be asked: Has vice, as Krishna stated in his description of an *avatar*, been in the ascendant in the present age?

The answer must be a resounding, "*Yes!*" When Yogananda came to America in 1920 as a young man, much of the civilized world was staggering (as it still is, though perhaps a little less so) under the impact of materialistic science. Man had lost his bearing, a fact which has become evident in every aspect of modern life: in music, in painting, in sculpture, in literature, in ethics—well, in virtually everything.

Religion had been so overwhelmed by science that its representatives simply haven't known how to respond to what has now become an entirely new perception of the universe.

Darwin seemed to have eliminated every possibility of a Conscious Creator.

Freud had undermined people's faith in aspiration of any kind: Everything man did, he said, derived from subconscious influences; in fact, it was all affected by the sex impulse.

Adam Smith had convinced many that self-interest is the only "morality."

Physics had revealed a universe in which man's part is so infinitesimal as to seem quite insignificant in the great scheme of things.

Could God—if He really exists—even be interested in us mere human beings? Could He listen, and respond, to our prayers? Could there really be a consciousness behind this vast, sprawling universe?

Almost coincidental with Yogananda's arrival in America, the astronomer Hubble, in 1918, discovered that what astronomers had thought to be a great cloud of gas in the Andromeda Constellation was actually a complete star system. Since then, the universe has been found to consist of over one hundred billion such star systems—now named "galaxies." Even with the vast number of stars (again, some one hundred billion of them) in our own galaxy, it seemed absurd to materialistic minds to think that there could be a conscious entity behind it all.

Biologists decided, in keeping with the "revelations" of Charles Darwin, that the very evolution of life has been a mere accident.

Physicists discovered that matter is not solid, but only a vibration of energy.

The earth was discovered not to have been created (as certain Christians believed) about the year 4000 BC, but to be several billion years old. The birth of civilization is even now being pushed back so far that it seems to vanish in the mists of tens of thousands of years (and getting older with many current archeological digs). (Christians may begin to doubt: Could God's "only son" really have waited so long to bring man salvation for the first time?) Great ancient civilizations are constantly being unearthed throughout the world.

The earth, far from being the center of the universe, seems to be but one of countless billions, perhaps, of inhabited planets in one galaxy.

Space is being demolished: through radio, television, ever-more rapid travel—even space travel—and countless preconceptions are being demolished.

What, people wonder nowadays, is even real?

Too many, in their confusion, have concluded that it doesn't really matter what we do: that we might as well just "eat, drink, and be merry, for tomorrow we die." What thinking person, they ask, could make any real sense of anything? Even in human life, vice in 1920 was "in the ascendant." Who could stop it?

The world had then just emerged from "the war to end all wars"—and seemed less stable politically than ever.

Communism, in 1917, had just taken over in Russia, killing all aristocrats and any "bourgeoisie" who didn't manage to escape to other countries. Under the inspiration of Karl Marx, the world was offered a new, false "faith" in which religion itself was condemned as "the opiate of the people," and the supposedly "enlightened" communistic system, created to bring about a Paradise on earth, instead brought social slavery, misery, and a new symbol: the hammer and the sickle, glorifying the most crudely physical and the least spiritual aspects of human consciousness.

Materialism had all but uprooted people's faith in morality, what to speak of in God? Jean-Paul Sartre, the "high priest" of Existentialism, was soon to declare—symptomizing an already-existing evil—that moral values are entirely man-made, and have no relevance except as individuals decide for themselves.

Money, and its partner, avarice, became the new "road to happiness." Widespread monetary greed, a quality that had already drawn a curse on human happiness, took on fresh impetus with the creation of the Federal Reserve Board and the free printing of money, which resulted in the concept that wealth can be produced "out of thin air." Avarice brought the earth's nations into a downward spiral of depression during the 1930s, and now (in 2009) seems destined (as Yogananda often predicted very forcefully) to put mankind through the "wringer" of a much deeper depression. What he predicted then is now becoming a reality, with a still-hidden deficit of over a quadrillion dollars in derivatives. Yogananda said that money, eventually, would not be "worth the paper it is printed on."

Human beings as a whole seemed on all fronts to be heading toward disaster—and all because, as the Bhagavad Gita put it, "vice is in the ascendant." The suffering that awaits mankind will be purgative. But Paramhansa Yogananda's mission was to show people how that suffering can be alleviated and a new era of progress, prosperity, and high ideals ushered in by practical and spiritual means.

Again, one short lifetime was not enough to declare his mission fully. His accomplishments, as I shall explain in the next chapter, were phenomenal. He needed, however, another person to come after him, as William's mission had needed Henry to complete it. For Yogananda, this successor was Swami Kriyananda.

Kriyananda's books explain the importance to modern times of his guru's teachings, and how they resolve every single one of the dilemmas I described above; how they can also affect education, family life, and business. Some of his books address the problems raised by the materialistic sciences, psychology, and social philosophy. In fact, I am at a loss to think of fields that Kriyananda has not addressed pertinently. He has even shown how all the great spiritual figures of the past really did have, as Yogananda clearly pointed out, essentially the same message.

Finally, Kriyananda has given to the world Yogananda's teachings on some of the great world scriptures: the Bhagavad Gita; the teachings of Jesus Christ and other books of the Bible; the Sufi work called the *Rubaiyat of Omar Khayyam*: all these in a manner so clear, simple, and convincing that the greatest skeptic, having read any one of them, must cry, "Then after all there *is* meaning in life! And how glorious that meaning!"

Interestingly, there was a hiatus after Yogananda's passing in 1952, before Kriyananda could begin his own mission. In the same way, there was a pause between William's life and Henry's. It was as though the impact of those great men's message needed a few years to become clarified and mentally digested before it could be addressed in earnest.

Even though "vice is in the ascendant," we live in an age in which awareness is ascending also. Yogananda's message came with a clarity that could only be delivered when people everywhere were ready to receive it.

Ours is, as I said, an age of energy. There has been a rapid shift in human awareness. Yogananda came to address that shift, and to "re-establish virtue" on earth. That is to say, he brought a new, deeper rationale for more spiritual ways of thinking and acting.

CHAPTER 43

The Spiritual "Invasion" of America

Swami (**his title at** that time) Yogananda was sent to America in 1920 by his spiritual teachers in India. The invasion he launched did not consist of armed might, like William's. Still, he was armed with even-more powerful "weapons": revolutionary concepts and insights that had the power to change people's outlook on everything.

There was no Harold Godwinson waiting on America's shores to oppose him. On the other hand, we may say—perhaps more than fancifully—that Yogananda was met by a similarly resistant "shield wall" of dogmas, preconceptions, and entrenched ideas regarding what Christianity, religion, and life itself are all about. He brought new insights into the life hereafter; into the pilgrimage every soul makes through the twisting by-ways of maya (delusion). He brought deeper understanding of the underlying purpose of life.

Yogananda confronted the concepts I listed in the last chapter, and gave mankind a new way of looking at everything.

Before he even came to America, he wrote a concise book titled, *The Science of Religion*. In its pages he proclaimed that his primary purpose in coming to the West was to show—contrary to the basic claims of most religionists everywhere—that belief is not an essential factor in religion; that the true essence of religion is *experience*.

Yogananda also pointed to the universal basis of religious experience—not, as he put it, in the mystical visions and ecstatic transports of a select few, but in an easily ascertainable truth: that human action is determined by only two factors: the desire,

304

on the one hand, to escape pain, and the compensating desire to find happiness.

The young yogi's mastery of English was not up to the task of writing out his ideas in a book. He therefore gave this task to his disciple, Swami Dhirananda, outlining for him a complete précis of what he wanted to say in *The Science of Religion*. Dhirananda put those thoughts into English. Although Dhirananda's writing was heavy, pedantic, and difficult to follow, he succeeded in stating Yogananda's concepts well enough for those who would later hear the young yogi express them in person.

Many years later, Swami Kriyananda re-wrote this book, titling it, *God Is for Everyone*. The book finally expresses his guru's central message—simply, clearly, and convincingly: in fact, thrillingly.

When Yogananda brought this new concept to America, he arrived like a bombshell! His charisma drew countless thousands to listen to his message wherever he went. Lecture halls large enough to accommodate five thousand were filled to overflowing. In his early years in America, Swami Yogananda was the most popular speaker in the whole country.

A photographer in Washington, D.C., kept a life-sized photograph of the master on the sidewalk outside his studio. Kriyananda, years later, received from Louise Royston, a fellow disciple, a fascinating account of the master's visit to that city. Her account appears in Swami Kriyananda's published record of his years with Paramhansa Yogananda, *The New Path*. This vivid portrait is worth sharing in full.

> Louise Royston, an elderly disciple who first met him during those early years, described [Yogananda] to me as a man so alive with divine joy that he sometimes actually came running out onto the lecture platform, his long hair streaming out behind him, his orange robe flapping about his body as if with kindred enthusiasm.
>
> "How is everybody?" he would cry.

"Awake and ready!" came the eager response, in which he led them.

"How *feels* everybody?"

Again the shout: "Awake and ready!"

Only in such a charged atmosphere was he willing to talk about God, whom he described as the most dynamic, joy-inspiring reality in the universe. Dry, theoretical lectures were not for him. He had not come to America to philosophize, but to awaken in people an ardent love for God, and an urgent longing to *know* Him. The forceful, inspiring personality of this teacher from India utterly captivated his audiences.

Louise Royston told me a charming little story from Yogananda's 1927 visit to Washington, D.C. There Mme. Amelita Galli-Curci, the world-renowned opera singer, became his disciple. At this time Galli-Curci had reached the pinnacle of her own extraordinary fame. One evening, while singing before a packed concert hall, she spotted her guru seated in the balcony. Interrupting the performance, she pulled out a handkerchief and waved it eagerly in his direction. The swami in his turn rose and waved back at her. The audience, finally, seeing whose presence it was that had interrupted the program, broke into enthusiastic cheers and applause, sustaining the acclamation for several minutes.

There is a photograph of Yogananda meeting the U.S. President, Calvin Coolidge. He also met many other prominent people.

Truly it may be said of Swami Yogananda that he took America by storm. In 1925, the *Los Angeles Times* reported: "Thousands being turned away from the three thousand seat philharmonic auditorium. . . . Swami Yogananda is the attraction. A Hindu invading the United States to bring God in the midst of a Christian community, preaching the essence of Christian Doctrine." The swami was an unprecedented sensation.

Later that same year, 1925, he bought Mt. Washington Estates, above Los Angeles, as his international headquarters, and settled there. To Kriyananda he described Los Angeles as "the Benares of America." (Benares might justifiably be called the spiritual center in India for devout Hindus). His international headquarters overlooked downtown Los Angeles from a height of about one thousand feet. It was a perfect location from which to spread his message throughout the world.

Interestingly—turning this account for the moment to Swami Kriyananda, his son "Henry" in the present life—it was during the year of the master's acquisition of this property that Kriyananda (Donald Walters) was conceived. Baby Donald was born on May 19, 1926—in Romania, but of American parents; his father's work as a geologist kept him in that country until Donald was thirteen. This, however, is for the moment a sidelight.

Yogananda's spiritual "invasion" of America was more in the realm of ideas than of outward achievements, although these, too, were considerable. Outwardly too (it should be added), he faced countless obstacles, much persecution, and many betrayals— just as he had during his life as William. Swami Dhirananda— whom Yogananda invited from India to help him with his work in America—developed the same treacherous attitude toward Yogananda that Robert Curthose had shown toward William in at least that one life we know about that they shared together. (After all—Dhirananda may have thought self-justifyingly—hadn't he been the actual writer of Yogananda's book, the master's major publication to date?)

Yogananda returned from a highly successful "campaign" lecture tour to find Dhirananda, like Curthose, in rebellion against him. This man left his guru's work; drew many people away with him; endeavored to gain control of all of Yogananda's money (leaving his own guru almost destitute); and did his best to destroy his guru's work.

A statement Yogananda made during his boyhood to Tulsi Bose, a mutual friend of Yogananda's and Dhirananda's, showed that the master was aware from the beginning of their relationship that Dhirananda would disappoint him. ("Some day he will betray me, and marry a white woman.") Why, then—a natural question—did he bring this disciple to America in the first place? We might as well ask, Why did Jesus accept Judas Iscariot as a disciple? In both cases those masters knew what the consequences would be. This single fact suffices to show their complete absence of attachment. They played their roles as God wanted, freely accepting the karmic play with all its consequences. In their souls, however, they remained ever untouched. Jesus Christ's suffering on the cross was not for himself: He suffered because of people's blindness and closed hearts which, as he said on the Mount of Olives while gazing out over Jerusalem, induces them to persecute the prophets and scorn those who come to them in God's name.

Yogananda had to suffer many betrayals in his life. He never lost his unconditional love, however, no matter what happened to him outwardly. Of Dhirananda he once said, "He will never find God except through this instrument, sent to him by God." To express his unconditional love, he sent a box of mangoes every year to him at Ann Arbor, Michigan. Every year, that faithless disciple sent the box back, unopened.

Think of the pain! A master's heart is soft, tender, and unconditionally forgiving. Never does it become hardened, for it flows with God's love. Indeed, a master's heart knows no other reality. Yes, he suffers—never for himself, but for others who, in their blind self-interest, reject God. Christians usually focus on the physical pain of the Crucifixion: they little realize how deeply, even today, Jesus and all great masters suffer for the sorrows which, Yogananda said, all humanity suffers in its ignorance.

I won't list every hardship Yogananda had to endure. Indeed, I myself know only a tithe of them. They do reflect the hardships that William, too, had to undergo, but having listed so many of those in this book I feel that another catalogue of suffering and betrayal won't accomplish any useful objective. The important thing is what Yogananda did for humanity. In any case, a liberated master, having worked out all his personal karma, will be similar from life to life—more so in his basic characteristics than in the episodes through which he lives.

The important thing is the great impact both men had on their times. Yogananda's life was, in fact, too recent for a prolonged discussion of its effects, some of which have yet to achieve their full impact. I can attempt, however, to show cogently some of the sweeping issues he addressed.

CHAPTER 44

Yogananda's Contribution

The first task the master addressed as a young man was the issue of providing an education that taught children spiritual and moral values. For today's children become tomorrow's citizens. Modern education, Yogananda lamented, is basically atheistic. In the name of preserving their own integrity, children are not asked to believe in anything. What can such a system produce but cynicism, selfishness, despair—and, of course, atheism? Suicide among the young has become a serious problem. Its cause is only partly the force with which information is crammed into their aching brains. The other part is that, being given nothing in which to believe, they naturally grow up thinking that life has no meaning—unless mere existence, procreation, and a better income can be equated with meaning.

In 1918 in India, Yogananda started a school at Ranchi, Bihar, where he taught universal values, which didn't depend on children's religious or social beliefs, but were based on their actual experience of life. Yogananda tried to give them that experience.

Again, I'll share an amusing story as related by Swami Kriyananda, who heard it firsthand. Yogananda told about two boys in his school who kept arguing and fighting together. He had them sleep in the same bed! "From then on," he said, "it was either constant warfare, or enforced peace. After a time, they became friends.

"Then I decided to see how deep their new friendship was. While they were asleep, I went silently and stood against the wall at the head of their bed. Both boys were sound asleep. I leaned down and rapped one of them on the forehead with my knuckles. He sat up angrily.

"'Why did you do that?' he demanded of the other boy.

"'I—I didn't do anything!' stuttered the other, sleepily opening his eyes.

"Well, they both settled back to sleep. After some time, I leaned down and rapped the other boy the same way.

"'I *told* you I didn't do anything!' the first boy woke up and shouted. They were on the point of coming to blows when they looked up and saw me.

"'Oh— *you!*' they understood immediately that I'd been testing them. From then on they became the best of friends."

Yogananda taught the boys faith in a formless, non-sectarian God. He taught them to meditate. He showed them from their own experience the importance of sharing, and of kindness, and of high ideals. Within a year the applications for enrollment had reached two thousand: far more boys than the school could accommodate.

Years later, Swami Kriyananda presented his own version of his guru's education principles in a book which he titled, *Education for Life*. This book is gradually gaining a worldwide reputation. Ananda itself, which Kriyananda founded, has several schools that teach all the way from preschool to college, and have inspired educators everywhere.

In 1925, Yogananda proposed to start a school at Mt. Washington. Of course, parents needed first to be convinced of the rightness of his teachings before they would send their children to his school. The proposal, therefore, never got off the ground. He must have known this would be the outcome.

There were several other projects that he tried to accomplish during his lifetime—not with the expectation of completing them, but simply to start a trend which others, later on, would be able to bring to fruition. In this case (as in others), Kriyananda has been the one to complete them.

Yogananda adopted a new way of spreading the yoga teachings: by means of a correspondence course. Again, he set the pattern, but didn't work out the details. Like William, his vision was too broad for him to concern himself constantly with the "hows." He left it to Louise Royston (the disciple I mentioned earlier) to take excerpts from lectures he had given and articles he had written, and make a course of lessons out of them. Mrs. Royston, however, had never taught anyone, personally. She didn't know what the beginning yoga student's first interest would be; she only thought in terms of preparing lessons to keep students connected to Self-Realization Fellowship as long as possible.

Years later, Yogananda gave to Kriyananda—then very new on the path—the job of studying the lessons, then of grading the answers students sent in answer to the exam questions that appeared at the end of each step in the seven-step course, which lasted nearly four years.

The master increasingly gave Kriyananda the job of sharing the teachings with others. The young man was still only twenty-two when he started this undertaking. He soon realized, however, that teaching should concern itself with helping others to *understand* what they were being given, and not merely to ladle it out to them ("like soup," is the expression he uses). Years later, in India, Kriyananda rearranged the lessons to follow the students' natural flow of interest. (It should be noted that the lessons in the format he gave them have yet to be adopted by SRF.) Years later, he wrote a complementary Raja Yoga home-study course, based on Yogananda's teachings, which has been well received around the world.

Yogananda started a magazine, which, four months after Kriyananda's arrival in 1948, he asked this disciple to "spruce up" with practical articles on how to live. In all ways, Yogananda tried to reach out to the world with a message that would inspire a new understanding. More and more it was becoming obvious that he counted on Kriyananda to bring that message to others.

His main mission, however, was not the specific things he started so much as the message he tried to convey through those channels. That message, and not the organization he founded, was what would change and uplift the world. Getting disciples who were capable of grasping and promoting this central purpose was more difficult.

One of the master's basic themes was what he called "world brotherhood colonies": places where people would live together; share the same high ideals; work cooperatively; study and worship together; grow their own food; live simply; and establish a new communal lifestyle together in an age when more and more people were forsaking the land to live in crowded cities. Yogananda felt, with Mahatma Gandhi, that the cities of our day are in themselves a disease which breeds mass indifference, ruthless competition, and selfish ambition.

At a garden party in Beverley Hills in 1949 Yogananda gave so stirring a lecture on this subject that, years later, Kriyananda stated, "It was the most stirring talk I have heard in my life." The master addressed eight hundred guests, most of whom had come for tea and entertainment! Speaking at full volume, he cried, "I am sowing my thoughts in the ether—in the Spirit of God, and my words shall not die! Thousands of youths must go North, South, East, and West" to spread this ideal new way of life. Kriyananda says he vowed that day to make this vision a reality. Since then, he has fulfilled that vow.

In 1958 he asked Daya Mata, by then the President of Self-Realization Fellowship (SRF), "When will we be able to begin carrying out Master's ideal of world brotherhood colonies?"

"Frankly," she replied, "I'm not interested."

Yogananda once said to her, "How you all will change this work after I am gone! I just wonder, if I were to come back in a hundred years, whether I would even recognize it."

Robert Curthose, William Rufus, and others have incarnated in other bodies, but the karma remains: It has been Kriyananda's task to do what Henry did: fulfill his father's (in this case, his guru's) mission. Yogananda's main social purpose—outwardly speaking— may indeed have been the creation of "world brotherhood colonies"

as a means of changing all of society in time. He said that this idea
would someday "spread through the world like wildfire." Already,
as economic depression intrudes more and more on the present-day
scene, voices are being raised in increasing number in support of
the creation of small, intentional communities as a solution to the
problem. Yet Daya Mata, through the monks in the organization of
which she is president, has declared publicly that the guru came to
the West "to start a monastery." This amounts, surely, to a betrayal
of his intentions. As we shall see later on, in her incarnation also as
William's daughter Agatha she betrayed his wishes for her, though
her betrayal was not personal, as Curthose's was.

Yogananda's vision, indeed, was even more sweeping in ways
that only Kriyananda seems to have fully recognized and accepted. (He was, for example, the only disciple present at that garden
party who dedicated himself to fulfilling the master's words on
that occasion.) Schools, also, were outward plans of the guru's that
Kriyananda has succeeded in putting into effect.

Yogananda said he had been sent to show the underlying oneness
of the teachings of Jesus Christ and those of Krishna in the favorite
Hindu scripture, the Bhagavad Gita. Through Yogananda's explanations he hoped to show that all true religions have, as their goal,
the realization of God, who is the underlying Self of all beings.
Indeed, there is, and can only be, in the entire universe, one religion. Everything came from God, and everything will eventually
return to him. Yogananda taught also that that is the best religion
which most scientifically works with reality, and with the human
mind and body, as they actually are—as proved, that is to say, by
direct experience.

Yogananda wrote commentaries on the Bhagavad Gita which are,
to the minds of many people, unsurpassed in scriptural literature. He
wrote commentaries on the Bible that merit his name for them: "The
Second Coming of Christ."* For they explain clearly the universal
teachings of Jesus Christ the man and also Son of God.

* These commentaries are available now in the book *Revelations of Christ,
Proclaimed by Paramhansa Yogananda*, Presented by his disciple, Swami
Kriyananda. Available from Crystal Clarity Publishers.

The question has arisen in some people's minds: Was Yogananda himself a reincarnation of Jesus Christ? Did he have a hidden meaning in naming his mission, "The Second Coming of Christ"? To many Christians, the very question would seem a blasphemy. All I can offer is Kriyananda's comment: "Their characters seem far more alike than one might expect who was influenced only by the comments of orthodox priests and ministers." When Kriyananda asked his guru this question directly one day, however, Yogananda responded only, "What difference would it make?"

Yogananda did, however, answer the question: Has Jesus Christ reincarnated? His response was, "Of course he has! A master of such great compassion would have returned to earth not only once, but many times."

Yogananda was not a scholar. It has therefore astounded Kriyananda, to whom scholarship comes more naturally, to see that *every single teaching* that has appeared in the long history of Christianity was addressed clearly and insightfully by his guru— from the Arian heresy of the fourth century to the present-day heresy of materialism. Always Yogananda came down on the side of the divinity of Christ, his universality, his omnipresence, and the need to tune into the Christ consciousness in order to know God. He explained the Trinity in a way that finally makes sense, and showed its parallel to the Hindu teaching—not that of Brahma, Vishnu, and Shiva (which he said are personalized aspects of *AUM*)—but of *AUM, Tat, Sat. AUM*, he explained, is the Cosmic Vibration, or Word, which produced the manifested universe; *Tat* is the Christ consciousness (*Kutastha Chaitanya*); and *Sat* is the Supreme, Motionless Spirit beyond all cosmic manifestation.

It would be straying too far from our present theme to explain the many similarities he pointed out between Christ's teachings and the teachings in all great religions. They were not superficial, but basic.

Because religion, although central to human life, is not man's only activity, he showed how everything else that man does can be directed toward its supreme fulfillment in God.

He showed the underlying validity of the caste system in India, which has been all but lost in that country. Caste, originally, was not defined by heredity; it indicated, rather, the right *direction* of growth for everybody. He also said that a truer explanation of the different races of man has nothing to do with the color of a person's skin. It depends, instead, on his personal outlook on life. It is a matter of different levels of consciousness, in other words, not of bodily color or structure. One may have more in common with someone on his own level of consciousness who lives on the other side of the world than with a member of his own family! The distinctions depend, then, on whether a person's personal outlook on life is body-bound; inclined to use the gift of intelligence for ego-fulfillment; desirous of expanding his self-identity to include others; or interested only in serving and expressing God in his life.

He showed that the true basis of morality lies not in social or religious beliefs, but in true self-fulfillment. And he showed that this fulfillment is achieved by self-expanding sympathy for others—as opposed to actions that, by shrinking the ego inward upon itself (through greed, lust, selfishness, and other similar vices), cause one pain and suffering. All the ethical teachings that have been taught only heretofore in terms of obedience to certain outer norms, he showed to have their basis in human nature itself. Thus, he pointed out that when Jesus said, "It is more blessed to give than to receive," he was proclaiming true, because spiritual, morality. Why is giving more blessed? for the simple reason that the giver himself feels blessed—that is to say, more blissful and more fulfilled.

Yogananda taught that the reason for sexual self-control is not social correctness or to please God, but true versus false fulfillment: the one bestowing an increase of energy, inner peace, and happiness; the other, depleting one's energy and inner peace, bringing inner tension and increasing nervousness, and developing a gnawing loss of inner unhappiness.

Yogananda showed the importance *to oneself* of controlling anger and other self-harmful emotions, which, when curbed, bring one happiness.

He taught the limitations of Freud's teachings, showing the difference between suppression and transcendence; between surrendering to one's lower appetites in the name of inner freedom, and aspiring to higher-than-human realities in oneself.

He taught that the writings of Charles Darwin address only the mechanism of evolution, but don't show its true goal: the evolution of *consciousness*. He also, very interestingly, insisted that man is indeed, as the Bible says, a special creation, and that a "missing link" between the lower animals and mankind will never be found. Indeed, Yogananda's entire account of Adam and Eve and the garden of Eden in his Bible commentaries is a direct challenge to, as well as a fulfillment of, the orthodox teachings on the subject.

He was a master psychologist, but said the only way really to understand people is not by psychoanalysis, but by heartfelt empathy.

Indeed, he pointed out that, without calming the heart's feelings and thereby developing one's intuition, nothing can be rightly understood.

He stated that patriotism should not be limited to what he called man's "fancy-frozen boundaries"—that our love and loyalty should include the whole human race.

He wholeheartedly endorsed the Biblical teaching that we should love God with heart, mind, soul, and strength (which, he explained, means energy), and love all beings equally as expressions of God. Often, too, he quoted the words of Jesus: "Seek the kingdom of God first, and His righteousness, and all these things shall be added unto you."

He showed how very *practical* it is to live more for God, because there alone lies the path to true fulfillment.

He taught that selfishness must not be excoriated, but spiritualized. "Everyone has most closely at heart his own interests," he said. "It would be hypocrisy to pretend otherwise. However, we can best fulfill that interest if we expand it to include the well-being and happiness of all."

He taught that leadership does not mean bossing others about, but *leading* them to greater fulfillment for themselves. Thus, a true leader does his best to *serve* others, never to dominate them.

He taught parents to respect their children's freedom of will, for they are souls, and each one is seeking in his own way to fulfill his nature and to emerge, finally, from the darkness of delusion.

He was deeply interested in politics—an interest which he said he had, in fact, carried over from such incarnations as that of William the Conqueror. Kriyananda recalls many discussions with him on such subjects as presidential elections in America. My friend once asked him, "Who was Roosevelt in a past life?" Yogananda responded, "I've never told anybody." With a wry smile he added, "I was afraid I'd get into trouble." When Truman was elected, he commented deprecatingly on his lack of dignity as a president in refusing to shake hands with those who had opposed him. Yogananda was very much opposed to Roosevelt's huge centralized government, and for that reason opposed the "liberal" policies of many Democrats, which he considered not liberal at all, but as showing a tendency toward the destruction of people's liberties in the name of doing everything for them.

He was very much against communism: no doubt above all for its atheistic assumptions, but also for the absolute control it seeks to exert over everyone—people who, for all that, are ironically named, "comrades"! He condemned communism for elevating the animal in man above his higher, spiritual nature (witness, as I said before, the banner of communism: the hammer and sickle as its supreme symbol, suggestive of glorifying manual labor over intelligent thought, sensitivity, and refinement). Communism exalts all that is most base, most animalistic, and most purely instinctual in human nature. In its insistence that all land belongs "to the people"—which, in Russia's case, soon came to mean, "to those who *control* the people"—communism is a religion of darkness, not of light.

When North Korea invaded South Korea, Yogananda told some of his disciples, "I myself put the thought in President Truman's

mind to go to the defense of South Korea. Otherwise, commu-
nists would have spread their system to Japan, then to the Aleutian
Islands, and finally into America. Communism is the greatest curse
of our age."

Would he have supported the defense of South Vietnam?
Kriyananda very much doubts it. That part of the world is too
distant from American interests for the U.S. forces to be sent there.
The job of the United States of America is not to police the whole
world. It *is*, certainly, to protect its own true interests, but there
are many ways of protecting those interests without seeking the
military "solution."

America, Yogananda said, has basically very good karma. Its
self-perceived mission is to be helpful to others. He said this good
karma would protect us, and would enable America to emerge victorious, in the end, from every global upheaval.

One mark of that good karma may be seen in the fact that
America alone, for the first time in known history, having been
attacked by a foe, beat it, and then did its best to uplift that foe
again. The enemies in this case came from two sides: from Japan to
the west, and from Germany to the east. America's Marshall Plan
program after the war was designed largely to raise vanquished
countries to their feet again.

Cynics sneered, "Well, of course it was in America's *interest* to do
so!" Well, of course it was, in that helping others is always in one's
own interest also! But how many other countries have ever shown
such enlightened self-interest? Yogananda, to repeat, never spoke
against self-interest: he only spoke of contractive versus expansive
self-interest. He was a realist, not a dreamer. He dealt with human
nature as it is, not as one might wish that it were.

What would he have said to the modern conviction, which
has been virtually shouted from the housetops: "Communism is
dead!" Is it? The same group of people are in control as before.
I personally believe (and feel intuitively that Yogananda would offer
a similar warning) that this quiescence is only a temporary strategic
retreat, with an all-out assault planned again for the future.

Yogananda said the world would eventually become one, and that its unity would constitute more a spiritual change than a political one. Specifically, he said that the United States and India would some day lead the world toward a more balanced way of living: a combination of material and spiritual "efficiency." And he worked particularly to bring harmony between those two countries: America and India.

As India's ambassador, Binay R. Sen, said to Yogananda on the master's last day on earth, "Ambassadors come and ambassadors go, but you, Paramhansaji, are India's true ambassador."

Yogananda—"Paramhansaji"—made predictions for the world in keeping with his interest in world conditions. He spoke of future world wars involving atomic bombs, in which "no corner of the world will be safe." Europe, he said, will be devastated; Russia, "annihilated." On the subject of future atomic wars, it is frightening to contemplate that there are *known* to be at least 30,000 atomic weapons stockpiled in the world.

The times of turmoil seem to be looming ever closer, but when they are finally over, Yogananda said that the world would finally be so fed up with fighting that it would know three hundred years of peace, harmony, and prosperity. "I prophesy," he declared, "you will see a new world, very different from the one you now live in."

His interests extended to every aspect of life. He showed that true practicality lifts human consciousness toward its eventual destiny: oneness with God.

CHAPTER 45

Past Karma and Present Challenges

Kriyananda, like Henry, came late in his predecessor's life. In their guiding karmas, Henry and Kriyananda shared much in common. In their individual or personal karmas, however, a greater difference may be seen between their lives than in those of William and Yogananda. For whereas the older men were *avatars*, and had no karma of their own to expiate, Henry/Kriyananda, though obviously advanced enough to have been selected for the roles he played in those lives, was still struggling toward inner freedom.

Thus, we see between Henry and Kriyananda not only many striking similarities, but also a few clear *dis*similarities, these last suggesting an ongoing evolution of consciousness.

As for William/Yogananda, who was spiritually free, how can we account for the amazing similarities of tests and challenges they faced in both their lives? The similarities of character must be there, of course, because the basic nature of the soul remains the same. What happens to a person in his life is due mostly to his own karma, or past actions. A master, however, is free from all karma. How then to account for what happens to him? Much of it must be due to the karma of others—perhaps to his taking onto himself their karmic burdens, as Jesus Christ did in suffering "for the sins of the world." It could be explained also in terms of the consciousness a master emanates: a positive flow which attracts to him an equal and opposite negative reaction.

Surely it was the fundamental character of William/Yogananda which attracted the extraordinary opposition both men encountered. Perhaps this accounts also for the similarities in the tests and challenges experienced by Henry/Kriyananda. Some of those challenges must of course be attributed to past karmas; in these, one would expect to see some evolutional change. But the similarities in their tests and challenges are so striking that we may have to account for them also as I've done in the case of William/Yogananda: a close similarity of character which attracted to them almost identical reactions.

Has there been a difference of evolution from the life of Henry to that of Kriyananda? If so, it seems likely that the changes would be toward greater soul-freedom.

What about more superficial similarities—let us say, of likes and dislikes, rather than of soul characteristics? An example would be money, since the handling of it played a large part in both lives.

Henry loaned his brother, Robert Curthose, three thousand pounds. Later, he was deliberately deprived of it. Did he show attachment to that money? When he was robbed of his countship, it would seem he took the loss calmly, expressing neither resentment nor a desire for vengeance. In his calm acceptance of the facts and determination to make the best of difficulties, we see a striking resemblance between the two men.

Kriyananda's lack of attachment to money may be seen in many ways, perhaps most strikingly in his calm reaction to the *loss* of money. For example, I have never seen him ruffled by the many financial vicissitudes he has faced in founding the eight Ananda communities worldwide. Once in the early years, when Ananda Village was threatened with imminent foreclosure, his hands were shaking. Some friends of his said to him, "Come home with us; we'll give you a cup of tea. That way, you'll feel better." He replied, "I'm not interested in how I *feel* about this! I'm thinking, 'What can I *do* about it?'" The first thing he did was get the trustees to grant him a postponement. Then he worked extra hard to raise the necessary money. One day before the foreclosure date, he sent the trustees the needed check for the required amount.

Even then, however, he remained loyal to high principles. One place that owed him for a class series he'd given there failed to pay him what they owed. He said nothing about it. "If God wants me to pay this debt, He will arrange matters for me without my having to insist on my rights."

Kriyananda has always had an aversion to gambling. Once, when he was visiting his parents, they asked him to join them in a game of bridge for "a penny a point." He wanted whenever possible to be obedient to them (especially since he'd totally ignored their wishes regarding the path he should follow in life!), but he had a strong aversion to gambling even for such a small sum. "Divine Mother," he prayed (he usually visualizes God in this feminine aspect), "please handle this matter for me!" His score, at the end of the game, was zero. As far as I know, the odds against such an outcome are astronomical.

In 1969, at Ananda's beginnings, a young man came to Kriyananda and said, "I would like your advice. I've come into a certain inheritance, and am wondering whether I should use this money to go to India, or stay here at Ananda, in which case I'd give my money to Ananda." (I should note here that Ananda never asks this of its members.) Under most circumstances, this would have been a naive question, but evidently this man trusted Kriyananda's integrity.

Kriyananda asked him, "How large is your inheritance?"; he wanted to ascertain whether the young man could afford to go to India.

"Two hundred thousand dollars," the other replied. The dollar was worth much more in those days than it is now; the present equivalent to that sum would be closer to a million dollars: enough to place the newly established community firmly on the road to success.

Kriyananda said later, "I wasn't even tempted. I told him, 'Use it to go to India.' My reasoning was that if he'd really wanted to

join Ananda, he wouldn't have come to me with that question."
Kriyananda was under great stress at the time to earn the money,
through classes, to get his community fairly launched.

Kriyananda has certainly had his share of financial burdens and
crises, as did Henry, but this is of course normal for anyone who
engages in large enterprises. Those men's non-attached reactions,
however, have been unusual, and I think show great similarity.

Both men met every problem, moreover, no matter how great,
with enormous courage.

In 1990, a huge lawsuit was filed against Kriyananda by his fellow disciples in Self-Realization Fellowship (SRF). Over the years
since they dismissed him in 1962, they had behaved toward him in
ways similar to Robert Curthose and William Rufus's treatment of
Henry. The lawsuit lasted twelve years, and cost SRF an estimated
fifty million dollars. Ananda itself ended up spending twelve million—a huge sum indeed, though much smaller for the reason that
Ananda hired as its lawyer a sole practitioner, and Ananda members
themselves did much of the legal work. SRF, on the other hand,
hired one of the largest law firms in the world. SRF lost decision
after decision, and appealed every one with the obvious purpose of
bankrupting Kriyananda and the Ananda community. Somehow
Ananda not only survived, but thrived. It won on ninety-five percent of the issues. SRF, in trying to ruin Ananda financially, ended
up losing most of their copyrights for Yogananda's books—even for
his main book, *Autobiography of a Yogi*. (They tried, in revenge, to take
away all of Kriyananda's copyrights on his own books! Whereas he
wanted to release Yogananda's original writings, so that the whole
world might benefit from the master's unexpurgated thoughts, what
SRF wanted to do was simply bury Kriyananda's writings.)

Daya Mata once told Kriyananda, "Master once said to me,
'God has given you great power in this lifetime. No one will be
able to stand against you.'" Interestingly, in Hindu tradition there
are examples of persons to whom God gave the boon of invincibil-
ity, who later went against dharma, or righteousness. God always
found a way for those who later slipped into *adharma* to be defeated,

despite the boon He had given them. In the present case, however, Kriyananda said, "I never stood against her. All I did was protect Ananda from her attempt to destroy it."

Daya had once told Kriyananda, "I called a meeting of all the monks and nuns and told them, 'I know you've heard that Kriyananda was dismissed. He was NOT dismissed: he *resigned!*'" She wanted Kriyananda to back that statement.

"I can't do that!" he exclaimed. "It isn't true, and you *know* it isn't true."

"Well," she replied after a moment of repressed frustration, "you *should have* resigned!"

During the lawsuit years, she evidently counted on her guru's promise to see her through to victory. Kriyananda was always very conscious of the fact that his struggle was not against her, personally: It was in the name of truth, against untruth.

Daya once said to him, about the lawsuit, "This isn't personal, you know." To him, however, SRF's attempt to destroy him did seem very personal. At one point in the legal struggle the magistrate appointed a settlement lawyer, a Mr. Lombardini. After one or two hours sequestered with Daya Mata and a few other SRF board members, Mr. Lombardini then saw Kriyananda and the Ananda legal team. Partway into the discussion, he said to Kriyananda, "Are you Mr. Walters?" Assured that such was indeed the case, Lombardini exclaimed, "Boy! You sure aren't anything like what I've been led to believe."

SRF tried to ruin Kriyananda—finally, to use the law to bankrupt him and Ananda, and even, as I said, to take away the copyrights for his books and music—in other words, much of his life's work. They failed, because he took his stand on the truth alone. Even his copyrights were insignificant to him: he wanted only to share the truth with others. Kriyananda has never thought in monetary terms primarily, and has accepted no royalties from his books and music. His entire purpose has been to support true principles.

Never in his life has money been his center of interest. One time, when Kriyananda (Donald, at that time) was sixteen years old, his father offered to buy him a tuxedo. Donald replied, "Don't bother, Dad. I'd never wear it. In fact, I'm never going to earn enough money to pay income taxes." Mr. Walters senior dismissed his son's prediction as a "teenage fantasy," but in fact, at the age of twenty-two, Kriyananda met Yogananda and was accepted by him as a monastic disciple. He has never had sufficient personal income to need to pay taxes.

I can think of one difference between Henry and Kriyananda, which suggests an evolution of consciousness. Henry had sometimes to force his will on people. Had he not done so, they would have ridden roughshod over him and over the laws of the land. It seems somewhat doubtful that Kriyananda could ever have behaved similarly. Perhaps he has recoiled from that past tendency in himself. At any rate, in my thirty-two years of working with him, I have never known him to impose his will on anyone, even if the consequence of not doing so resulted in great inconvenience for himself.

One time—a little incident, merely—while Kriyananda was spending some time at his parents' home, a woman phoned him every evening, just as he was about to sit down to his evening dinner. With every phone call she asked him long and perfectly pointless questions. His mother remonstrated to him one evening, "You've just got to tell her to stop pestering you like this!" Kriyananda answered, "But she has a right"—then finished lamely—"to pester me if she wants to." Where principles are concerned, however, he is no doormat. Several times people have threatened Ananda's very existence, or challenged its integrity. In all cases, Kriyananda has stood firmly by his ideals no matter how high the stakes. He has often said, "I would rather Ananda itself failed than give in, where principles are concerned."

He has fought against evil, and against unscrupulosity in people, but has never cut corners where the issue was success vs. high principle. Moreover, it has been his principle never to defend himself personally. "I'm trying to get out of my ego," he says, "not to affirm it."

Henry had to spend his life fighting. However, he seems never to have initiated a war out of personal ambition. In this respect, is Kriyananda different? As a child, as I said earlier, though he never initiated a fight, he never ran away from one. The same thing may be said of the later difficulties he faced. In this respect he was very much like King Henry. He never courted high position, but when his guru placed him in one, he accepted the charge and took it seriously, defending his position as a duty, not as something to which he was attached. Like Henry, whom his companions had mockingly called "Stagfoot," Kriyananda, as a young man, was mockingly called, "The Monk." Through thick and thin, however, he stuck to what he had accepted as his duty.

To convince the monks under him (many of them were much older than he) to follow the simple rules he had instituted, he said, "Monastic tradition insists on obedience to one's superior, but I won't ask that of you. All I request is your cooperation. In return, moreover, I will do anything that any one of you asks of me, provided it doesn't go against my conscience, or against the rules of our calling." Cynics might make of this statement what they like, as historians have done when writing about Henry, because the attitude itself is so unusual, but both men have rigidly insisted on service to others over self-aggrandizement, which was never their consideration at all.

Henry was described by his contemporaries as being in every respect self-controlled. He never drank to excess, and disapproved of drunkenness in others. He was abstemious in his diet. (The tradition that he died from eating an excess of lamprey eels is now generally conceded to be an invention.) I know of no instance of his getting angry or hating anyone. All these qualities are evident in Kriyananda, too. I have never seen or heard of him getting angry, even as a show to impress his wishes on anyone. As for hatred, he tells us that he doesn't even understand this emotion; he has never felt even a suggestion of it.

There is one quality, however, in which he seems to have evolved since his lifetime as Henry, and indeed since his youth in this life.

Henry is said to have had more illegitimate children than any other English king. The reason may be simply that Henry forthrightly acknowledged, as his own, offspring that other rulers tried to conceal or deny for the sake of their own convenience. When I read, however, about his supposedly remarkable self-control, I wonder whether he can justifiably be said to have overcome lust. Perhaps that quality was so common in his time as not to have seemed to merit attention. His children may also, as the contemporary chronicler William of Malmesbury firmly stated, have been a way of making sure that he had enough loyal supporters in an age rife with treachery and deceit. All of his children, legitimate or not, were well brought up, educated, and married to high nobility—to their own benefit and that of the kingdom. (And even so, one natural daughter, Juliana, tried to kill him with a crossbow!) He may have produced children for such worthy purposes. One cannot assume, however, that he did so without any sexual desire. Sexual desire—perhaps even more so than any other kind of desire—is a great impediment to soul-liberation. Yogananda called it "the greatest delusion." Henry was open, truthful, and forthright—yes, to all of these qualities—but his sexual self-control must surely be in question. Even though it does seem that he was almost wholly faithful to Edith Matilda throughout their marriage, there remains that word, "almost."

Sexual desire is man's second strongest nature-implanted impulse, after self-preservation. It would need to be so, to insure the continuation of the species. "Otherwise," Yogananda said, not mincing words, "who would indulge in such a dirty act?"

In this lifetime, Kriyananda has felt his share of attraction to the opposite sex. Yet he wanted very badly to overcome this tendency, and always resisted it mentally. His guru, to whom he frankly admitted this struggle, told him, "This quality isn't deep in you. You *will* overcome it."

When Kriyananda was thrown out of SRF ("the best thing that ever happened to me," he has since then said; "it has freed me to do all the things my Guru asked of me"), he lost the supportive environment of monks and a monastic setting. Until very recently, even at Ananda, he has been the only monk—in a community of evenly mixed men and women. "With God's grace," he says today, "I have completely lost all sexual desire. Now, I see and feel no difference between men and women: to me, they are simply my brothers and sisters in God." Indeed, having known him for over thirty years, I can say—and women have an intuition in these matters—that he has seemed always, throughout this time, to have been remarkably immune to feminine attraction. Such inner struggles as he has undergone have not been evident on the surface.

"When one has once come out of a delusion," he says, "it is amazing to look back. One wonders, then, what on earth attracted him in the first place? It seems ridiculous to have ever been drawn in that direction."

He found the same thing with pride: once he had truly overcome it, he says, he couldn't see anything even to be proud about!

"In recent years," he says, "I have felt a bliss so intense that sometimes I can hardly contain it. I try to hide it by not speaking, but when I'm obliged to speak—for instance, to give a lecture—I sometimes find that I simply can't contain my feelings. To shed tears before others is intensely embarrassing to me." This nearly overwhelming divine joy emanating from Kriyananda is evident now to even the most casual observer.

I have shown some of the ways in which Kriyananda's character resembles that of Henry I. In the last chapter I shall list many more. I have also shown ways in which that character has evolved toward the spiritual goal of final liberation in God. Both the similarities and the dissimilarities can be attributed very reasonably to a basic identity of character.

My next task will be to see what Yogananda told him personally, in terms of the young man's future service to his mission.

CHAPTER 46

A Guru-Given Destiny

After Yogananda accepted young Donald on September 12, 1948, as a disciple, the guru came out onto the lecture platform and, with evident satisfaction, announced to those who were present, "We have a new brother." The very tone of the master's voice conveyed the fact that this was an important event in Yogananda's life, as well as in the new monk's.

The next time Donald saw his guru was again at that Hollywood church. I will quote here from Kriyananda's book, *The New Path*:

Following [Yogananda's] sermon, [a disciple] made a few announcements. He concluded by recommending *Autobiography of a Yogi* to newcomers. At this point Master interrupted him to say, "Many are coming from afar after reading the book. One man recently read it in New York, and—Walter, please stand up."

I glanced around to see this "Walter" who, like me, had read the book recently in New York. No one had stood up. Turning back to Master, I found him smiling at me! *Walter?!* "Ah, well," I thought philosophically, "a rose by any other name. . . ." Self-consciously I rose to my feet.

"Walter," Master continued affectionately, "read the book in New York, and left everything to come here. Now he has become one of us."

Members, lay and renunciate alike, smiled at me in blessing.

"Walter" was the name Master called me ever thereafter. No one else used this name, until, after Master's earthly passing, I longed for every possible reminder of those precious years with him. I then asked my brothers and sisters on the path to call me by that name.

The master seems to have singled out "Walter" from the beginning for special attention. Hardly a month after accepting him, he invited his new disciple to come to his desert retreat at Twenty-Nine Palms. There Walter (as I'll call him for this phase of his life) was present during a new dictation by the master on the technique of Kriya Yoga, which normally is given only during a special initiation ceremony. Again, I'll share this event in Kriyananda's own words:

"Say—Walter!" the master suddenly exclaimed. "You haven't had Kriya yet."

"No, sir," the young man replied, smiling a little smugly. He had heard enough already to understand the essence of this important technique.

"In that case," the master said, "I'll have to initiate you right now." He instructed those present to sit up straight, with closed eyes. "I am sending the divine light through your brain," he told Walter, "preparing you for this sacred practice." The disciple felt a spiritual blessing pass through his brain. Afterward, his guru told him not to practice the technique until the formal initiation, the day after Christmas.

The day before Christmas, there was an all-day meditation at Mt. Washington. The guru had told Walter not to practice Kriya, but during that dictation he had said, "One isn't really practicing Kriya until he does it slowly." Walter thought, "In that case, if I do it quickly I won't be disobeying him." Kriya initiation was to come the day after Christmas. Before the long meditation, therefore, the young monk asked his master, "Sir, would it be all right, during the all-day meditation, if I practiced Kriya?"

"Yes," replied the master with a significant look, "but do it *slowly!*"

At the initiation two days later, he said, "Of those present, there will be a few *siddhas* (those who are finally liberated), and quite a few *jivan muktas* ('freed while living'; a *jivan mukta* has united his soul with God, but still has some past karma to overcome).

This, of course, did not single out Walter, specifically, but it thrilled the young monk to think that such heights might be attainable in this life.

During the all-day Christmas meditation the following year, the master addressed a handful of the disciples, saying, "God is very pleased with you." To Bernard, another disciple, he said, "Be very careful, Bernard. You have accomplished much, but now you *must* be careful!" (Bernard later fell into a deep delusion, and left the path.)

Then the master declared, "Walter, you must try hard, for God will bless you very much."

One day, perhaps a month earlier, he had been speaking to two of the men disciples: Walter, and another monk whom he was sending as minister to the SRF church in Phoenix, Arizona. At one point he hesitated, then added, "You have a great work to do." Walter turned to his companion with a smile of felicitation.

"It's you I'm talking to, Walter," the master said, (Walter was nearsighted and hadn't been able to see where the master was directing his gaze.)

From then on, the master made the same prediction to Walter many times—always, however (except for the first time) when no one else was present to hear him. This interesting fact recalls to mind William's deathbed prediction to Henry, when only a few of those present could hear what William was saying. ("Be patient, my son. For in time you shall have all that your brothers now have, and shall be greater than they.")

Why did William utter that prediction seemingly only for Henry's ears? As we said earlier, had he announced it openly Henry's brothers might have done their best to deny him that destiny—even, perhaps, by killing him.

And why did Yogananda speak to "Walter" only when they were alone, on the subject of the "great work" the young disciple was to do? He must have done so for very similar reasons. Walter's senior disciples in the work (all of them women) had a fault—one which all must eventually overcome—that Swami Sri Yukteswar mentioned in his book, *The Holy Science*: "pride of pedigree." They could not imagine that such a young "upstart" could have anything of value to contribute to their guru's cause—that great master, with whom some of them had resided personally for thirty and more years, and whom they regarded practically as their own property.

Kriyananda once mentioned to Daya (years after Yogananda's passing), "Master told me I have a great work to do."

"Yes," she said, "we all have a great work to do."

There really seems to have been a certain jealousy toward him in the attitude of his superiors. He was obviously a man of great ability, and kept coming up with new ideas for the spread of their guru's mission. They would often expostulate to one another, "Why can't he just wait to be *told* what to do?!"

In fact, as we shall see, when they saw Kriyananda trying to fulfill the charge their guru had given him (unknown to them, however), they lost no time in dismissing him from the organization. We shall discuss that story in its proper place in this book.

Yes, there had to be some jealousy in that mix. There was also, perhaps, an attachment to power.

There is also a difference between some of the attitudes that are natural to men and to women. Women are more protective, more concerned with the things close to them. As Yogananda once said about women to a small group of men disciples, "They have more attachment to *maya* (delusion)." (He'd been scolding the men, however, for their more single-minded attraction to sex. It was in this context that he added, "Well, women have their problem, too: they have. . . ." It was here he referred to their greater attachment to *maya*.) Masculine energy, however, was what the launching of such a great new mission as his required.

One day, Yogananda and "Walter" were alone on the retreat grounds at Twenty-Nine Palms. The master said, "Of the men disciples, apart from Saint Lynn [his most advanced male disciple], every man has disappointed me. And *you mustn't disappoint me!*" He spoke these words fervently. Kriyananda knew it was not the master's meaning that many men had disappointed him *spiritually*. He understood the meaning to be, ". . . disappointed me in their lack of zeal for sharing this mission."

It was Kriyananda alone who, like Henry I, really understood that mission, and did his best to complete what his guru/father had initiated.

Interestingly, Saint Lynn (Rajarshi Janakananda) once told "Walter" also, in a whisper so that none of the other monks could hear him, "Master has a great work to do through you, Walter, and he will give you the strength to do it."

Thus, when Yogananda said to Walter shortly before his own departure from this world, "You have pleased me very much. I want you to know that," the disciple felt a great burden lifted from his heart. The master had given him many responsibilities, including placing him in charge of the other monks, making him a minister, and consulting him (as well as confiding in him) on diverse aspects of the work. "Walter" had been longing for some reassurance that, so far at least, his guru was satisfied with him. He has always kept these words as a treasure in his heart. They have served him as a lifeline whenever his monastic superiors have tried to convince him he was working *against* their guru's wishes.

CHAPTER 47

After Yogananda's Passing

Kriyananda thought—indeed, he couldn't imagine otherwise—that the "great work" his guru had given him to do would be within the confines of his organization. Yet Yogananda had said to him at Twenty-Nine Palms, "Your work in this life is lecturing, editing, and writing." The master didn't mention communities. Perhaps, had he done so, the young disciple's mind would have moved in that direction too soon. Yet Kriyananda always remembered the silent vow he had made at that garden party in 1949: to fulfill his guru's charge someday and help in spreading this "world brotherhood colony" idea.

On the point of the guru's words to him at Twenty-Nine Palms that his work would be writing, the disciple asked, "But Sir, haven't you written enough books already?"

"Don't say that!" the master remonstrated. "*Much more* is needed." Kriyananda has said that his guru even seemed slightly shocked at the suggestion.

Now that the guru had left his body, Kriyananda wondered what he could write that would be meaningful. Before meeting Yogananda, he had once wanted to be a playwright and a poet. He had abandoned that ambition when he realized that he didn't himself know the truth—which was the only thing he wanted to share with people. Thus, he had concluded, "If I write now, I'll only be imposing my own ignorance on others. I must give up writing." Not a few people had predicted a shining career for him in the

335

theater. Success to him, however, didn't mean fame or money: it meant helping others to find true happiness. He didn't yet feel that he knew enough of the truth to help others through writing.

Another problem faced him, moreover: How, in SRF, would he ever find the time to write? And even if he did write anything, would SRF ever agree to publish it? Certainly not!

Daya wouldn't permit him to devote the necessary time to writing books. She actually tried once to get him to accept a job in the printshop, working with the presses.

"That isn't my work at all!" he exclaimed in dismay.

"Why *not*?!" she cried in exasperation. The printshop may have seemed to her a good way of getting him out of her hair—with all those suggestions of his for furthering the work! She'd paid no attention to what he'd said about Master's charge to him personally. Probably she didn't believe Kriyananda had even told the truth in saying so.

The young man had, then, to fall back on another perfectly valid explanation. "Any machinery I work with," he told her, "would almost certainly break down the moment I touched it!"

As the years passed, however, he realized that there was an even greater problem connected with any hopes that SRF might publish his books. Tara Mata, the senior editor, wouldn't let anything through her hands that she hadn't edited carefully herself. Moreover, she wasn't even close to getting out Yogananda's own books—many of which remained unpublished even years after his death.

"What do people need with more books?" she once demanded rhetorically of Kriyananda. She'd received criticism for not getting out the master's later writings. "They already have everything they need for their own salvation!"

In Tara's mind, any zeal to spread the work could only be motivated by deep, personal ambition.

Publication of such extremely important books as Yogananda's commentaries on the Bible and the Bhagavad Gita was delayed for decades while Tara interfered with Daya's work as president. No one could prevent her, for Tara was senior to them all.

Kriyananda felt increasingly frustrated. Daya had told him, on the subject of founding communities, "Frankly, I'm not interested." Tara had scoffed at the idea of getting out "more books," even though those books were central to Paramhansa Yogananda's mission. (She had also laughed, in speaking to Kriyananda, at what she considered their guru's lack of touch with reality in his plans for founding communities.) What could Kriyananda ever do, to fulfill his guru's commission to him?

Even the things their guru had told him concerning his wishes for the monks were scoffed at by the senior women disciples. Yogananda had insisted more than once, for example, that the monks have a separate community of their own. When Kriyananda later repeated these words to his women superiors, their only reaction—as it emerged later—was to conclude that he was maneuvering to get the monks "out from under Daya Mata's control."

Daya Mata, as a leader, attempted to control everything—not only to hold the reins, but also (as Kriyananda has since put it wryly) to act as the horse! Increasingly frustrated by her inability to delegate authority, he once wrote to her, "I suppose I must resign myself to living with ulcers for the rest of my life!" He found himself blocked at every turn.

As we noted above, in the life of William the Great, Daya had been his daughter Agatha, whom William sent to be married to Alfonso VI, the heir to the throne of Leon and later king of Castille. She had wanted to be a nun, and had adamantly rejected the role assigned to her by her father—who was also, however, her guru. In rejecting his wishes for her, she was also, in effect, rejecting God's will.

It is said that when the ship reached port, Agatha was found in her cabin, kneeling in prayer, dead. She remarked once to Kriyananda, "Ever since then, I've had trouble with my knees." Kriyananda later reflected: If her determination not to be queen had been God's will, would not her knees have been, if anything, strengthened by that death? As queen, she would have learned much about leadership, which would have helped her in her present incarnation, as president. Instead, she has shown a degree of self-involvement that no competent leader could afford to entertain, or would even be likely to feel. In her treatment of Kriyananda, even when she gave him permission to follow a line of action, she would withdraw that permission if anyone objected, later on, to what he was doing. Thus more than once she effectively severed the line on which he'd been left dangling.

Hope came to him at last in June of 1962, when he read an article in *SPAN,* the United States Information Service magazine in India, written by the head of the philosophy department at Massachusetts Institute of Technology (MIT). The article described modern trends in philosophy, and made a number of startling declarations: 1) that life has no meaning, no purpose, no direction; 2) that there is no consciousness underlying creation, and that everything just "happened" as it were by cosmic accident; 3) that there is no meaning in evolution, which, too, is accidental; 4) there are no moral values. The article quoted heavily from Jean-Paul Sartre, the French nihilist, whose book *Saint Genet* described a French thief and male prostitute, whom Sartre described as a saint because he "honestly" admitted—in fact, boasted about—his activities. Sartre praised Genet as a man who had "created his own values, and remained true to them," because Sartre himself denied the existence of any absolute values.

This article stirred in Kriyananda the serious thought: "Master gave clear answers to every single one of these preposterous tenets. Wouldn't it be wonderful if I could write a book in answer to them!"

The thought was fortuitous, and also fortunate. One month later, Kriyananda was flung out of the monastery and of his guru's organization altogether—as he puts it, "on my ear."

CHAPTER 48

The Storm Breaks

Surely one of God's greatest tests is when one's own nearest and dearest spurn him—especially when they do so virulently. This is what happened to Kriyananda. Summoned by Daya and Tara Mata in July 1962, from India to New York, a "safe" three thousand miles (as he couldn't help observing) from SRF's headquarters in Los Angeles, he was excoriated by them in terms more damning and deeply hurtful that he could have thought possible. Tara did most of the talking, though Daya chimed in supportively from time to time. Clearly, Tara was determined to destroy his faith in himself, so as to get him out of their hair once and forever. (Shades of Curthose and Rufus!)

Through much of that one-and-a-half-hour interview, Kriyananda knelt on the floor before his older sister disciples, his arms crossed over his heart in a gesture of surrender and unbearable anguish. He hardly spoke. Like Henry after Mont-Saint-Michel, it seemed to him that the entire purpose of his life had just been destroyed. Like Henry, he found himself, too, banished from everything he had known (in Kriyananda's case) for the past fourteen years. At the age of thirty-six, he found himself suddenly stranded in New York City, with only the money in his wallet to keep him alive until he could find "any old job that comes along," as Tara put it to him unfeelingly. (He had been a monk all of his adult life up to that moment.)

For many years, Kriyananda, on principle, never described that meeting to anyone. Only in 1990, when SRF forced him to do so by their lawsuit against him and Ananda, and he was deposed under oath, did he find it necessary to relate his past history with his sister disciples.

Curiously, although Curthose and Rufus incarnated, as we know, in their most recent lifetime in other bodies, it was Kriyananda's destiny to be placed under two persons who in certain respects closely resembled his former brothers. Daya, like Curthose, could be charming, but she was also a weak leader, and unreliable. In Kriyananda's case, she never showed any hesitation in betraying him. Tara, like Rufus, had a tendency to judge others ruthlessly, and apparently took pleasure in denouncing them in the most drastic terms possible, displaying complete indifference to whatever shriveled corpses she left in her wake.

Tara told Kriyananda in New York, "You'd stop at nothing short of murder to get what you want!" Then, as he related, evidently pleased with the sound of that denunciation, she repeated it with added emphasis, carefully emphasizing each word: "*Nothing - short - of - murder!*"

It was the most outrageous thing anyone had ever said to him. He had always carefully avoided doing anything that wasn't scrupulously *dharmic* (righteous). But Tara wasn't concerned with the truth. As we've noted, what she wanted to do was utterly to destroy Kriyananda's faith in himself, and even in his discipleship to his guru. She hoped her words would so infuriate him that he'd fulfill a prediction she'd made before the meeting: that he'd storm out the room, slamming the door behind him as he went. In fact, she insisted to him at that meeting that this was exactly how he'd have treated their guru—"if you'd come to him earlier than you did."

Another statement she made was, "From now on, we want to forget that you ever lived!"

The sequel to that story was that Kriyananda's parents had happened just then to land in New York. (Tara's comment to

Kriyananda in New York over the phone: "Isn't it *wonderful* how Master has worked this whole thing out!") They'd been vacationing in Europe. Kriyananda was able to contact them in Scarsdale, and drove back with them to their Atherton home in California, just south of San Francisco. (Daya's outraged comment to him on the phone when she heard where he now lived: "You've settled *right on our doorstep!*")

At first, all Kriyananda could do was lie on his bed and stare at the ceiling, wondering what he could possibly do with his life now, and praying for the grace of death. He'd dedicated himself entirely to serving his guru.

After about a month, he accompanied his parents to the home of a friend of theirs for tea. At that home he met Dr. Haridas Chaudhuri, a scholar, philosopher, and the founder of Cultural Integration Fellowship, an ashram in San Francisco. Dr. Chaudhuri finally succeeded, after great effort, in persuading this "lost sheep" to sing at his ashram for an anniversary in celebration of the birth of Mahatma Gandhi. The ashram became Kriyananda's "Domfront"—the town that welcomed Henry when he was debarred from every other part of Normandy or England. Gradually, thereafter, the young man began regaining his strength, and also his faith—not in his guru (which he had never lost), but in his guru's love for him, which had been badly shaken. (He had prayed daily to his guru, "Even if you forsake me, I will never forsake you, and will always love you!")

He continued gradually, from this time on, inwardly to be shown ways in which he might serve God and his guru. Tara, in New York, had told him very firmly never to do anything in his guru's name—nor even to tell anyone he was Yogananda's disciple. She had added, "We don't want people to know that Master had such a *despicable* disciple! Moreover, until you do something about that atrocious personality of yours we want you to keep as far away from his work as possible! You are not to contact any SRF member." (Always when speaking she punctuated every sentence with an invisible exclamation mark.)

The one thing Kriyananda could not do for his guru was nothing at all. Slowly, he regained the momentum he had lost, and the faith—not in himself, but in what he might still do to serve his guru.

The first thing he decided was to pursue the inspiration that had come to him when he'd read that article in *SPAN* magazine. He went—as he puts it—"into the camp of the enemy": the skeptics, the materialists, the atheists, the nihilists, and all those who used science and reason to persuade themselves and others that there is no purpose or meaning to anything; that values are entirely subjective; that evolution is a complete accident; that there is no intelligence or consciousness anywhere except that which is produced by the brain; that life must simply be endured as well as possible, for at death one passes into eternal non-existence.

Kriyananda told himself, "The people who hold these thoughts are educated and intelligent. If they were stupid, they wouldn't even try to express their absurd opinions so lucidly. I can't combat them by merely scoffing at them and denying the things they say. If I am to undermine their conclusions with the truths my guru taught me, I must learn to reason *from their point of view.*"

For years Kriyananda studied the rationale behind atheism, purposelessness, accidental evolution, and nihilism. He went to the public library and read books that, to one of his nature, could only be completely incompatible; that offended his deepest beliefs—indeed, they were wholly inimical to them. He tried, however, to maintain an open mind, keeping faith in the depth of his own convictions, that he might *use their own logic against them.*

In the end, he wrote a book, now titled, *Out of the Labyrinth* (the first edition was called, *Crises in Modern Thought*). Years later he wrote another book, *Hope for a Better World*, which showed the fallacies of still other men on whose conclusions most of Western civilization has been based. He ended up taking on Western philosophy itself, and showed how, reasoning *in its own terms*, it betrays itself as a house constructed on sand.

We, the observers of this time period in Swami Kriyananda's life, cannot but stand in awe of this choice of a project at a time when it would have been natural for most people in his position to seek some activity that would be familiar and spiritually self-nurturing. For Kriyananda, as for Henry, the first consideration was never how he himself felt about anything, even if he was struggling against the deepest inner anguish. (Consider King Henry after the traumatic losses he sustained in the sinking of the White Ship. He directed all his energies toward helping others by carrying out his God-given responsibilities as king and duke.) Rather, Kriyananda, like Henry, has always thrown himself into doing whatever he felt his guru (or God) was asking of him. Concerning this dark period (at least of comparable anguish to the White Ship disaster), Kriyananda would say that the inner guidance he felt to pursue writing this book amounted to the only thread—a very slim one—of guidance he received. But he took up that thread with all the energy his battered heart permitted him.

Few people realize what a profound service Kriyananda performed for humanity in writing those two books. Though he went on to write nearly a hundred other books, these two form the basis of his, and of Yogananda's, special gift to mankind.

His other books cover the whole gamut of the guru's teachings, as I presented them in the foregoing chapter.

Education for Life, Kriyananda's treatise on education, is drawing increasing support from educators around the world.

Art as a Hidden Message, which represents another of his guru's teachings, is convincing people everywhere that art should not be merely "for art's sake," but should serve the needs of all men for inspiration and understanding. Art should always, in other words, subserve *truth*.

He wrote an important work for married couples: *How to Spiritualize Your Marriage*.

Another book he called, *The Art of Supportive Leadership*, which has been ordered in large quantities by leading businesses to serve as a training manual for management personnel.

He also wrote another small book, geared especially to business-men: *Money Magnetism*, explaining how to attract money when you need it.

He wrote plays; poems; and books on how to spiritualize every aspect of life. It would be tedious for the reader were I to list all the one hundred books Kriyananda has written. His books alone represent what would be a major achievement in anyone's life. And they have sold, so far, well over three million copies.

In addition, he has composed over four hundred pieces of music: songs, instrumental pieces, choir pieces (including a full-length ora-torio, "Christ Lives"). Among the instrumental pieces is a piano sonata, a string quartet, and several trios for piano, strings, and flute.

It might be interesting to learn how he came to compose music, for he had never thought of himself as a composer, and in fact, though he did take a semester on music composition in college, he hardly ever went to class, and did almost no homework assign-ments. His mind was becoming set ever more firmly in the direc-tion of finding truth.

Once, two years after he was dismissed by SRF, he spent a week in Yosemite Park, in the mountains of central California. The day before his scheduled departure, he happened to see two young men seated on the railing of a bridge, singing to the accompaniment of a guitar. Kriyananda was a gifted singer. His singing teacher when he was eighteen, an old lady in her seventies, had told him one day, "I'm living for only one thing now: to see you become a *great* singer!" She raised her hands dramatically, to reinforce her mean-ing. It was the last lesson he ever took from her; he didn't want to hurt her feelings, but he hadn't the slightest desire for name and fame, and singing songs that expressed sentiments with which he didn't even agree seemed to him like wasting his life. All he wanted was to find the truth about life, the soul, and God.

In India, too, where he had served SRF for nearly four years, he had become well known as a singer of *bhajans* (devotional songs) in Bengali, Hindi, and Sanskrit, as well as of the chants composed in English by his guru.

That afternoon at Yosemite, he for some reason felt in a mood to sing, and offered to do so for the boys. When they accepted gladly, he selected a song, in English, with at least a modicum of spiritual meaning: "Swing Low, Sweet Chariot." The boys were so pleased that they pleaded with him to come and sing for a party they were having that evening on a beach by the lake. Swami sang there also—the same song, however; his repertoire of folk songs in English was drastically limited. Everyone loved it. Unfortunately, he could think of no more songs they might like.

The next day, as he was driving home, the thought came to him, "I'm looking for unobtrusive ways—which won't compete with anything SRF is doing—of serving my guru. Maybe singing would be one solution." Then he thought, "What's the use? I can't sing the classical songs I know in French, German, and Italian; no one would understand them. Besides, their message is completely worldly, and is rarely even good poetry. I can't sing devotional songs. What kind of 'service' would it be to Master if I sang only to show off my own voice?"

He was about to drop the whole idea, when suddenly the thought came to him: "Maybe I can write my own songs, songs that would convey messages I *want* to convey?" The moment this thought occurred to him, a song appeared full-blown in his mind, complete with melody and lyrics. He liked it, and, stopping at a milk shake stand, he wrote down the words and music on a paper napkin.

He had been driving to his parents' home. There, he found that his brother Dick had left behind a valuable Martin guitar. Kriyananda bought a book on how to play the guitar. And there he was: a budding composer! He visualized himself touring the country, singing songs, especially to young people, sharing his guru's message through the medium of song.

This too, then—apart from the book he was writing—became a means by which he could keep on serving his guru. He wrote two more songs that month. Then a visitor to the Cultural Integration Fellowship, where he was now living and lecturing, asked him if he wouldn't give a concert at the local Unitarian Church. Kriyananda had only been playing the guitar (far from well) for a month, and had a very small repertoire of his own compositions. As in Henry's case, however, fear was not in Kriyananda's makeup. Thinking, "At least it will force me to practice!" he accepted, then plucked doggedly at his guitar for a week.

The big event arrived. The hall was filled: two hundred people! The organizers, seeking to create "atmosphere," had turned off all the lights, leaving one candle lit on the mantelpiece— *behind* the singer. If there was one thing Kriyananda absolutely needed it was to be able to see the guitar strings! In that relative darkness he could hardly *find* the strings. Nevertheless, he managed to pull the event off, adding stories and a few Indian chants. His musical "career" was now truly launched.

Another way of serving his guru appeared to him. Some years later, he wanted to put together a slide show about Ananda Village. Several people had taken photographs, but these didn't say anything meaningful about the community. He bought a camera and took other pictures himself. He then went on to take numerous photographs around the world, some of which were later (and still are) used as covers for his books, while others have sold well as enlargements. All his photographs show vividly that one can also share states of consciousness through the camera, and thereby inspire people to seek higher states themselves. When he was informed one day that the number of his photographs had reached 15,000, he decided, "That's quite enough." Since then, he hasn't taken another photograph.

About ten years ago he reached the same conclusion with his music compositions. "I've said what I had to say through music," he declared one day. Since then, he hasn't written a note. His music continues to inspire thousands, however, and choirs have traveled as far as Europe expressly to sing it.

His own view of action is to see it as a road to inner freedom. His goal is to pass beyond action to the "actionless state" of freedom in God. Otherwise, except as a service to his guru, he would much rather have been a hermit. It was his guru's prompting that drove him to seek so many ways of serving God. Nothing he has done as a disciple has been with the motive of finding personal fulfillment in that act.

Like King Henry, however, his interests are wide-ranging, as he has shown also by his many-faceted writings. Those interests include architecture; history (especially ancient); languages; psychology; the psychological basis for accents in speech; the limitations and true purpose of government; national economy; different social systems; the equality of men and women, and their different complementary qualities; good leadership; writing style as a means of conveying vibrations of consciousness; travel, and the vibrations that people have left in the various places they lived in; humor as a way of keeping human consciousness from becoming too solemn and heavy (he loves, as I said earlier, the kindly humor of P.G. Wodehouse); the psychological and spiritual influence of music and the arts; astronomy; astrology; physics; biology; geology; ancient sites. Indeed, the list is virtually endless. Primarily, of course, he is interested in the spiritual destiny of man, and in finding ways of helping people to fulfill that destiny.

Daya Mata, whose focus is very singular, used to scold him for his many interests. One must, however, be true to one's own nature.

Kriyananda is averse to violence of all kinds. As a young teenager, he was once talked into studying boxing, but he felt no desire to hit anybody, and soon abandoned that study. Interestingly, when he was much younger, he did love to play games that featured knights in armor. Once when he was nine, on a visit to America, he organized a medieval jousting tournament for the children around him. Cardboard boxes from the grocery store were used as "armor," cut and molded to form breastplates and whatever else the children's fancy supplied. On his own breastplate were printed the words, "Handle with Care." He claimed for himself, therefore, the solemn sobriquet, "The valiant knight Sir Handle-with-Care."

Whether his interest in knighthood can be traced back to his life as Henry I, or whether knights in armor are simply a game many boys play, I am unable to say. I wonder how many boys have such knightly memories, brought over from the past. Perhaps the game is common among them. What I can state with certainty is that I've never known Kriyananda to shirk any necessary confrontation. On the other hand, in the midst of what has often been a highly stressful life, I've always seen him seek peaceful means, first, of resolving every conflict. His deep inclination is not to inflict pain on anyone. Henry, too, was clearly of the same temperament, preferring—as his main chronicler William of Malmesbury put it—to "contend by council" rather than by the sword.

Perhaps this is a reaction to his incarnation as Henry, when it was necessary for him to inflict pain on so many in order simply to rule at all. Kriyananda's oft-stated "bottom line" is peace. "No matter how many things I have to do, and how many decisions I have to make, I never let anything rob me of my inner peace." Here again, as Henry's good friend Hugh of Amiens wrote just after the king's death: "God grant him peace, for peace he loved."

One time, in a legal deposition demanded of him during the 12-year lawsuit with SRF, the opposing lawyer, anxious to "rattle" Kriyananda, insisted that a video camera be brought closer and closer to his face until it was nearly touching him. Kriyananda paid no attention to it at all. The opposing lawyers deliberately insulted, ridiculed, and whispered to each other derogatory comments about Kriyananda during those eighty hours of deposition. They failed completely to "get his goat." He remained calm and polite, either ignoring their remarks or responding graciously to their questions, despite the sneering innuendos.

His greatest interest in life has always been one for which he is now famous: the founding of intentional communities. Kriyananda, like Henry, is a natural leader, but—again like Henry—he tries to *win* people to his ideas, rather than force acceptance on others. This disinclination toward hurting anyone has certainly been increased by the treatment he has received from his fellow disciples. One suspects that part of Henry's compassion was due, similarly, to the ruthless way his brothers had treated him. It was a positive response to situations that would have aroused hostility and resentment in most people.

Indeed, there are only two natural reactions to hurts of this kind: either a desire to inflict pain in punishment or revenge for what one has suffered, or an attempt—born of compassion—to spare others what one has suffered, oneself. Sensitive people—among whom one must certainly include Swami Kriyananda and, almost as certainly, King Henry—cannot but select the second alternative.

Thus, Kriyananda, like Henry, has tried to create an alternative to injustice: in Henry's case, a kingdom ruled by law; in Ananda's case, a place that would serve as an example of peace, harmony, and prosperity for people everywhere. Kriyananda has succeeded in this attempt by creating several such societies: proofs that this ideal offers a practical solution for many of the troubles now being faced in the modern world.

CHAPTER 49

Intentional Communities

As I stated earlier, one of Paramhansa Yogananda's principal ideas for the upliftment of society was to form little self-sustaining "world brotherhood colonies," as he called them. He tried to found such a community in the 1940s in Encinitas, but the time then was not ripe; people, generally speaking, were simply not interested in the idea.

If the timing then was not right, this fact did not mean, as the master's women disciples claimed later, that he'd "changed his mind." Yes, he did lament, "Encinitas is gone!" It may well have been that this lament was directed to the lack of interest in the idea among his own women disciples. He was still talking with fervor of the need for communities, however, until shortly before he left his body.

In 1969, Kriyananda founded the first Ananda community near Nevada City, California. The public interest in such a venture had increased greatly by then, as may be seen from the thousands of failed experiments at the time, and from Ananda's own outstanding success. Today, with the world entering a serious economic depression, more and more statements are again appearing in print that boost the need for a "return to the land," where people can grow their own food, and pursue this experiment in company with others.

Kriyananda had no wealthy friends to support him when he decided to found Ananda. In fact, he stood virtually alone with his dream, which was much more high-minded than the concepts held by groups of hippies, some of whom he initially attracted. A few of his family members questioned his sanity. Everyone, it seemed, was opposed to the idea. In this regard he was like King Henry, who met opposition on all sides, even from his own magnates. Henry succeeded only gradually in winning people to his side. In the same way, Kriyananda had to convince people that his concept of communal life, lived together harmoniously, might work.

It takes success to attract people. And it takes people to attract success. A closed circle! It takes money, moreover, to make an idea practical. On this last front, at least, Kriyananda thought he might be able to work his way out of that "circle of covered wagons." For years in the 1960s he gave nightly classes in many cities, and was probably the best-known yoga teacher in northern California. For five years, in San Francisco and Sacramento, he had a weekly radio program. He gave innumerable lectures. He never debarred anyone from taking his classes, for which he charged a nominal fee of fifteen dollars for six classes (once a week) in either *hatha* or *raja yoga*; twenty-five dollars, for those who enrolled in both series. If people couldn't afford to pay even that small amount, he always let them study in exchange for some minor service such as setting up chairs between classes.

He did insist, however, that people who desired to study with him must do *something* in exchange for what they received. In every case, he found that those who were allowed to study free of charge could easily have paid. He never took them to task about it, however. His generosity had been primarily to satisfy his own conscience.

On July 4, 1969—America's Independence Day!—the purchase agreement was signed for the main land at Ananda Village. Today, that land totals some one thousand acres; all of it has been paid off. Ananda's reputation has become worldwide, with guests coming from countries even on the other side of the globe, to see how hundreds of people are able to live together in peace, harmony, and willing cooperation. Kriyananda, in proving that his system works, has wrought a miracle.

The Ananda communities accomplish for mankind what William and Henry tried to do for England. The present age, which is seeing the emergence of energy-consciousness, is showing itself far more open to qualitative endeavors. Both Yogananda and Kriyananda dreamed from early in their lives of starting intentional communities. They saw these as an important step toward uniting the world—not under one law, but under lofty ideals of love, brotherhood, and shared endeavor. Perhaps both men had the same mission: to materialize this vision. It is certainly not coincidental that Kriyananda, it may again be said, has come into Yogananda's mission late enough to bring the idea to fruition.

Henry and Kriyananda had similar ways of working. Henry was noted for delegating authority. That is how Kriyananda has worked also. Many other communities have failed because their founders insisted on making every decision themselves. Kriyananda's approach has been to ensure that people's *spirit* be right. Assured of that, he knew that their decisions also would be good. There is no such thing, however, as *one and only way to do things*. His interest, therefore, has lain in developing the right spirit.

Both Henry and Kriyananda won loyalty from others not by demanding it, but by *giving* loyalty to them first. In the same way they won friendship, support, and acceptance. Henry forgave "even to the point of foolhardiness," to quote his biographer C. Warren Hollister. Kriyananda is the same way. Even when he knows that a person will betray him—and many have done so, some of them repeatedly—he has never harbored a grudge. Needless to add, he doesn't give people responsibility if they've shown themselves incapable of handling it. Is this what Hollister meant by saying, ". . . to the point of foolhardiness"? If so, we may say that Kriyananda has learned well that particular lesson!

Kriyananda says, "If a dog bites you, you may make friends with it, but you never forget that it once bit you." He is always willing, on the other hand, to give everyone a chance, and never denies that chance to anyone. He simply allows them back into the scheme of things at a level where any harm they might inflict will be minimal. A little harm he accepts willingly, however, if he thinks the result may benefit the individual.

Both William and Henry understood the need for devotion to God as essential to well-grounded ideals. Both gave much attention to monasteries and to sincere devotion, as opposed to mechanically performed rituals, in the priests. Kriyananda also attributes the success of Ananda to his unabashed insistence that members live for God, above all.

William and Henry both worked to bring England into the orbit of Rome, instead of letting the country drift spiritually between Nordic and Roman influences.

In the same way, Kriyananda also found that devotion to a single spiritual path is important for *cohesive* devotion in a community. All Ananda members, therefore—or at least one member of a couple—have to look upon themselves as disciples of Paramhansa Yogananda. In the case of one member of a couple being of a different persuasion, Kriyananda has insisted that that person at least respect Yogananda, his path, and his teachings.

In his public talks, Kriyananda always says, "I am not trying to convert you to anything but your own highest Self." In a community, however, he feels that it is important for everyone to follow the same path. "The failure of communities in the past," he says, "was due at least partly to the fact that they held lower ideals, such as new social systems. Those, on the other hand, that were based on spiritual principles failed by settling for mere beliefs, not insisting on direct spiritual experience, or at least on *aspiration* to such experience."

In the beginning of Ananda he was more lenient in some respects. Soon, however, he found too much leniency didn't work. "Who wants to tiptoe around out of respect for others' disbelief in tenets, such as reincarnation, that one holds dear?" There were also disagreements in the kitchen regarding food that was "taboo" in some religions, and not in others. Ananda is vegetarian, but doesn't insist that its members follow such a diet in their own homes. (Nevertheless, almost all, and perhaps indeed all of them, are vegetarians.) Most moral and spiritual precepts don't even need to be insisted on, because everyone who comes to Ananda does so out of a desire to improve himself. In this way, what Kriyananda has accomplished works much better than the system William and Henry had no choice but to accept, and to work with.

People are people, of course. They can't be herded, like cattle. A formula that Kriyananda has insisted on from the beginning is, "People are more important than things, or projects, or the need for efficiency, or than any fixed social pattern."

Another principle he has insisted on—it is the *only* other one—was phrased in Bengali on the wall of the palace of the maharaja of Cooch Behar: "*Jato dharma, tato jaya*" (or, in Sanskrit, "*Yata dharma, sthata jaya*")—"Where there is righteous action, therein lies victory." Ananda's very survival has sometimes been threatened: always, Kriyananda has insisted on this principle. He has never cut, even slightly, any ethical corner, even if adhering to truth might mean the failure of everything which he has dedicated his life to accomplish.

CHAPTER 50

King Henry and Swami Kriyananda: Similarities

I have, at many places in this text, described a number of shared qualities in the natures of King Henry and Swami Kriyananda. Let me attempt in this final chapter to sum up these similarities. I'll include many others that emerge from a careful study of both lives. That the same soul animated them both is, surely, an inevitable conclusion. The similarities are too unusual to be tossed off casually.

Similarities of Physical Features

Yogananda said that the embodied soul often carries forward from lifetime to lifetime the same physical characteristics. Although those outer characteristics do change over many lifetimes, something about the eyes, at least, remains always the same.

No reliable portrait exists of King Henry, but we have two descriptions of him from his contemporaries. William of Malmesbury, who almost certainly saw Henry and heard him speak, wrote the following words about him:

"[Henry] was taller than short men, and shorter than tall ones [of average height, in other words]. His hair was black [Kriyananda's was brown], and [like Kriyananda's] receding from his forehead. His eyes were sweetly serene [a very good description of Kriyananda's eyes]. His chest was muscular [another shared characteristic]; his body, fleshy [Kriyananda has been described as robust]. He was witty at appropriate times, nor did the press of business cause

355

him to be any less genial [this is a very accurate description of Kriyananda's behavior]. . . . He was plain in diet [true of the man I know], and rather satisfied the calls of hunger than surfeiting himself [with] a variety of delicacies. He never drank [alcohol] except to allay thirst, execrating the least departure from temperance, both in himself and in those about him. [Kriyananda never drinks anything alcoholic, and avoids whatever might affect his mental clarity.] . . . His speech was informal, not oratorical—easy paced, not rapid, but deliberate [this exactly describes Kriyananda's manner of speaking. He never prepares his lectures, and delivers them in a conversational style, as though speaking with friends]."

Another contemporary of Henry's, Peter of Blois, gave this assessment of Henry: "[He is] a young man of extreme beauty [something that many have said about Kriyananda]."

Similarities of Action

1. Henry saved his father's legacy, and Kriyananda saved his guru's—in both cases from betrayal by uncomprehending and self-centered thinking. I refer, of course, to Henry's older brothers, and to Kriyananda's religious superiors.

2. Both men worked with no other desire than to complete their father's/guru's missions.

3. Both Henry and Kriyananda won people easily to their own points of view, not by careful diplomacy (which to Kriyananda seems "manipulative"), but by the magnetism of friendship and of their own deep interest in the subjects under discussion. They could be very firm in defense of what they felt to be their duty. Henry wrote to Pope Paschal II (as I stated earlier) on the subject of clerical investitures, "Your holiness should be aware that as long as I live, with God's help, the privileges and usages of the Kingdom of England shall not be diminished." And regarding the treacherous Robert of Bellême Henry averred, "I will not tolerate anyone in my kingdom who is not my man." Kriyananda was equally firm when it came to defending what

he felt his guru wanted of him. People sometimes called him stubborn for not budging on certain issues, but he once frankly told a rebel in the community, "I didn't start Ananda just to turn it over to *you!*" Yet both men won others by showing them kindness and respect, and by their willingness to consider all aspects of a subject—as long as the subject was still in the considering stage. Rarely did either man allow further discussion once the time for action began, but I sometimes knew Kriyananda to "turn on a dime" when he saw sufficient reason to change a course of action, even when the first direction had been widely publicized. He was not bound to any commitment, in other words, once he saw it was wrong, especially ethically or spiritually. Kriyananda often quoted a saying from the Indian scriptures: "If a duty conflicts with a higher duty, it ceases to be a duty." As for Henry, this is how I have understood his withdrawal from the siege of Falaise campaign, which historians have ascribed to indecisiveness.

4. Both men built enduring relationships with others. Their ability, especially, to see and appreciate points of view very different from their own indicates exceptional clarity of mind and feeling.

5. Both men recognized the need (as neither of Henry's brothers in that lifetime, nor Kriyananda's organizational superiors in this one, ever did) to develop people by giving them a chance to express themselves. Both men appreciated the fact that an organization's strength depends on the strength of its individual members.

6. Both men won loyalty from others by first giving it, themselves. King Henry's loyalty to his men was legendary even in his own day. Kriyananda never failed to support others when he could, though at times he was sorely tested. One man turned against him for thwarting his will on several impractical projects that Kriyananda would have had to fund personally. They met years later, and Kriyananda said to him,

"J___, I might be the devil himself, but it just wouldn't be *your* problem!" "I know," the other replied. "I just can't help my anger." His self-esteem had been offended, but Kriyananda continued to offer him sincere friendship.

7. Both men took the time to offer explanations and give reasons for what they did, giving others thereby a chance to learn and to think things through for themselves, instead of giving mindless obedience.

8. Both men had great tolerance of situations and people, allowing considerable diversity of action and opinion, and never forcing others to conform to their own personal preferences.

9. Both showed a deep and abiding commitment to expanding the spiritual consciousness of not only a few, but of all those who could be touched by their influence.

10. Both found great pleasure in the company of people of noble character. When in the company of persons less refined than themselves, they showed kindness and respect. Both men, moreover, actively sought the company of saintly people.

11. Both showed an ability to make things happen without their own direct, personal involvement. This trait is part of what I said earlier in these pages: their ability to delegate authority. Both men could set energies in motion which later gained a momentum of their own.

12. Both men showed an ability to recognize and appreciate talent and greatness in others. In this quality they differed greatly from people who try jealously to repress outstanding qualities in others in order to safeguard their own status and power.

13. Both men had the ability to step outside the prevailing modes of thinking, and to see things in fresh, new ways.

14. Both men loved order, peace, and refinement.

15. Both men worked joyfully for human upliftment. They didn't approach duty as a burden, but embraced their great responsibilities wholeheartedly.

16. Neither man showed a desire to shine, personally. One woman with whom Swami Kriyananda was conversing after a public event, asked him his name. When he told her, she exclaimed in astonishment, "Swami Kriyananda! But—you're famous!" "Perhaps so," he replied, "but why that word, 'but'?" She answered in some confusion: "Well, all the other famous people I've met seemed important." Kriyananda knew she meant "self-important," but he was delighted to be called un-important, because he was always conscious of his own lack of importance. This same trait in Henry may explain why he is considered the least-known king of England despite thirty-five years marked by peace and great innovations in govern-ment. Neither man was "flashy"; both simply wanted to do what needed to be done.

17. By their force of character, and by working in harmony with divine grace (never, in other words, opposing their own will to God's will) both men overcame what sometimes seemed like impossible odds against them.

18. Both men were utterly fair in their dealings with others.

19. Both were impervious to flattery.

20. Neither man ever resorted to insincerity in trying to obtain an objective. Both eschewed that pitfall into which leaders so often fall: the thought that the end justifies the means.

21. Both men, as leaders of others, were highly charismatic in the enthusiasm they brought to their work, and to their con-sideration for others. They not only encouraged initiative in others, but supported them also in *their* dedication.

22. Both men had the ability to work very hard, with great con-centration and self-discipline. Both too, however, enjoyed beauty in the arts (especially music), beauty in Nature, and high thoughts. Walter Map, whom I mentioned earlier, said that the days at Henry's court had an established rhythm, and were evenly divided between work in the morning, sports and relaxation, and "decent merriment" in the afternoon.

23. Neither depended on approval from others, though Swami Kriyananda, at least, always listened to people's opinions and suggestions, and accepted them if they felt *right* to him. Both men depended greatly on their own *inner* feelings about things.

24. Both men gave willingly to causes in which they believed, and to people who were in need—for the sake of helping, and not to impress anyone. Thus, the benefits they bestowed often remained not only unheralded, but (in Kriyananda's case certainly) unknown—gifts, for example, to two Roman Catholic missions in Sri Lanka. Henry gave, among other donations, to tiny groups of ascetics who lived alone in the woods and to monastic foundations outside the Anglo-Norman borders.

25. Both men gave credit freely to others. Kriyananda never accepted personal credit for himself. "God is the Doer" was his invariable answer when people praised him. Often, moreover, when someone came up with an idea that he himself had already had, he happily gave that person the credit for it.

26. Both men showed enormous courage, whether in action, in relationships, or in willingness to sacrifice everything when they felt they were on a right course and doing something that needed to be done. Fear never seemed to be a part of either man's nature. Henry has been accused of cowardice for changing bedrooms every night when, in his most difficult years in Normandy, he found himself surrounded by treachery. There is a vast difference, however, between fearfulness and sensible caution.

27. Kriyananda and Henry carried many others with them in their own development, accomplishments, and manifestation of talents. Others would not have developed so highly in those areas had they been on their own. What both men did was *inspire* others to reach up toward the best in themselves.

28. Both men infused others, and even the atmosphere around them, with their own idealism, selflessness, and expansive

vision. We saw earlier how Henry "busied himself with train-ing his foot soldiers," and "went to special lengths to teach them the techniques of warfare." Kriyananda likewise dis-dained no activity, mental or manual, as the needs arose.

29. Both were deeply appreciated, loved, and respected by those who worked under them, or who knew them well. In this way, too, they won people's unconditional loyalty.

30. Both created societies unique for their times in which people found it a joy to live.

31. Both led by their own example, and never asked anyone to do what they themselves were unwilling to do.

32. Both men were satisfied with subordinate positions, but showed themselves willing to accept posts of authority when they felt that to do so might be helpful to others. Once they accepted those positions, they took full responsibility for them, and never gloried in their elevated importance.

33. Both men traveled constantly. Kriyananda was only six months old when his parents first took him from Romania to America. As he put it, "I've hardly stopped traveling since then!" King Henry not only crossed the Channel repeatedly, but itinerated constantly within England and Normandy.

34. Both men were able to make friends with a wide variety of people, by giving everyone, even strangers, complete respect and appreciation.

35. Both men treated others thoughtfully, and responded quickly to their needs and interests. They talked *with* others, rath-er than *at* them. We are forced to infer this characteristic in Henry. However, it would have been impossible for him to judge character as unerringly as he is reputed to have done unless he had been a careful, open-minded listener.

36. Both were highly practical, not sentimental like Robert Curthose. They were willing and able to make hard decisions, and to back those decisions by risking their own well-being.

They saw situations as they really were, not through others' eyes or through their prejudices.

37. Neither man was deterred by temporary setbacks; both showed an ability to chart a new course, if the way they were going seemed to be leading toward a dead end.

38. The consciousness which both men projected seemed to state, "Don't look at me: look at the principles I represent." Both men, therefore, though loved by those who knew them, tended to grow obscure with distance. Neither man was "colorful" in the sense that many prominent people demonstrate, whether they be monarchs or public figures, as they seek to draw attention to themselves. Henry has been labeled "the least-known king of England"—an opinion which has degenerated more recently to a frequent assumption that his character was repellant. Kriyananda, similarly, was loved by those who knew him, but has not had or sought the public prominence that more colorful public speakers have achieved. How history will treat him remains, of course, to be seen.

39. Both men had astute legal minds. Henry's Coronation Charter led, in time, to the Magna Carta—the "foundation stone," we may call it, for today's government in England, and the English government shared its fundamentals with the world, through its worldwide empire. Henry became known as "The Lion of Justice." Kriyananda, on the other hand, was the strategist for Ananda's legal battles—more so even than the lawyers themselves. He amazed Ananda's legal team with how well he understood legal tactics, though he'd never had prior training or experience in the field of law.

40. Both men were given the years they needed to complete their missions—Henry, nearly four decades, and Kriyananda nearly six. This is rare for both kings and spiritual leaders. It gave both men enough time to mold a new generation in fresh and enlightened ways of thinking, for which their father/guru had only had time to plant a seed.

41. Both men remained calm and free from rancor in the face of defeat. When Henry's brothers drove him from Mont-Saint-Michel, then out of Normandy altogether, he calmly waited for an opportunity to return. When Kriyananda was thrown out of SRF, he waited until God Himself resolved matters for him. When a lawsuit was filed against him years later, and Kriyananda was faced with an unscrupulous (and untruthful) lawyer and a biased judge, and denied the opportunity to defend himself, he had to deal with relentless antagonism. Accepting this treatment as God's will, feeling no emotion of any kind, not even anger, at being treated so unfairly. To him, whatever happened came as a blessing from God.

42. Both Henry and Kriyananda showed an ability not only to convey insights to others, but actually to share with others their own state of consciousness. People often remarked to Kriyananda, "In your presence, I feel different." Henry, by his dignity, courtesy, insistence on order and on mutual respect, brought a refinement of consciousness that was not known at the court of Rufus. Perhaps it is no coincidence that Geoffrey of Monmouth's writing on chivalry was first "published" only one year after Henry's death.

43. Neither Henry nor Kriyananda was democratic in the modern sense. They never considered calling for a majority vote except in matters they saw as inconsequential. Where principles were concerned, they simply felt that their God-given purpose was to guide others, not to receive guidance from them.

44. Both were "noblemen" in the truest and best sense of the word: refined, but not pretentious; dignified, but never aloof from others; appreciative of beauty, but without attachment; natural leaders, but concerned for those whom they led. Henry was a king, obviously, but Kriyananda lived in a democratic age, and still he carried himself with a certain kingly dignity, and emanated a regal aura that was somehow utterly unself-conscious, and at the same time humble. A close friend of

his parents during Kriyananda's high school days remarked many years later, "He was always different from his brothers and their friends—as though he were a young prince."

45. Both Henry and Kriyananda had to live, act, and make their decisions without the advantage of having any peers.

Similarities of Temperament

1. Kriyananda has said, "Usually, when I think about historic figures, I see them objectively, in the third person. When contemplating King Henry and the events of his life, however, I feel as though I were looking out *through his eyes.*"

2. Both men had great clarity of over-all vision. They were able to see what would help to materialize that vision, and what would be detrimental to it, long before others even knew there was a vision to be considered!

3. Both men from a young age displayed strong moral character—a fact which suggests spiritual advancement from previous lifetimes.

4. Both men were capable of thinking in terms of longer rhythms. Neither was impatient for immediate results; instead, both of them bided their time, building gradually toward the desired ends. It is easy to see, in their deliberateness, why men whose energies are more scattered saw in both Henry and Kriyananda a sort of ruthless deliberation, like Professor Moriarty "weaving his web of evil" in the Sherlock Holmes stories. That image, however, simply doesn't apply here. Both men, rather, awaited patiently the dawn of understanding in those who were recalcitrant, and for the wind-shifts of circumstance to turn in their favor.

5. Both men sought ways of turning their opponents' tactics against themselves, rather than fighting them. Kriyananda once entered a chess tournament against a reputed champion, whose expertise was said to lie in his pawn movements. Kriyananda—who was no expert—decided therefore to

confuse his opponent by moving his own pawns haphazardly. He won the first game, tied the second, and never got to play a third, since the other man, realizing he'd been hoodwinked, rose and stalked angrily off the scene. In combating the meaninglessness of modern materialism, when writing *Out of the Labyrinth*, Kriyananda studied that philosophy *from inside, in its own terms*, and turned that reasoning against itself. King Henry won the compromise he needed on the clerical investiture issue in part by demonstrating his great support for many aspects of church reform, then showing logically that, where the land they occupied belonged to England, they owed fealty for that land to the king. Surely only those people who refuse common sense in the name of their own convictions would call either man, for these reasons, manipulative.

6. Both men were impersonal in their appraisal of people and of situations. They never allowed any thought of personal gain or advantage, or any personal feeling, to cloud their thinking.

7. Both men were capable of deep feeling, but they directed their feelings toward greater clarity and higher understanding. Henry's dedication to completing his father's mission, and Kriyananda's to rendering his guru the same service, could have sprung only from deep devotion.

8. Both men were by nature completely loyal. Henry remained loyal to his brothers despite the way they treated him. Kriyananda remained loyal to his monastic superiors, even after they'd done their best to destroy him.

9. Both men had noble natures—outstandingly so among their contemporaries.

10. Both men had naturally joyful temperaments.

11. Both men, though deeply ambitious, were never so for themselves. They sought only to advance the causes to which they'd dedicated their lives.

12. Both men were much better educated than most others of their time.

13. Both men had, as I said earlier, a vast range not only of interests, but of talents. Kriyananda sang beautifully; wrote music that somehow conveyed his states of consciousness; painted; designed buildings; had a writing style that was concise, clear, and rhythmic; took beautiful photographs; decorated his homes with good taste; spoke many languages, several of them well enough to give public lectures in them: all these talents and more, apart from those he showed in working with people. Henry, too, as we've shown, embraced a wide variety of interests, including many that added beauty and noble architecture to the land.

14. Both men, though realistic, were basically optimistic in their assessment of human nature and of destiny. They were unwilling to give up on anyone until their faith was proved wrong. And they were willing to give others a chance, even long after other people had given up on them. Both were willing, however, to accept that some people cannot be dissuaded from wrong action; they never clung naively to the thought that everybody can be helped. Still, it wasn't in their nature to give up trying. I noticed that this trait became more marked in Kriyananda in his later years. It seemed that no one was outside his love and compassionate interest, long after that person had pushed him away.

15. Both were fun to be with—exciting, stimulating, and forever offering new ideas and insights. They expanded the consciousness of others by the expansiveness of their own. From the chroniclers' accounts, it seems that Henry very consciously kept a flow of new people, projects, and ideas coming into his court—a setting that already kept everyone "on his toes" with the sheer amount of activity that was the daily business.

16. Both Kriyananda and Henry were able, in the midst of personal troubles, to think first of others' needs. The White

Ship disaster is a dramatic example in Henry's life, when the king, despite his own deep sorrow, still tried to raise the morale of others. As I mentioned earlier, historian Frank Barlow expressed the awe of many historians through the centuries who contemplated the spirit in which King Henry met the disaster: "It was an almost annihilating blow; and that Henry recovered, planned anew, indomitably pursued his new aims, and appeared to regain control reveals the true qualities of the man." There are countless examples from Kriyananda's life also, where, to serve others, he disregarded his own well-being.

17. Both men were brilliant organizers, but held things together more by personal magnetism than by systems and rules.

18. Both were extremely forgiving of others; they never nourished grudges. Even when others were treacherous, these two men wished those same people well, and never viewed them with personal animosity. I can't imagine Kriyananda ever wanting, or trying, to hurt anyone.

19. Both men showed an active desire to escape ego-attachment. Yogananda even scolded Kriyananda for not taking himself seriously enough. But the disciple very deeply wanted to overcome the sense of egoic doership. Everything he accomplished can be understood best by keeping this one point clearly in mind.

20. Both were, in a sense, men "without a country." Kriyananda was more obviously so, having been born in Romania of American parents, and having lived in Romania, Switzerland, England, and (briefly) Holland before moving to America in 1939; then having lived in Italy and India as an adult; and with his fluency in several languages. But Henry, too, knew French; the evolving English language of his day; Latin; and Greek. From my deep study of his life, I am convinced that he did not identify with being either Norman or English. Moreover, the help he offered others transcended national

boundaries, with the help he extended to monasteries outside of Normandy, and his interest in creating a trans-Alpine road between Switzerland and Italy.

21. Both men had a good sense of humor. Let me finish, in fact, by telling two jokes that Kriyananda loved. A person's sense of humor, after all—above all, its kindliness and refinement—speaks volumes about who he is. These stories are not his own:

> a) A priest in Ireland once visited a farmer and complimented him on many accomplishments, in each case giving credit first to God. When the priest complimented the man on his abundant crops, however, and remarked, "What a beautiful farm you and God have made here," the farmer replied, "Well, Father, you may be right, but you should have seen it when God had it all to Himself!"

> b) An Irish woman was coming through New York customs. The officer spied among her possessions a suspicious-looking bottle, and cried, "Aha! What have we here?"
>
> "Please sir, it's only holy water."
>
> The man opened the bottle, sniffed, and exclaimed, "Just as I thought: Irish whiskey!"
>
> "Glory be to God!" cried the woman. "A miracle!"

Points of Dissimilarity

1. Henry seems to have enjoyed hunting. Everyone in those days, evidently, seems to have taken pleasure in this "sport." Kriyananda, however, as a child of six, was taken fishing by his father on nearby Lake Snagov, in Romania. They caught two very little fish. Little Donny, as he beheld them wriggling helplessly on the end of the line, felt so much pity for them that he could never bring himself to go fishing again. Some years later, his father took him and his brothers out on a rabbit hunt. Young Donald was greatly relieved when they failed to rouse any game. After growing up, and upon reading in

Yogananda's book that the master was a vegetarian, Donald at once became a vegetarian also, and has remained so ever since.

2. Henry's death left a vacuum of power, and was followed by twenty years of anarchy. Kriyananda, on the other hand, trained and empowered dozens of capable leaders to carry on his guru's work smoothly on three continents. This difference may reflect a lesson he learned from the chaos that followed his life as Henry.

3. Kriyananda has said, "King Henry, during the week before he died, confessed his sins and received absolution for them three times. Henry needed to model, even at the time of his death, the appropriate expressions of devotion to God of his times. For myself, however, I can only say that I feel free in my heart. When I leave this world, it will be without a single regret. I have done my best. Yes, I have made mistakes, and I do regret the times (fortunately, I think they were few) when I've hurt others. But I am grateful for everything. Many years ago I offered my life to God, and now I want nothing for myself except to merge in Him."

4. Any other differences would indicate to my mind an evolution of awareness toward greater, inner soul-freedom.

One Overarching Similarity

Finally, there is the over-arching quality of single-minded devotion to God, which I see as the supremely defining quality not only in William and Yogananda, but also in Henry and Kriyananda. While obvious in the lives of Yogananda and Kriyananda, it may also be described as the polestar of William the Great's and of Henry's life. For though in those long-gone times those kings' love was often forced into subterranean channels, devotion to God was central to their natures. The cynical interpretations of many historians have somewhat obscured the noble qualities of William and Henry, two of England's greatest kings. However, if their actions and decisions are sensitively reconsidered in the context of their times, as we have done here, the evidence is abundant: God was the central reality of both men, in all four of their lives.

Conclusion

Dear reader, my aim in writing this book, finally, has been to offer you inspiration for yourself. The contemplation of true nobility in others helps all men to become more noble, themselves. By noble I don't mean stuffy, pompous, self-important, or arrogant. True nobility means to seek gain first, not for oneself, but for others. It is, above all, to live for duty, without personal attachment or desire. A truly noble person has no other motive than to be of use to others, to bring them peace, harmony, happiness, and personal fulfillment. Such persons, as I have tried to make clear in these pages, are often misunderstood by others. For those persons have come to realize that true fulfillment *cannot* be found in ego-fulfillment.

William and Henry; Yogananda and Kriyananda: both souls, in all four of their lives, understood that by self-denial alone—by curbing the natural selfishness and turbulence of human nature— can one find the inner peace all humanity craves.

The two great souls whose lives we have contemplated had not the back-slapping, ego-pleasing natures of lesser and therefore, quite often, more popular men. They were also somewhat stern, as the dedicated ascetic is stern, for in curbing human ambition they sought to help others to gratify their deeper, soul-need for divine bliss.

It is this aspect of their natures that has made many ego-centered historians and commentators adjudge them cold, unfeeling, even ruthless. We read in Isaiah 55:8: "For my thoughts are not your thoughts, neither are your ways my ways, saith the Lord." And in the Bhagavad Gita, II:69, we read: "That which is night for the unenlightened is day for the yogi [the enlightened being]."

Both William and Henry in their lifetime, and Yogananda and Kriyananda (very clearly so) in this lifetime, lived for others; and were often misunderstood for this very fact—sometimes even by people whom they did their best to help.

But what I hope you will take from this study of their lives is the encouragement not to seek popularity, selfish gain, personal power, or self-aggrandizement in your own life, but the conviction that to live nobly for others, and for God, is the highest destiny of all human beings.

APPENDIX

Fernando III and Alfonso X

I stated in the main text of this book that certain disciples of Yogananda researched possibilities for who might have been that incarnation he spoke about when he was a Spanish king who helped to drive the Moors out of Spain. It is noteworthy that he came in at least two lives to strengthen and unify Christianity, this having been also his supreme purpose in coming to the West as Paramhansa Yogananda. Perhaps it was necessary for him to come this time from outside of Christendom, with what he called the true message of Christ—or, as he put it, "the Second Coming of Christ"—to a society that had lost touch with many of the original teachings of Jesus Christ. Yogananda himself told people, "Jesus Christ appeared to Babaji in the Himalayas and asked him, rhetorically, 'What has happened to my church? My followers do good works, but they have forgotten the importance of inner communion with God. Let us send someone to the West to bring them once more my complete message.'" Yogananda told his disciples that he himself was that "someone."

What I will state now is only, I grant you, my personal belief. I word it therefore as a question: Could it be that Yogananda actually *was*, himself, Jesus Christ? Yogananda said that a master of such deep compassion would certainly have returned to earth more than once since that lifetime. I have other reasons also for my opinion, one of them being the great similarity I find between the personalities of those two great masters—both of them strong, magnetic

372

leaders who were also very approachable as men, and who both (this may surprise a few readers) had a delightful sense of humor.

Swami Kriyananda once asked his guru, "Sir, were you Jesus Christ?" The master replied, "What difference would it make?" But at least he didn't say, "No."

Could it be that Jesus himself came back to earth to strengthen and protect his religion? It seems almost inevitable that he would have done so.

An interesting fact about the lives of both William I of England and Fernando III of Spain is that both saw their mission as one of bringing unity. William unified England and made it a country where God was more widely worshiped. Fernando accomplished that same mission for Spain. Even before both those lives, Yogananda, as Arjuna, brought unity to India.

Fernando III (1198–1252) was later given the epithet, "El Santo" (the Saint). His body, like William's, and again like Yogananda's, was incorrupt. Again like William, Fernando insisted that his soldiers be morally righteous—a principle which, to him, was more important than military skill or martial valor. I am reminded here of the Sanskrit saying, "*Yata dharma, sthata jaya*: Where there is righteousness (and right living), there [alone] is victory."

The highest aims of Fernando's life were twofold: the strong unity of Christendom, and, as a prerequisite, Spain's liberation from the Moorish yoke. He succeeded to a great extent in both of these aims, bringing political unity, building churches and monasteries, and reestablishing Catholic worship everywhere.

Fernando III was intensely spiritual, and lived amid the tumult of a military camp like a religious in his cloister, actually wearing a hair shirt in penance, and praying for God's grace and guidance before every battle. An excellent administrator and just ruler, he often pardoned those who had worked against him and the Crown. History describes him as a ruler who won every battle, but who never sought personal glory or a personal increase of possessions. He called himself un *caballero de Jesu Cristo* (a knight of

Jesus Christ), and a servant of the Virgin Mary. Always his actions were for the glory of God.

Fernando III was canonized in 1671 as a saint by Pope Clement X. Since his death, many miracles have occurred at his tomb, which is opened every year on the 30th of May, at which time all can see his body, which remains incorrupt to this day.

Like Paramhansa Yogananda, Fernando was a warrior for Truth, a poet, musician, and a ruler who placed great emphasis on literature and the arts.

Fernando's firstborn son and heir helped, as Henry did in England, to complete his father's mission. He helped to drive out the Moors from Spain, and brought religious and cultural unity to a country with several rulers. This son was Alfonso X, "El Sabio" (the Wise, 1221–1284), who shared with his father a deep devotion to God, and demonstrated a special devotion to the Virgin Mary (a picture of whom he always carried on his person).

He also shared his father's devotion to the arts and to literature, which he promoted assiduously in his court. Alfonso was a noted astronomer, astrologer, and composer of music. (Kriyananda, too, first wanted to become an astronomer, and later wrote what is considered a classic in its field, *Your Sun Sign as a Spiritual Guide*. He has also written over 400 pieces of spiritual music, both vocal and instrumental.)

Alfonso prepared what are known in astronomy as the Alfonsine tables, because of which one of the craters on the moon has been named after him: the Alphonsus crater. He wrote many spiritual poems and music compositions, 420 of them dedicated to the Blessed Virgin and called the *Cantigas de Santa Maria*. His works on philosophy were highly regarded. His music is still listened to and loved in Spain, and is also available on Amazon.com. Alfonso founded the School of Translators of Toledo, which had the effect of fixing the forms of the Spanish language. Swami Kriyananda has also made many suggestions for improving one's clarity in the writing of English.

It is said of Alfonso that he tended to be "impractical in his idealism." Yogananda once counseled Kriyananda: "You must learn to be practical in your idealism." It must be said of Kriyananda, however, that if he was a dreamer, he also succeeded in materializing those dreams in this lifetime.

Many similarities of both circumstance and personality can be found between all three lives—Henry I, Alfonso X, and Swami Kriyananda—enough, perhaps, for another book! That job, however, if ever it becomes attempted, would be better left to someone who can do his research in Spanish.

DRAMATIS PERSONAE

This list is intended to serve as a quick reminder of who's who—especially in differentiating among the many Roberts, Williams, and Matildas. It is not intended to be an exhaustive listing of all the people mentioned in the text. In some cases a quick glance at one of the genealogical charts may prove helpful.

Agatha – One of the elder daughters of William the Conqueror. Possibly betrothed to Harold Godwinson in 1064, and later, more definitely, to Alphonse of Leon in Spain. According to a contemporary chronicler: "Died a virgin," before her marriage to Alphonse.

Adeliza of Louvain 1103-1151 – The second queen of King Henry I, whom she wed in 1121. The union produced no children, which intensified the succession problem in the last years of Henry's reign. Ironically, Adeliza and her second husband had at least seven children.

Alfred the Atheling (prince) – Son of King Ethelred II of England and Queen Emma (of Normandy). After Ethelred's death, exiled with his brother, Edward, to the court of Normandy. Alfred was murdered by Earl Godwin's henchmen when he attempted a visit to his mother, Queen Emma.

Amaury III de Montfort d.1137 – Thwarted initially by King Henry in succeeding to the Evreux lands in Normandy because of his close ties to the French king, Amaury repeatedly stirred up rebellion among the Norman barons. Even though Henry's forces defeated Amaury, ultimately King Henry bestowed the Evreux lands on him, in order to promote future peace.

Anselm of Bec c.1033-1109 – A student of Lanfranc at Bec Abbey, Anselm succeeded his great teacher in a leadership role at Bec,

376

and later, as archbishop of Canterbury. Though circumstances placed Anselm and the king on opposing sides of the church-wide controversy over a lay prince's right to invest clerics with the symbols of office, the two men were able to create a compromise. In the West Anselm is perhaps most famous as the originator of the ontological argument for the existence of God—something he undertook because of his deep compassion for his doubting brethren. Later canonized and declared a Doctor of the Church.

Boso of Bec – Saintly abbot (from 1124) of Bec, and a close friend of King Henry I.

Edward the Confessor king of England born c.1003-1066 – Son of Ethelred II king of England and Queen Emma; brought from long exile in Normandy and crowned king of England in 1042. King Edward chose Duke William of Normandy as his successor.

Emma of Normandy queen of England (born c.985-1052) – Wife and queen of King Ethelred II to whom she bore two sons, Alfred and Edward (the Confessor). After Ethelred's death in 1016, Emma married his conqueror and successor, Cnut 'the Great,' simultaneously king of England, Denmark, and Norway. (See the genealogical charts for offspring of these two fateful marriages, and her relationship to William the Conqueror.)

Godwin earl of Wessex c.993-1052 – Became earl of Wessex under Danish king of England, Cnut 'the Great.' Through ruthlessness and by establishing his many sons in positions of power in England, Godwin's cachet as "king maker" was established. He forced King Edward the Confessor to marry his daughter Edith, though the marriage was childless.

Harold Godwinson earl of Wessex (c.1022-1066) – Second son and heir to Godwin family power; seized the throne of England upon the death of King Edward the Confessor in January 1066. Defeated by William the Conqueror at the Battle of Hastings.

Helias count of Maine – Count of Maine (on Normandy's southern border) and supporter of King Henry I in battles with Curthose for control of the Normandy.

Helias of Saint-Saen – Son-in-law of Duke Robert Curthhose, chosen by King Henry I to be the guardian of the child William

Clito, Curthose's only son, after the latter's decisive defeat at Tinchebray.

Henry I king of France (1008-1060; king from 1031) – Though he initially supported the boy William (the Conqueror) as duke of Normandy, King Henry soon betrayed his vassal, and supported a succession of challenges to Duke William's authority.

Herleve c.1003-c.1050 – More recent research suggests that Herleve's father, Fulbert, was probably a burgher, rather than a tanner as originally believed. Herleve was the mother of William the Conqueror by Robert I duke of Normandy. Subsequently, she married a minor nobleman, Herluin, by whom she had at least two sons, Odo (later bishop of Bayeux) and Robert (later count of Mortain).

Lanfranc of Pavia c.1005-1089 – Born in Pavia, Italy, trained in law, and a scholar of great renown. In 1042 Lanfranc became a monk at the new abbey of Bec. His first three years were spent in strict seclusion. To help Bec financially he was persuaded to open a school, which drew devout, talented monastics. The Conqueror appointed Lanfranc to be the first abbot of his new foundation, St. Stephen's at Caen. After the Conquest, William called Lanfranc to England to assume the primacy of the church as archbishop of Canterbury. King and archbishop worked closely to unite and revitalize the English church, and bring it under the beneficial influence of the Church of Rome. When the Conqueror died, it was Lanfranc who ensured the succession of William Rufus to the throne of England.

Matilda of Flanders d.1083 – Wife of William the Conqueror and daughter of Baldwin V count of Flanders; married c1051. Crowned queen of England in 1068, before the birth of their youngest son, Henry.

Matilda (Edith-Matilda) c.1081-1118 – Daughter of Malcolm Canmore king of Scotland and his wife, St. Margaret. Through her mother, Edith-Matilda was a direct descendant of England's West Saxon royal line. Mother of King Henry I's two legitimate children, Matilda (Empress Maud) and William Adelin.

Matilda (Maud), Empress b.1102-1167 – Married to Henry V

Holy Roman Emperor in 1114. After the death of Maud's brother, William Adelin in the White Ship, and the death of her husband a few years later, Maud was recalled to England by King Henry, her father, and groomed by him to assume the throne. Married to Geoffrey count of Anjou in 1128. With Geoffrey's support she waged ceaseless war against the usurper of the English throne, Stephen of Blois, until, war-wearied, King Stephen agreed that the throne would pass to Maud's eldest son upon Stephen's death. This eldest son became King Henry II (Plantagenet) in 1154.

Matilda of Anjou – Daughter of Fulk V count of Anjou; married in 1119 to Henry's heir, William Adelin. After the prince's death in the White Ship disaster, Matilda of Anjou, still a very young girl, entered a convent.

Odo bishop of Bayeux – Half-brother of William the Conqueror, through their mother, Herleve of Falaise. Odo was promoted by his half-brother to the bishopric of Bayeux when the young Duke William needed trustworthy kinsmen in high positions within Normandy. A warrior and an able administrator, Odo's ambitions ultimately proved dangerous to the security of the Anglo-Norman kingdom, and he was imprisoned by the Conqueror. As William lay dying, he was persuaded, though greatly reluctant, to release Odo, who continued to foment division within the nobility during the reign of King William II (Rufus).

Ralph d'Escures archbishop of Canterbury – Followed Anselm of Bec as archbishop of Canterbury. It's likely that he suffered a stroke that rendered him moderately senile and querulous in his later years.

Ralph the Red – One of the great heroes of Henry's military household during the war of 1118-19. Ralph drowned in the White Ship catastrophe and was much mourned by King Henry.

Ranulf Flambard bishop of Durham – King William Rufus' unscrupulous right-hand man, with a genius for extorting money from every situation to enrich the king and himself. Imprisoned by the newly crowned King Henry, Ranulf escaped from the Tower of London and offered his services to Duke Robert Curthose in the latter's attempt to invade England. Probably helped broker the final treaty that confirmed Henry's kingship and allowed Flambard to remain bishop of Durham.

Richard earl of Chester – Son of Henry's loyal *familiaris* Hugh of Chester. Upon Hugh's death in 1101, Richard, aged seven, became Henry's ward. Richard, whose land interests in Normandy were vigorously defended by Henry, was a loyal supporter. Drowned in the sinking of the White Ship.

Richard bastard son of King Henry – One of the heroes of Henry's struggle in 1118-19 to put down the rebellion of certain Norman barons who were aided by Louis VI of France. Died in the White Ship disaster.

Richard of Redvers – A landholder in western Normandy during young Henry's countship of that area. Supported Henry from the beginning and remained a *familiaris* throughout his life. Under Henry, he also prospered as a moderate landholder in England.

Robert I 'the Magnificent' duke of Normandy – Father of William the Conqueror, by his mistress, Herleve. Died in 1032 on pilgrimage to Jerusalem.

Robert of Bellême – Heir to the vast cross-Channel domains of the Montgomery-Bellême family. Though his father, Roger of Montgomery, had been a *familiaris* of William the Conqueror, Robert of Bellême was vilified even by his contemporaries for his cruelty, including his use of torture. Disseised of his English lands by King Henry I for waging private warfare, Robert became Henry's implacable enemy. Imprisoned by Henry in 1111.

Robert "Curthose" duke of Normandy 1087-1106 – Eldest son of William the Conqueror. Betrayed and made war on his father beginning in 1078, with a final break in 1083. After the Conqueror's death, Robert's misrule of Normandy threw the duchy into violence and chaos. He was defeated by his brother, Henry, at the battle of Tinchebray in 1106, and imprisoned in relative luxury for the rest of his very long life.

Robert count of Meulan, lord of the Beaumont, earl of Leicester (1049-1118) – During his long career, Robert of Meulan served as chief advisor to both King William Rufus and King Henry I. In Henry Robert found a lord whose leadership, and love of peace and justice, resonated with his more philosophical nature.

Unwaveringly loyal to Henry, Robert had his twin sons, Waleran and Robert, raised at Henry's court.

Robert Bloet bishop of Lincoln – Chronicler Henry of Huntingdon wrote that Bishop Robert, a close advisor to King Henry, had fallen from Henry's favor over a legal matter. However, the evidence suggests otherwise: Bishop Robert witnessed many royal writs right up to his death from stroke in 1123.

Robert count of Mortain c.1031-1090 – Half-brother of William the Conqueror, through their mother, Herleve. (Odo bishop of Bayeux was Robert's full brother.) Robert was the wealthiest magnate of post-Conquest England, and steadily loyal to his half-brother, William. However, after the Conqueror's death, both Robert and Odo joined the rebellion against Rufus, William's chosen successor to the throne of England.

Robert earl of Gloucester c.1090-1147 – Thought to be the eldest of King Henry's illegitimate children, Robert was highly regarded by his contemporaries and greatly elevated by his father. Though his illegitimacy prevented him from being his father's heir, Robert provided crucial military support for his half-sister, Maud, in her fight for the English throne against King Stephen.

Robert of Jumieges archbishop of Canterbury – A respected Norman ecclesiastic who was appointed archbishop of Canterbury in 1051 by King Edward the Confessor. Archbishop Robert attempted to regain Canterbury lands seized by the Godwin family. Earl Godwin's faction later drove Robert from England.

Robert earl of Leicester 1104-1168 – Together with his twin brother, Waleran count of Meulan, raised and educated at the court of King Henry I, as the heirs of their father, Robert of Meulan (see above). Earl Robert, who inherited the family's English lands, remained loyal to King Henry, even as Waleran, as lord of the Beaumont in Normandy, led a rebellion against Henry.

Robert fitz Hamon – King William Rufus gave the lands which comprised Henry's maternal inheritance to Robert fitz Hamon. However, Henry, it seems, bore him no ill will and Robert became a *fidelis* of Henry. King Henry rescued Robert from imprisonment in Normandy in 1105. Just weeks later, Robert sustained a head wound that left him a near idiot. King Henry kept Robert in his care until the latter's death.

Roger bishop of Salisbury – The "poor priest of Avranches [an area of western Normandy]" whom young Henry befriended probably soon after he purchased his countship of western Normandy from Curthose in 1088. Roger's loyalty and genius for administration were steadily rewarded by Henry. In the latter years of King Henry's reign, Bishop Roger served as regent of England when Henry was in Normandy, and was perceived as "second only to the king."

Stephen of Blois (later King Stephen I of England) – Youngest son of Henry's favorite sister, Adela countess of Bois. Stephen was loyal to his uncle who enriched him to the point that Stephen could make a successful bid for the throne when Henry died. The seventeen years of war between Henry's designated heir, the Empress Maud, and King Stephen plunged England into anarchy.

Stigand archbishop of Canterbury from 1052-1070 – The "man" of the Godwin family, who installed him as archbishop and who kept him at Canterbury despite the fact that Stigand was excommunicated by five successive popes. By 1066 Stigand's personal wealth was second only to that of the Godwin family.

Suger abbot of St. Denis – A peasant boy given to the church as an oblate, Suger's genius expressed itself in grand new forms of monumental architecture for the period. His writings included an invaluable biography of King Louis VI of France, for whom Suger served as regent when Louis VI was absent on campaign. Despite his deep attachment to King Louis, a jealous rival of King Henry, Abbot Suger was a life-long admirer of Henry.

Waltheof earl of Northumbria – Son of Siward, earl of Northumbria at the time of the Conquest, Waltheof submitted to William, retained his lands, and remained at the Conqueror's court for two years. However, Waltheof joined forces several times with Scandinavians invading the north of England. Despite pardoning for his first offense, the Conqueror sadly concluded that Waltheof must be executed for his second act of treachery.

William Adelin 1103-1120 – The only legitimate son of King Henry I, and undisputed heir to the Anglo-Norman kingdom until William was drowned with many other aristocratic youth when the White Ship sank in 1120.

William count of Arques – A half-uncle of William the Conqueror, William, together with his brother Mauger archbishop of Rouen, seized control of Upper Normandy from the very young Duke William. The young duke's ultimate defeat of William of Arques in 1054 was a milestone in establishing his own authority.

William Clito 1103-1128 – The only legitimate son of Duke Robert (Curthose), Clito fought his uncle King Henry I for Normandy, which Curthose's son considered his paternal inheritance. Henry offered to enrich Clito and train him in the "art of government," but Clito refused.

William count of Mortain and earl of Cornwall, died after 1140 – Heir of the great Conquest family founded by the Conqueror's half-brother, Robert of Mortain. Despite his vast wealth, William's demands for more English land and his backing of Curthose's claims to the entire Anglo-Norman kingdom, caused a break with King Henry in 1103. William was captured by Henry at the Battle of Tinchebray and comfortably imprisoned until 1140, when he was released to the monastery at Bermondsey. The charge that King Henry blinded William is now widely considered to be false.

William II Crispin – A Norman aristocrat and an implacable enemy of King Henry I. He was twice pardoned by Henry after being defeated in battle. When faced with a third capture by Henry in 1119, William charged through battlefield "mop up" operations by Henry's victorious forces in a particularly vicious attack on the dismounted king.

William II of Warenne earl of Surrey d.1138 – A powerful Anglo-Norman baron, William of Warenne supported Curthose's invasion of England in 1101 and was soon after disseised of his English earldom for conducting private warfare. Importuned ceaselessly by William to recover his lost earldom, Curthose willingly transferred Warenne's vassalage to King Henry I, who reinvested William with Surrey. Thereafter, William was loyal to King

Henry, led a contingent of the king's army at Tinchebray, and was at Henry's deathbed in 1135.

William Talvas lord of Bellême d.1171 – The son and heir of Robert of Bellême, William showed himself to be as cruel in nature and as disloyal to Henry's leadership as his father. Nevertheless, after temporarily disseising William Talvas of his vast lands in Normandy, King Henry eventually reinstated him to most of the Bellême inheritance.

William Warelwast bishop of Exeter – The tireless diplomat who served as envoy from King Henry to the pope in Rome. In his later years he was blind and still served the king in this capacity.

GENEALOGICAL CHARTS

WILLIAM THE CONQUEROR'S LINEAGE

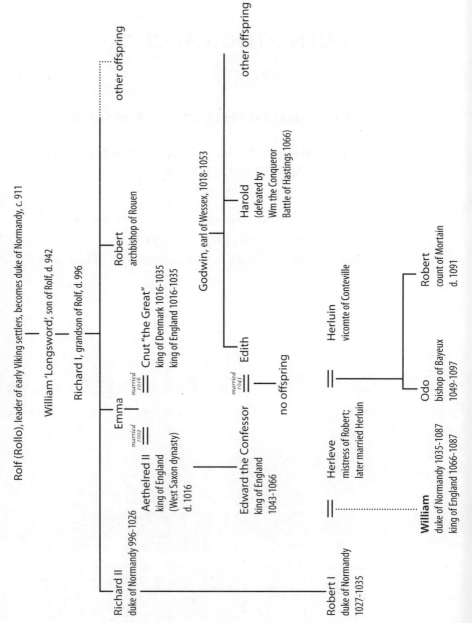

WILLIAM THE CONQUEROR CHILDREN AND GRANDCHILDREN

(A select genealogy)

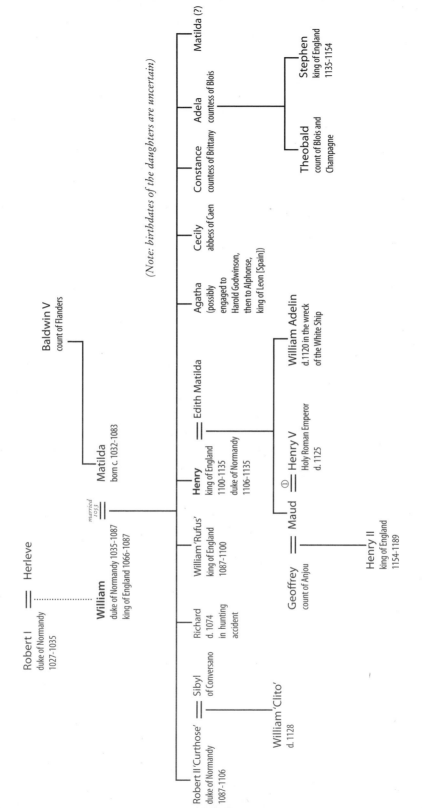

(Note: birthdates of the daughters are uncertain)

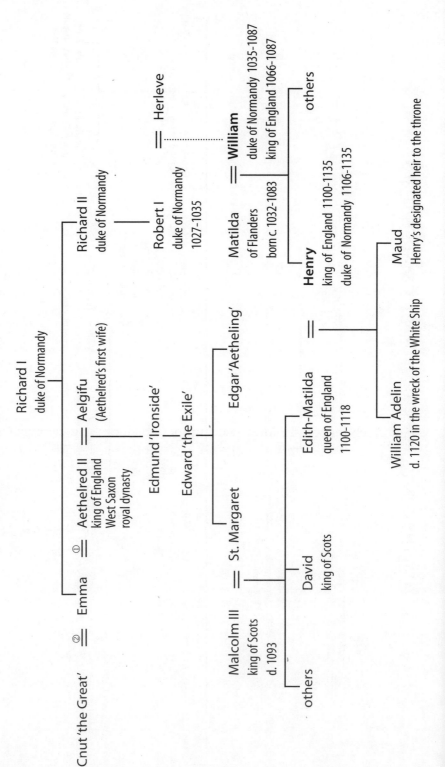

THE MARRIAGE OF KING HENRY I AND EDITH-MATILDA
Norman Kingship United to Anglo-Saxon Royal Dynasty

Cnut 'the Great' ② = Emma ① = Aethelred II
king of England
West Saxon
royal dynasty

Richard I
duke of Normandy

Richard II
duke of Normandy

Herleve

Aelgifu
(Aethelred's first wife)

Robert I
duke of Normandy
1027-1035

William
duke of Normandy 1035-1087
king of England 1066-1087

Edmund 'Ironside'

Edward 'the Exile'

Edgar 'Aetheling'

Matilda
of Flanders
born c. 1032-1083

Henry
king of England 1100-1135
duke of Normandy 1106-1135

others

Malcolm III
king of Scots
d. 1093

= St. Margaret

Edith-Matilda
queen of England
1100-1118

=

Maud
Henry's designated heir to the throne

David
king of Scots

William Adelin
d. 1120 in the wreck of the White Ship

others

GLOSSARY

Special terms and their meaning in the High Middle Ages.

Abbey–A large monastery or convent, governed by an abbot or abbess, often with a church associated with it.

Antipope–An individual who, in opposition to a sitting pope (the bishop of Rome), claims for himself the authority of the pope. Usually the term "antipope" is reserved for those claimants who had some substantial backing. The most numerous antipopes occurred during the eleventh and twelfth centuries and were candidates put forward by the Holy Roman Emperors of this period to further their own causes against the church.

Archdeacon–In Medieval Europe a high-ranking clergyman, under the authority of a bishop, who was responsible for the administration of a diocese.

Augustinian Canons (Canons Regular)–Canons, unlike monks, came together to live in apostolic community and minister to the public through sharing liturgy and prayer with those who visited their churches. Many communities of canons were established by Henry and his great men.

Baron–A nobleman who was a tenant-in-chief of the king. That is, a baron held his lands directly from the king, as opposed to being the subtenant of another nobleman.

Bishopric–Refers either to the office of bishop or to the see/ diocese encompassed by his ecclesiastical authority.

Burgher–A merchant or a person of some standing (and usually of some wealth) in a city.

Canon–An ecclesiastical rule, often with the force of law within the church, for those who fall under its jurisdiction.

Castellan–An individual appointed to be responsible for the administration and defense of a castle.

Chamberlain–In the time of Henry I, a high-ranking official (and often a significant landholder) who was in charge of the financial administration of the large royal household. Though this official might offer personal attendance on the king, as the office evolved, the chamberlain became the administrator of large sums of money, particularly in times of warfare, as the chamberlain drew revenue from the treasury to pay both the regular household knights and the mercenaries.

Churl–An Anglo-Saxon term for a free man who held land, under the authority of a thegn. This word has gained a pejorative meaning that it did not originally carry.

Cleric–A member of the clergy; someone who is set apart, by ordination, to the service of the church.

Count–A landholder who, when William and Henry were the dukes of Normandy, held his land directly of the duke. This relationship between duke and count was a constant point of contention in the duchy, with many counts militating for independence from ducal authority.

Curia (courtiers)–Those who derived their authority directly from their close connection with the king. These men were often called upon by the king to serve as his advisors, as he chose to involve them. (Individuals within the curia: curialis, curiales.)

Danegeld–A tax originally devised by Anglo-Saxon King Ethelred II in 991 to buy off the Danes (Vikings) who were threatening a devastating invasion of England. The first Norman kings continued intermittently to collect Danegeld within England as one source of royal revenue.

Danelaw–That part of England in which Danish law prevailed because conquered and settled by people of recent Scandinavian (Viking) descent. By the year 1000 the Danelaw encompassed the land north of the Thames River to the border of Scotland, excluding Wales and the rest of southwestern England.

Demesne–The land farmed directly by the lord who held it or by those who owed that lord labor. The royal demesne was comprised of all those lands not held by the church or directly of the king by his tenants-in-chief.

Disseise–To deprive a man of land that he had rightfully held, either of the king or of another nobleman. Though technically the word carried the connotation of an unlawful seizure of land, it is often used, as we have used it, to apply to those instances when the king reasonably reclaimed the land that he had formerly bestowed on a now-rebellious baron.

Duchy–The territory encompassed by the authority of a duke or a duchess.

Earl–An Anglo-Saxon term denoting those few noblemen who held the largest domains directly of the king. Among the lay aristocracy, the earls were second in power to the king.

Ecclesiastic–Those persons or matters having to do with the church as an institution.

Exchequer–The court, convened twice a year, which was responsible for auditing and overseeing the collection of revenues due to the king from all sources. During the reign of Henry I, the royal treasury in England was located at Winchester. When the Exchequer was in session, county sheriffs and others responsible for the collection of taxes and other royal revenue came to give an accounting. Though some kind of regular audit may have existed before the reign of King Henry I, it is agreed that it was he who gave the Exchequer its authority and well-defined role.

Familiaris, familiares–In our context the term identifies those who enjoyed the friendship of the king and were often in his company.

Fealty–An oath of fidelity sworn to a lord, often on the Bible or on saints' relics. Fealty did not necessarily involve the bestowal of land or any privileges by the lord on his fidelis. Fealty in this sense is not to be confused with homage, and fealty to the king took precedence over homage to lesser lords.

Feudalism–A term applied (with a wide variety of meanings) to the economic and political system present in varying degrees in the High Middle Ages in Western Europe whereby one man (an inferior) was obligated to fulfill one or a multitude of duties (financial or his labor) to another man (his superior) by virtue of his holding land from his superior/lord.

Fidelis, fideles–A man/men who owed fealty to the king or his lord. (In this book, we've used the term to denote those men who not only owed fealty, but who demonstrated their loyalty as well.)

Fyrd–The Anglo-Saxon militia, drawn from the whole free male population, mobilized during times of national danger; the *fyrd* could be called up by the king or by a local lord.

Gregorian Reform–A series of reforms associated with Pope Gregory VII (though named for Gregory the Great) between 1050-80 that had to do with the moral integrity and independence of the clergy from the power of the lay princes. The Reform's campaign to eliminate simony (see below), insistence on clerical celibacy, and the elimination of the practice of clerics being invested with the symbols of their ecclesiastical office by lay princes and doing homage to those same princes caused enormous turmoil in the High Middle Ages.

Hide/hyde–An Anglo-Saxon unit/measurement of land use in some parts of England in our time period. It was originally calculated to be the amount of land needed to support one family for one year, and has been estimated to be between eighty and 120 acres.

Holy Roman Empire–Charlemagne, the first prince in the Dark Ages to restore some semblance of order to Europe, was crowned the first Holy Roman Emperor in 800 by Pope Leo III. Pope Leo's hope was that this Emperor would be a protector and champion for the Roman church. In fact the Holy Roman Empire, a loose confederation of Germanic states, conceived of by the pope, was perennially unstable after Charlemagne's death, and the Emperor and Pope were in serious conflict by the twelfth century over Gregorian Reform issues.

Homage–An oath by which a man became the vassal of another, now his lord. The vassal became "the man" of the lord and bound himself to fulfill the duties associated with holding a fief of the lord.

Investiture–The ceremony by which the king (or another authority) bestowed on a candidate for a high ecclesiastical office the ring and staff that were symbols of authority for that office.

Legate (papal legate)–A representative of the pope, commissioned to act with papal authority.

Liege/liege lord–The loyalty and obligations due to that lord of whom a vassal holds land or other privileges.

Magna Carta–A landmark document that King John was forced to sign by his barons in 1215. The Magna Carta set boundaries on the king of England's ability to act arbitrarily, and bound the king to certain laws. The noblemen and ecclesiastics who composed the Magna Carta drew heavily from King Henry I's Coronation Charter.

Magnate–One of the wealthier landholders.

Murdrum fine–Under Anglo-Saxon law, a fine, the amount of which varied, paid by a murderer, usually to his victim's kin. Immediately after the Conquest, this fine became more punitive, sometimes with consequences to a whole community, in order to curtail the ambush of individual Normans. Under King Henry I, the fine reverted to its less onerous, pre-Conquest application.

Pallium–An ecclesiastical vestment conferred on an archbishop by the pope.

Pipe roll–Each pipe roll, set on animal skin parchment that was stitched end-to-end, recorded royal income in England for the period of one year. This precocious written financial record, unique in Europe, was probably begun around the middle of King Henry I's reign, but only the Pipe Roll of 1130 survives.

Prelate–One who holds an exalted ecclesiastical rank, such as archbishop, bishop, abbot, or prior.

Primate/primacy–The Roman church's highest ecclesiastic within a country. The contest between the archbishop of Canterbury and the archbishop of York to be recognized as primate of the church in England was a major issue throughout the reign of King Henry I.

Primogeniture–The practice (by law or tradition) of passing land or titles to the next of kin of a deceased lord, with the eldest male child considered the most eligible heir.

Priory–A smaller monastery, often an offshoot of (and dependent on) a larger abbey.

Regent/regency–An individual (or small group) who temporarily discharge the responsibilities of a prince or lord who is absent, disabled, or still a minor.

See–The jurisdiction of a bishop, a diocese.

Servicium debitum–Military services owed to a ruler, especially by the landholding class, or, as the High Middle Ages progressed, payment to the ruler in lieu of the military service owed.

Simony/simoniac–To obtain an ecclesiastical office in exchange for money. A simoniac was an ecclesiastic who was judged to be guilty of purchasing his position in the church.

Steward–One who managed a fief on behalf of the lawful landholder.

Tenants-in-chief–Landholders who received their domains directly from the king.

Thegn–The Anglo-Saxon term for someone who held a moderate amount of land in exchange for military service; below an earl in rank.

Vassal–"The man" of a greater lord, by virtue of his having sworn to fulfill obligations to the lord in exchange for land or other privileges.

Vicomte–A position within the aristocracy in the duchy of Normandy. Particularly during William's era and that of his immediate predecessors, the vicomte was associated with the administrative interests of the duke within a countship in Normandy, though under the authority of the count.

BIBLIOGRAPHY

Select Primary Sources
Chronicles from the Eleventh and Twelfth Centuries

Anglo-Saxon Chronicle, translated and edited by Michael Swanton. London, 1966.

Eadmer. *Life of St Anselm*. Ed. and trans. R.W. Southern. Oxford, 1962.

Gesta Normannorum Ducum: The Deeds of the Norman Dukes. William of Jumieges, Orderic Vitalis, and Robert of Torigni. Vol. II. Ed. and trans. Elisabeth M.C. Van Houts. Oxford, 2001.

Henry of Huntingdon. *The History of the English People 1000-1154.* Trans. Diana Greenway. Oxford, 2002.

Orderic Vitalis. *The Ecclesiastical History of Orderic Vitalis.* Vols. II and III. Ed. and trans. Marjorie Chibnall. Oxford, 1969-1972.

Wace. *Le Roman de Rou: The History of the Norman People.* Trans. Glyn S. Burgess. Woodbridge, Suffolk, 1964.

William of Malmesbury. *Chronicle of the Kings of England: From the Earliest Period to the Reign of King Stephen.* Trans. J.A. Giles. New York, 1968.

William of Malmesbury. *The Deeds of the Bishops of England.* Trans. David Preest. Woodbridge, Suffolk, 2002.

William of Poitiers. *Gesta Guillelmi: The Deeds of William.* Eds. and trans. R.H.C. Davis and Marjorie Chibnall. Oxford, 2006.

Select Secondary Sources

Barlow, Frank. *The Feudal Kingdom of England 1042-1216.* 5th edition. New York, 1999.

——. *The Godwins: The Rise and Fall of a Noble Dynasty.* Edinburgh, 2002.

——. *William Rufus.* Berkeley, 1983.

Bartlett, Robert. *England under the Norman and Angevin Kings 1075-1225.* Oxford, 2002.

Bates, David. *William the Conqueror.* London, 1989.

Belloc, Hilaire, *William the Conqueror,* Rockford, Ill., 1992.

Brett, Martin. *The English Church under Henry I.* Oxford, 1975.

Brewer, Clifford. *The Death of Kings: A Medical History of the Kings and Queens of England.* London, 2004.

Chibnall, Marjorie. *Anglo-Norman England 1066-1166.* Oxford, 1990.

——. *The Empress Matilda: Queen Consort, Queen Mother and Lady of the English.* Cambridge, Mass., 1993.

Churchill, Winston S. *The Birth of Britain: A History of the English-Speaking Peoples,* Vol. I. New York, 2005.

Clanchy, M.T. *England and Its Rulers 1066-1272.* 2nd edition. Oxford, 1998.

Clark, Kenneth. *Civilisation: A Personal View.* New York, 1969.

Cowdrey, H.E.J. *Lanfranc: Scholar, Monk, and Archbishop.* Oxford, 2003.

Daniell, Christopher. *From Norman Conquest to Magna Carta: England 1066-1215.* London, 2003.

Danziger, Danny and John Gillingham. *1215: The Year of Magna Carta.* New York, 2003.

David, Charles Wendell. *Robert Curthose, Duke of Normandy.* Cambridge, Mass., 1920.

Davis, R.H.C. *King Stephen 1135-1154.* 3rd edn. New York, 1990.

Douglas, David C. *The Norman Fate, 1100-1154.* Berkeley, 1976.

— . *William the Conqueror: The Norman Impact upon England.* Berkeley, 1964.

Fettu, Annie. *Queen Matilda: Portrait of Queen Matilda, Spouse of Duke William.* Trans. Heather Costil. Paris, 2005.

Finn, R. Welldon. *Domesday Book: A Guide.* London, 1973.

Fleming, Donald F. and Janet M. Pope, eds. *Henry I and the Anglo-Norman World: Studies in Memory of C. Warren Hollister.*

Freeman, Edward A. *William the Conqueror.* Charleston, South Carolina, 2006.

Gravett, Christopher and David Nicolle. *The Normans: Warrior Knights and their Castles.* Oxford, 2006.

Green, Judith A. *The Government of England under Henry I.* Cambridge, England, 1986.

Haskins Society Journal, 17. Woodbridge, Suffolk, 2007.

— . *Henry I: King of England and Duke of Normandy.* Cambridge, 2006.

Hollister, C. Warren, ed. *Anglo-Norman Political Culture and the Twelfth-Century Renaissance: Proceedings of the Borchard Conference on Anglo-Norman History, 1995.* Woodbridge, Suffolk, 1997.

— , ed. and completed by Amanda Clark Frost. *Henry I.* New Haven, Conn., 2001.

— , ed. *The Impact of the Norman Conquest.* New York, 1969.

— . *Monarchy, Magnates and Institutions in the Anglo-Norman World.* London, 1986.

— , ed. *The Twelfth-Century Renaissance.* New York, 1969.

Huneycutt, Lois L. *Matilda of Scotland: A Study in Medieval Queenship.* Woodbridge, Suffolk, 2003.

Kealey, Edward J. *Roger of Salisbury, Viceroy of England.* Berkeley, 1972.

Liddiard, Robert, ed. *Anglo-Norman Castles.* Woodbridge, Suffolk, 2003.

Mason, Emma. *"Henry I: Decoding an Enigma." Headstart History: Medieval History,* Vol I, No. 3 (1991): 17-33.

Mayr-Harting, Henry, ed. *Studies in Medieval History Presented to R.H.C. Davis.* London, 1985.

O'Brien, Harriet. *Queen Emma and the Vikings.* New York, 2005.

Southern, R.W. *The Making of the Middle Ages.* New Haven, 1953.

— . "The Place of Henry I in English History." *Proceedings of the British Academy* 48 (1962): 127-169.

Strickland, Matthew. *War and Chivalry: The Conduct and Perception of War in England and Normandy, 1066-1217.* Cambridge, 1996.

Tyerman, Christopher. *Who's Who in Early Medieval England 1066-1272.* London, 1996.

Vaughn, Sally N. *Anselm of Bec and Robert of Meulan: The Innocence of the Dove and the Wisdom of the Serpent.* Berkeley, 1987.

Select Bibliography of Books
By and About Paramhansa Yogananda
and Swami Kriyananda

Novak, Devi. *Faith Is My Armor: The Life of Swami Kriyananda.* New Delhi, India and Nevada City, Calif., 2005.

Praver, Asha. *Swami Kriyananda As We Have Known Him.* Nevada City, Calif., 2006.

Paramhansa Yogananda. *Autobiography of a Yogi.* (Reprint of the Philosophical Library 1946 First Edition.) Nevada City, Calif., 1995.

— . *Karma and Reincarnation. The Wisdom of Yogananda* series, Volume 2. Eds. Swami Kriyananda and Anandi Cornell. Nevada City, Calif., 2007.

— . *Whispers from Eternity.* Ed. Swami Kriyananda (J. Donald Walters). Nevada City, Calif., 2008.

Swami Kriyananda (J. Donald Walters). *Conversations with Yogananda.* Nevada City, Calif., 2004.

— . *Education for Life: Preparing Children to Meet the Challenges..* Nevada City, Calif., 2003.

— . *The Essence of the Bhagavad Gita Explained by Paramhansa Yogananda.* 2nd edn. Nevada City, Calif., 2007.

— . *God Is for Everyone.* Nevada City, Calif., 2003.

— . *Hope for a Better World! The Small Communities Solution.* 4th, revised, edn. Nevada City, Calif., 2003.

— . *The New Path: My Life with Paramhansa Yogananda.* 2nd edn. Nevada City, Calif., 2009.

— . *Out of the Labyrinth–For Those Who Want to Believe, But Can't.* 3rd, revised, edn. Nevada City, Calif., 2001.

— . *The Peace Treaty: A Plya in Three Acts,* Nevada City, Calif., 1991.

— . *Religion in the New Age.* Nevada City, Calif., 2008.

— . *Revelations of Christ Proclaimed by Paramhansa Yogananda.* Nevada City, Calif., 2007.

INDEX

ABOUT THE AUTHOR

Catherine Kairavi's life path has taken her from Indiana, where she grew up, to international tours, including extensive travel in England. She became interested in reincarnation and yoga philosophy in her twenties when she moved to Ananda, a yoga community in the Sierra Nevada foothills of Northern California.

For thirty-plus years she has continued her studies under the guidance of Swami Kriyananda, a direct disciple of Paramhansa Yogananda (the great spiritual master and author of the classic, *Autobiography of a Yogi*). An author and minister, Catherine has given hundreds of lectures on yoga philosophy, reincarnation, and history in the United States and in Europe.

About ten years ago, Catherine received the inspiration to write a book based on Yogananda's statement that he was William the Conqueror in a past life, and Kriyananda's belief that he had been William's son, Henry I of England. Catherine has had a lifelong interest in medieval history, and she was deeply impressed by the evidence she uncovered during her ten years of research.

Catherine writes, "The connections between Yogananda and William revealed a depth and breadth to the way God works in the world that I found utterly inspiring. In contemplating Swami Kriyananda's role as Henry, I saw a thrilling example of a disciple's dedication, over countless centuries, to his guru's vision. *Two Souls: Four Lives* was an opportunity to meditate on what it means to act with soul freedom, even while doing what is practical and appropriate to a particular time and place."

Ms. Kairavi has a B.A. in English literature, and is an amateur historian. She is also an expert on yoga philosophy, meditation, and reincarnation. Some of her articles and lectures have been published online.

PARAMHANSA YOGANANDA

"As a bright light shining in the midst of darkness, so was Yogananda's presence in this world. Such a great soul comes on earth only rarely, when there is a real need among men."

—The Shankaracharya of Kanchipuram

Born in India in 1893, Paramhansa Yogananda was trained from his early years to bring India's ancient science of Self-realization to the West. In 1920 he moved to the United States to begin what was to develop into a worldwide work touching millions of lives. Americans were hungry for India's spiritual teachings, and for the liberating techniques of yoga.

In 1946 he published what has become a spiritual classic and one of the best-loved books of the twentieth century, *Autobiography of a Yogi*. In addition, Yogananda established headquarters for a worldwide work, wrote a number of books and study courses, gave lectures to thousands in most major cities across the United States, wrote music and poetry, and trained disciples. He was invited to the White House by Calvin Coolidge, and he initiated Mahatma Gandhi into Kriya Yoga, his most advanced technique of meditation.

Yogananda's message to the West highlighted the unity of all religions, and the importance of love for God combined with scientific techniques of meditation.

SWAMI KRIYANANDA

"Swami Kriyananda is a man of wisdom and compassion in action, truly one of the leading lights in the spiritual world today."

—Lama Surya Das, Dzogchen Center, author of *Awakening the Buddha Within*

A prolific author, accomplished composer, playwright, and artist, and a world-renowned spiritual teacher, Swami Kriyananda refers to himself simply as "a humble disciple" of the great God-realized master, Paramhansa Yogananda. He met his guru at the young age of twenty-two, and served him during the last four years of the Master's life. And he has done so continuously ever since.

Kriyananda was born in Rumania of American parents, and educated in Europe, England, and the United States. Philosophically and artistically inclined from youth, he soon came to question life's meaning and society's values. During a period of intense inward reflection, he discovered Yogananda's *Autobiography of a Yogi*, and immediately traveled three thousand miles from New York to California to meet the Master, who accepted him as a monastic disciple. Yogananda appointed him as the head of the monastery, authorized him to teach in his name and to give initiation into Kriya

Yoga, and entrusted him with the missions of writing and developing what he called "world brotherhood colonies." Recognized as the "father of the spiritual communities movement" in the United States, Swami Kriyananda founded Ananda World Brotherhood Community in 1968. It has served as a model for a number of communities founded subsequently in the United States and Europe.

In 2003 Swami Kriyananda, then in his seventy-eighth year, moved to India with a small international group of disciples, to dedicate his remaining years to making his guru's teachings better known. To this end he appeared daily on Indian national television with his program, *A Way of Awakening.* He has established Ananda Sangha Publications, which publishes many of his one hundred literary works and spreads the teachings of Kriya Yoga throughout India. His vision for the next years includes founding cooperative spiritual communities in Pune, India with a temple of all religions dedicated to Paramhansa Yogananda, and a retreat center; a school system, and a monastery, as well as a university-level Yoga Institute of Living Wisdom.

FURTHER EXPLORATIONS

If you are inspired by *Two Souls: Four Lives* and would like to learn more about **Paramhansa Yogananda** and his teachings, or **Swami Kriyananda**, **Crystal Clarity Publishers** offers many additional resources to assist you:

Crystal Clarity publishes the **original 1946, unedited edition** of Paramhansa Yogananda's spiritual masterpiece

Autobiography of a Yogi

Paramhansa Yogananda

Autobiography of a Yogi is one of the best-selling Eastern philosophy titles of all time, with millions of copies sold, named one of the best and most influential books of the twentieth century. This highly prized reprinting of the original 1946 edition is the only one available free from textual changes made after Yogananda's death.

Yogananda was the first yoga master of India whose mission was to live and teach in the West. His account of his life experiences includes childhood revelations, stories of his visits to saints and masters in India, and long-secret teachings of Self-realization that he made available to the Western reader.

In this updated edition are bonus materials, including a last chapter that Yogananda wrote in 1951, without posthumous changes. This new edition also includes the eulogy that Yogananda wrote for Gandhi, and a new foreword and afterword by Swami Kriyananda, one of Yogananda's close direct disciples.

PRAISE FOR *Autobiography of a Yogi*

"In the original edition, published during Yogananda's life, one is more in contact with Yogananda himself. While Yogananda founded centers and organizations, his concern was more with guiding individuals to direct communion with Divinity rather than with promoting any one church as opposed to another. This spirit is easier to grasp in the original edition of this great spiritual and yogic classic."

–David Frawley, Director, American Institute of Vedic Studies, author of *Yoga and Ayurveda*

THIS TITLE IS ALSO AVAILABLE IN:
52-Card Deck and Booklet
Unabridged Audiobook (MP3 format)

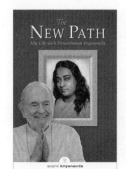

The New Path
My Life With Paramhansa Yogananda
Swami Kriyananda

This is the moving story of Kriyananda's years with Paramhansa Yogananda, India's emissary to the West and the first yoga master to spend the greater part of his life in America.

When Swami Kriyananda discovered *Autobiography of a Yogi* in 1948, he was totally new to Eastern teachings. This is a great advantage to the Western reader, since Kriyananda walks us along the yogic path as he discovers it from the moment of his initiation as a disciple of Yogananda. With winning honesty, humor, and deep insight, he shares his journey along the spiritual path through personal stories and experiences.

Through more than four hundred stories of life with Yogananda, we tune in more deeply to this great master and to the teachings he brought to the West. This book is an ideal complement to *Autobiography of a Yogi.*

"Reading Autobiography of a Yogi *by Yogananda was a transformative experience for me and for millions of others. In* The New Path, *Kriyananda carries on this great tradition. Highly recommended."*
–Dean Ornish, M.D., Founder and President, Preventative Medicine Research Institute, Clinical Professor of Medicine, University of California, San Francisco, author of *The Spectrum*

"Kriyananda has written a compelling and insightful account of his own life, as well as revealing his remembrances of Paramhansa Yogananda. Completely revised and updated, The New Path *is filled with profound reflections, insights, experiences, challenges, and spiritual wisdom. Required reading for every spiritual seeker. I heartily recommend it."*
–Michael Toms, Founder, New Dimensions Media, and author of *True Work* and *An Open Life: Joseph Campbell in Conversation with Michael Toms*

THIS TITLE IS ALSO AVAILABLE IN:
Unabridged Audiobook (MP3 format)

Revelations of Christ
Proclaimed by Paramhansa Yogananda,
Presented by His Disciple, Swami Kriyananda

Over the past years, our faith has been severely shaken by experiences such as the breakdown of church authority, discoveries of ancient texts that supposedly contradict long-held beliefs, and the sometimes outlandish historical analyses of Scripture by academics. Together, these forces have helped create confusion and uncertainty about the true teachings and meanings of Christ's life.

This soul-stirring book, presenting the teachings of Christ from the experience and perspective of Yogananda, finally offers the fresh understanding of Christ's teachings for which the world has been waiting, in a more reliable way than any other: by learning from those saints who have communed directly, in deep ecstasy, with Christ and God.

"This is a great gift to humanity. It is a spiritual treasure to cherish and to pass on to children for generations. This remarkable and magnificent book brings us to the doorway of a deeper, richer embracing of Eternal Truth."
–Neale Donald Walsch, author of *Conversations with God*

"Kriyananda's revelatory book gives us the enlightened, timeless wisdom of Jesus the Christ in a way that addresses the challenges of twenty-first century living."

–Michael Beckwith, founder and Spiritual Director, Agape International Spiritual Center, author of *Inspirations of the Heart*

THIS TITLE IS ALSO AVAILABLE IN:
Unabridged Audiobook (MP3 format)

The Essence of the Bhagavad Gita
Explained by Paramhansa Yogananda
As Remembered by His Disciple, Swami Kriyananda

Rarely in a lifetime does a new spiritual classic appear that has the power to change people's lives and transform future generations. This is such a book.

This revelation of India's best-loved scripture approaches it from a fresh perspective, showing its deep allegorical meaning and its down-to-earth practicality. The themes presented are universal: how to achieve victory in life in union with the divine; how to prepare for life's "final exam," death, and what happens afterward; how to triumph over all pain and suffering.

PRAISE FOR *The Essence of the Bhagavad Gita*

"The Essence of the Bhagavad Gita *is a brilliant text that will greatly enhance the spiritual life of every reader."*

–Caroline Myss, author of *Anatomy of the Spirit* and *Sacred Contracts*

"It is doubtful that there has been a more important spiritual writing in the last 50 years than this soul-stirring, monumental work. What a gift! What a treasure!"

–Neale Donald Walsch, author of *Conversations with God*

THIS TITLE IS ALSO AVAILABLE IN:
Unabridged Audiobook (MP3 format)
Also available as paperback without commentary,
    titled *The Bhagavad Gita.*

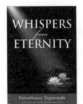

Whispers from Eternity
Paramhansa Yogananda
Edited by his disciple, Swami Kriyananda

Many poetic works can inspire, but few, like this one, have the power to change your life. Yogananda was not only a spiritual master, but a master poet, whose poems revealed the hidden divine presence behind even everyday things.

Open this book, pick a poem at random, and read it. Mentally repeat whatever phrase appeals to you. Within a short time, you will feel your consciousness transformed. This book has the power to rapidly accelerate your spiritual growth, and provides hundreds of delightful ways for you to begin your own conversation with God.

THIS TITLE IS ALSO AVAILABLE IN:
Unabridged Audiobook (MP3 format)

The Wisdom of Yogananda Series

This series features writings of Paramhansa Yogananda not available elsewhere. These books include writings from his earliest years in America, in an approachable, easy-to-read format. The words of the Master are presented with minimal editing, to capture his expansive and compassionate wisdom, his sense of fun, and his practical spiritual guidance.

How to Be Happy All the Time
The Wisdom of Yogananda Series, Volume 1
Paramhansa Yogananda

Yogananda powerfully explains virtually everything needed to lead a happier, more fulfilling life. Topics include: looking for happiness in the right places; choosing to be happy; tools and techniques for achieving happiness; sharing happiness with others; balancing success and happiness, and many more.

Karma and Reincarnation
The Wisdom of Yogananda Series, Volume 2
Paramhansa Yogananda

Yogananda reveals the truth behind karma, death, reincarnation, and the afterlife. With clarity and simplicity, he makes the mysterious understandable. Topics include: why we see a world of suffering and inequality; how to handle the challenges in our lives; what happens at death, and after death; and the origin and purpose of reincarnation.

Spiritual Relationships
The Wisdom of Yogananda Series, Volume 3
Paramhansa Yogananda

Topics include: how to cure bad habits that spell the death of true friendship; how to choose the right partner and create a lasting marriage; sex in marriage and how to conceive a spiritual child; problems that arise in marriage and what to do about them; the divine plan uniting parents and children; the Universal Love behind all your relationships.

How to Be a Success
The Wisdom of Yogananda Series, Volume 4
Paramhansa Yogananda

This book includes the complete text of *The Attributes of Success*, the original booklet later published as *The Law of Success*. In addition, you will learn how to find your purpose in life, develop habits of success and eradicate habits of failure, develop your will power and magnetism, and thrive in the right job.

How to Have Courage, Calmness, & Confidence
The Wisdom of Yogananda Series, Volume 5
Paramhansa Yogananda

This book shows you how to transform your life. Dislodge negative thoughts and depression. Uproot fear and thoughts of failure. Cure nervousness and systematically eliminate worry from your life. Overcome anger, sorrow, over-sensitivity, and a host of other troublesome emotional responses. And much more.

The Essence of Self-Realization
The Wisdom of Paramhansa Yogananda
Edited and compiled by Swami Kriyananda

A fantastic volume of the stories, sayings, and wisdom of Paramhansa Yogananda, this book covers more than twenty essential topics about the spiritual path and practices. Subjects include: the true purpose of life, the folly of materialism, the essential unity of all religions, the laws of karma and reincarnation, grace vs. self-effort, the need for a guru, how to pray effectively, meditation, and many more.

Conversations with Yogananda
Edited with commentary by Swami Kriyananda

This is an unparalleled, first-hand account of the teachings of Paramhansa Yogananda. Featuring nearly five hundred never-before-released stories, sayings, and insights, this is an extensive, yet eminently accessible treasure trove of wisdom from one of the twentieth century's most famous yoga masters. Compiled and edited with commentary by Swami Kriyananda, one of Yogananda's closest direct disciples.

Religion in the New Age
Swami Kriyananda

Our planet has entered an "Age of Energy" that will affect us for centuries to come. We can see evidence of this all around us: in ultra-fast computers, the quickening of communication and transportation, and the shrinking of time and space. This fascinating book of essays explores how this new age will change our lives, especially our spiritual seeking. Covers a wide range of upcoming societal shifts—in leadership, relationships, and self-development—including the movement away from organized religion to inner experience.

God Is for Everyone
Swami Kriyananda

This book is the core of Yogananda's teachings. It presents a concept of God and spiritual meaning that will broadly appeal to everyone, from the uncertain agnostic to the most fervent believer. Clearly and simply written, thoroughly nonsectarian and non-dogmatic in its approach, it is the perfect introduction to the spiritual path.

"This book makes accessible the inspired pursuit of Bliss in simple, understandable ways. Written as an introduction for those just starting on the spiritual path, it is also a re-juvenating and inspiring boost for experienced seekers. Clear, practical techniques are offered to enhance personal spiritual practices. The author maintains that "everyone in the world is on the spiritual path" whether they know it or not, even if they are temporarily merely seeking pleasure and avoiding pain. Sooner or later, "They will want to experience Him (God)." Experiencing God—and specifically experiencing God as Bliss—is that underlying goal of this work, based on the teachings of a self-realized teacher. It hits the mark for contemporary spirituality."
—*ForeWord* Magazine

Meditation for Starters
Swami Kriyananda

Have you wanted to learn to meditate, but just never got around to it? Or tried "sitting in the silence" only to find yourself too restless to stay more than a few moments? If so, *Meditation for Starters* is just what you've been looking for, and with a companion CD, it provides everything you need to begin a meditation practice. It is filled with easy-to-follow instructions, beautiful guided visualizations, and answers to important questions on meditation such as: what meditation is (and isn't); how to relax your body and prepare yourself for going within; and techniques for interiorizing and focusing the mind.

PRAISE FOR *Meditation for Starters*

"A gentle guide to entering the most majestic, fulfilling dimensions of consciousness. Kriyananda is a wise teacher whose words convey love and compassion. Read and listen and allow your life to change."
—Larry Dossey, M.D., author of *Prayer Is Good Medicine*

Awaken to Superconsciousness
How to Use Meditation for Inner Peace, Intuitive Guidance, and Greater Awareness
Swami Kriyananda

This popular guide includes everything you need to know about the philosophy and practice of meditation, and how to apply the meditative mind to resolving common daily conflicts in uncommon, superconscious ways. Superconsciousness is the source of intuition, spiritual healing, solutions to problems, and deep and lasting joy.

PRAISE FOR *Awaken to Superconsciousness*

"A brilliant, thoroughly enjoyable guide to the art and science of meditation. [Swami Kriyananda] entertains, informs, and inspires—his enthusiasm for the subject is contagious. This book is a joy to read from beginning to end."
— *Yoga International*

ALSO AVAILABLE IN THIS SERIES:
Music to Awaken Superconsciousness (CD)
Meditations to Awaken Superconsciousness, spoken word (CD)

Affirmations for Self-Healing
Swami Kriyananda

This inspirational book contains fifty-two affirmations and prayers, each pair devoted to improving a quality in ourselves. Strengthen your will power; cultivate forgiveness, patience, health, enthusiasm; and more. A powerful tool for self-transformation.

PRAISE FOR *Affirmations for Self-Healing*

"[This book] has become a meditation friend to me. The inspiring messages and prayers, plus the physical beauty of the book, help me start my day uplifted and focused."
—Sue Patton Thoele, author of *Growing Hope*

THIS TITLE IS ALSO AVAILABLE IN:
Unabridged Audiobook (MP3 format)

Music and Audiobooks

We offer many of our book titles in unabridged MP3 format audiobooks. To purchase these titles and to see more music and audiobook offerings, visit our website: www.crystalclarity.com. Or look for us in the popular online download sites.

Metaphysical Meditations
Swami Kriyananda

Kriyananda's soothing voice guides you in thirteen different meditations based on the soul-inspiring, mystical poetry of Paramhansa Yogananda. Each meditation is accompanied by beautiful classical music to help you quiet your thoughts and prepare for deep states of meditation. Includes a full recitation of Yogananda's poem "Samadhi," which appears in *Autobiography of a Yogi.* A great aid to the serious meditator, as well as to those just beginning their practice.

Meditations to Awaken Superconsciousness
Guided Meditations on the Light
Swami Kriyananda

Featuring two beautiful guided meditations as well as an introductory section to help prepare the listener for meditation, this extraordinary recording of visualizations can be used either by itself, or as a companion to the book, *Awaken to Superconsciousness.* The soothing, transformative words, spoken over inspiring sitar background music, creates one of the most unique guided meditation products available.

Music to Awaken Superconsciousness
Donald Walters (Swami Kriyananda)

A companion to the book, *Awaken to Superconsciousness*. Each of the lush instrumental selections is designed to help the listener more easily access higher states of awareness—deep calmness, joy, radiant health, and self-transcendence. This beautiful recording can be used simply as background music for relaxation and meditation. Or, you can follow the instructions in the liner notes to actively achieve superconsciousness.

Relax: Meditations for Flute and Cello
Donald Walters (Swami Kriyananda)
Featuring David Eby and Sharon Nani

This CD is specifically designed to slow respiration and heart rate, bringing listeners to their calm center. This recording features fifteen melodies for flute and cello, accompanied by harp, guitar, keyboard, and strings.

Bliss Chants
Ananda Kirtan

Chanting focuses and lifts the mind to higher states of consciousness. *Bliss Chants* features chants written by Yogananda and his direct disciple, Swami Kriyananda. They're performed by Ananda Kirtan, a group of singers and musicians from Ananda, one of the world's most respected yoga communities. Chanting is accompanied by guitar, harmonium, kirtals, and tabla.

Other titles in the Chant Series:

Divine Mother Chants	*Power Chants*
Love Chants	*Peace Chants*
Wisdom Chants*	*Wellness Chants**

*Available starting in summer 2010

AUM: Mantra of Eternity
Swami Kriyananda

This recording features nearly seventy minutes of continuous vocal chanting of AUM, the Sanskrit word meaning peace and oneness of spirit. AUM, the cosmic creative vibration, is extensively discussed by Yogananda in *Autobiography of a Yogi*. Chanted here by his disciple, Kriyananda, this recording is a stirring way to tune into this cosmic power.

Other titles in the Mantra Series:
Gayatri Mantra*
Mahamrityanjaya Mantra*
Maha Mantra*

The Complete Audio Catalog
We offer a complete audio catalog, which includes all of our music and audiobooks in one convenient collection.

Set is in *MP3 format,* on two DVDs.

*Available starting in summer 2010

ANANDA SANGHA WORLDWIDE

A **nanda Sangha is a** worldwide fellowship of kindred souls following the teachings of Paramhansa Yogananda. The Sangha embraces the search for higher consciousness through the practice of meditation, and through the ideal of service to others in their quest for Self-realization. Approximately ten thousand spiritual seekers are affiliated with Ananda Sangha throughout the world.

Founded in 1968 by Swami Kriyananda, a direct disciple of Paramhansa Yogananda, Ananda includes seven communities in the United States, Europe, and in India. Worldwide, about one thousand devotees live in these spiritual communities, which are based on Yogananda's ideals of "plain living and high thinking."

"Thousands of youths must go north, south, east and west to cover the earth with little colonies, demonstrating that simplicity of living plus high thinking lead to the greatest happiness!" After pronouncing these words at a garden party in Beverly Hills, California in 1949, Paramhansa Yogananda raised his arms, and chanting the sacred cosmic vibration AUM, he "registered in the ether" his blessings on what has become the spiritual communities movement. From that moment on, Swami Kriyananda dedicated himself to bringing this vision from inspiration to reality by establishing communities where home, job, school, worship, family, friends, and recreation could evolve together as part of the interwoven fabric of harmonious, balanced living. Yogananda predicted that these communities would "spread like wildfire," becoming the model lifestyle for the coming millennium.

Swami Kriyananda lived with his guru during the last four years of the Master's life, and continued to serve his organization

443

for another ten years, bringing the teachings of Kriya Yoga and Self-realization to audiences in the United States, Europe, Australia, and, from 1958–1962, India. In 1968, together with a small group of close friends and students, he founded the first "world brotherhood community" in the foothills of the Sierra Nevada Mountains in Northern California. Initially a meditation retreat center located on sixty-seven acres of forested land, Ananda World Brotherhood Village today encompasses eight hundred acres where about 250 people live a dynamic, fulfilling life based on the principles and practices of spiritual, mental, and physical development, cooperation, respect, and divine friendship.

After more then forty years of existence, Ananda is one of the most successful networks of intentional communities in the world. Urban communities have been developed in Palo Alto and Sacramento, California; Portland, Oregon; and Seattle, Washington. In Europe, near Assisi, Italy, a spiritual retreat and community was established in 1983, where today nearly one hundred residents from eight countries live. Swami Kriyananda currently lives in Pune, India where work has begun to develop both urban and rural communities, a retreat center, schools, and a temple dedicated to Paramhansa Yogananda. Ananda Sangha also supports more than one hundred meditation groups worldwide.

Contact Information:

mail:	14618 Tyler Foote Rd., Nevada City, CA 95959
phone:	530-478-7560
online:	www.ananda.org
email:	sanghainfo@ananda.org

EXPANDING LIGHT RETREAT

Visited **by over two** thousand people each year, the Expanding Light welcomes seekers from all backgrounds. Here you will find a loving, accepting environment, ideal for personal growth and spiritual renewal. We offer a varied, year-round schedule of classes and workshops. Offerings include: yoga, meditation, spiritual practices, yoga and meditation teacher training, and personal renewal retreats.

We strive to create an ideal relaxing and supportive environment for people to explore their own spiritual growth. We share the nonsectarian meditation practices and yoga philosophy of Paramhansa Yogananda and his direct disciple, Ananda's founder, Swami Kriyananda. Yogananda called his path "Self-realization," and our goal is to help our guests tune in to their own higher Self.

Guests at The Expanding Light can learn the four practices that comprise Yogananda's teachings of Kriya Yoga: the Energization Exercises, the *Hong Sau* technique of concentration, the AUM technique, and Kriya Yoga. The first two techniques are available for all guests; the second two are available to those interested in pursuing this path more deeply.

Contact Information:

mail: 14618 Tyler Foote Rd., Nevada City, CA 95959
phone: 800-346-5350
online: www.expandinglight.org
email: info@expandinglight.org

CRYSTAL CLARITY PUBLISHERS

When you're seeking a book on practical spiritual living, you want to know it's based on an authentic tradition of timeless teachings, and that it resonates with integrity. This is the goal of Crystal Clarity Publishers: to offer you books of practical wisdom filled with true spiritual principles that have not only been tested through the ages, but also through personal experience. We publish only books that combine creative thinking, universal principles, and a timeless message. Crystal Clarity books will open doors to help you discover more fulfillment and joy by living and acting from the center of peace within you.

Crystal Clarity Publishers—recognized worldwide for its best-selling, original, unaltered edition of Paramhansa Yogananda's classic *Autobiography of a Yogi*—offers many additional resources to assist you in your spiritual journey, including over ninety books, a wide variety of inspirational and relaxation music composed by Swami Kriyananda, Yogananda's direct disciple, and yoga and meditation DVDs.

For our online catalog, complete with secure ordering, please visit us on the web at:

www.crystalclarity.com

To request a catalog, place an order for the products you read about in the Further Explorations section of this book, or to find out more information about us and our products, please contact us:

Contact Information:
   mail: 14618 Tyler Foote Rd., Nevada City, CA 95959
   phone: 800-424-1055 *or* 530-478-7600
   online: www.crystalclarity.com
   email: clarity@crystalclarity.com